Computers and Programming
A System/360–370 Assembler Language Approach

Computers and Programming

A System / 360-370 Assembler Language Approach

Reino Hannula

California Polytechnic State University
San Luis Obispo

Houghton Mifflin Company · **Boston**
Atlanta
Dallas
Geneva, Illinois
Hopewell, New Jersey
Palo Alto
London

To my wife, Alice,
who made it all possible

Printed in the United States of America

Library of Congress Catalog Card Number: 73–9192

ISBN: 0–395–16796–5

Preface

This work covers thoroughly the Basic Assembler Language of System/360–370 as well as many programming techniques useful to the assembly programmer. The writing style has purposely been kept informal, and humor has been used occasionally to lighten the tone. The organization of the book maintains a logical continuity, the reader being taken through the Basic Assembler Language repertoire and System/360–370 concepts step by step.

The book is divided into two parts. The first part consists of Chaps. 1, 2, and 3. These chapters are an introduction to computers and computing with an emphasis on the symbol table and its use in the assembly process. Those who do not have an adequate background with respect to the symbol table and its use in the assembly process should start with Chap. 1. Others might want to start their study with the second part of the book, Chap. 4. Chapter 4 is a fairly comprehensive discussion of number systems with emphasis on the hexadecimal number system and the two's complement representation of negative numbers.

Chapter 5 introduces the Define Constant and Define Storage pseudo instructions. Opportunity is also given to program the concepts studied.

Chapter 6 introduces the basic full-word binary instructions—load, store, and arithmetic. Also, parts of all five types of the BAL instructions are introduced.

Chapter 7 is a comprehensive discussion of the machine language format and the methods by which the effective addresses of the instruction operands are determined.

Chapter 8 is an action chapter. Data is read in, converted, processed, converted back to printable form, and printed. There will be an opportunity to perform input/output operations.

Chapter 9 is devoted to the study of loops and the various BAL instructions which monitor them. The concept of an effective address pointer (EFP) is introduced. An instructor will find this pointer a useful teaching and programming technique for any language.

Chapter 10 thoroughly explores the condition code and the Branch on Condition instructions. The programming concepts concomitant with the need for a base register are considered in some depth. The student should, after completion of this chapter, be quite conversant with basic System/360–370 concepts.

Chapter 11 explains the subroutine conventions used by System/360–370.

One section of this chapter is devoted to a discussion of the *levels* of subroutines.

Chapter 12 presents the floating-point instruction repertoire. An algorithmic approach is used to present the action of the floating-point instructions. We believe this approach gives the student a deep insight into this subset of BAL.

Chapter 13 presents the packed decimal instructions. Edit and Edit and Mark, which edit packed decimal operands, are discussed in this chapter.

Chapter 14 is an introduction to input/output routines. Upon reading this chapter, the user should be able to write his own QSAM and QISAM I/O packages. He should also gain sufficient background so that his research into IBM manuals will be more meaningful.

Chapter 15 is a study of the specialized instructions Translate, Translate and Test, and Execute. In a sense, this chapter might be considered an introduction to compiler writing.

Chapter 16 explores the powerful macro and conditional assembly facilities of System/360–370. An attempt is made to display the great power of the macro.

Chapter 17 is an introduction to the Operating System, the program status word, the privileged instructions, the concepts of interrupts, and channel programming. The discussion is both thorough and logical. The final topic uses the Execute Channel Program supervisor macro instruction to print a message.

Other topics, which are integral parts of some chapters but which do not fit the "flow of logic" are placed in a separate section called the Computer Notebook. These topics generally fall into one of three categories:

1. In-depth items
2. Extensions of System/360–370 concepts
3. Topics unrelated to the main subject matter of concepts considered at that point

All the topics in the Computer Notebook—with the possible exception of the half-word binary integer instructions—should be discussed in class.

Those topics in the Notebook which are not directly related to the subject matter of any chapter appear in later parts of the text. Since these topics are independent of the chapter in which they appear, the instructor might choose to teach such topics as the subject matter of the zero-, one-, two-, and three-address machines in the beginning of the course.

This book adheres to the "Course B2, Computers and Programming Course." (See the 1968 curriculum recommendation by the ACM Curriculum Committee on Computer Science.) It is also suitable for the reader with no prior background if the first three chapters are included.

There is sufficient material in this book for two 10-week quarter courses. Chapters 14, 15, and 16 can easily be expanded so that the book can be used as the basic text for a two-semester course. The text could be covered in one semester by omitting chapters 12, 13, 15, 16, and 17, which are independent of the main text.

I wish to express my appreciation to those who have helped in my work. Kenneth Skewes has given much of his time to this text. James Sturch gave me a great many ideas about the input/output routines. Charty Beam was always helpful in developing the diagrams for most of the figures. Tania Shwetz and Sharon Ernstrom typed the manuscript. My appreciation also to the reviewers who aided me considerably with their comments: Professor Robert M. Aiken, University of Tennessee (Knoxville); Professor Bernard M. Levine, Middlesex County College; Professor Dan W. Scott, North Texas State College; and Professor Nelson Weiderman, University of Rhode Island.

My special thanks are due to my colleagues who have encouraged my writing. I appreciate the help given me by my colleague, Robert Dourson. I also appreciate the cooperative attitude and the help given by the personnel in the Computer Center at California Polytechnic State University. Credit is also due to my students in my department who have taught me so much.

My greatest debt is to my wife, Alice Beatrice Hannula, who has contributed so much by her patience and love and putting up with a task that seemed never to end.

February, 1974   Reino Hannula

Contents

Computers and Programming
A System/360–370 Assembler Language Approach

1 | Introduction

1.1 Ten Thousand Gas Bills

Suppose we are in charge of an operation for a gas company which must produce monthly gas bills for 10,000 customers. We are given the *old* meter reading, the *new* meter reading, and the price per cubic foot. The gas bill for the amount of gas used for the month will be equal to the price per cubic foot times the number of cubic feet used. (The number of cubic feet used is, of course, the difference between the two readings.) To simplify matters for the moment, we will assume that the new reading is always greater than the old reading.

Our job, then, is to compute the gas bill, which we can write as follows: a gas bill is equal to the difference between the two readings times the price per cubic foot. Or, we might write it as a formula:

gas bill = (new reading − old reading) × price per cubic foot

We can develop a more algebraic formula:

let B = gas bill
let R1 = new reading
let R2 = old reading
let C = price per cubic foot

Then

$$B = (R1 - R2) \times C$$

Now that we have developed this formula, the preparation of the gas bills is merely a tedious job involving a good deal of repetition.

1.2 Robert

Who do we hire to process this vast batch of bills? All we really need is someone, perhaps of minimum intelligence, who can memorize a simple routine and who can perform a sequence of instructions we will prepare for him. (We will, henceforth, call this sequence of prepared instructions the *Gas Bill Program*.)

Let us suppose that we find a person named Robert who satisfies the requirements for our job. We will provide Robert with an arrow-shaped

1

pointer, some blank bill forms, a pen, an in-tray, an out-tray, and a calculating machine. We will also give Robert a simple routine which he must memorize.

When Robert reports to work, he will sit at a table. The in-tray will be on his right, the out-tray on his left. The blank bill forms, his pencil, the arrow-shaped pointer, and the calculating machine will all be in handy positions.

We will put the cost per cubic foot (C), the old reading (R2), and the new reading (R1) for each customer into the in-tray. Please note that the order in which these are put into the in-tray is of crucial importance. R1, R2, and C for customer 1 are immediately followed by R1, R2, and C for customer 2, then R1, R2, and C for customer 3, and so on.

Notice that for each customer we have put in the data item called C. If the price per cubic foot (C) is the same for all 10,000 customers (which it should be), then we have repeated C 10,000 times. As we develop our story, we will find a way to avoid this.

We place the Gas Bill Program on top of all data items in the in-tray. Remember, our Gas Bill Program is the list of prepared instructions which Robert is to follow in his preparation of the 10,000 bills.

1.3 The Preparation of the Gas Bills

When Robert reports to work, he will sit down at the table, take the first item, the program, from the in-tray, and place it in front of himself. Then he will work in a systematic fashion following the routine he has memorized. The list below gives this routine.

Memorized Routine

1. He takes the arrow-shaped pointer and points it to the first instruction of the Gas Bill Program.
2. He reads, interprets, and memorizes the instruction indicated by the arrow-shaped pointer.
3. He moves the pointer so that it points to the next instruction in the program.
4. He does what the instruction he just memorized told him to do.
5. He goes back to step 2.

The important concept in the memorized routine is that Robert does not execute the instruction to which the arrow points. Rather, he memorizes, "digests," the instruction and moves the pointer to the next instruction in the program. *Then,* and not until then, does he execute the instruction he memorized.

Now, in order to understand how the gas bills are being prepared, we must look at the Gas Bill Program—that list of prepared instructions which is supposed to guide Robert to a successful completion of our job.

TABLE 1.1   Gas Bill Program

Number	Instruction
0*	Take a data item.
1	Enter this data item.
2	Take a data item.
3	Subtract this data item.
4	Take a data item.
5	Multiply this data item.
6	Write the number in the accumulator.
7	Put out this number.
8	Stop.
9	Do nothing.

* Note that the numbered instructions start with 0. It is customary in computer science to number starting with 0. As the student gains insight into the discipline, the rationale behind this will become obvious.

1.4   The Program

Robert, of course, will be so trained that he will know the meaning of each instruction. However, the action which takes place as an instruction is executed will not be so obvious to the casual reader. We, therefore, repeat in Table 1.2 the program along with an explanation of the action which will take place as Robert executes that instruction.

Our program will not produce 10,000 gas bills, but it will produce one. And, if Robert can make one bill with our program, we can easily modify it to make any number, but we will leave that for a moment.

We will run through one set of data to see how well our program works. Before we do that, however, remember that if our job is to produce 10,000 bills after modification of our program, we need 10,000 sets of data. The data must be in the order R1, R2, C; there is no way around it. We call this the responsibility of the programmer.

Now, let us go through one set of data with Robert. Assume R1 = 9864, R2 = 7612, and C = .03. Table 1.3 depicts the action as Robert produces the gas bill from our data. Note that when the arrow points to the first instruction in the Gas Bill Program, no instruction will be executed.

Some items in Table 1.3 need clarification.

1. C(IN-TRAY) is read, "Contents of the in-tray."
2. C(ACCUMULATOR) is read, "Contents of the accumulator."
3. The value given in the C(IN-TRAY) column has the value of the top data item in the in-tray.
4. The column headed by ⟶ has the number of the instruction which the arrow points to.

TABLE 1.2 The Instruction Set

Program	Explanation
0 Take a data item.	Robert takes a card which contains a data item from the in-tray. (The data item should be R1.)
1 Enter this data item.	Robert clears the accumulator of the calculator. He then enters the value R1 into the accumulator.
2 Take a data item.	Robert takes the next card from the in-tray. (This should contain the value R2.)
3 Subtract this data item.	Robert causes the calculating machine to subtract the value R2 from the value in the accumulator.
4 Take a data item.	Robert takes a card from the in-tray. (This should have the value C on it.)
5 Multiply this data item.	Robert causes the calculating machine to multiply the value in the accumulator by C. (The product will be in the accumulator.)
6 Write the number in the accumulator.	Robert writes the value which is in the accumulator onto a blank bill form.
7 Put out this number.	Robert puts the bill into the out-tray.
8 Stop.	Robert stops working.
9 Do nothing.	Robert relaxes.

TABLE 1.3 The First Run

Instruction executed	Instruction statement	C(IN-TRAY)	C(ACCUMULATOR)
0 —	—	9864	?
1 0	Take a data item.	7612	?
2 1	Enter this data item.	7612	9864
3 2	Take a data item.	.03	9864
4 3	Subtract this data item.	.03	2252
5 4	Take a data item.	? or empty	2252
6 5	Multiply this data item.	? or empty	6756
7 6	Write the number in the accumulator	? or empty	6756
8 7	Put out this number.	? or empty	6756
9 8	Stop.	? or empty	6756

5. The C(ACCUMULATOR) column has the value in the accumulator after the execution of the instruction in the same row.
6. The amount of the bill is on a bill form after the execution of instruction 6.
7. The bill is placed in the out-tray by instruction 7. We say that the bill is an output value.
8. The value in the accumulator is, of course, unchanged after Robert copies its contents.

Loops.   We have succeeded in producing one bill with our human computer. How can we modify our program so that we can produce more than one? We do so by making our computer perform a *loop*.

We must not let Robert execute the Stop instruction. That is, we do not want that particular instruction executed until he has produced a sufficient number of bills. The modified program appears in Table 1.4.

TABLE 1.4   Modified Gas Bill Program

0	Take a data item.
1	Enter this data item.
2	Take a data item.
3	Subtract this data item.
4	Take a data item.
5	Multiply this data item.
6	Write the number in the accumulator.
7	Put out this number.
8	Make the pointer point to instruction 0.
9	Stop.
10	Do nothing.

(Note that throughout this text, the present instruction will be designated by P. The next instruction in sequence is, then, P + 1. Therefore, the student should always remember that the arrow-shaped pointer points to P + 1 while P is being executed.)

Is it obvious now why Robert moves the pointer to P + 1 before he executes the instruction he memorized? Perhaps not. In any case, we suggest that the reader take a few sets of data—R1, R2, C—and run through the program. When you run through the program, keep track of the contents of the various devices. There are only three important values: the top value in the in-tray, the number in the accumulator, and the top bill in the out-tray. Try it once using the sequence memorized by Robert. Then try it while moving the pointer *after* the instruction has been executed.

But now another question comes to mind. How does Robert get out of the loop? Since Robert is human, he will stop working when the in-tray is

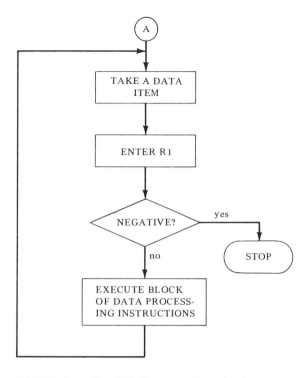

FIGURE 1.1 Gas Bill Program Flowchart

empty. That's natural. However, this solution is not very elegant when we are writing programs for a computer.

One way to exit from the loop would be to put a negative value for the last data item in the in-tray. Robert would consider this item to be an R1 value. He would enter it into the accumulator as he does any R1 value.

We would then have Robert check the value in the accumulator after he enters *each* R1. If the value is positive, then he proceeds in the usual manner. If, however, the value is negative, then he must move the pointer to the *Stop* instruction. Hence, *STOP* will be the next instruction executed. Robert has exited from the loop.

We present a flowchart of the logic in Figure 1.1.

1.5 The Gas Meter Completes a Cycle

What if the old reading is greater than the new reading? Consider the odometer in an automobile. Eventually it will hit 999999. Then when we drive 1/10 of a mile more, our odometer will be set to 000000. Similarly, the gas meter at some time will reset itself to zero. Hence, it is possible that an old reading might be 9998 and a new reading might be 0012 for a meter with a

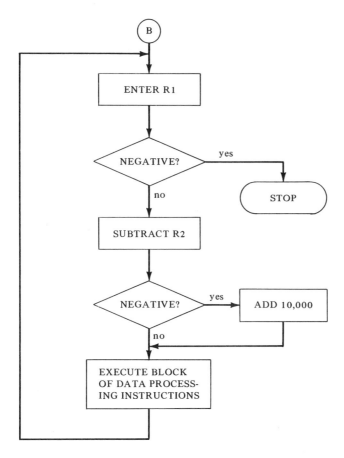

FIGURE 1.2   The Modified Gas Bill Program Flowchart

capacity of 10,000 cubic feet. When we subtract the old from the new, our difference will be a negative number.

Since it is logically possible for R1 − R2 (R1 minus R2) to be negative, we must modify our program to handle this situation. (Programmers must consider all logical possibilities no matter how small the probability.)

Exercise 4 asks you to submit a program which modifies our Gas Bill Program so that this event (R2 > R1), if it occurs, is handled correctly and expeditiously. You may find Figure 1.2 useful as an aid in modifying the program. However, use Figure 1.2 only as an aid in writing a more detailed flowchart. Then write your program using your own flowchart.

EXERCISES

1. Write a set of instructions for Robert which is more concise. For example, "ENTER DATA" might easily replace "ENTER THIS DATA ITEM."

2. Make a detailed flowchart of the Gas Bill Program. Include an exit from the loop. (See Figure 1.2.)

3. Consider Figure 1.1. Invent a new instruction which can be used to force an exit from the loop. Write a Gas Bill Program which utilizes this new instruction. (Use the flowchart from exercise 2 as an aid in writing the code.)

4. Consider Section 1.5. Write the Gas Bill Program which allows an old reading to be greater than a new reading. Invent the instructions which may be necessary to complete the program.

5. Write a program which produces bills for a car rental agency. The bill for each customer is determined by the formula:

   bill = mileage $\times$ price per mile + \$5 per day

6. Modify the program written for exercise 5 if the minimum bill for car hire is \$25. Invent instructions, if necessary, to complete the code. Submit a complete flowchart with the solution.

7. Consider the quadratic equation $y = 3x^2 + 2x - 4$. Write a program which will enable Robert to find the value of y for any given x. Hint: consider Horner's form, $y = (3x + 2)x - 4$.

2 | A Simple Computer

Since both System/360 and System/370 computers are extremely complicated, we would be faced with unnecessary difficulties if we started our review of some important principles of computer science using these computers as models. Hence, in this chapter and in Chapter 3, we will discuss some attributes of computer science using a simple computer as a reference. The attributes we will discuss are common to all computers. Our discussion of System/360 and System/370 Assembler Language will begin in Chapter 4.

One of the things we will do in this chapter is describe the various physical components of a computer. These components are often called the computer *hardware*. We will, however, limit our discussion to the basic components: the CARDREADER, the PRINTER, MEMORY, and the CENTRAL PROCESSING UNIT (usually abbreviated to CPU). This discussion begins in Section 2.1.

A computer obeys only those commands that are written in its own language—the *machine language* of that particular computer. Humans find it very difficult to write a program in machine language, since it is a numeric code consisting of ones and zeros. Each computer manufacturer has, therefore, developed a language, called an *assembly language,* that a human can use when writing the instructions that comprise a computer program. We will discuss a common attribute of all assembly languages in Section 2.2.

The set of instructions that comprise the assembly language of our simple computer appears in Section 2.4. Section 2.3 is devoted to a discussion of the definitions of various terms that are associated with an assembly language instruction.

The computer cannot, of course, understand the assembly language instructions. How can it then execute a program which consists of assembly language instructions? It cannot. The computer manufacturer also supplies a program, called the *Assembler,* which will translate the assembly language instructions into the computer's machine language. We say the Assembler *encodes* the machine language instruction from the assembly language instruction. The process of translating the entire assembly language program is called *assembly*.

The Assembler and the other programs (such as a Fortran compiler) supplied by the computer manufacturer (or which are developed by the computer installation) to facilitate the operation of the computer are called

9

software. Together, the hardware and the software constitute the *computer system.*

We follow a simple convention in this text which should make it easy to distinguish a hardware element from a software item. All the letters in the name of a hardware element are capitalized, while only the initial letter in the name of a software item is capitalized (for example, PRINTER and Assembler).

We feel that the key to understanding an assembly language is the *symbol table.* Hence, our presentation of the elementary principles of computer science will emphasize the symbol table. We will discuss its organization and how it is used by the Assembler to translate the assembly language instruction into the computer's machine language.

We recognize that we have not, at this point, defined the symbol table concept. We assure those readers who are not familiar with the concept that by the time Chapter 3 has been covered, they will be thoroughly conversant with the symbol table concept.

We also feel that a good understanding of the other concepts presented in this chapter and the next chapter will pay handsome dividends when we present the Assembler Language of System/360 and System/370.

2.1 The Anatomy of a Simple Computer

Our first task in this section is to choose some computer as a model. The machine we pick should have attributes common to all computers. And, most important, we want the first attributes we study to be simple and easy to understand.

Therefore, let us choose a fictitious computer. Its name? FINAC. What does FINAC stand for? Nothing really. It just happened that the author was in Finland when he decided to write this text.

Now let us look at the anatomy of our simple computer. We divide the anatomy of FINAC into four basic components. They are INPUT, OUTPUT, MEMORY, and the CENTRAL PROCESSING UNIT. (Note that these hardware elements appear in capital letters following the convention given in the introduction to this chapter.)

In our discussion we will divide the CENTRAL PROCESSING UNIT (which we will usually abbreviate to CPU) into its two major parts—CONTROL and the ARITHMETIC-LOGICAL UNIT (abbreviation: ALU). As is common in computer science, we will, at times, refer to the ARITHMETIC-LOGICAL UNIT as the CPU. We will do this, however, only when it is obvious that we are referring to the ALU, not to CONTROL.

Since all input for FINAC is in the form of punched cards we will often refer to INPUT as READER or CARDREADER. Likewise, PRINTER will be a substitute for OUTPUT.

Figure 2.1 is a diagram of FINAC. It will be worthwhile for the student

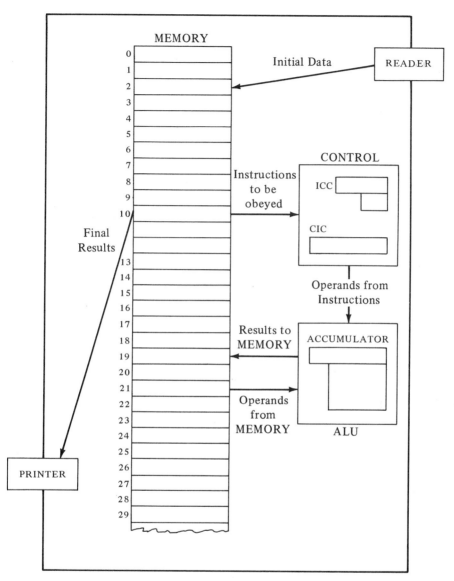

FIGURE 2.1

to refer to this diagram when we discuss these hardware components in greater detail.

INPUT. READER (INPUT) corresponds to Robert's in-tray. The READER is a device which allows the programmer to communicate with the computer via punched cards. All data (including programs) are entered into FINAC's MEMORY via the READER.

There are, of course, other types of input devices which can enter data into the MEMORY of a computer. The computer operator can, for example, enter data via the typewriter console. Data can also be moved into MEMORY from tapes, disks, drums, etc. A detailed discussion of these input devices is beyond the scope of this text, although a discussion of disk packs does appear in Topic 1 of the Computer Notebook for Chapter 14.

Note the arrows in the diagram which connect the READER with MEMORY. These lines are called *DATA BUSES*. It is via these DATA BUSES that our input items (including our program) will enter MEMORY from READER.

OUTPUT.   PRINTER (OUTPUT) is the hardware device which enables FINAC to return printed results to the user. We might say that it is one of the computer's "voices" to the outside world. (Note the DATA BUSES along which items from MEMORY move to the PRINTER.)

Again it is important to note that output can be received by several devices. There are devices which will place output results onto tapes, disks, punched cards, drums, etc. We note again that a detailed discussion of these input/output (I/O) devices is beyond the scope of this text.

MEMORY.   MEMORY has many aliases; it is often referred to as MAIN STORAGE, CORE, CENTRAL MEMORY, STORE, MAIN CORE, etc.

MEMORY is that component of the computer where we store data items (including instructions of our program). Although data and programs can be stored in other devices—the disks, drums, tapes, etc., which are part of the computer system—the CPU can access only those items which reside in MEMORY. That is, data must reside in MEMORY before it, the data, can be processed by the CPU. An instruction which does not reside in MEMORY cannot be executed. Why? Because CONTROL, which executes the instruction, cannot "access" it.

We might say *accessibility* differentiates MEMORY from all other storage devices available to the computer system. There must be *input* into MEMORY before data, which resides on a disk, a tape, or a drum, can be processed by the CPU. Any data item brought into MEMORY from anywhere (except the CPU) is *input*. Any data item copied from MEMORY and stored on any other device (except the CPU) is *output*.

We will have more to say about MEMORY and about some concepts which involve MEMORY after the discussion on CONTROL and the ALU.

ARITHMETIC-LOGICAL UNIT.   The ARITHMETIC-LOGICAL UNIT is the calculating machine of the computer. The ALU has, however, greater capabilities than Robert's calculator since it can perform logical operations as well as the familiar arithmetic ones.

The ALU may have one or more registers in which it keeps the results of its arithmetic operations. A data item may also be *loaded* into a register from MEMORY. Or the contents of a register may be *stored* (copied) into a specific location in MEMORY.

The load and store operations are nondestructive. That is, if a data item which is in a register is stored into a MEMORY location, the data item still exists in the register. The data item now is in two places—the register and the MEMORY location. This is true of the load operation also.

FINAC's CPU has exactly one register whose name should be familiar. It is called the *ACCUMULATOR*. Many computers have two registers, often called the ACCUMULATOR and the *QUOTIENT*. System/360 and System/370 computers have sixteen general purpose registers and four floating-point registers. (Imagine Robert with all those registers—accumulators—in his calculating machine!) We have limited FINAC's CPU to one register in order to simplify our discussion of FINAC's instruction repertoire.

Note the arrows (see Figure 2.1) which go from the ARITHMETIC-LOGICAL UNIT to MEMORY. These are the DATA BUSES which transfer data between MEMORY and the ALU. The DATA BUSES also return results from the ACCUMULATOR to MEMORY. CONTROL, which we discuss next, monitors the transfer of data along these lines.

CONTROL.   CONTROL corresponds to Robert himself. It is the hardware element which monitors the behavior of the computer. CONTROL causes the execution of instructions, supervises the ARITHMETIC-LOGICAL UNIT, and monitors itself.

CONTROL has two very interesting and important registers which aid it in the execution of a computer program. One, the *INSTRUCTION COUNTER CELL* (abbreviated to ICC), corresponds to Robert's arrow-shaped pointer. The ICC points to the next instruction to be executed just as Robert's arrow-shaped pointer does. (Many computer scientists call this register *INSTRUCTION ADDRESS REGISTER*. The other register, *CURRENT INSTRUCTION CELL* (abbreviated to CIC), contains the instruction which is being interpreted and executed at the moment.

CONTROL also has two other registers to help it move data into and out of the CPU. The *MEMORY ADDRESS REGISTER* (MAR) points to the location in MEMORY into which or from which data is to be transferred. The other register, *MEMORY DATA REGISTER* (MDR), holds the data during the transfer.

More about Some MEMORY Concepts.   MEMORY is divided into elements called *words*. Each word has an *address*. The address of the first word is zero. If FINAC has a 5,000-word MEMORY, then the highest address is 4,999. The address of a word is the unique label by which that word can be referenced. *Location* 12 has the same meaning as address 12.

It is important to distinguish between the concept of "contents of" a location and the numeric address of a location. Suppose, for instance, that the value contained in location 12 is 125. We write: C(location 12) = 125. We read: "The contents of location 12 is 125." The important thing to remember is that we can change the value of the contents of location 12, but we cannot change the value of the address of location 12.

A programmer, however, seldom refers to a MEMORY location by a numeric value, since it is possible to associate a name with a MEMORY location. We can associate, say, BLUE with the numeric address 12. If we do, then we write C(BLUE) = 125, which has the same meaning as C(location 12) = 125. Names for locations, such as BLUE, are called *symbolic addresses*. We use symbolic addresses in the examples of FINAC assembly instructions which follow Table 2.1.

A large part of Chapter 3 is devoted to the method by which the programmer and the Assembler associate a symbolic name with a numeric address. We begin this discussion in Section 2.5 of this chapter. We now turn to a discussion of assembly language.

2.2   An Attribute of an Assembly Language

We pointed out earlier in the chapter that the instructions executed by a computer are in a numeric code called the machine language of that particular computer. The instructions of all programs, which are written in any other language, will be converted by software programs—a compiler and/or an Assembler—into the machine language understood by the computer.

There is, however, a one-to-one relationship between the computer's assembly language and its machine language. That is, there exists a unique command in the machine language for each assembler language instruction. This one-to-one relationship does not exist between any high level language such as Fortran, Cobol, or PL/I and the machine language. One Fortran statement, for example, will usually translate to more than one machine language command.

Since there is one and only one machine language instruction for each assembly instruction, each command we issue in assembly language will cause a particular action in the computer. Further, this action will be the same each time we give the instruction. We can, therefore, assume when we give the assembler command that we are actually issuing a machine language instruction. In a sense, we are "closer" to the computer and we can observe its action in much greater detail than if we write our program in, say, Fortran.

The numeric code associated with an assembly instruction is usually listed in the *printout* of an assembly program. Figure 2.2 is an example of such a printout. The column marked OBJECT CODE is the machine language equivalent of the assembly language SOURCE STATEMENT in the same row. For instance, the machine language code 5830C16E is equivalent to the assembly language instruction L 3,BLUE (see statement 24).

The printout in Figure 2.2 is from a standard System/360 Assembler Language program. We have, however, removed three columns from the regular

OBJECT CODE		STMT		SOURCE STATEMENT	
		1		PRINT	NOGEN
		2		SETUP	END = SAM
5830	C16E	24		L	3,BLUE
5A30	C16A	25		A	3,RED
5830	C172	26		S	3,TAN
5030	C17A	27		ST	3,BLACK
5850	C16A	28		L	5,RED
5040	C16E	29		M	4,BLUE
5050	C17E	30		ST	5,PINK
5840	C16A	31		L	4,RED
8E40	0020	32		SRDA	4,32
5040	C16E	33		D	4,BLUE
5050	C176	34		ST	5,GREEN
5040	C182	35		ST	4,YELLOW
		36	SAM	GOBACK	
0000000A		43	RED	DC	F'10'
00000005		44	BLUE	DC	F'5'
00000004		45	TAN	DC	F'4'
		46	GREEN	DS	F
		47	BLACK	DS	F
		48	PINK	DS	F
		49	YELLOW	DS	F
		50		END	

FIGURE 2.2

printout in order to simplify our illustration of the relationship between assembly language instructions and the machine language code.

2.3 Some Important Definitions

A data item is composed of *fields*. An assembly language instruction is a data item composed of four fields. Many data items, however, are composed of exactly one field. The values R1, R2, and C used by Robert in preparing the gas bill are each examples of single field data items. If we were preparing our gas bill data for a System/360 computer, we would punch all three values onto a single card. In this case our punched card might be considered a data item with three fields.

In computer science we call a data item a *record*. A record may consist of a single data item, or the record may be packed with several pieces of information. Each piece of information would be in its own field in the record.

The set of data items {R1, R2, C} punched on a single punch card might be called a gas bill record. Because of the limited capabilities of our FINAC computer, we will be forced to punch each value on a separate card. Hence, to us R1 is a record, R2 is a record, and so is C.

Fields may have names. That is, we might refer to the R1 field of the gas bill record. Suppose, for instance, we have a set of records such that each record contains the name and address of some individual. Then each record is composed of exactly two fields—the *name* field and the *address* field. And further, these fields might be independent in the sense that we can alter the value in the address field without affecting the contents of the name field.

Instructions in FINAC assembly language and in the Basic Assembler Language of System/360 and System/370 are composed of four fields. These fields are:

1. name or label
2. operation
3. location or operand
4. remarks

We will discuss these fields in greater detail in the next chapter.

Machine language instructions in both FINAC and System/360 and 370 are composed of two fields—the *operation code* field and the *operand* field. The contents of the operation code field will be interpreted by CONTROL. The numeric code in this field will determine the action that will occur in the computer. The contents of the operand field may give the address in MEMORY of the data item—this data item is now called an *operand*—which will be used by the CPU in the execution of the command.

If no data is needed in the execution of the instruction, then, of course, CONTROL may ignore the contents of the operand field. Or we might say, "The contents of the operand field are meaningless."

2.4 FINAC Assembly Instructions

Table 2.1 gives the complete FINAC assembly language instruction set. Note that the action caused by the instruction is given in two ways, in English prose and then in computer science notation. Some of the instructions, such as TESTN Y, may not make sense at the moment, but be patient. When we run the Gas Bill Program in FINAC Assembly Language, the action of all FAL instructions will become clear. We will also gain insight into how a computer works.

We have kept the FAL instruction repertoire as small as possible, since its only purpose in this text is to help review some basic computer science concepts. The mnemonics we have chosen are pretty straightforward. They should be easy to remember. But bear in mind as you read this section that these instructions *will not be used after Chapter 3*. At that time the concept of a symbol table and the insight into how a computer works should make the discussion of the System/360 computer architecture and its assembly language much easier to understand. An example of each instruction except the test instructions is given after the table. The examples involving the test instructions appear in the programs in Chapter 3.

TABLE 2.1   FAL Instructions

Instruction	Action (English prose)	Action (CSc notation)
READ X	The first data item in the READER is placed into location X.	$X \leftarrow$ INPUT
PRINT X	The data item at location X is printed.	OUTPUT $\leftarrow$ C(X)
LOAD X	The contents of location X are copied into the ACCUMULATOR. The former contents of the ACCUMULATOR are lost.	ACC $\leftarrow$ C(X)
STORE X	The contents of the ACCUMULATOR are copied into location X. The former contents of X are destroyed.	$X \leftarrow$ C(ACC)
ADD X	The contents of location X are added to the contents of the ACCUMULATOR. The sum replaces the former contents of the ACCUMULATOR.	ACC $\leftarrow$ C(X) + C(ACC)
SUB X	The contents of location X are subtracted from the ACCUMULATOR. The difference replaces the former value held in the ACCUMULATOR.	ACC $\leftarrow$ C(ACC) − C(X)
MUL X	The contents of the ACCUMULATOR are multiplied by the contents of location X. The product replaces the former contents of the ACCUMULATOR. If the product is too large for the ACCUMULATOR, then the most significant digits of the product are lost.	ACC $\leftarrow$ C(ACC) * C(X)
DIV X	The integral part of the quotient of the contents of ACCUMULATOR divided by contents of location X replaces the dividend in the ACCUMULATOR. The remainder is lost.	Quotient of C(ACC) / C(X) $\rightarrow$ ACC Remainder is lost
TESTN Y	If the contents of the ACCUMULATOR are less than zero, the next instruction is taken from location Y. If the contents of the ACCUMULATOR are equal to or greater than zero, the next instruction in sequence will be executed.	If C(ACC) < 0, then RNI from location Y; otherwise RNI from P + 1 Read RNI as "Read next instruction"
TESTZ Y	If the contents of the ACCUMULATOR are equal to zero, then transfer control to location Y. If the contents of the ACCUMULATOR are not zero, the next instruction in sequence is obeyed.	If C(ACC) = 0, RNI from location X; otherwise RNI from P + 1
GOTO Y	An unconditional branch. The next instruction will be taken from location Y.	RNI from location Y

TABLE 2.1 (Cont.)

Instruction	Action (English prose)	Action (CSc notation)
STOP	The computer is told that the user's program is done. Control will pass to the Operating System.	Branch to Operating System

We now give an example of each instruction in the FAL repertoire.

Example 2.1

a. LOAD SAM

Before execution	Action	After execution
C(SAM) = 433		C(SAM) = 433
C(BLUE) = 747	ACC ← C(SAM)	C(BLUE) = 747
C(ACC) = 100		C(ACC) = 433

The data item 433 is in both location SAM and the ACCUMULATOR after execution. The previous contents of the ACCUMULATOR have been lost. We say LOAD is nondestructive to the operand field but destructive to the ACCUMULATOR.

b. ADD BLUE

Before execution	Action	After execution
C(SAM) = 433		C(SAM) = 433
C(BLUE) = 747	ACC ← C(ACC) + C(BLUE)	C(BLUE) = 747
C(ACC) = 433		C(ACC) = 1180

c. STORE SAM

Before execution	Action	After execution
C(SAM) = 433		C(SAM) = 1180
C(BLUE) = 747	SAM ← C(ACC)	C(BLUE) = 747
C(ACC) = 1180		C(ACC) = 1180

d. SUB BLUE

Before execution	Action	After execution
C(SAM) = 1180		C(SAM) = 1180
C(BLUE) = 747	ACC ← C(ACC) − C(BLUE)	C(BLUE) = 747
C(ACC) = 1180		C(ACC) = 433

e. MUL BLUE

Before execution	Action	After execution
C(SAM) = 1180		C(SAM) = 1180
C(BLUE) = 747	ACC ← C(ACC) * C(BLUE)	C(BLUE) = 747
C(ACC) = 433		C(ACC) = 323451

f. DIV SAM

Before execution	*Action*	*After execution*
C(SAM) = 1180	Quotient of	C(SAM) = 1180
C(BLUE) = 747	C(ACC) / C(SAM) → ACC	C(BLUE) = 747
C(ACC) = 323451		C(ACC) = 274

The remainder 131 is lost. In most computers the remainder is available in some register. But in order to simplify our review of computer science, we have devised a computer which does not save the remainder. Even so, the remainder can be determined by the programmer. See exercise 5.

g. Assume the first value in the READER is 453.
    READ SAM

Before execution	*Action*	*After execution*
C(SAM) = 1180		C(SAM) = 453
C(BLUE) = 747	SAM ← 453	C(BLUE) = 747
C(ACC) = 274		C(ACC) = 274

READ is destructive. The value in the READER is replaced by the next value in the READER queue. The original value in SAM is lost.

h. PRINT BLUE

Before execution	*Action*	*After execution*
C(BLUE) = 747	C(BLUE) are printed	C(BLUE) = 747

PRINT is nondestructive. The contents of BLUE are copied into a buffer. Eventually CONTROL will initiate the output routine. Hence, C(BLUE) will be printed.

We defer the examples of the TESTN and TESTZ instructions to a more appropriate point in our discussion.

2.5 The Assembler

When our Gas Bill Program is read into the computer, it will become data for the Assembler. Each instruction, if correctly written, will be converted to the numeric code which is its machine language counterpart. If the code is incorrectly written, the Assembler will return a message to the programmer in the printout. Such a message is called a *diagnostic.*

If the programmer commits too many errors in writing the assembly language program (or makes a single error which is too serious), CONTROL will not be allowed to execute the machine language code that has been assembled.

Once an instruction is in machine language, the FINAC Assembler stores it into MEMORY at an address which immediately follows the previous instruction. In FINAC, the first instruction is always stored into location 100. Hence, at execution time, CONTROL will take the first instruction to be executed in the program from location 100.

The System/360 Assembler will store the ML (machine language) code on a disk or tape. Then, if the program has been assembled without too many diagnostics, this converted program will be loaded into MEMORY by a software program called, appropriately, the *Loader*. The location of the first ML instruction depends on many factors related to the status of the computer at load time. (The Loader keeps a record of these conditions or it can ascertain them. Hence, the address of the first instruction may vary from time to time.)

All Assemblers, including those of System/360, must keep track of the storage locations used in the assembling process. That is, the Assembler must know the address of the next storage location which is available to the program being converted. The System/360 Assemblers, even if they store the processed ML instructions on a disk, must know, relative to location 0, the address of the next location available to the program.

Hence, all Assemblers maintain a *pointer* in a register called the *LOCATION COUNTER*. This register is used only during the Assembly; it points to the next available storage location in MEMORY. That is, the address in the LOCATION COUNTER is the address of the next available location for the program being assembled.

Note that a register or a location which contains the address of another cell is called a *pointer*. A pointer *points* to the location whose address it contains. For example, if the LOCATION COUNTER contains the value 110, then we say it points to location 110.

Consider the assembly language programmer. Must he keep track of the addresses where his instructions will be located? Yes. He must do so in some cases. But it is difficult, if not impossible, for a programmer to keep track of the *numeric addresses* in the computer where his instructions might be stored. In fact, with respect to most computers, the programmer will not know the numeric address of either his program or his data. The programmer gives a *symbolic address* (*symbolic name* is a synonym) to any assembly language instruction he wants to refer to. The Assembler will associate the symbolic name with the numeric address of the corresponding machine language instruction. Let us see how the Assembler does this.

An assembly language allows a programmer to choose an *alphanumeric* name (a name composed of alphabetic letters and arabic numerals) to associate with any instruction or data item in his program. This symbolic address is placed in the name field of the assembly language instruction.

The Assembler, when it translates the assembly code to machine language, creates a table called the *symbol table*. All symbolic names assigned to assembly language instructions are associated in this table with the numeric address of the corresponding machine language instruction. If a programmer refers to a symbolic name in the *operand* field of an assembly language instruction, the Assembler will, when encoding, search the symbol table for the numeric address associated with that symbolic name. This numeric address is then inserted into the machine language code.

There is one almost universal restriction with respect to an alphanumeric name that may be used as a symbolic address: all alphanumeric names must begin with an alphabetic character. The allowable length for this name will vary, but the maximum length in a FINAC (as well as a System/360 or System/370) computer is eight characters. These characters may be arabic numerals or alphabetic letters. Remember, however, the first character must be alphabetic.

We shall return to a discussion of these symbolic addresses and the symbol table in the next chapter.

Computer Notebook

TOPIC 1   Some Vocabulary and Some Concepts

The Assembler does not translate some assembly language statements into machine language. Such statements are often called *pseudo instructions.* They fall into two classes:

1. assembly control statements
2. declaratives

If we pick the name *imperatives* for the instructions which are converted into machine language, then an assembly language repertoire might be classified as given in Schedule A.

Schedule A

   I. Instructions
     1. imperatives
  II. Pseudo instructions
     1. declaratives
     2. assembly control statements

Our choice is, however, arbitrary. Some computer scientists prefer to group the declaratives and imperatives into the same subset. Their classification might be as in Schedule B. Here an assembly statement is considered an instruction if

1. it is converted into a machine language instruction, or
2. it requests the Assembler to allocate MEMORY space.

Schedule B

   I. Assembler instructions
     1. imperatives
     2. declaratives
  II. Assembly control statements

There is still a third classification which divides the repertoire into three main subsets. These are listed in Schedule C. In this text we have chosen the terminology given in Schedule A.

Schedule C
- I. Instructions (imperatives)
- II. Pseudo instructions (declaratives)
- III. Quasi-instructions (assembly control statements)

What is the difference between an imperative and a pseudo instruction? (Consider Schedule A.) We know that an imperative is translated by the Assembler into a machine language instruction. But what happens to a pseudo instruction?

A pseudo instruction is either a message to the Assembler or a request by the programmer for some special service by the Assembler. When the Assembler receives the message or fulfills the service request, the work of the pseudo instruction is done. It is no longer needed. The examples which follow in the discussion of the difference between a declarative and an assembly control statement should help clarify the concept.

Neither pseudo instruction—the declarative or the assembly control statement—requires MEMORY space for itself. The declarative, however, asks the Assembler to allocate storage space for the variables. FINAC has one declarative statement—Define Storage, which has the mnemonic DS—which, please note, is not listed in Table 2.1. This FINAC declarative requests the Assembler to set aside (allocate) storage. Example 2.2 shows how this is accomplished.

Example 2.2

Let us assume that the LOCATION COUNTER is pointing to the address 150 when the Assembler encounters our declarative (given below) in the assembly program. That is, C(LOCATION COUNTER) = 150.

(1) BLUE DS 2

1. The circled numeral, (1), is not part of the instruction. We use such circled numbers as reference numbers in the text.
2. The Assembler responds to the pseudo instruction by:
   a. associating the symbolic name BLUE with the numeric address in the LOCATION COUNTER.
   b. allocating two words of storage starting at location 150. This is done by adding two to the value in the LOCATION COUNTER. We say that the LOCATION COUNTER is "moved" so that it points to the second word beyond 150.
3. Although the declarative (1) does not itself require MEMORY space (and hence is not executable), the declarative requests storage allocation. In this sense space is required.
4. When the Assembler has associated the symbolic name BLUE with the numeric address 150 in the symbol table *and* the LOCATION COUNTER has been "moved," the work of (1) is done. It is no longer needed in the program.

We classify pseudo instructions which request allocation of space in MEMORY (for any reason) as *declaratives*. We classify the other pseudo instructions, those which pass a message to the Assembler or which issue a command to the Assembler, as *assembly control statements*.

TOPIC 2   The End Control Statement

FINAC has one assembly control statement in its repertoire: the End control statement.

Our assembly language program is read into MEMORY. The program is data for the Assembler. If our program is a logical sequence of instructions which will accomplish a specified task, then the Assembler will translate this program, instruction by instruction, into a logical sequence of machine language instructions.

But how does the Assembler recognize the end of our program? Each AL instruction in our program will reside in a word in MEMORY. These instructions will occupy consecutive MEMORY locations in ascending order.

Now suppose our AL program is stored in locations 300 to 350. The Assembler proceeds to encode the AL instruction at 349, then 350. The Assembler will assume that the contents of location 351 are part of our program. How can it assume anything else?

The chances are very good that the contents of location 351 will not be recognizable to the Assembler. Hence the Assembler will issue a diagnostic stating that the bit of code in that location was not a legitimate AL instruction. How do we avoid this? Simple. All we do is provide, in our assembly language instruction set, an assembly control statement which informs the Assembler that our program is ended.

END seems to be an appropriate word to use in order to pass this information to the Assembler. END, itself, will not be converted into a machine language instruction. This statement is a message from the programmer to the Assembler. The work of the END statement is done when the Assembler ceases its conversion process.

Note that both FAL (FINAC Assembly Language) and BAL (Basic Assembler Language) of System/360 and System/370 require the programmer to use the END control statement. It is the last statement of every program.

TOPIC 3   A Glimpse at the Operating System

In this topic we discuss some elementary attributes of the Operating System. We take the opportunity to define some important computer science concepts that will be used in the text that follows. We divide the Operating System into two basic parts—the *control program* and the *processing programs*.

The processing programs translate user programs which are written in Fortran, Cobol, PL/I, or Assembly into machine language. Those processing programs that convert a high level language into machine language are called *compilers*. The Cobol, the Fortran, and the PL/I compilers *compile* (translate) programs (called *source programs* or *source decks*) written in Cobol, Fortran, and PL/I, respectively, into machine language. The Assembler, as we have seen, translates an assembly language source deck into machine language. The duration of the compilation process (or the assembly process) is called *compile time*.

The compiled program is called the *object program, object deck,* or *object module*. It is usually stored on a disk until *load time*. A program, called the *Loader,* which belongs to the control program part of the Operating System processes the object deck into a *load module*. The Loader *loads* the load module into MEMORY. Control of the CPU is then transferred to the user load module. The duration of time when the user program has control of the CPU is called *execution time*. If the user program successfully completes its task, then the user program should in its last instruction transfer control back to the control program. Let us now consider the control program in greater detail.

The control program, as its name implies, maintains control of the computer system's resources. If we define *routine* as a sequence of machine language instructions which carry out a well-defined function, then we might say that the control program is a *set of routines* which maximizes the utilization of the computer resources. When we use the term *Operating System* in this text we are, in general, referring to the function performed by the control program routines.

We call the program that monitors the routines which comprise the Operating System by the name *Supervisor*. The Supervisor has many aliases. Among them are *Monitor, Director,* and *Executive Program*. Bear in mind, though, that the Supervisor is one of the routines (a synonym is *module*) which comprise the Operating System.

If the Operating System is to maximize the utilization of the computer system's resources, then it must, since humans are so "slow," minimize the need for human intervention. Hence, in a sense, the Supervisor must never lose control of the computer system even when the effective control of the CPU has been transferred to a user program.

Facilities are, therefore, provided so that CONTROL can signal the Supervisor whenever the user program commits an "error." (An error committed during execution time is called an *exception*.) This facility is called the *program interrupt mechanism*. The signal, itself, is called a *program interrupt* or just an *interrupt*.

The Supervisor (notice: no human intervention) will assign an interrupt handling routine to process the error. If the interrupt routine can rectify the error, then control of the CPU will be returned to the user program. That is, the user program will start to execute again at the point where the interrupt occurred. If, however, the error cannot be rectified, then the user program will be *abnormally terminated*. That is, the execution of the user program will stop. The Supervisor will direct an *Initiator* routine to introduce a new user program to the computer.

When a program is terminated abnormally, the Operating System will cause information pertinent to the program to be printed by the PRINTER. This printed information is called an *indicative dump*. It includes the name of the exception that caused the interrupt along with a good deal of other information which may be useful to the programmer when he attempts to diagnose (debug) the program. Further discussion of the indicative dump appears in Topic 2 of the Computer Notebook in Chapter 8.

Additional features of the System/360 Operating System will be introduced as needed.

TOPIC 4   Data Sets

We used the word *record* in Section 2.3 as a synonym for the concept of data item. We pointed out that a record could contain several pieces of information such that each piece of information was contained in its own field.

Now let us go a little further. Records are elements of a set called a *file* or a *data set*. The set of all data items (records) in Robert's in-tray is a data set. An appropriate name for it might be the Gas Bill Input data set. Even the set of gas bills produced by Robert is a data set. Each gas bill is a record in that data set which we might label the Gas Bill Output.

Figure 2.3 is an example of a water bill mailed by a water company in California. The name of the record is WATER. METER, CONSUMED, and AMOUNT are the three fields of the record. The METER field is divided into two subfields named PRESENT and PREVIOUS.

All of the bills mailed by the company might be called the Water Bill data set.

One last comment. The record of a water bill does not differ very much from the record of a gas bill, does it?

FIGURE 2.3

561	546	15	7	07
PRESENT	PREVIOUS	CONSUMED	AMOUNT	
METER		1000 GAL.		
WATER				

EXERCISES

1. Write a program in Fortran or in any high level language of your choice. Get an assembly language listing. After studying the printout, what is your guess as to the average number of ML instructions generated by your high level language statements.

2. Learn the input/output configuration of the computer(s) in your installation.

3. Pick the name of a computer not in the IBM System/300 series. Go to the library to do some research on the computer of your choice. Discuss the five components of that computer.

4. FINAC has only one register in its CPU that is accessible to the programmer. Suppose there were two. How would you now modify the action caused by the instruction DIV X?

5. Suppose location SAM contains 44 and C(BLUE) = 144. Consider the code:

   LOAD   BLUE   C(ACC) = 144
   DIV   SAM   C(ACC) =   3
   The remainder 12 has been lost.

   Write a piece of code which will "retrieve" this lost remainder. Assume that the program has defined two storage locations by RED DS 2. Store the remainder in RED+1 and the quotient in RED.

6. FINAC does not possess a pseudo instruction which will enable the programmer to define a constant for his program. Invent a mnemonic for a Define Constant declarative for FINAC. Explain the action of the Assembler when it encounters your declarative.

7. Consider the End pseudo instruction in Topic 2 of the Computer Notebook. When we use END, the Assembler knows when to stop assembling the machine language code. Now our question. How does the Assembler know where to start assembling? Do we need an assembly control statement for that purpose?

8 The largest value that a register can hold in any computer is certainly a finite number. It should be clear that a register in the CPU can overflow. For example, let C(ACC) = X where X is the maximum value that can be held by the register. If we add one to the ACCUMULATOR, clearly we will have an overflow.

   The most significant digits are lost if the ACCUMULATOR overflows in multiplication. Is this the usual practice of the registers in the ARITHMETIC-LOGICAL UNIT of computers with which you are familiar?

3 | The Program

In this chapter we will write the Gas Bill Program in FINAC Assembly Language and watch the execution of the program by CONTROL after the program has been converted into machine language. Before we do that, however, we must consider a few details about the format of an assembly language instruction. That is, we must answer the question: How do we punch the cards that constitute the assembly language source deck?

We note here that all of the discussion about the format of a FINAC Assembly Language instruction applies also to the System/360 Basic Assembler Language as well; the System/360 Assembler Language instructions have exactly the same format of instructions as in the FINAC language. The information given here will, therefore, be useful when we write in System/360 Basic Assembler Language.

3.1 The Assembly Language Format

Each instruction has four fields, two of which are optional. The four fields are:

1. symbolic address (optional)
2. operation
3. location
4. remarks (optional)

The symbolic address, location, and remarks fields are often called the *name, operand,* and *comments* fields, respectively. We say the symbolic address and remarks fields are optional because these fields may be left blank in an assembly language instruction.

The format rules are listed in Table 3.1. These rather liberal rules are replaced in practice by the set of conventions listed below in Table 3.2. Please note that these conventions, although a bit more stringent, do help to give us a much more readable printout than if each programmer followed his own fancy.

Most instructions will fit on a single punch card. If a statement must be continued onto a second card (called a *continuation card*), then column 72 of the first card must contain any nonblank character. The continuation on the second card must start in column 16. The maximum number of cards

TABLE 3.1 Assembly Language Format Rules

---

1. At least one blank must be inserted between fields.
2. No blanks may appear within any field except the remarks field. (When the Assembler encounters a blank in the instruction, it assumes the programmer desires to start a new field. In other words, a new field in the instruction begins with the first nonblank character which is encountered after any blank.)
3. A symbolic address, if nonblank, must begin in column 1. If column 1 is blank, the Assembler will assume that the name field has been omitted.
4. A symbolic address must not be longer than eight characters and must not include any special characters. The following characters and numbers are acceptable: #, @, $, 1, 2, 3, 4, 5, 6, 7, 8, 9, 0; any letters of the alphabet are also acceptable.
5. A symbolic address, if nonblank, must begin with an alphabetic character.

TABLE 3.2 Assembly Language Format Conventions

---

1. The name field (symbolic address), if present, must begin in column 1.
2. The operation field must begin in column 10.
3. The first entry in the location field must be in column 16, if possible.
4. Remarks begin in column 30.

---

allowed for one instruction is three. Or, we might say each instruction is allowed two continuation cards.

Note that an assembly language instruction must be contained in columns 1 through 71 (inclusive) of a punched card. If any nonblank character appears in column 72, the Assembler will expect a continuation card. This is true even if the programmer is writing a comment.

3.2 Writing the Program

We have the formula $B = (R1 - R2) \times C$ where, as the reader will recall,

R1 is the new reading
R2 is the old reading
C is the price per cubic foot
B is the calculated value of the gas bill

The values R1, R2, and C are input variables. That is, we must read them into storage locations which we will have to ask the Assembler to allocate by the DS pseudo instruction. Since we have to refer to these locations, we will be forced to choose a symbolic address for each of the pseudo instructions we use.

It is not difficult to choose the symbolic names for the locations into which we read R1, R2, and C. The Assembler will allocate the three locations and associate these locations with their symbolic names if we merely write

R1	DS	1
R2	DS	1
C	DS	1

Table 3.3 illustrates how these pseudo instructions are incorporated into the program.

B is an output variable. When B is calculated by the CPU we must have a storage location where we can put the value. Again, we must use a Define Storage statement to accomplish this.

TABLE 3.3   The Gas Bill Program

	READ	R1	THE VALUE OF THE VARIABLE R1 → LOCATION R1
	READ	R2	THE VALUE OF THE VARIABLE R2 → LOCATION R2
	READ	C	THE VALUE OF THE VARIABLE C → LOCATION C
	LOAD	R1	ACC ← C(R1)
	SUB	R2	ACC ← C(ACC) − C(R2)
	MUL	C	ACC ← C(ACC) * C(C)
	STORE	B	LOCATION B ← C(ACC)
	PRINT	B	THE BILL IS PRINTED
	STOP		
R1	DS	1	
R2	DS	1	
C	DS	1	
B	DS	1	

Let us peek inside the computer right after our program has been assembled and just before execution starts. We assume that the first set of data, {R1, R2, C} to be read in is {9246, 8743, 3}. The second set is {147, 92, 3}. The Assembler has resolved all symbolic addresses. That is, each symbolic name has been converted to the numeric address associated with it. See Table 3.4.

The address of the first instruction in our program has been placed into the INSTRUCTION COUNTER CELL by the Operating System. (Remember the ICC, which is the abbreviation for this register, points to the next instruction which will be *fetched* by CONTROL.)

When our program starts to execute, the contents of location 100 will be copied into the CURRENT INSTRUCTION CELL. At that moment our program is in control of the computer.

Our program will remain in control until the computer senses the Stop instruction or until the computer encounters an error which the software error routines cannot handle.

If the computer senses the Stop instruction, we will relinquish control of

TABLE 3.4   The Program in MEMORY

Location	Code	
100	READ	109
101	READ	110
102	READ	111
103	LOAD	109
104	SUB	110
105	MUL	111
106	STORE	112
107	PRINT	112
108	STOP	
109	?*	
110	?	
111	?	
112	?	

* The question marks in the last four locations indicate that we do not know the contents of those locations.

the computer in an elegant manner. If we relinquish control in any other manner, it is said we have been terminated abnormally.

When READ 109, which is the instruction at location 100, is copied into the CIC, CONTROL increases the value in the ICC by one. Now the two registers have the following appearance:

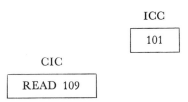

and CONTROL has completed the "fetch" cycle of the next instruction.

Now that the ICC has been updated, CONTROL interprets and causes the execution of the machine language instruction in the CIC.

The execution of an instruction is divided into two intervals called the *fetch cycle* and the *execute cycle*. In the fetch cycle, CONTROL fetches the instruction from the address pointed to by the INSTRUCTION COUNTER CELL. This instruction is copied into the CURRENT INSTRUCTION CELL. Then, still in the fetch cycle, CONTROL adds one to the ICC. The ICC now points to the next instruction in sequence. In the execute cycle CONTROL interprets and causes the execution of the instruction in the CIC.

The reader is strongly urged to interrupt his perusal of this text to run through the program. Use the first set of data {9246, 8743, 3} for the values R1, R2, and C. Keep track of all values in all MEMORY locations and in

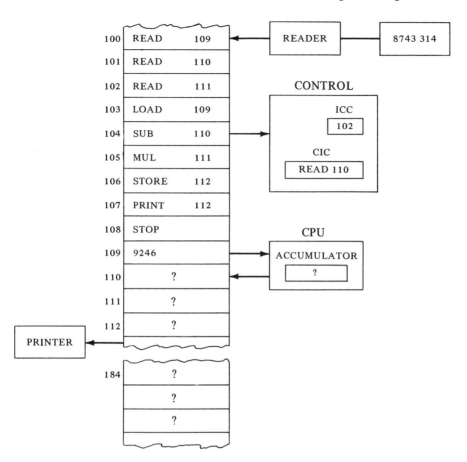

FIGURE 3.1 FINAC After Execution of READ 109

all hardware items which are affected by the code. Figure 3.1 illustrates one suggested technique. The figure is a snapshot of the pertinent components of the computer after the execution of READ 109 and after completion of the fetch cycle of the next instruction.

What has changed? The contents of location 109 now is the value R1. The ICC has been updated to 102. The instruction at location 101 is the new content of CIC. The R2 value, 8743, is now first in the READER queue.

Figure 3.2 is a view of the same components just after the computer has finished the execution of the entire program. Note that the PRINTER has printed a bill. The next set of data is in place in the READER queue ready to be read into their respective locations. ICC points to 10. The instruction in the CIC is STOP.

The computer does not "stop" when it encounters the command STOP. Actually, the Stop instruction is a branch to the Operating System subroutine

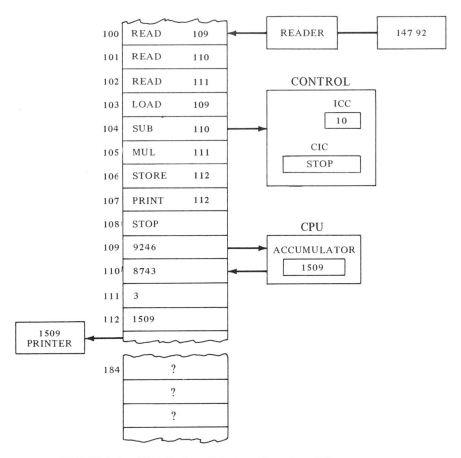

FIGURE 3.2 FINAC after Printing One Gas Bill

which is given control when a program terminates normally. CONTROL interprets STOP simply as "put the address of location 10 into the ICC." This is the address of the first instruction of the Operating System subroutine which takes control of the computer. However, with respect to our program, the computer has stopped.

3.3 The Loop Using an Unconditional Branch

FINAC Assembly Language has an unconditional branch instruction, GOTO Y. (See Table 2.1.) It will be easy to insert this instruction into our program so that we can produce 10,000 gas bills.

Before we do, however, consider the variable C, the cost per cubic foot for gas. Certainly it should be the same for each customer. If it is and if we loop 10,000 lines to the first instruction, we will read in the same value 10,000 times. What a waste! It does not make good sense, which implies it is not a good programming practice. Think of all the times, for instance, that the value C must be punched on a card. How can we avoid this? All we need to do is interchange instruction 1 and instruction 3. If our program is already punched, we merely interchange card 1 and card 3. Now our program will read C first, then R1, then R2. We will insert our unconditional branch immediately following PRINT B. This instruction should transfer control to the second instruction of the code. The result? The computer, instead of reading in 10,000 sets of {R1, R2, C}, will read in *one* C and 10,000 sets of {R1, R2}. (See Table 3.5.)

TABLE 3.5 The Modified Gas Bill Program

	READ	C
BLUE	READ	R1
	READ	R2
	LØAD	R1
	SUB	R2
	MUL	C
	STØRE	B
	PRINT	B
	GØTØ	BLUE
	STØP	
R1	DS	1
R2	DS	1
C	DS	1
B	DS	1

Note that we did not have to change the order in which the storage locations R1, R2, C, and B were defined. When we peek into the computer's MEMORY to look at the machine language program, we will see that the numeric addresses of R1, R2, C, and B have increased by one. The instruction GOTO BLUE pushed them farther "down" into MEMORY.

The symbolic address BLUE which we have put in the name field of the second instruction will now be associated with the numeric address of that location.

Table 3.6 is a peek into MEMORY just before our modified program executes for the first time.

How does the computer accomplish the branch? The remark "Branch to location BLUE" is computer science jargon for a fascinating sequence of events. A moment ago, we said that when our program begins to execute, it is in control of the computer. The unconditional branch illustrates vividly how CONTROL does our bidding.

Let us look at the values in the ICC and CIC registers as CONTROL goes through both the fetch cycle and the execute cycle of each instruction. We divide the fetch cycle into two intervals. We will look at the registers

TABLE 3.6 The Loop

100	READ	112
101	READ	110
102	READ	111
103	LØAD	110
104	SUB	111
105	MUL	112
106	STØRE	113
107	PRINT	113
108	GØTØ	101
109	STØP	
110	?	
111	?	
112	?	
113	?	

just before CONTROL updates the value in the ICC and just after the pointer, ICC, has been "moved." That is, we begin where PRINT 113 has been copied into the CIC but CONTROL has not updated the value in the CIC.

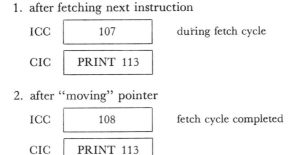

1. after fetching next instruction

ICC   107   during fetch cycle

CIC   PRINT 113

2. after "moving" pointer

ICC   108   fetch cycle completed

CIC   PRINT 113

Since ICC points to location 108, the next instruction to be fetched is in location 108.

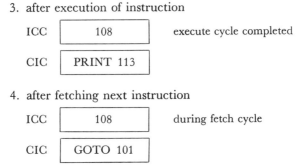

3. after execution of instruction

ICC   108   execute cycle completed

CIC   PRINT 113

4. after fetching next instruction

ICC   108   during fetch cycle

CIC   GOTO 101

5. after "moving" pointer

| ICC | 109 | fetch cycle completed |
| CIC | GOTO 101 | |

We interrupt our sequence at this crucial point. ICC points to the instruction STOP. One may well ask, "Won't STOP be brought into the CIC in the next fetch cycle?" No. Because CONTROL interprets GOTO 101 in this sense: the value in the instruction's operand field is copied into the ICC. That value is 101. And the value 101 replaces 109 in the INSTRUCTION COUNTER CELL.

6. after execution of instruction

| ICC | 101 | execution cycle completed |
| CIC | GOTO 101 | |

It is the fetch cycle again. CONTROL must fetch the next instruction. That is, CONTROL must fetch the instruction that the ICC points to. That instruction is in location 101.

7. after fetching instruction

| ICC | 101 | during fetch cycle |
| CIC | READ 110 | |

The instruction has been brought into the CURRENT INSTRUCTION CELL. Before the instruction is executed, however, the value in the ICC is increased by one.

8. after "moving" pointer

| ICC | 102 | fetch cycle completed |
| CIC | READ 110 | |

Now the computer is in a loop.

3.4 Conditional Branch and End-of-File Test

Our program works. It produces gas bill after gas bill. But it never stops. It is in an endless loop. What we are trying to say is that our program will not stop itself. A software program, part of the Operating System, will finally "bomb" us out.

Why? Well, for one thing, we will reach the end of the data set. Our file of records {R1, R2} will eventually be exhausted. When we execute the instruction READ 110 and there is no R1 available for input in the CARD-READER, our program will be interrupted. An error has occurred.

What happens next depends to a large extent on what kind of Operating System we devise for FINAC. In any case, our program will be forced to relinquish control of the computer. Let us assume that Error-Subroutine, a software subroutine of the Operating System, takes over.

If the interruption has been caused by a rectifiable error, then Error-Subroutine will make the necessary corrections. When they have been made, control of the computer will be returned to our program.

If Error-Subroutine needs to use the ACCUMULATOR, it will save the contents by copying the value into some specific location in MEMORY. Error-Subroutine will also remember the instruction address—the point at which the interrupt occurred. Control will be returned to our program at that point. Since the value of the ACCUMULATOR will have been restored, our program will not even know it has been interrupted.

But, alas! No such luck for us. Our type of interrupt is not rectifiable. Our program will be terminated abnormally. Along with the error message, we will receive an indicative dump which we neither desire nor need.

There is, however, nothing wrong with our program proper. We just didn't provide an end-of-file condition check. We can easily do that by using one of the two available conditional branches provided in the FINAC Assembly Language—TESTN and TESTZ.

System/360 uses the delimiter card, /*, to denote the end of a data set. (The slash is in column 1 and the asterisk is in column 2.) The user is expected to provide a symbolic address to which the computer may transfer control when and if the user's program reads the /* card. An unrectifiable error will result if the user's program reads /* without the stipulation of such an end-of-file address. In Fortran, for example, the programmer can provide for this exigency by coding READ (5, 40, END = 10). If the /* is read now, a branch will be made to symbolic address 10.

When CONTROL encounters the instruction TESTN Y at execution time, CONTROL will check the value in the ACCUMULATOR. If that value is negative, CONTROL will copy the operand Y into the ICC. Hence, the next instruction fetched will be the one at location Y. A branch will have been made. If, however, the value in the ACCUMULATOR is nonnegative, then CONTROL will do nothing more in that execute cycle. That is, the execute cycle of TESTN Y has been completed. CONTROL will now fetch the next instruction in sequence $P + 1$. No branch has been made. (P is the present instruction, the instruction being executed right now. $P + 1$ is the next instruction in the regular sequence.)

It is quite simple to incorporate this end-of-file condition test into our program. First, however, we must add one new record to our data set. In this record, R1 will be set to -1, although any negative number would be acceptable. This record will, of course, be the last record in the file.

The end-of-file test will force us to change the order of our instructions. We will read in R1, load R1 into the ACCUMULATOR, and check for end-of-file before we read in R2. If R1 is negative, we have exhausted our data set. Then we want to branch to STOP. Hence we must give the Stop instruction a symbolic name to which TESTN can refer. (See Table 3.7.)

TABLE 3.7   The Gas Bill Program: Modification 2

	READ	C	
LOOP	READ	R1	
	LØAD	R1	LOAD AND TEST BEFORE READING IN R2
	TESTN	EXIT	IF NEGATIVE, BRANCH TO EXIT
	READ	R2	
	SUB	R2	
	MUL	C	
	STØRE	B	
	PRINT	B	
	GØTØ	LØØP	UNCONDITIONAL BRANCH TO LOOP
EXIT	STØP		
R1	DS	1	
R2	DS	1	
C	DS	1	
B	DS	1	
	END		

Consider the code

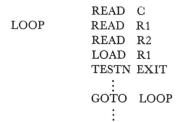

```
         READ   C
LOOP     READ   R1
         READ   R2
         LOAD   R1
         TESTN  EXIT
           ⋮
         GOTO   LOOP
           ⋮
```

This code will cause an interrupt and the program will be terminated abnormally. Why? The negative test appears in the program a little too late.

R1 is read into MEMORY. The instruction READ R2 appears before the test for negativity. If R1 is negative, then we have exhausted our data set. Control, however, must try to execute READ R2. Since the instruction cannot be executed, an interrupt occurs. The program is terminated.

Let us now consider the machine language coding of our modified GAS BILL PROGRAM which appears in Table 3.8. We will observe how the program uses the *trailer card* (an impossible data item such as our negative R1 is often called a trailer card) to exit from the loop when all gas bills have

TABLE 3.8   The Gas Bill Program in MEMORY

100	READ	113
101	READ	111
102	LØAD	111
103	TESTN	110
104	READ	112
105	SUB	112
106	MUL	113
107	STØRE	114
108	PRINT	114
109	GØTØ	101
110	STØP	
111	?	
112	?	
113	?	
114	?	
115	?	

been printed. Assume that in the 1497th loop of the program the value of R1 is 4012. The first snapshot of the series given below has been taken just after the fetch cycle of LOAD 111 has been completed.

1. after fetching LOAD 111

The value in the ACCUMULATOR is the amount of the last gas bill computed.

2. after execution of instruction

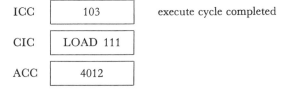

3. after fetching next instruction

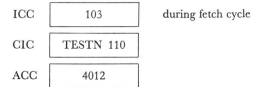

4. after "moving" pointer

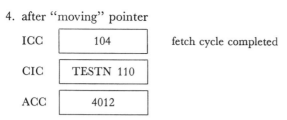

ICC | 104 | fetch cycle completed

CIC | TESTN 110 |

ACC | 4012 |

After the ICC has been updated, CONTROL must interpret and execute the instruction TESTN 110. This instruction forces CONTROL to determine if the value in the ACCUMULATOR is negative. If the value is not negative, no action is taken. Since, in this case, the value is positive, CONTROL goes into the fetch cycle of the next instruction. That is, CONTROL will bring in instruction 104—READ 112—and then he will update the ICC to 105.

5. after fetching instruction

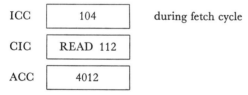

ICC | 104 | during fetch cycle

CIC | READ 112 |

ACC | 4012 |

6. after "moving" pointer

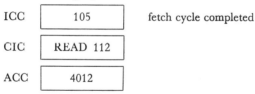

ICC | 105 | fetch cycle completed

CIC | READ 112 |

ACC | 4012 |

In this execution of the loop no branch was made. The variable R1 was an authentic meter reading. A new gas bill will be calculated and then printed.

Suppose 10,041 loops later the value of R1 is −1. The first snapshot of ICC, CIC, and the ACCUMULATOR in the new series given below again has been taken just after the fetch cycle of LOAD 111 has been completed.

1. after fetching LOAD 111

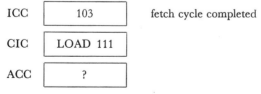

ICC | 103 | fetch cycle completed

CIC | LOAD 111 |

ACC | ? |

2. after execution of the instruction

ICC | 103 | execute cycle completed

3. after fetching next instruction

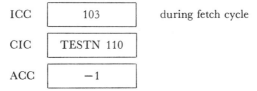

4. after moving pointer

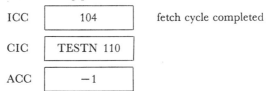

CONTROL executed the instruction TESTN 110 in each pass through the loop. In each of those cases, the value in the ACCUMULATOR was nonnegative. Hence the execution cycle of the instruction ended when CONTROL determined that the value in the ACCUMULATOR was nonnegative.

This time the value in the ACCUMULATOR is negative; hence, CONTROL must put the value 110—the value in the operand field of the instruction—into the ICC. The ICC now points to location 110.

5. after execution of the instruction

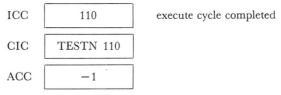

CONTROL will now bring in the instruction that the ICC points to.

6. after fetching next instruction

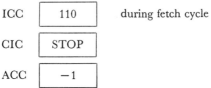

7. after moving pointer

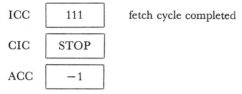

ICC   111   fetch cycle completed

CIC   STOP

ACC   −1

The Stop instruction must not be taken literally. CONTROL does not stop the computer. Rather, CONTROL puts the address of the first instruction of a software program called the Supervisor (a subroutine belonging to the Operating System) into the INSTRUCTION COUNTER CELL. That is all there is to the execute cycle of the instruction.

The next instruction to be executed will be taken from the Supervisor program. It is true, however, that the Gas Bill Program has been completed. The execution of that program has stopped.

8. after execution of STOP

ICC   10   execute cycle completed

CIC   STOP

ACC   −1

Our program has gracefully relinquished control of the computer. The next instruction to be executed, which comes from location 10, will undoubtedly initiate a routine (program) which will direct the computer to some other task. Our job is done.

Computer Notebook

TOPIC 1   The Assembler at Work

How does the Assembler go about its job of converting a piece of assembly code to machine language? Consider the program segment in Table 3.9. Let us follow the steps the Assembler takes to convert this fragment into numeric code.

The Assembler will make two passes through our code. In the first pass it will construct a symbol table where it will list all the symbolic addresses along with their associated numeric values. The symbol table will also contain other attributes associated with symbolic addresses, such as length and type. These attributes, however, are beyond the scope of this discussion.

Now let us assume that the Assembler will put the ML (machine language) code equivalent to our AL (assembly language) instructions into MEMORY starting at location 100. That is, our program will start executing at location

TABLE 3.9 A Program to Encode

	Name field	Operation field	Location field
①		READ	ABLE
②		LØAD	ABLE
③	LØØP	READ	RED
④		ADD	RED
⑤		TESTN	EXIT
⑥		GØTØ	LØØP
⑦	EXIT	STØP	
⑧	ABLE	DS	1
⑨	RED	DS	1
⑩		END	

100. Hence, when the assembly process begins, the LOCATION COUNTER will point to the address 100.

In the first pass, the Assembler will scan the first character of the name field of each instruction. If this character is a blank, the symbolic address has been omitted. (If this remark puzzles the reader, we suggest he review the assembly language format which is discussed in Section 3.1.)

FINAC has fixed word length instructions. Each and every ML instruction requires one word of STORAGE. Once the Assembler has determined that the name field is blank and that the instruction is an imperative—that is, it is not a Define Storage pseudo—then it allocates one word in MEMORY for the ML instruction. It does this by simply adding one to the LOCATION COUNTER.

If the assembly language instruction is the pseudo, Define Storage, then the Assembler must scan the operand to ascertain the number of words which must be allocated. The allocation is made by adding the value found in the operand field to the LOCATION COUNTER.

Some computers, System/360, for example, have variable length instructions. The numeric code associated with the mnemonic informs the Assembler whether the ML instruction will require one-half, one, or one and one-half words in STORAGE. The Assembler will respond by adding the appropriate amount to the LOCATION COUNTER.

Let us take a close look at the first pass and second pass made by the Assembler through our program segment in Table 3.9.

First Pass. The name field of ① is blank. Since ① is not a DS, the Assembler merely adds 1 to the LOCATION COUNTER. Now it points to location 101. Again in ② we find a blank name field. The pointer is moved to location 102. In ③, the Assembler encounters L-O-O-P-blank in the name field.

The Assembler first determines if the symbolic name is legitimate. There are three basic rules this label must satisfy:

1. Is the first character alphabetic? It is. Okay.
2. Are there any illegal characters in the name? There aren't. Okay.
3. How many characters are there? Four. Is four less than nine? Yes. Okay.

The label has passed inspection. Now the Assembler must check the symbol table to see if this label is unique. That is, has the programmer used this label in the name field of any previous instruction? If he has, then he has given the same label to two different locations. That is illegal, since the Assembler cannot differentiate between the two locations. If, however, this label is unique, then the Assembler will accept it by listing it in the symbol table. So let's look at the symbol table.

At this time the symbol table is empty. So the symbolic name is unique. LOOP is accepted. The Assembler enters it in the first column. In the second column and in the same row, it will put the address to which the LO-CATION COUNTER is pointing. That value is 102.

The Assembler will associate LOOP with the numeric value 102 in the assembly process. Here is how the entry appears:

LOOP 102

Now the Assembler must add one to the LOCATION COUNTER, and then it is done with that instruction with respect to the first pass.

When the symbolic name RED has been finally entered, the symbol table is complete. It is presented in Table 3.10.

TABLE 3.10   Symbol Table

LOOP	102
EXIT	106
ABLE	107
RED	108

When the Assembler senses the END statement, the first pass is completed.

The Assembler has an *Operation Table* (Optable) to help it in the second pass. The Optable lists each FAL (FINAC Assembly Language) mnemonic with the associated numeric code for the machine language instruction. Table 3.11 gives the FINAC Optable.

Second Pass.   The second pass begins. The Assembler scans just the operation and operand fields. In ①, it encounters R-E-A-D-blank. The blank signifies the end of the operation field.

If READ is in the Optable, then it is a legitimate mnemonic. Its machine language numeric code, in this case 40, will be copied from the Optable and

TABLE 3.11 Optable

Mnemonic	Code
ADD	50
DIV	53
GØTØ	72
LØAD	60
MUL	52
PRINT	41
READ	40
STØP	01
STØRE	61
SUB	51
TESTN	71
TESTZ	70

placed into the first field of the address pointed to by the LOCATION COUNTER. This is location 100. So we have

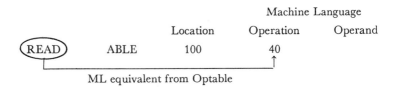

Now the Assembler will scan the operand field. The first nonblank in this field is A, then B, then L, then E, then blank. ABLE.

Since this is the Assembler's second pass, its only concern is to determine if the label ABLE is listed in the symbol table. Or, we might say, "Is ABLE defined?" The Assembler considers a label to be defined when it has been used in the name field of an assembly language instruction. Of course, it must be defined exactly once. The Assembler picks up all defined labels in the first pass.

If ABLE is a legitimate label, then the Assembler will enter the numeric value associated with it in the symbol table into the operand field of the machine language instruction that it is encoding. That's all there is to it.

The numeric value attached to ABLE is 107. Hence 107 is copied into the operand field of location 100. Now we have

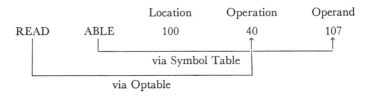

and then

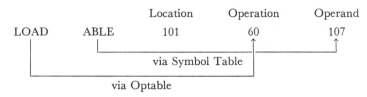

		Location	Operation	Operand
LOAD	ABLE	101	60	107

via Symbol Table

via Optable

The Assembler must search the symbol table for ABLE each time the programmer places ABLE into the operand field. When the Assembler encounters ABLE in ②, it repeats the question: Is ABLE legitimate? Or, has it been defined? When ABLE is once again found in the symbol table, the associated numeric value is copied into the ML operand field.

The operation and operand columns in Table 3.12 are the machine language code for our program segment of Table 3.9. The addresses in the location column are not part of the ML program.

TABLE 3.12   The Machine Language Program

Location	Operation	Operand
100	40	107
101	60	107
102	40	108
103	50	108
104	71	106
105	72	102
106	01	
107	?	
108	?	
109	?	

The question marks in the operation field of the last three instructions signify that we do not know the contents of these locations. The Assembler has allocated these locations for use by our program, but the Assembler has not changed the contents. The value of the contents of these locations was left by a previous program. This value, however, is immaterial to our program.

EXERCISES

1. Consider the polynomial

$$y = 4x^3 - 3x^2 + x - 7$$

Write a program in FAL (FINAC Assembly Language) which computes y for any x where $-20 < x < 20$. Use Horner's method. See exercise 7 in Chapter 1. Let the end-of-file condition test check for an *x* whose value is greater than 20. Invent instructions if necessary.

2. Modify the Gas Bill Program in Table 3.3 so that R1 is allowed to be less than R2. Submit a detailed flowchart with the program.

3. Play the Assembler Game. Convert the assembly program you wrote for exercise 2 into machine language code. Assume that the ML program will be assembled starting at location 100. Use the Optable in Table 3.11, but construct your own symbol table.

   Turn in the symbol table with your machine language program. The ML program should have the form:

Location	*Operation field*	*Operand field*
100	opcode	value

4. The Assembler will, of course, issue a diagnostic to the programmer when it encounters an illegal symbolic name. There are many ways for a symbolic name to be in error. (Can you list them?) Should the Assembler issue one blanket statement when it encounters an illegal symbolic name, for example, BLUE is illegal? Or should the Assembler attempt to pinpoint the cause? Justify your answer.

5. Consider exercise 4.
   a. Assume that we have chosen the first alternative. The Assembler will issue a single blanket statement, such as "BLUE is illegal," when we use an illegal symbolic name. Suppose you are allowed to receive one additional piece of information concerning the error. What additional piece of information would you choose to receive?
   b. Assume that we have chosen the pinpoint alternative. The Assembler will pinpoint, to the best of its ability, the cause of the error. List the types of possible errors. Give the diagnostic you would like to receive from the Assembler for each type.

6. Fortran handles the end-of-file condition by the clause END = symbolic address, which is inserted into the WRITE statement.
   a. How do the PL/I, COBOL, and ALGOL languages handle the end-of-file condition?
   b. Pick any computer not in the System/360 series. Find out how the computer you chose handles the end-of-file condition in its I/O routines.

7. Write a program which will produce the bills for a car rental agency. The bill for each customer is determined by the formula:

   Bill = mileage × price per mile + $5.00 per day.

But the following conditions must be met:
a. The minimum charge is $25.00.
b. A discount of 10 per cent is given if the bill exceeds $100.00
Submit a flowchart with your solution.

8. Play the Assembler Game again. Assemble the following program into machine language. Assume that the first instruction of ML code will be placed in location 100. Use the Optable given in Table 3.11. Construct your own symbol table. Issue Assembler diagnostics in the form given below. Use short, pithy comments in the diagnostics. Submit the symbol table and the diagnostics as your solution to the problem.

      Error number   Diagnostic

Play the Assembler Program

	READ	ØNE	VARIABLE → ØNE
	READ	FØUR	VARIABLE → FØUR
	READ	BLUE	VARIABLE → BLUE
	READ	SAM	VARIABLE → SAM
	LØAD	BLUE	ACC ← C(BLUE)
	DIVIDE	SAM	ACC ← C(ACC) / C(SAM)
	PUT	QUØT	QUØT ← C(ACC)
	WRITE	QUØT	C(QUØT) PRINTED
	LØAD	FØUR	ACC ← C(FØUR)
	SUB	ØNE	ACC ← C(ACC) − C(ØNE)
	TEST2	LØØP1	BRANCH IF ZERO
	STØP		
ØNE	DS	1	
BLUE	DS	2	
SAM	DS	1	
	END		

9. Consider the computer you picked to satisfy exercise 6. Compare the format of its assembly language to that of FINAC and System/360. How many fields are there in the machine language of your choice?

4 | The Representation of Information

The MEMORY of many modern computers is composed of tiny doughnut-shaped ferrite elements called *cores*. These cores have wires threaded through the holes in their center. Whenever a current of sufficient amperes is passed through the wire, the core is magnetized. The direction of the current flow determines the polarity of the magnetic field induced in the core. When the current is removed the core will retain both the magnetism and the polarity. The polarity of the core's magnetic field can be changed by causing current to flow through the wire in the opposite direction. (We might say information retrieval from MEMORY—LOAD, PRINT—is the process of sensing the magnetic state. Information storage—READ, STORE—is the magnetization of the core.)

Since the cores can be placed in one of exactly two magnetic states or orientations, it is natural to label these states as zero and one. And since zero and one are the two binary digits, we are led quite easily into the binary number system. The information stored in one core is called a *bit,* which is short for binary digit. And henceforth, we will talk about *bits,* the information possessed by the core, rather than the state of the core. We will refer to the core itself as the *bit position* and, as is the usual practice in computer science, shorten bit position to bit when it is clear in the context that we are referring to the bit position and not the information possessed by it.

Since a single bit position holds very little information—either zero or one—the bits are grouped into larger sets called *bytes.* A byte in a System/360 computer is a set of eight consecutive bits. Since each bit position in a byte can take on one of two different values, we find that there are 256 different patterns that a byte can assume. Hence a byte may possess any 1 of 256 pieces of information.

A byte might appear as

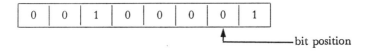

or

1	1	0	0	1	1	0	1

or in any of the 254 other patterns.

The byte is the smallest set of addressable bits. That is, each byte has a unique address. The addresses run, as is usual in computer science, from 0 to n − 1, where n is the number of bytes in the MEMORY of the computer.

The bit, byte, word configuration varies from computer to computer. The smallest set of addressable bits is called a *word* with respect to the FINAC computer. In the CDC 3000 series computers, a byte is a set of six bits. And, further, in this series we may speak of a byte address in one context but of a word address in another.

A word in the 360 series is a set of four consecutive bytes such that the address of the low order byte is divisible by four, or we might say that the address of a word is always divisible by four. Figure 4.1 is a schema of a full-word.

A *half-word* is a set of two consecutive bytes such that the address of the low order byte is divisible by two. The first two bytes and the last two bytes in Figure 4.1 are both examples of half-words.

A *double-word* is a set of eight consecutive bytes such that the address of the low order byte is divisible by eight. A schema of a double-word appears in Figure 4.2.

Whenever there might be confusion between word and half-word or word and double-word, we will use the phrase full-word as a substitute for word.

4.1 Number Systems

All data in a computer is stored in binary form. Characters, such as the letters of the alphabet, are in a binary code. One byte is usually necessary to

FIGURE 4.1

byte 0	byte 1	byte 2	byte 3
000464	000465	000466	000467

address

FIGURE 4.2

byte 0	byte 1	byte 2	byte 3	byte 4	byte 5	byte 6	byte 7
000800	000801	000802	000803	000804	000805	000806	000807

address

hold the binary code which will represent any character. The letter "A," for example, is represented in EBCDIC (Extended Binary Coded Decimal Interchange Code) by 11000001.

Integers, however, do not usually appear in code. (We will study one form —the packed decimal numbers—which might be considered a binary code for the integers.) A decimal (base 10) number appears in the computer as a binary (base 2) number. A decimal number will be converted to its binary equivalent by the computer.

The binary number system is common to all computers. Other number systems, such as octal (base 8) or hexadecimal (base 16) are used with a computer depending on the bit, byte, and word structure of the particular computer. Therefore, the student of computer science must become familiar with the nature of the various number systems.

If the student is programming in the Compass language for the CDC 3000 series which has a six-bit byte structure, he must possess a good knowledge of the octal, base 8, number system. Octal is required because six binary digits are so readily converted to two octal digits (see Table 4.2).

In System/360, the 8 bit byte structure leads us to the base 16 or the hexadecimal (hex) number system. The conversion between hex and binary is easy to do because 8 binary digits (1 byte) converts to 2 hex digits. The reason for this conversion will become apparent as we gain a background in Basic Assembler Language of System/360.

One attribute all number systems have in common is positional representation. The position of a digit in a numeral determines the value of that digit in the numeral. In 469_{10}, the value of the digit 4 is 400 because 4 appears in the third position from the right. To find the true value of 4 in the numeral, we multiply 4 by the square of the radix. The radix or base is 10. Hence the numeral's value is $4 \times 10^2 = 400$.

If we write a numeral in a power series, the value of each digit is easily ascertained. For example,

$$4 \times 10^2 + 6 \times 10^1 + 9 \times 10^0 = 400 + 60 + 9$$

The conversion of a number which is written in any base to decimal is done handily using the power series technique, with all arithmetic being done in base 10.

Algorithm 1

standard form → power series → positional values → base 10

Example 4.1

Convert 764_8 to base 10.

Using the power series technique, we find

$$764_8 = 7 \times 8^2 + 6 \times 8^1 + 4 \times 8^0 = 448 + 48 + 4 = 500_{10}$$

Example 4.2

Convert 1011110_2 to base 10.

Using the power series technique, we find

$$1011110_2 = 1 \times 2^6 + 0 \times 2^5 + 1 \times 2^4 + 1 \times 2^3 + 1 \times 2^2 + 1 \times 2^1 + 0 \times 2^0$$
$$= 64 + 0 + 16 + 8 + 4 + 2 + 0 = 94_{10}$$

Another attribute all number systems have in common is the fact that the number of digits possessed by the system is equal to the value of the radix of the system. Binary whose radix is 2 has 2 digits. There are 8 digits in the octal system. The hexadecimal system has 16; they are 0, 1, 2, 3, 4, 5, 6, 7, 8, 9, A, B, C, D, E, and F. The unfamiliar digits have values as follows:

Hex	Decimal
A	10
B	11
C	12
D	13
E	14
F	15

We count to 25 in 4 different bases in Table 4.1 on page 52.

The conversion procedure from hex to decimal follows the algorithm outlined above. Bear in mind that all arithmetic is done in base 10.

Example 4.3

Convert $49AB_X$* to decimal.

Using the power series technique, we find

$$49AB_X = 4 \times 16^3 + 9 \times 16^2 + 10 \times 16^1 + 11 \times 16^0$$
$$= 4 \times 4096 + 9 \times 256 + 10 \times 16 + 11$$
$$= 16384 + 2304 + 160 + 11$$
$$= 18859_{10}$$

We have inserted one extra step in the solution in order to clarify the procedure.

The algorithm to convert a decimal numeral to a numeral in some other radix is a division process. The technique is not difficult, but the statement of the algorithm is a little cumbersome. We present a *Decimal to Hexadecimal Conversion Algorithm*. The student is asked to generalize this algorithm in exercise 5 at the end of this chapter.

---

* $49AB_X$ is equivalent to $49AB_{16}$. The subscript x is used to denote that 49AB is a hexadecimal numeral.

TABLE 4.1 Four Number Systems

Decimal	Binary	Octal	Hexadecimal
1	1	1	1
2	10	2	2
3	11	3	3
4	100	4	4
5	101	5	5
6	110	6	6
7	111	7	7
8	1000	10	8
9	1001	11	9
10	1010	12	A
11	1011	13	B
12	1100	14	C
13	1101	15	D
14	1110	16	E
15	1111	17	F
16	10000	20	10
17	10001	21	11
18	10010	22	12
19	10011	23	13
20	10100	24	14
21	10101	25	15
22	10110	26	16
23	10111	27	17
24	11000	30	18
25	11001	31	19

We use the following notation in the algorithm:

1. DIVI is a number written in base 10.
2. The value of RADIX is set to 16—the value of the hexadecimal radix when it is written as a base 10 numeral.
3. NUMBER is the base 10 numeral which will be converted.
4. i is a subscript. It will be initialized to 0.
5. R_i is a digit in the new base.
6. QUOT is the quotient of the division.
7. REM_{10} and REM_{16} are the remainder of the division written in base 10 and base 16, respectively.

$$
\begin{array}{r}
28 \longleftarrow\text{QUOT} \\
\text{RADIX}\longrightarrow 16\overline{\smash)463}\longleftarrow\text{DIVI} \\
\underline{32} \\
143 \\
\underline{128} \\
15 \longleftarrow\text{REM}_{10}
\end{array}
$$

The work of the algorithm is done when QUOT equals zero. The result will be in the form

$$R_n R_{n-1} \ldots R_3 R_2 R_1 R_0$$

where the R_i's are digits in the new base.

The Decimal to Hexadecimal Conversion Algorithm

Step 0: Set $i = 0$.
Step 1: Set RADIX equal to 16.
Step 2: Set DIVI equal to NUMBER.
Step 3: Let QUOT equal the quotient of DIVI/RADIX.
Step 4: Let REM_{10} equal the remainder of DIVI/RADIX.
Step 5: Convert REM_{10} to REM_{16}.
Step 6: Set $R_i = REM_{16}$.
Step 7: If QUOT equals zero, go to step 11.
Step 8: Set DIVI equal to QUOT.
Step 9: Set $i = i + 1$.
Step 10: Go to step 3.
Step 11: Stop.

Example 4.4

Convert 474_{10} to hexadecimal.

Using the Decimal to Hexadecimal Conversion Algorithm, we find:

Step 0: $i = 0$
Step 1: RADIX $= 16$
Step 2: DIVI $= 474$
Step 3: QUOT $= 29$
Step 4: $REM_{10} = 10_{10}$
Step 5: $REM_{10} = 10_{10} \Rightarrow REM_{16} = A_{16}$
Step 6: $R_0 = A_{16}$
Step 7: QUOT $\neq 0$
Step 8: DIVI $= 29$
Step 9: $i = 1$
Step 3: QUOT $= 1$
Step 4: $REM_{10} = 13_{10}$
Step 5: $REM_{10} = 13_{10} \Rightarrow REM_{16} = D_{16}$
Step 6: $R_1 = D_{16}$
Step 7: QUOT $\neq 0$
Step 8: DIVI $= 1$
Step 9: $i = 2$
Step 3: QUOT $= 0$
Step 4: $REM_{10} = 1$
Step 5: $REM_{10} = 1_{10} \Rightarrow REM_{16} = 1_{16}$
Step 6: $R_2 = 1_{16}$
Step 7: QUOT $= 0$
Step 11: Stop

The result is $1DA_{16}$ since $R_0 = A_{16}$, $R_1 = D_{16}$, $R_2 = 1_{16}$.

An illustration of the technique to convert 474_{10} to **HEX** is given below:

$$16)\overline{474}$$
$16)\underline{29}$ remainder 10_{10} = A in hex
$16)\underline{1}$ remainder 13_{10} = D in hex
0 remainder 1 = 1 in hex
Solution: $474_{10} = 1DA_x$

The two remaining examples show how to convert a base 10 integer to octal or binary. The examples should be helpful in developing a generalized algorithm for the conversion of a decimal integer to an integer in any base.

Example 4.5

Convert 474_{10} to octal.

The decimal numeral is the dividend in the process given below. The radix value is the divisor. The integral remainder is the first digit in the numeral of the new base.

$$
\begin{array}{r}
59 \\
8)\overline{474} \\
\underline{40} \\
74 \\
\underline{72} \\
2 \end{array}
$$
$2\longleftarrow$ first digit in base 8 numeral

The quotient 59 is the new dividend for the next division. The divisor will again be the radix value.

$$
\begin{array}{r}
7 \\
8)\overline{59} \\
\underline{56} \\
3 \end{array}
$$
$3\longleftarrow$ second digit in base 8 numeral

The quotient 7 is the new dividend for the next division. We will continue this division process until the quotient is zero.

$$
\begin{array}{r}
0 \\
8)\overline{7} \\
\underline{0} \\
7 \end{array}
$$
$7\longleftarrow$ third digit in base 8 numeral

The quotient is zero. We are done. $474_{10} = 732_8$.

Let us combine all steps into a single picture.

$8)\overline{474}$
$8)\underline{59}$ with a remainder of 2 ────┐
$8)\underline{7}$ with a remainder of 3 ───┐│
0 with a remainder of 7 ──┐↓↓↓
732_8

Example 4.6

Convert 474_{10} to binary.

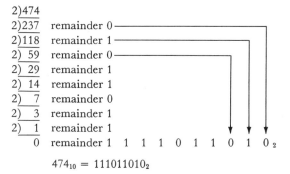

$$474_{10} = 111011010_2$$

Octal and Binary Conversions. Conversions between octal and binary is, to use an old phrase, "easy as pie." No division is necessary. No multiplication is involved. All that is required is a little mental effort. Every octal digit has a three-digit binary value. Consider Table 4.2.

TABLE 4.2 Binary-Octal Conversion Table

3-digit Binary	Octal
000	0
001	1
010	2
011	3
100	4
101	5
110	6
111	7

To convert *from octal to binary*, simply write the binary equivalent of each octal digit.

Example 4.7

Convert 474_8 to binary.

$$474_8 = 100\ 111\ 100 = 100111100_2$$

Example 4.8

Convert 1247_8 to binary.

$$1247_8 = \underbrace{001}\ \underbrace{010}\ \underbrace{100}\ \underbrace{111} = 001010100111_2 = 1010100111_2$$

In the last step, we merely dropped the unnecessary leading zeros.

The conversion *from binary to octal* is simple too. Group the binary digits into sets of three starting at the right. (Add leading zeros if necessary.) Write the octal equivalent of each set of binary digits.

Example 4.9

Convert 110111101_2 to octal.

$$110111101_2 = \underbrace{110}\ \underbrace{111}\ \underbrace{101} = 675_8$$

Example 4.10

Convert 1111011111_2 to octal.

$$1111011111_2 = \underbrace{001}\ \underbrace{111}\ \underbrace{011}\ \underbrace{111} = 1737_8$$

Conversions Between Hex and Binary.   The conversions *from hex to binary* can be accomplished quite rapidly also. Since $16 = 2^4$, each hex digit can be represented by four binary digits. Consider the four-digit binary representation of a hex digit given in Table 4.3.

Example 4.11

Convert $AB1_x$ to binary.

$$AB1_x = 1010\ 1011\ 0001 = 101010110001_2$$

Example 4.12

Convert $7AF_x$ to binary.

$$7AF_x = 0111\ 1010\ 1111 = 11110101111_2$$

TABLE 4.3 Binary-Hex Conversion Table

4-digit Binary	Hex
0000	0
0001	1
0010	2
0011	3
0100	4
0101	5
0110	6
0111	7
1000	8
1001	9
1010	A
1011	B
1100	C
1101	D
1110	E
1111	F

To convert *from binary to hex,* group the digits in the binary numeral into sets of four starting at the right. Write the hex equivalent of each set of four binary digits.

Example 4.13

Convert 101111111011_2 to hex.

$$101111111011_2 = 1011 \ 1111 \ 1011 = BFB_x$$

Example 4.14

Convert 10111_2 to hex.

$$10111_2 = 0001 \ 0111 = 17_x$$

4.2 The Conversion of Fractions

It is interesting to note that the base 10 integer 55 converts to the hex integer 37, while the base 10 decimal fraction .55 converts to the repeating hex fraction $.8CCCC\cdots$. That is, $55_{10} = 37_x$ and $.55_{10} = .8CCC\cdots_x$.

This should suggest that the procedure followed to convert the fractional part of a numeral in one base to another is significantly different than the conversion of the integer part. And it is.

The conversion of fractions from one base to another is a multiplicative process, and it is a relatively easy one.

We present an algorithm, the *Fraction Conversion Algorithm*, which explains the details of the conversion. The algorithm follows the explanation of the terminology.

RADIX is the numerical value of the "new" base written in the "old" base. For example, if we wish to convert a fraction from base 10 to base 16, then RADIX equals 16. If we wish to convert from base 16 to base 10, then RADIX equals hex A.

A terminating fraction in base 10 may not terminate in some other base. And this statement can be generalized: A terminating fraction in base Y may not terminate in base X. The following statement, however, is true: If t is a terminating fraction in base X and t does not terminate in base Y, then t will be a *repeating* decimal in base Y. For example, $.44_{10} = .70A3D70A3D70\text{-}A3D_X \cdot \cdot \cdot \cdot$

We must, therefore, decide, before converting, how many digits we want in the fraction of the new base. The variable EXTENT (in the algorithm) is set to the number of digits desired in the new base.

The new fraction will be in the form $.X1X2X3X4X5 \cdot \cdot \cdot$ with the new radix point in front of X1. One digit, Xi, will be generated in each pass through the algorithm. These digits will be generated in the order X1, X2, X3, etc. A subscript variable i will be initialized to one at the beginning of the algorithm; i will be increased by one in each pass. When, for example, i = 3, then Xi = X3. When i > EXTENT, the generation of digits stops.

If the fraction terminates in the new base, the algorithm will stop generating digits even if i ≤ EXTENT. That is, the algorithm will not generate trailing zeros. For example, if we wish to convert $.5_{10}$ to a five-digit hex fraction, the result given by the algorithm will be $.8_x$ since the fraction terminated. It is, however, simple to "tack on" the four trailing zeros and get $.80000_x$ if that is necessary.

All multiplication performed in the algorithm is done in the old base. The product of the multiplication will have two parts—the integral part and the fractional part. These parts are labeled $INTEGER_{OLD}$ and $FRACTION_{OLD}$, respectively. Examples follow the algorithm.

The Fraction Conversion Algorithm

Step 0: Set EXTENT equal to the number of digits desired in the new fraction.

Step 1: Set i = 1.

Step 2: Set RADIX equal to the value of the new base.

Step 3: Set FRACTION equal to the fraction in the old base.

Step 4: Multiply FRACTION by RADIX.

Step 5: Convert $INTEGER_{OLD}$ to $INTEGER_{NEW}$.

Step 6: Let Xi = $INTEGER_{NEW}$

Step 7: If $FRACTION_{OLD}$ equals zero, go to step 12.

Step 8: Let i = i + 1.

Step 9:   If i is greater than EXTENT, go to step 12.
Step 10: Let FRACTION equal FRACTION$_{\text{OLD}}$.
Step 11: Go to step 4.
Step 12: Stop.

Note that we limit our examples to conversions from base 10 to some other base.

Example 4.15

Convert .24 to a three-digit binary fraction.

Following the Fraction Conversion Algorithm, we obtain:

   0. EXTENT = 3
   1. i = 1
   2. RADIX = 2
   3. FRACTION = .24
   4. RADIX times FRACTION = 0.48
   5. $0_2 = 0_{10}$
   6. X1 = 0
   7. FRACTION$_{\text{OLD}}$ is not equal to 0
   8. i = 2
   9. i is not greater than EXTENT
  10. FRACTION = .48
   4. RADIX times FRACTION = 0.96
   5. $0_2 = 0_{10}$
   6. X2 = 0
   7. FRACTION$_{\text{OLD}}$ is not equal to 0
   8. i = 3
   9. i is not greater than EXTENT
  10. FRACTION = .96
   4. RADIX times FRACTION = 1.92
   5. $1_2 = 1_{10}$
   6. X3 = 1
   7. FRACTION$_{\text{OLD}}$ is not equal to 0
   8. i = 4
   9. i is greater than EXTENT
  12. stop
  Result: .X1X2X3 = .001

or

   $.24_{10} \cong .001_2$

The algorithmic process is illustrated below.

.24	.48	.96
$\times 2$	$\times 2$	$\times 2$
0.48	0.96	1.92
X̃1 F̄RACTION$_{\text{OLD}}$	X̃2 F̄RACTION$_{\text{OLD}}$	X̃3

$.24_{10} \cong .X1X2X3 \cong .001_2$ (to three digits)

Example 4.16

Convert $.5625_{10}$ to a hex fraction with no more than 6 digits.

Using the Fraction Conversion Algorithm, we obtain:

> 0. EXTENT = 6
> 1. i = 1
> 2. RADIX = 16
> 3. FRACTION = .5625
> 4. RADIX times FRACTION = 9.0000
> 5. $9_x = 9_{10}$
> 6. X1 = 9
> 7. FRACTION$_{OLD}$ equals 0
> 12. Stop
> Result: .X1 = .9

or

> $.5625_{10} = .9_x$

The algorithmic process resulted in only one division. It is illustrated below.

$$
\begin{array}{r}
.5625 \\
\times 16 \\
\hline
33750 \\
5625 \\
\hline
9{.}0000 \\
\end{array}
$$

X1   FRACTION$_{OLD}$ = 0

Hence,

> $.5625_{10} = .X1 = .9_x$

Example 4.17

Convert $.44_{10}$ to a 3 digit hex fraction.

Using the Fraction Conversion Algorithm, we find:

> 0. EXTENT = 3
> 1. i = 1
> 2. RADIX = 16
> 3. FRACTION = .44
> 4. RADIX times FRACTION = 7.04
> 5. $7_x = 7_{10}$
> 6. X1 = 7
> 7. FRACTION$_{OLD}$ $\neq$ 0
> 8. i = 2
> 9. i $\not>$ EXTENT
> 10. FRACTION = .04

4. RADIX times FRACTION = 0.64
5. $0_x = 0_{10}$
6. X2 = 0
7. $FRACTION_{OLD} \neq 0$
8. i = 3
9. i $\not>$ EXTENT
10. FRACTION = .64
4. RADIX times FRACTION = 10.24
5. $A_x = 10_{10}$
6. X3 = A
7. $FRACTION_{OLD} \neq 0$
8. i = 4
9. i > EXTENT
12. Stop
Result: .X1X2X3 = .70A

or

$.44_{10} \cong .70A_x$

4.3   The Hex Number System

What is the rationale behind the use of hexadecimal in System/360? We certainly need to understand the relationship between decimal and binary. Binary is, after all, the language of the computers. And the decimal number system is the basic number system used in society. But why hexadecimal?

Recall the snapshots we had of FINAC's memory when the computer was executing the gas bill. Those contents were pictured in English prose. In actuality, as the reader knows, the contents of those memory locations and those registers we looked at were in binary. The binary, however, would have been incomprehensible to us. Hence we took poetic license and wrote the contents in English prose.

The final results of a computer program, when printed, will usually be written in English prose. The numerals used in the output will be "good old" decimal. However, there is another type of output which is important to the computer scientist. This output is the *dump* of MEMORY or the registers of the computer or both. Any dump is usually restricted to those cells in MEMORY which are pertinent to the program being executed. These dumps may be especially important when a program does not run as anticipated. The Operating System provides these dumps on request.

Now suppose we request a dump of 100 words or we are given an abnormal termination dump. It doesn't matter which. Suppose further that this dump is in binary. The contents of 100 words printed in binary would consist of 3200 characters. If the dump were in hex, only 800 characters need be printed.

The savings in paper and time are impressive. Remember that the conversion from binary to hex is done almost without effort. There are four binary digits to one hex digit, four bits to a hex digit, thirty-two bits to eight hex digits. Suppose location BLUE has the following bit pattern:

01001001100001000001000000100000

The binary dump would be a faithful replica of the above pattern. But 32 bits mean 32 characters. Here is a hex dump of location BLUE:

49841020

Our snapshots of MEMORY or the registers or both will be given, at first, in both binary and hex. Eventually, the snapshots in this text will be given only in hex. However, by that time, this policy should not work any hardship on the reader.

We now turn to a discussion of the full-word binary representation of a decimal integer.

4.4 Full-word Representation of Decimal Integers

Consider the decimal integer 43: $43_{10} = 101011_2$. The full-word binary representation of decimal 43 is:

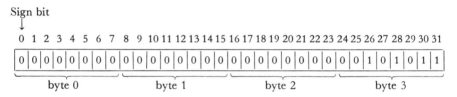

Bit 0 is the sign bit. If the sign bit equals zero, the integer is positive. If the sign bit equals one, the integer is negative.

The hex form of the contents of this word is

0000002B

The full-word binary representation of decimal 148 is

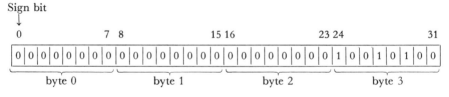

The hex form is 00000094.

A negative integer is represented in two's complement form. Some computers store negative numbers in one's complement form. Since these two forms are so closely related we will discuss both.

Algorithm 2 gives one method of finding the two's complement of a decimal integer. Note that on the way to the two's complement we must pass through the one's complement form.

Algorithm 2

Decimal Integer $\rightarrow$ Absolute Value of Decimal Integer $\rightarrow$
Full-word Binary $\rightarrow$ One's Complement $\rightarrow$ Two's Complement

We offer two definitions; the first is of the one's complement form, and the second is of the two's complement form. Then we demonstrate how to use Algorithm 2 to find the two's complement of a negative decimal integer.

Definition of One's Complement

Let x be a binary integer.
Let y be the binary integer which results from the following manipulation on x:
1. Replace each zero digit in x by one.
2. Replace each one digit in x by zero.
Then y is called the one's complement of x.

For example, let $x = 10101011$. Then the one's complement of x is 01010100.

Definition of Two's Complement

Let x be a binary integer.
Let y be the one's complement of x.
Then y plus one is the two's complement of x.

For example, let $x = 10111111$. The one's complement of x is 01000000, and the two's complement of x is 01000001.

Example 4.18

Write the full-word two's complement of -25.

We follow Algorithm 2 step by step.

1. Find the absolute value of -25.

   $|-25| = 25$

2. Convert to full-word binary.

   $25_{10} = 0000\ 0000\ 0000\ 0000\ 0000\ 0000\ 0001\ 1001_2$

3. Complement.

   $1111\ 1111\ 1111\ 1111\ 1111\ 1111\ 1110\ 0110_2$

4. Add 1.

   $\underset{\text{Sign bit}}{\underline{1}}111\ 1111\ 1111\ 1111\ 1111\ 1111\ 1110\ 0111_2$

Note the one in the sign bit which signifies a negative number. The hex representation of the above is FFFFFFE7.

In Example 4.19 we convert -43 to full-word two's complement form. We follow Algorithm 2, but all results are given in hex.

Example 4.19

Convert -43 to two's complement.

Solution:

    1. Find absolute value.

       $|-43| = 43$

    2. Convert to full-word binary (hex).

       $43_{10} = 0000002B_x$

    3. Complement.

       FFFFFFD4

    4. Add 1.

       FFFFFFD5

One advantage of writing negative integers in two's complement form is that the CPU does *not* have to sense the sign bit of the addends when adding. The numbers are merely added. If the sum is positive, the result will be in sign-absolute value form of positive binary integers. If the sum is negative, the result will be in two's complement form.

Example 4.20

Add -27 and $+17$. (Our illustration will be written in hex. Our thinking is in binary, but our output is in hex.)

Solution:

$$17_{10} = 00000011$$
$$-27_{10} = \underline{FFFFFFE5}$$
$$\overline{FFFFFFF6}$$

Is that the correct answer? If it is, then FFFFFFF6, when converted to binary, is the two's complement of -10.

Algorithm 3, given below, gives one technique by which we can find the signed decimal equivalent of a two's complement value.

Algorithm 3

Two's Complement $\rightarrow$ One's Complement $\rightarrow$ Sign-absolute
Value Binary $\rightarrow$ Decimal $\rightarrow$ Signed Decimal

We now find the signed decimal equivalent of FFFFFFF6 using Algorithm 3.

1. Start.

   FFFFFFF6

2. Subtract 1.

   FFFFFFF5

3. Complement.

   0000000A

4. Convert to decimal.

   10

5. Replace sign.

   -10

Our solution in Example 4.20 was correct.

Example 4.21

Add -17 and $+27$.

Solution:

$$
\begin{array}{rl}
27_{10} = & 0000001\mathrm{B} \\
-17_{10} = & \mathrm{FFFFFFEF} \\
\hline
① & 0000000\mathrm{A}
\end{array}
$$

overflow

There is overflow. The overflow is ignored by the CPU. The answer which remains is equal to a positive 10_{10}.

Another advantage of two's complement notation occurs in subtraction. The CPU is able to ignore the sign of the subtrahend and the minuend. (Can you recall the rather elaborate subtraction algorithm associated with signed numbers?) When negative numbers are written in two's complement form, the CPU is able to accomplish subtraction of signed numbers by merely "complementing" the subtrahend and adding that value to the minuend. That is, if X is positive and X is the subtrahend, then the two's complement of X is added to the minuend. If the subtrahend is negative, the absolute value of the subtrahend is added to the minuend.

We omit any examples of subtraction employing the above technique since it is so similar to two's complement addition. Example 4.22 illustrates that two's complement subtraction is interesting in its own right. Remember, however, that the CPU of most computers performs subtraction using the technique discussed in the previous paragraph.

Example 4.22

Subtract -27 from $+17$.

Solution:

$$\overset{\textcircled{1}\,\text{Borrowing from ``thin air!''}}{\begin{array}{r} +17_{10} = 00000011 \\ -27_{10} = \text{FFFFFFE5} \\ \hline 0000002\text{C} \end{array}}$$

Did you notice the "borrowing from thin air"? In order to subtract five from the first digit in the minuend, one was borrowed from the second digit (1 in this case is 16_{10}). Five from seventeen $= 12_{10} = C_x$. Now continue the subtracting. The remaining digits are

$$\begin{array}{r} 0000000 \\ -\text{FFFFFFE} \end{array}$$

There is nothing to borrow from any digit on the left. So we borrow one for the leftmost digit from the "thin air." Then each preceding digit is able to borrow one, and the subtraction is accomplished.

Example 4.23

Subtract $+17$ from -17.

Solution:

$$\begin{array}{r} -17_{10} = \text{FFFFFFEF} \\ +17_{10} = 00000011 \\ \hline \text{FFFFFFDE} \end{array}$$

Is our answer correct? Apply Algorithm 3 to check this solution.

We conclude our discussion concerning the peculiarities of computer addition and subtraction in Topic 1 of the Computer Notebook.

Computer Notebook

TOPIC 1   One's Complement Arithmetic

Some computers, particularly CDC 3000 Series computers, store negative binary integers in one's complement form. The CPUs of these computers must, therefore, employ a slightly different technique than the CPUs of System/360 when adding binary integer operands.

In our discussion of some of the more interesting aspects of these techniques, we will assume that a byte is six bits long. Our words will be 4 bytes, or 24 bits, long. We will therefore use octal in our discussion.

Example 4.24

Add $+37_{10}$ and $-26_{10}.$*

Solution:

$$
\begin{array}{rll}
+37_{10} = & 45_8 & \text{or} \quad 00000045 \\
-26_{10} = & -32_8 & \text{or} \quad 77777745 \\
\end{array}
$$

$$
\begin{array}{r}
\llcorner 00000012 \\
\text{End} \qquad \quad \longrightarrow 1 \\
\text{around} \quad \overline{00000013} \\
\text{carry}
\end{array}
$$

The answer is $+11$. Correct? Note the "end around carry" in one's complement addition. Overflow is ignored in two's complement addition.

Example 4.25

Add -37_{10} and $+12_{10}.$

Solution:

$$
\begin{array}{rll}
-37_{10} = & -45_8 = & 77777732 \\
12_{10} = & 14_8 = & 00000014 \\
\hline
 & & 77777746
\end{array}
$$

Modify Algorithm 3 to convert one's complement integers to signed decimals. Then check the solution to this example.

We must, at times, employ "end around borrow" to accomplish a one's complement subtraction. This technique is illustrated in Example 4.27. (Bear in mind, though, that the CPU, when it performs the subtraction, will complement the subtrahend and add that value to the minuend.)

Example 4.26

Subtract 46_{10} from $-32_{10}.$

Solution:

$$
\begin{array}{rll}
-32_{10} = & -40_8 = & 77777737 \\
46_{10} = & 56_8 = & 00000056 \\
\hline
 & & 77777661
\end{array}
$$

Is the answer correct?

---

* -26_{10} will be in one's complement form when stored in a full word.

Example 4.27

Subtract -32_{10} from 46_{10}.

Solution:

$$46_{10} = 56_8 = 00000056$$
$$-32_{10} = -40_8 = \underline{77777737}$$
$$17$$

We have no problem subtracting the first two digits in the problem. Then we must subtract seven from zero, which we can't do. We must "borrow" from some high order digit on the left. But no digit on the left has anything to "lend."

The one's complement subtraction algorithm states, "borrow one, if necessary, from the units digit of the difference." Consider:

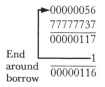

We have no problem subtracting the first two digits in the problem. Then we
End
around
borrow

TOPIC 2 EBCDIC Character Representation

In Section 4.1 we stated that characters are stored in MEMORY in the Extended Binary Coded Decimal Interchange Code. Each character requires one byte of storage. Since a byte may assume any 1 of 256 patterns, the EBCDIC code can define up to 256 characters.

A fairly complete list of the EBCDIC characters can be found in Appendix A. For your convenience, we have repeated a portion of that list in Table 4.4. You may find it quite useful to refer to this table during the course of the discussion which follows.

Note that

1. A blank is a character.
2. The digits 0, 1, 2, 3, 4, 5, 6, 7, 8, 9 are also called *zoned decimals* when they are represented in EBCDIC. The computer *CANNOT* perform arithmetic operations on zoned decimal numbers.
3. The data punched on an IBM card is in Hollerith code. The channel which controls the READER causes the conversion of the data from Hollerith to EBCDIC. It is the programmer's responsibility to convert numerical data from zoned decimal to an appropriate form which the computer can process.
4. The data which the programmer expects the PRINTER to print must be in EBCDIC. It is the programmer's responsibility to convert

TABLE 4.4   Some EBCDIC Representations

Character	Binary code	Hex code
blank	0100 0000	40
A	1100 0001	C1
B	1100 0010	C2
C	1100 0011	C3
D	1100 0100	C4
E	1100 0101	C5
F	1100 0110	C6
G	1100 0111	C7
H	1100 1000	C8
I	1100 1001	C9
J	1101 0001	D1
K	1101 0010	D2
L	1101 0011	D3
M	1101 0100	D4
N	1101 0101	D5
O	1101 0110	D6
P	1101 0111	D7
Q	1101 1000	D8
R	1101 1001	D9
S	1110 0010	E2
T	1110 0011	E3
U	1110 0100	E4
V	1110 0101	E5
W	1110 0110	E6
X	1110 0111	E7
Y	1110 1000	E8
Z	1110 1001	E9
0	1111 0000	F0
1	1111 0001	F1
2	1111 0010	F2
3	1111 0011	F3
4	1111 0100	F4
5	1111 0101	F5
6	1111 0110	F6
7	1111 0111	F7
8	1111 1000	F8
9	1111 1001	F9

the results of his data processing to EBCDIC before he issues a write command.

5. Consider the column called *Binary code*. If the EBCDIC representation of the letters and of the decimal integers is considered a binary number, then the values of those numbers increase as we proceed

through the alphabet. This is called the *collating sequence*. Table 4.4 is in the EBCDIC collating sequence. Note that "blank" comes before any letter and the zone decimals follow the alphabetic characters. The entire set of characters which are listed in Appendix A are given in the collating sequence of EBCDIC.

A set of characters is often called a *character string* or *character constant*. The Basic Assembler Language has a pseudo instruction, Define Constant, which allows the programmer to define a character string of up to 256 bytes in length.

The general form of Define Constant when used for character definition is:

label   DC   C'string or value'

The label in the name field is optional. The string or value is required and must be enclosed in apostrophes. For example:

BLUE   DC   C'APRIL FOOL'

The reply of the Assembler will be the generation of the EBCDIC code for APRIL FOOL. That code will be stored into the byte locations starting at BLUE.

BLUE

C1	D7	D9	C9	D3	40	C6	D6	D6	D3

Example 4.28

What will the Assembler reply to the pseudo

RED   DC   C'THE SUM IS'

Solution: The Assembler will generate the following code, starting at location RED.

RED

E3	C8	C5	40	E2	E4	D4	40	C9	E2

Some of the above discussion will be repeated and extended in the next chapter.

TOPIC 3   Packed Decimal Numbers

Consider the following four-bit binary representation of the decimal integers given in Table 4.5.

TABLE 4.5   Four-bit Binary Integers

Four-bit Binary	Decimal
0000	0
0001	1
0010	2
0011	3
0100	4
0101	5
0110	6
0111	7
1000	8
1001	9

If we use the four-bit binary code to represent a decimal integer, then we can "pack" two decimal integers into one byte. For example, 95 packed into one byte would appear as:

0	2	2	3	4	5	6	7
1	0	0	1	0	1	0	1

9	5

The digit 9 is in the left nibble, and 5 is in the right nibble of the byte. Bits 0–3 of a byte are sometimes referred to as the *left nibble,* and bits 4–7 as the *right nibble.*

Example 4.29

Write 1237 as a packed decimal number.

Solution:

0001	0010	0011	0111
1	2	3	7

What about the sign of a decimal number? System/360 places the sign into the right nibble of the rightmost byte. For example, −843 would appear in the packed decimal format as

1000	0100	0011	1101
8	4	3	D

where D represents a minus sign.

A hex digit in the right nibble of the rightmost byte of a packed decimal field represents a sign. The computer recognizes A, C, E, and F as plus signs, while B and D are regarded as minus signs. The computer itself, however, generates C for plus and D for minus.

Example 4.30

Write −943 as a signed packed decimal number.
Solution:

1001	0100	0011	1101
9	4	3	D

Example 4.31

Write 12346 as a signed packed decimal number.
Solution:

0001	0010	0011	0100	0110	1100
1	2	3	4	6	C

Let x be a decimal integer. Let n be the number of digits in x. Then if n is odd, the number of bytes needed to store x in packed decimal representation is given by $(n + 1)/2$. For example, let $x = 56747$, which is 5 digits long. Hence the number of bytes necessary to represent x in packed decimal is three.

0101	0110	0111	0100	0111	1100
5	6	7	4	7	C

If n, the number of digits in x, is even, then the number of bytes needed to store x in packed decimal is given by $(n + 2)/2$.

Example 4.32

Write 1268 in packed decimal representation.
Solution:

0000	0001	0010	0110	1000	1100
0	1	2	6	8	C

All packed decimal numbers are of odd parity with respect to the number of digits. The computer supplies a leading zero for all decimal integers which have an even number of digits.

System/360 computers can perform arithmetic and logical operations with packed decimal operands. A full discussion of the instructions in the packed decimal repertoire appears in a later chapter.

TOPIC 4   Floating-point Representation of Real Numbers

The floating-point numbers of computer science are quite similar in structure to the numbers written in scientific notation. For example, 2.4×10^{-27} is a real number in scientific notation standard form. A floating-point number differs merely in that the "normalized" form, the point (hex point, not decimal point) is placed before the first nonzero digit. Still, 2.4×10^{-27} might be considered an unnormalized floating-point number in base 10.

The sign, the mantissa, and the characteristic[2] of the floating-point number are all stored in the same cell. The length of the cell may be one or two words. A short, or single-precision, floating-point number can be stored in one word. The long, or double-precision, type requires a double-word in storage.

The sign of both types is stored into bit 0 of their respective cells. If bit 0 is equal to zero, then the mantissa is positive. If bit 0 is equal to one, then the mantissa is negative. Unlike the binary representation of integers, in which negative values are in two's complement, the floating-point representation of real numbers is in sign-absolute value form.

For example, negative six and positive six have exactly the same representation except for the value in the sign bit, which will be one for minus six and zero for plus six.

Both types, single- and double-precision, store the characteristic into bits 1 through 7 of their respective cells. The mantissa, or fraction, of the short form occupies bits 8–31 of its word, while the mantissa of the long form occupies bits 8–63 of its double-word.

A schema of a single-precision number is given below.

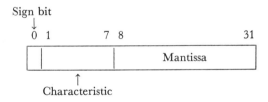

The schema of a double-precision number follows.

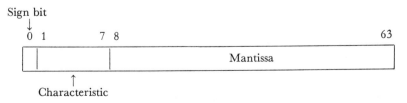

[2] The exponent of a floating-point number is equal to the characteristic minus sixty-four.

The above schemata clearly illustrate the fact that while there are two types of floating-point numbers, they differ merely in the number of the digits in their respective mantissas. Since the length of the mantissa is not pertinent to the discussion that follows, we will limit our illustrations and examples to the single-precision, or short, form.

The exponent, which is a power of 16, has a bias value of 64. The *true* exponent associated with the mantissa is found by subtracting this bias value from the value of the characteristic given in bits 1–7. If the true exponent is negative, then the value of the real number represented is between minus one and plus one.

The conversion from floating-point to signed decimal which is illustrated in Example 4.33 should clarify the bias value concept.

Example 4.33

The contents of location SAM is 41100000. Find the real number represented.

Solution:

1. Convert to binary.

41	10	00	00	=	0	100 0001	0001 0000	0000 0000	0000 0000

$$0\ 1 \qquad 7\ 8 \qquad\qquad\qquad\qquad\qquad 31$$

2. Determine sign: bit 0 = 0; hence, value is positive.
3. Determine characteristic: the value in bits 1–7 is $1000001 = 65_{10}$.
4. Find true exponent:

   (characteristic − biased value = true exponent)
   $65 - 64 = 1$

5. Express magnitude of real number as mantissa times exponent: $.0001_2 \times 16^1 = .0001_2 \times 2^4$.
6. Multiply (shift binary point to the right): $.0001 \times 2^4 = 0001. = 1$.

The point is a binary point. Each positive power of two "moves" the point one place to the right. A negative power of two will "move" the point one place to the left. If the mantissa is written in hexadecimal, the point will be a hexadecimal point. Each positive power of the exponent as determined in step 4 will move the hex point one hex digit place to the right.

Example 4.34

The content of location BLUE is $BF800000_x$. Find the real number represented.

Solution:

1. Convert to binary.

BF	80	00	00	=	1	011 1111	1000 0000	0000 0000	0000 0000

$$0 \qquad 1 \qquad 7 \quad 8 \qquad\qquad\qquad\qquad\qquad 31$$

2. Determine sign: bit 0 = 1; hence, value is negative.

3. Determine biased exponent: the value in bits 1–7 is $0111111_2 = 63_{10}$.

4. Determine true exponent: $63 - 64 = -1$.

5. Express magnitude of real number as a product: $.10000000_2 \times 16_{10}^{-1} = .1000_2 \times 2^{-4}$.

6. Multiply: $.1000 \times 2^{-4} = .00001 = 0 \times 2^{-1} + 0 \times 2^{-2} + 0 \times 2^{-3} + 0 \times 2^{-4} + 1 \times 2^{-5} = 1/32$.

7. Attach sign: $-1/32$.

We now present the definition of a Basic Assembler Language *normalized* floating-point number. We use this definition in Example 4.35. Note that the definition of a normalized floating-point number will vary depending on the computer manufacturer and computer model.

Normalized Floating-point Number

A floating-point number is said to be normalized if the first hex digit which follows the hex point is nonzero.

Example 4.35

Express 14.5 as a single-precision floating-point number.

Solution:

1. Convert to binary: $14.5_{10} = 1110.1_2$.

2. Normalize (in hex: E.8 = .E8 × 16¹): $1110.1_2 = .11101 \times 2^4 = .11101_2 \times 16^1$. Hence, exponent equals one.

3. Find characteristic: $1 + 64 = 65$.

4. Express characteristic as a seven-bit binary integer: $65_{10} = 1000001$.

5. Find sign: 14.5 is positive; hence, move zero into sign bit.

6. Put sign, mantissa, and characteristic into their proper fields in a full word:

0	100 0001	1110 1000	0000 0000	0000 0000
↑				
Sign bit	Exponent		Characteristic	

7. Convert to hex: 41E80000.

EXERCISES

1. Convert the following numerals to the specified base.

   a. 474_8 to base 10   f. 569_{10} to base 16

   b. ACD_{16} to base 10   g. 10101111_2 to base 16

   c. 10101011_2 to base 8   h. 77760_8 to base 2

   d. 346_7 to base 10   i. $ABCD_{16}$ to base 8

   e. 444_{10} to base 8   j. 77760_8 to base 16

2. a. Write the full-word binary integer representation of 125, -125, 37, 43, -12.

   b. Convert the results of part (a) to hex.

3. Express 47 as a full-word binary integer. Show how this 32 bit integer would be added to the full-word representation of -19.

4. Find the value of the signed decimal integers represented in locations A, BLUE, and BLACK, if the respective hex representations of these locations are: (a) FFFF6413, (b) FFFFFF12, and (c) FFFFFFF1.

5. State an algorithm which, if followed, will convert a numeral written in base 10 into a numeral of any base.

6. Express the following two decimal integers in twenty-four-bit word form. Use one's complement form for negative integers. Show how the addition of the two integers is accomplished in one's complement arithmetic. Subtract (a) from (b) using one's complement arithmetic.
   a. 55
   b. -31

7. Give the computer reply in hex for each of the following character strings. The reply should be in EBCDIC.

BLUE	DC	C'HAPPY NEW YEAR'
RED	DC	C'HAUSKAA JOULUA'
BLACK	DC	C'THE SUM IS'
GREEN	DC	C'EBCDIC'

8. What is the character string in location SAM if the hex representation of SAM is

C8	C1	E5	C5	40	C1	40	C7	D6	D6	C4	40	C4	C1	E8

9. Write the following signed decimal integers in the IBM/360 packed decimal representation.
   a. -173 e. 427
   b. 46956   f. -185
   c. 45   g. $+625111$
   d. -1111 h. 84

10. Express the decimal integers in exercise 9 as full-word binary integers.

11. The analogous systems to one's complement and two's complement of binary are nine's complement and ten's complement of the decimal system. Express -1456 in (a) nine's complement and (b) ten's complement.

12. Explain the fifteen's complement and the sixteen's complement representations of a hexadecimal negative number. Explain how these representations have been used in the examples in this chapter.

13. Suppose a computer uses one's complement form to represent negative numbers. Suppose the contents of locations BLUE and GREEN are as follows:

C(BLUE)   = 77777777_8
C(GREEN) = 00000000_8

Which location, BLUE or GREEN, contains the higher value? Or are the values equal?

14. a. Express 32 as a single-precision floating-point number.
    b. Express 1.75 as a double-precision floating-point number.

15. Find the real value represented by the following floating-point numbers. The snapshots are in hex.
    a. 42300000
    b. C1200000

16. Convert the following numbers to the base indicated. Use the Fraction Conversion Algorithm. Set EXTENT to a reasonable value.
    a. .77 to base 8   d. .569 to base 16
    b. .AB$_x$ to base 10   e. .142 to base 8
    c. 11.02 to base 2   f. 77.77 to base 2

5 | The Define Constant Instruction

At last we have arrived at a point in our discussion where the student may actually program the concepts we cover. And since in this chapter we study the Define Constant (DC) pseudo instruction, we suggest he do so.

There is a great deal of material a programmer must master before he can use the Define Constant pseudo effectively. As an aid to mastering this material, the student should, we feel, run at least one program in which he defines each type of constant in the Assembler Language repertoire. He should, in his definitions, exercise some of the various options available with this pseudo instruction.

As part of his program the student should request a dump of his constant area. He should then "read" this dump, designating in some way the constants he has defined in his program. This procedure, we believe, will facilitate the understanding of the rather complex material in this chapter.

Appendix C has some useful macros, a few of which simplify the housekeeping necessary in getting a program to run on a System/360 computer. Although the discussion of these macros has been placed in the appendix, we will use them in the examples with which we illustrate our topics. Notice in particular the QDUMP macro which enables the programmer to get a dump of a specified area in MEMORY.

Before we begin our discussion of the Define Constant pseudo instruction, let us take a closer look at some important System/360 architecture.

5.1 The Registers

There are 16 general purpose registers in the System/360 CPU. All 16 can be used to hold operands for and results of the binary integer arithmetic operations.

The addresses or names of these registers are 0, 1, 2, 3, 4, 5, 6, 7, 8, 9, 10, 11, 12, 13, 14, and 15. These are usually addressed in decimal, but they can be referred to in hex or binary.

Each program submitted in Assembler Language must specify at least one register which the Assembler will use as a base register. This designated base register is then not available for any other purpose. The SETUP and INIT macros of Appendix C both stipulate register 12 as the base register. Hence, if the programmer employs the SETUP or INIT macros, register 12 is not available. However, that still leaves up to 15 other registers. Can you imagine Robert with 15 accumulators in his calculating machine?

Each register is 32 bits long. Each is designed to hold the contents of one full word of storage. In fact, if we try to load anything else, we will usually run into an "alignment" error.

There is, however, a special byte (character) load operation and a special byte (character) store operation. There is also a set of half-word instructions. Still, we can say the main function of the general purpose registers is to hold full-word binary integers.

Floating-point Registers.   There are also four floating-point registers which hold the operands for and the results of floating-point arithmetic. These registers are 64 bits long. However, when single-precision commands are issued, bits 32–63 of the floating-point registers are ignored. When a double-precision instruction is specified, all 64 bits are used.

The names or addresses of these floating-point registers are 0, 2, 4, and 6. Although these addresses duplicate four of the addresses of the general purpose registers, there is no ambiguity with respect to which type of register is needed for an instruction. The machine language numeric value associated with the assembly mnemonic informs CONTROL as to which type of register is needed for the command.

5.2 Definition of Constants in Assembly Language

When we write the declarative Define Constant (DC), we are "talking" to the Assembler. Although the Assembler will allocate space into which it will generate the constant, the DC itself will not reside in MEMORY. In other words, the DC, Define Constant, statement is not executable. It is not part of the object module. Once the Assembler has generated the constant into its allocated space, the work of the DC is finished.

The general form of the Define Constant declarative is

> name   DC   operand.

The name field may be left blank. The operation field must specify DC. The operand field, which has four subfields, is required. However, some of these subfields are optional. The Assembler will assign default values to these optional subfields if the programmer chooses to omit them.

Remember that no blanks may appear in any field of any Assembler Language statement (see Chapter 2). How then are the subfields separated? They are not. The subfields of the operand run together. No blanks and no commas are permissible between them.

We have listed the four subfields of the DC operand in Table 5.1 along with the status and default value of each.

TABLE 5.1   Subfields of the DC Operand

Subfield	Status	Default value
duplication factor	optional	1
type of constant	required	none
length modifier	optional	see Table 5.2
value of constant	required	none

Table 5.2 gives a summary of useful information pertaining to most constants which can be generated by the DC declarative. We comment, following the table, on each of the column headings.

TABLE 5.2   Table of Constants

Type	Length range	Default	Truncation	Padding	Multiple constants
C	1–256	as needed	right	right	no
X	1–256	as needed	left	left	no
F	1–8	4	left	left	yes
H	1–8	2	left	left	yes
E	1–8	4	right	right	yes
D	1–8	8	right	right	yes
B	1–256	as needed	left	left	no
P	1–16	as needed	left	left	yes
A	3–4	4	left	left	yes
V	3–4	4	left	left	yes
Z	1–256	as needed	left	left	yes

Type.   Every constant has an attribute called *type*. The type of each constant defined is given by a single alphabetic character in the operand field. For example, the C in BLUE DC C'EXAMPLE' designates the constant named BLUE to be a character string in EBCDIC form.

The Assembler will place the type value into the symbol table along with the other attributes associated with BLUE. Table 5.3 expands the type column of Table 5.2.

Length.   Each constant has a length attribute. The number of bytes allocated for the constant determines its length. If four bytes are used to store a constant named SAM, then the length attribute associated with SAM is four. The length attribute given at definition time becomes the *implied* length of that constant.

Again we note that if the programmer has assigned a symbolic name to his constant, for example, SAM, then the Assembler will place the implied length into the symbol table. If necessary, the programmer may reference this length attribute by writing L'SAM.

TABLE 5.3 Table of Types

Letter	Type
F	full-word binary integer
H	half-word binary integer
C	character (EBCDIC)
E	single-precision floating-point number
D	double-precision floating-point number
B	binary integer
X	hexadecimal integer
A	address constant
V	external address constant
Z	zoned decimal
P	packed decimal

A constant may be assigned an implied length by default. In most cases, the programmer should omit the length subfield in his definition, thereby allowing the Assembler to assign the length attribute.

The default value for a full-word binary integer, for example, is four. The default value for an EBCDIC character constant is equal to the number of bytes needed to code the character string. This value is, of course, equal to the number of characters in the string. For example, the length attribute associated with BLUE in the symbol table after the Assembler encounters

BLUE   DC   C'HAVE A GOOD DAY'

is 15 since there are 15 characters in the string—12 letters and 3 blanks.

The range of the permitted length varies from type to type. The length range given in Table 5.2 gives the upper and lower limits allowed for any particular type of constant. The implied length of a character string may, for example, vary from 1 to 256 bytes.

Alignment. Full-word binary integers are always placed by the Assembler on a word boundary if the length modifier is omitted in the DC statement. That is, the Assembler will align full-word constants on an address divisible by four. Characters, on the other hand, are placed into the first available MEMORY location. If the length modifier is not omitted, then the Assembler will generate the constant into the first available byte in MEMORY. If, for instance, we define a full-word binary integer without omitting the length attribute, then the Assembler will generate the integer into the first available byte. Since the address of this byte may not be divisible by four, we may have "lost" our constant; that is, the CPU may not be able to perform arithmetic with our constant. We suggest, therefore, omitting the length subfield when defining full-word binary integers.

When the Assembler encounters the DC pseudo which defines a character string, the Assembler will check the contents of the LOCATION COUN-

TER. The character string will be generated starting at the address to which the LOCATION COUNTER points.

When the Assembler encounters an F-type DC definition, it must check the address pointed to by the LOCATION COUNTER. If that address is divisible by four, the constant will be generated into that address. If that address is not divisible by four, then the Assembler will move the pointer (increase the value in the LOCATION COUNTER) to the nearest higher address divisible by four. (So that the contents of the bytes skipped will not contain "garbage," the Assembler will store hex zeros in them.) The constant will then be generated and stored in this word-boundary address. (See Example 5.4 in Section 5.3.)

The Assembler will align H-type constants on a half-word boundary. Types F, A, V, and E will be aligned on a full-word boundary. D-type, double-precision floating-point constants, will be aligned on a double-word boundary. All other types will be aligned on the nearest byte. They will be stored in MEMORY starting at the address pointed to by the LOCATION COUNTER. If, however, any value appears in the length modifier subfield, then the Assembler will place that constant, no matter what its type, in the first available location in MEMORY.

Multiple Constants. The programmer may define more than one constant per DC statement for all types except C, X, and B. The symbolic address, if given, in a DC statement defining multiple constants is associated with the first constant in the set. Example 5.3 in Section 5.3 illustrates how to define multiple constants.

Truncation. If the length modifier is ignored by the user, the Assembler will always allocate just enough bytes to satisfy the default value for the constant defined. But, suppose that a programmer puts the value three in the length modifier subfield. Then suppose he punches 'ABCD' in the value subfield.

The character string requires four bytes of storage. The programmer has insisted that only three bytes be allocated. What should the Assembler do? Do we have an unrectifiable assembling error? A good Assembler assumes that a programmer knows what he is doing. For some reason, the user wants the Assembler to generate a four-byte character string into three bytes of storage. It is not the Assembler's role to reason why. So the Assembler allocates three bytes at the first available address. Then it causes the computer to generate the EBCDIC form for ABC. The D will not fit. The value of the constant will be ABC. We say the constant has been truncated on the right.

The column headed truncation in Table 5.2 shows whether a constant will be truncated on the right or the left.

Padding. The padding problem is the inverse of the truncation problem. Suppose the Assembler has been asked to allocate more than enough storage for a constant. Suppose, for example, the user specifies five bytes for the EBCDIC constant *ABCD*.

The Assembler will allocate five bytes. The constant is generated but it does not fill the allocated space. The user, certainly, does not have a hint of the value which is in that fifth byte. There's something there, though. One of the 256 possible patterns is in that byte, perhaps left by a previous program. What does the Assembler do? It puts the EBCDIC code (40 in hex) for a blank in that byte. The value of the constant is *ABCDb*. A dump of the constant would appear as C1C2C3C440. We say it has been padded on the right by a blank.

Numeric constants will not be padded with blanks. If the allocated space for a numeric constant is too large, the Assembler will pad with zeros—eight binary zeros or 2 hex zeros for each byte. The floating-point constants will be padded on the right. All other numeric fields will be padded on the left.

Specification. Types H, F, E, D, P, and Z are specified by writing decimal digits in the value field. C-type is specified by characters which belong to the Assembler Language character set. The X-type and B-type are specified by hex and binary digits, respectively. The A- and V-types are specified by expressions involving a symbolic address.

5.3 Examples of the DC Statement

We have discussed the C-type constant to some extent in Topic 2 of the Computer Notebook in Chapter 4. Therefore, in this section, we limit the examples of C-type constants to the use of the padding, truncation, and duplication factors.

C-Type Constants The default length of character constants is equal to the number of characters in the string. If the length modifier is not omitted in the DC statement, then, if necessary, padding or truncation occurs on the right.

Apostrophes and ampersands require special handling if they are to be inserted into a character string. Two ampersands must appear where one is desired. Two apostrophes must be punched to get one.

Example 5.1

Reply is given in character form. The hex reply is given at the end of the examples.

CHAR	DC	C'WHERE'	reply:	*WHERE*
CHAR1	DC	CL3'WHERE'	reply:	*WHE*
CHAR2	DC	3CL3'WHERE'	reply:	*WHEWHEWHE*
CHAR3	DC	2CL4'BIG'	reply:	*BIGb BIGb*

CHAR4	DC	C'WASN''T'	reply:	*WASN'T*
CHAR5	DC	C'&&ABC'	reply:	*&ABC*

Hex Reply

C(CHAR) = E6C8C5D9C5
C(CHAR1) = E6C8C5
C(CHAR2) = E6C8C5E6C8C5E6C8C5
C(CHAR3) = C2C9C740C2C9C740
C(CHAR4) = E6C1E2D57DE3
C(CHAR5) = 50C1C2C3

F-Type Constants

Example 5.2

SAM   DC   F'16'
reply: 00000010

Note that:

1. The duplication factor has been omitted by the user. One constant will be generated.
2. The length subfield has been omitted, hence SAM will have an implied length of four by default.
3. The numeric address associated with SAM will be divisible by four. Why?

Example 5.3

Generate the constants 7, 9, and −19 by one DC statement.

BLUE   DC   F'7,9,−19'
reply: 0000000700000009FFFFFFED

Note that: (1) BLUE+4 is the address of decimal 9, and (2) BLUE+8 is the address of decimal −19.

Example 5.4

BLACK   DC   FL3'7'
reply: 000007

A three-byte constant has been generated. It will be stored starting at the first available byte. It may or may not be on a full-word boundary.

Example 5.5

A1   DC   F'3.9'
reply: 00000004
A2   DC   F'1.76E1'
reply: 00000012
A3   DC   FL5'3.241E2'
reply: 0000000144

Note that a fixed-point constant may have a decimal point in the value field. All digits to the right of the decimal point are dropped by the Assembler after rounding.

The value field may have an exponent. The Assembler will scale the number as specified by the exponent. If a decimal point is present, all digits to the right of the point in the scaled number will be dropped.

F-type constants should be aligned on a word-boundary. The Assembler does this when the length modifier is omitted. Therefore, let the default value of four be the implied length of the fixed-point constant. Even if the user puts the value four, which is equal to the default value, the Assembler will not align the constant on a full-word boundary.

An F-type constant which is not on a word boundary cannot be used in binary integer arithmetic operations.

H-Type Constants   There are two differences between the H-type constants and the F-type:

1. H-type constants will be aligned on a half-word boundary.
2. The implied length of H-type constants should be two. Let the Assembler assign this value by default.

Example 5.6

RED   DC   H'4'
reply: 0004
HDATA   DC   H'123'
reply: 007B
MINUS   DC   H'-17'
reply: FFEF
BLUE   DC   H'7,19'
reply: 00070013

X-Type Constants   Every hex constant possesses an even number of digits. If n digits, n being even, are specified in the value subfield, then $n/2$ bytes are allocated to the constant by the Assembler. There is no problem. The digits fit exactly into the storage allocated.

If n digits, n being odd, are specified by the user, the Assembler allocates $(n + 1)/2$ bytes for the constant. The left nibble of the leftmost byte is padded with a leading zero.

The CPU does not perform arithmetic operations on hex constants. The user generally defines a hex constant in order to put a particular pattern into the allocated bytes. (See Edit instruction, Chapter 13.)

The Assembler places the defined hex constants into the first available MEMORY locations. If the user wants the Assembler to place the hex constant on a half-word, full-word, or double-word boundary, it is his responsibility to "force" alignment. We discuss *forcing alignment* in Section 5.4.

Example 5.7

a.   HEX1   DC   X'463'
        reply: 0463

b.   HEX2   DC   XL2'46'
        reply: 0046

Note the padding with leading zeros.

c.   HEX3   DC   2XL3'1289'
        reply: 001289001289

d.   PATTERN DC   X'402020216B2020'
        reply: 402020216B2020

B-Type Constants   Binary constants are strings of zeros and ones. The bits must be in sets of eight. If the number of elements in the value subfield is not divisible by eight, leading binary zeros will be added to the string until the number of elements is a multiple of eight.

Example 5.8

a.   BIN   DC   B'00010001'
        reply: 11_x

b.   BIN1   DC   B'00011'
        reply: 03_x

c.   BIN2   DC   3B'001100'
        reply: $0C0C0C_x$

Note that (1) the three leading binary zeros were added to BIN1, and (2) the two leading zeros were added to each of the three binary integers created by the DC in BIN2.

A-Type Constants   A symbolic name which has been defined in the program usually appears in the value subfield of an address (A-type) constant definition. The symbolic address may appear by itself or as part of an arithmetic expression.

The A-type constant is aligned by the Assembler on a full-word boundary. The default value for the implied length is four. The contents of the value subfield in the DC statement must be enclosed in parentheses, not apostrophes.

Since the reply of the computer is the numeric value associated with the symbolic name, we omit the reply in the following examples.

Example 5.9

ADCON   DC   A(SAM)

The reply is the numeric value associated with the symbolic name SAM. This address is generated and placed into ADCON. ADCON is now a pointer. It points to location SAM.

Example 5.10

BLUE   DC   A(SAM+8)

BLUE points to the location SAM+8.

Example 5.11

  ① POINTER DC   A(LIST)
  ② LIST   DC   A(A,B,C,D)

Note that:

  1. C(POINTER) = address of LIST
     C(LIST)   = address of A
     C(LIST+4) = address of B
     C(LIST+8) = address of C
     C(LIST+12) = address of D

  2. The DC in ② establishes a block of addresses. We might refer to this block as the *parameter address list*, where A, B, C, and D are parameters. POINTER points to the first element in this block.
  3. The diagram in Figure 5.1 illustrates the pointer concept. Note that all elements in the LIST block are pointers.

V-Type Constants   A V-type constant is a pointer to a location which is external to the program being assembled. Since the symbolic address which is

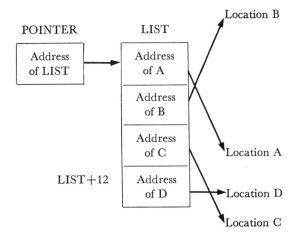

FIGURE 5.1

given in the value subfield of the DC pseudo is an external name, it does not appear in the symbol table. The Assembler, therefore, cannot know the numeric address associated with it. The Assembler inserts hex zeros into the space allocated to the pointer.

The V-type constant is used to link one program to another. The actual numeric address will be placed into the pointer when both modules are loaded prior to execution. The printout of the assembly process will, however, display the zeros inserted by the Assembler.

Example 5.12

EXTERN	DC	V(SUBA)
BLUE	DC	V(GREEN)

Additional information about the external address constant appears in Chapter 11.

P-Type Constants   The programmer should frequently exercise his option to modify the length of a packed decimal constant. The default length, assigned by the Assembler, will be just long enough to hold all the decimal digits listed in the value subfield of the DC pseudo. However, if the value assigned is merely the initialization of a packed decimal field, then the programmer should determine the length of the field by its use.

For example, suppose the user initializes a packed decimal constant to zero without modifying the length of the operand. Then the largest value which that field can hold is nine. If we add one to the operand, when the field holds its maximum value, then the operand will revert to zero. (See Example 5.14.)

The implied length of a packed decimal constant may not exceed 16 bytes, which means the maximum number of digits allowed is 31. The minimum is one. All packed decimal constants are aligned on the nearest byte.

System/360 computers can perform arithmetic on packed decimal operands in MEMORY. No registers are referenced when packed decimal arithmetic instructions are issued.

Chapter 13 is devoted to a discussion of the rules which regulate the arithmetic of these operands. We suggest you review Topic 3 of the Computer Notebook (Chapter 4) before considering the following examples.

Example 5.13

a.   PACKED   DC   P'17'
        reply: 017C

b.   PACK1   DC   P'−17'
        reply: 017D

c.   PACK2   DC   PL3'17'
        reply: 00017C

d.   PACK3   DC   2PL3'123'
        reply: 00123C00123C

e.   PACK4   DC   P'4.6'
        reply: 046C

The value field of the PACK4 definition has a decimal point—called an *assumed decimal point*—which is ignored by the Assembler. The programmer might use the assumed decimal point to remind himself that the constant PACK4 has to be scaled by the indicated factor.

Example 5.14

        COUNTER   DC   P'9'
        reply: 9C

If we add one to COUNTER, then the value will go to 0C. Why? Because the implied length of COUNTER is one (by default). COUNTER is a one-digit packed decimal field. The maximum value it can hold is nine! If we had written

        COUNTER   DC   PL2'9'
        reply: 009C

then COUNTER would be a three-digit field. COUNTER could then attain a maximum value of 999.

E-Type Constants The E-type short or single-precision floating-point constants are aligned on a full-word boundary. Multiple constants may be defined by one DC pseudo.

We suggest that the student review the discussion of floating-point constants which appears in Topic 4 of the preceding chapter.

Example 5.15

```
FLOAT1     DC     E'1'
reply:  41100000
FLOAT2     DC     E'.001E+3'
reply:  41100000
FLOAT3     DC     E'1500E-3'
reply:  41180000
FLOAT4     DC     E'4.5'
reply:  41480000
PI         DC     E'3,.5,1E+2'
reply:   413000004080000042640000
```

D-Type Constants The Assembler aligns the D-type double-precision floating-point constant on a double-word boundary. Except for the D in the type field, the D-type constant is defined in exactly the same manner as the E-type constant.

Example 5.16

```
FLOAT1     DC     D'1'
reply:  4110000000000000
FLOAT2     DC     D'1E+5'
reply:  45186A0000000000
FLOAT3     DC     D'1E-1'
reply:  4019999999999999
```

Z-Type Constants The Z-type constant is a *zoned decimal* representation of a base 10 integer. Table 5.4 gives the zoned decimal representation of the base 10 digits. The sign of a zoned decimal field is in the left nibble of the rightmost byte. The Assembler generates a hex C to signify a positive field, while a hex D is generated for a negative field. Example 5.17 will help clarify these concepts.

All zoned decimal fields are aligned to the nearest byte. Padding and truncation of the field by zeros occurs on the left.

TABLE 5.4

Decimal	Zoned decimal	Hex
0	1111 0000	F0
1	1111 0001	F1
2	1111 0010	F2
3	1111 0011	F3
4	1111 0100	F4
5	1111 0101	F5
6	1111 0110	F6
7	1111 0111	F7
8	1111 1000	F8
9	1111 1001	F9

Example 5.17

```
BLUE1       DC      Z'124'
reply:  F1F2C4
SAM         DC      Z'-124'
reply:  F1F2D4
BLACK       DC      Z'+1267'
reply:  F1F2F6C7
ROUND       DC      Z'1267'
reply:  F1F2F6C7
```

5.4   The Define Storage Statement

The Define Storage statement has the general form

    name   DS   operand

We note the following points about this declarative.

1. The name field is optional. If it is used, the symbolic address refers to the first byte of storage allocated.
2. DS is required in the operation field.
3. There are four subfields in the operand field of which only *type* is required. The *duplication* factor, if used, may be any nonnegative integer from 0 to 65,535. The default for this subfield is one.
4. The *length* option is usually exercised with the P-type and C-type storage assignment statements. A glance at Table 5.5, given below, will be instructive.

TABLE 5.5 DS Length Table

Type	Length default
C	1
B	1
P	1
F	4
H	2
Z	1
D	8
E	4
A	4
V	4

The *value* subfield should usually be omitted. Any entry in this subfield will *not* be generated. The Assembler will, however, use the constant to determine the number of bytes to allocate. Consider

    BLUE   DS   C'ABC'

The value ABC will *not* be generated. But since ABC requires three bytes of storage, BLUE will be given a length attribute of three.

Example 5.18

    SAM   DS   CL7

Note that seven bytes of storage are allocated by the Assembler. The Assembler makes this allocation by adding seven to the contents of the LOCATION COUNTER. The length attribute of SAM is seven.

Figure 5.2 is a diagram of the allotted storage.

We do not know the contents of the bytes.

FIGURE 5.2

byte 0	byte 1	byte 2	byte 3	byte 4	byte 5	byte 6

SAM   SAM+6

Example 5.19

a.   BLACK   DS   F

b.   BLACK1   DS   6F

BLACK is a full-word storage location. It is aligned on a word boundary. Its implied length is four.

BLACK1 is the first word of a block of six full-words of storage. Perhaps a one-dimensional matrix is being defined. The length attribute of BLACK1 is also four.

Example 5.20

```
DOUBLE    DS    D
```

DOUBLE is aligned on a double-word boundary.

Forcing Alignment.   Suppose we want the hex pattern 40202020216B2020 placed on a double-word boundary at definition time. The following code solves our problem.

```
①                 DS    0D
②    PATTERN   DC    X'40202020216B2020'
```

The D in the type field of ① forces the Assembler to "move" the LOCATION COUNTER to the first available MEMORY location divisible by eight. No storage, however, will be allocated because of the zero in the duplication subfield. We say that we have "forced alignment" to the nearest double-word boundary.

The code

```
          DS    0F
BELL    DC    C'ABCD'
```

forces the alignment of the constant BELL to the nearest full-word boundary.

Example 5.21

The last constant defined in a program was a one-byte binary pattern. This is located at *address* 004664. The LOCATION COUNTER now points to 004665. Write the code so that the constant, a hex pattern—X'404040F0'—will be generated on a word boundary.

```
Location
004664    B1      DC     B'01110000'
004668            DS     0F
004668    PAT     DC     X'404040F0'
```

We see that the pattern PAT is on a full-word boundary, location 004668. B1 is in location 004664. What is in locations 004665, 004666, and 004667? Garbage. Garbage left from a previous program. Is there anything wrong? No. But we must remember when we look at a dump of our data section that the contents of these three bytes do not pertain to our program.

We suggest, in order to reduce the number of forcing-alignment DS statements, that data and storage definitions be given in the following order: double-word, full-word, half-word, and then byte-aligned definitions.

Structure.   We will digress in Chapter 7, Topic 3, to discuss a programming technique which uses the "0" duplication factor in the DS statement to create interesting and useful data structures in MEMORY.

There is no question that this topic should follow "forcing alignment." However, a clear understanding of the technique is difficult to gain without a fair knowledge of some Basic Assembler Language instructions.

If the student has a fair background in BAL, we suggest he turn to this section now.

Computer Notebook

TOPIC 1   Some Additional Assembler Control Statements

We continue our discussion of assembly control statements. Recall that these statements do not produce object code. They do not take any space in MEMORY, nor do they cause the Assembler to generate items which might utilize storage.

The programmer uses control statements as a way of informing the Assembler about his needs or wishes with respect to the options available to him.

Title.   The general format of Title is

    name   TITLE   'character string'

The character string may consist of up to 100 characters enclosed in single apostrophes. The character string which is the title of the program is printed at the top of each page of the assembly printout. The user may change the contents of the operand field by issuing a new Title statement. Each Title statement, whether the contents of the operand field are changed or not changed, causes the printout to start at the top of a new page.

The name field may contain up to four alphabetic or numeric characters. These characters will be punched into columns 73–76 of every output card produced by the program. Only the first Title statement may have an entry in the name field.

Eject.   The general form of the Eject statement is

    EJECT

The Eject statement causes the printout of the program to skip to a new page. The name field and the operand field must be blank.

Print.   The Print assembly control statement has up to three operands. The operands are *keywords,* hence they may appear in any order.

The general form of the Print statement is

> PRINT   (1 to 3 operands)

The name field must be blank. The number of operands may vary from one to three. They are separated by commas. If an operand is omitted, then the default option for that operand will be assumed by the Assembler.

Table 5.6 lists the three sets of operands. The options in each set are mutually exclusive. The default options are italicized.

TABLE 5.6   The PRINT Option Table

SET I	
ON	A printout of the assembly program will be given.
OFF	No printout of the assembly program will be made.
SET II	
GEN	All instructions generated by the macros used in the program are listed in the printout.
NOGEN	The macro statement will be printed, but the code generated by the macro will be suppressed.
SET III	
DATA	All defined constants will be listed in full in the printout.
NODATA	Only the first 8 hex digits generated by a Define Constant pseudo instruction will be listed in the printout.

Note that if PRINT is omitted, then the Assembler will assume that the user has issued

> PRINT   GEN,NØDATA,ØN

The options chosen, by default or by an explicit declaration, will remain in force until the Assembler encounters a new Print statement.

Space.   The general form of Space is

> SPACE   (blank or a positive decimal integer)

The name field must be blank. If the operand field is blank, then the Assembler will cause a line to be skipped in the source printout. The skip will be made at the point the Space statement is encountered.

If a positive decimal integer, n, is inserted into the operand field, then the Assembler will skip n lines at the point the Space statement is encountered. SPACE will be equivalent to EJECT if the number of lines skipped would exceed the end of the page.

TOPIC 2   A Short Note on Macros

Basic Assembler Language has a facility which enables the programmer to incorporate any legitimate sequence of instructions into a macro. This process is called a *macro definition*. Once the macro has been defined, a single instruction—called the *macro instruction*—can be used by the programmer at any point in his program where he wishes to include the sequence of instructions which defined the macro.

The appearance of the macro instruction in the program is named a *macro call*. The macro call causes a software program named a *macro generator* to insert the sequence of instructions (which defined the macro instruction) at the point where the macro was *invoked* (where the macro call appeared). The insertion of the sequence of instructions is called the *macro generation*.

Certain sequences of instructions are used by many programmers. In order to avoid having each programmer define his own macro for the sequence, many installations have a macro library where macro definitions for commonly used sequences are placed. Once a macro is in the macro library, any programmer may invoke it by merely inserting the macro instruction into his program.

For example, in order to run a program on a System/360 computer (under OS) in Assembler Language, the programmer must issue instructions which perform some *housekeeping* for the Operating System. The following sequence of instructions, or a sequence similar to it, must be coded at the beginning of each program. (The symbolic name SAVE refers to an eighteen-word *save area*. This save area is discussed in Chapters 10 and 11.)

```
STM     14,12,12(13)
BALR    12,0
USING   *,12
ST      13,SAVE+4
LA      11,SAVE
ST      11,8(13)
LR      13,11
```

At the author's college installation, this sequence has been incorporated into a macro named INIT. All programmers, including student users, are able to accomplish the necessary housekeeping by using this single macro instruction.

The explanation of the housekeeping instructions to beginning students is cumbersome. With the use of the INIT or other such macros the student is able to run his program. After he has gained some background in computer science in general and the Assembler Language in particular, the explanation of the housekeeping instructions presents no problem. (See Chapter 11.)

If the user wishes to have the instructions which comprise a macro listed in his printout, then he may choose the GEN option in the Print assembly

```
54                  PRINT GEN
55                  INIT
56+SUBPGM           CSECT
57+                 USING SUBPGM,15 ESTABLISH INITIAL BASING
58+                 B       *+12 BRANCH AROUND ENTRY POINT ID
59+                 DC      AL1(7) CSECT NAME LENGTH
60+                 DC      CL7'SUBPGM' CSECT NAME
61+                 STM     14,12,12(13) SAVE REGISTERS IN OLD SAVE AREA
62+                 CNOP    0,4 ALIGN TO FULL WORD BOUNDARY
63+                 BAL     12,*+76 BRANCH AROUND SAVE AREA
64+                 DC      F'4096' SAVE AREA WORD 1
65+                 DC      17F'0' REGISTER SAVE AREA WORDS 2-18
66+                 ST      13,4(12) SAVE REGISTER 13 IN OUR SAVE AREA
67+                 ST      12,8(13) CHAIN SAVE AREAS
68+                 LR      13,12 POINT TO NEW SAVE AREA
69+                 LR      12,15 ESTABLISH NEW BASE REGISTER
70+                 DROP    15 DROP INITIAL BASING
71+                 USING SUBPGM,12 INFORM ASSEMBLER OF NEW BASE
72                  AR      2,4
```

FIGURE 5.3   The PRINT GEN Option

control statement. Figure 5.3 illustrates this option. The instructions which comprise the INIT macro are designated by a small plus sign.

If the user wishes to have the listing of the instructions which comprise the macro suppressed, then he must choose the NOGEN option in the Print statement. Figure 5.4 illustrates this option.

We suggest that the user choose the NOGEN option in most instances. Programs which contain all the macro listings are quite difficult to read.

FIGURE 5.4   The PRINT NOGEN Option

```
74                  PRINT NOGEN
75                  INIT
92                  AR      2,4
```

TOPIC 3   More about Data and Storage Definition Pseudos

All assembly languages allow the user to define constants for his program. The technique which accomplishes this is chosen from one of two available methods.

Some assembly languages have one Define Constant pseudo to cover all types of constants allowed in that assembly language. When this method is followed, the programmer modifies the Define Constant, along with its value, in the operand field. (We have discussed this method quite throughly in this chapter.)

In the second method, the assembly language has a Define Constant pseudo instruction for each type of constant permissible in that language. The Assembler is told in the operation field which type of constant is being defined. The operand field gives the value, length, and duplication factor. (In many assembly languages the length and duplication factor are not permissible options.) For example,

    BLUE   DEC   12

might define a full-word binary integer whose base 10 value is 12 in the assembly language of some computer.

The CDC 3000 series computers define character stirngs by a BCD pseudo.

    SAM   BCD   4,MERRY CHRISTMAS

would define the character string *MERRYbCHRISTMASb* in four words. The integer preceding the comma is the length of the character field. *b* indicates a blank. The constant in the value subfield of the BCD need not be enclosed in apostrophes. The Assembler knows that the characters that follow the comma represent the value to be generated into the 16 bytes which start at SAM. Note that the last character is a blank.

A tag in the operation field modifies the BCD pseudo.

    BLACK   BCD,C   15,MERRY CHRISTMAS

would cause the Assembler to generate the character string *MERRY bCHRISTMAS* into 15 bytes. The C following the comma in the operation field modifies the BCD pseudo instruction so that a byte character string is generated. BLACK is now a byte address, not a word address.

In our opinion neither method has any particular advantage over the other. The reader should note, however, that the DC pseudo of System/360 does give the programmer a great many options. There is a price to pay for these numerous options. The user must master a good deal of detail in order to avoid errors in assembling constants for his program.

The storage allocation techniques of the different assembly languages do not differ as much as the data definition methods. Perhaps the most common mnemonic in use, after DC, is BSS (Block Started by Symbol). For example,

    BLUE   BSS   4

will allocate a block of four words starting at symbolic address BLUE.

If we want a block of seven bytes instead of seven words, we might tag the BSS mnemonic by a C as in

    SAM   BSS,C   7

The tag C which modifies the BSS tells the Assembler that allocation should be in bytes, not words.

An assembly language which allows the allocation of bytes or words in its storage assignment statements must provide a method for word alignment.

Although this alignment will be handled by the Assembler, the programmer must understand how to align constants on a word boundary when it is required.

One last word. If a programmer masters the data definition and storage allocation techniques of one assembly language, the methods of another language, even if different, can be readily understood.

EXERCISES

1. Write an assembly language program in which each type of constant is defined at least once. Vary the options in the duplication and length fields. Get a dump of that part of MEMORY where the defined constants have been generated. Read the dump by designating the defined constants in some manner.

2. Give the reply to each of the following data definition statements:
   a. BLUE   DC   F'−125'
   b. GREEN   DC   CL4'HØME-RUN'
   c. ZERØ   DC   3F'0'
   d. DØUBLE   DC   D'.25'
   e. PACK   DC   PL4'−16'
   f. STRING   DC   CL5'SØRRY, ITS NØT HERE'
   g. ZØNE   DC   Z'−64'
   h. CHAR   DC   C'−64'
   i. HALF   DC   H'14,−14,6'
   j. TØØBIG   DC   3CL4'WHY'

3. Suppose the LOCATION COUNTER is pointing to 007000 at the time the Assembler encounters each of the following three sets of Define Constant statements. Give the address of each defined constant. (All work is in hex.)
   a. BLUE   DC   F'0,4'
      CHAR1   DC   CL5'ABC'
                  DS   0F
      PATTERN   DC   C'JØHN'
   b. SAM   DC   B'00011'
                  DS   0D
      HEX   DC   X'000000F0'
      PAT   DC   X'000001'
      TEN   DC   F'10'
   c. ABLE   DS   0F
      PACK   DC   PL5'6'
      CØUNTER   DC   PL2'0'
                  DS   0D
      BIG   DC   CL6'17'

4. It is not permissible to define multiple C-type constants in one DC pseudo.
   a. Why has this restriction been placed on the C-type DC pseudo?

b. Consider the pseudo

> BLACK   DC   C'BØY, GIRL'

Will the Assembler give an error message to the programmer?

5. Suppose the following block of data definitions and storage allocation statements appear in an assembly program.

X	DC	F'10'
BLUE	DS	10F
RED	DC	CL6'
BLACK	DC	3F'0'
SAM	DS	CL100
Y	DS	100F

What is the value of
a. X−Y?
b. BLUE−SAM?
c. SAM+4−Y? (Hint: Are we interested in contents or addresses?)

6. Pick any type of computer which has not been mentioned in this chapter (preferably a computer not manufactured by IBM or CDC). Prepare a short written discussion on the data definition and storage allocation methods used by the assembly language of that computer.

7. If the length subfield "overrides" the default length of a C-type constant, then the Assembler pads or truncates the character string on the right. Give the rationale for this procedure. Are there any advantages to padding or truncating a character string on the left?

8. Consider the following block of declaratives:

A	DC	B'0111'
B	DC	X'0F'
C	DC	Z'−7'
D	DC	C'LAST'

Insert the declarative

> RED   DC   X'20202120'

so that RED will be aligned on a double-word boundary.

9. Play the Assembler Game. Assume the role of the Assembler. Create the symbol table for the following block of declaratives. Include the numeric address, the length attribute, and the type attribute for each symbolic name in the table. The LOCATION COUNTER is pointing to 007200 at the start of assembly.

A1	DC	0D
A2	DC	C'12'
A3	DS	100F

A4	DC	PL5'−6'
A5	DS	5PL5
A6	DS	D'3.7E2'
A7	DS	2D
A8	DS	CL100
A9	DS	0CL10
A10	DS	CL5
A11	DS	CL5

10. Provide a good, workable definition for the word *pointer*, which we have used frequently.

11. Does the computer you chose in exercise 6 allow the user to define a macro for his program? If so, explain how the macro is defined.

6 | Some Assembler Instructions

We noted earlier that a one-to-one relationship exists between the assembly and machine languages of any computer. The relationship between these two languages means that the assembly programmer must become very conversant with the machine language of his computer.

Most textbooks on assembly programming devote at least one chapter to a detailed discussion of the formats of the related machine language. The usual practice is to present this material before any assembly instructions are introduced.

We feel, however, that the machine language formats of System/360 will be more easily understood if the reader has an opportunity to use some Assembler instructions first. We, therefore, present in this chapter the load and store, the binary arithmetic, and some storage move instructions.

In Chapter 7, we will give a detailed discussion of the machine language formats. By then, the student should have run a few practice programs in which he has used some of the instructions given in this chapter. This acquaintance, albeit slight, with the System/360 repertoire will facilitate his understanding of the machine language.

Before we begin our discussion, we will take a close look at the notation which we will use quite extensively from now on. The notation appears in the operand field of an Assembler Language instruction's general form.

All of the explanations may not be meaningful right now. However, the student should refer to this list whenever he is in doubt about the meaning of the notation used. A clear understanding of R1, R2, R3, S1, S2, and I2 will be useful, since they are used in this chapter. See Table 6.1.

6.1 Load and Store Instructions

The load and store instructions appear in Table 6.2. We will discuss all of the full-word binary integer load and store instructions in this section except Load and Test Register, which is discussed in Chapter 9. The half-word instructions are discussed in Topic 1 of the Computer Notebook.

TABLE 6.1 The Notation

Symbol	Meaning
R1	A register which is the first operand.
R2	A register which is the second operand.
R3	A register which is the third operand.
S1	The first operand which is in MEMORY.
S2	The second operand which is in MEMORY.
X2	The index register for the second operand.
B1	The base register for the first operand.
B2	The base register for the second operand.
I2	The second operand is an immediate one.
L	Length of the operands. (The number of bytes affected by the action of the instruction.)
L1	The length of the first operand. (The number of bytes in the first operand affected by the action of the instruction.)
L2	The length of the second operand. (The number of bytes in the second operand affected by the action of the instruction.)
D1	The displacement of the first operand.
D2	The displacement of the second operand.

TABLE 6.2 Load and Store Instructions

Instruction	Mnemonic	Action
Full-word		
Load Register	LR R1,R2	$R1 \leftarrow C(R2)$
Load Complement Register	LCR R1,R2	$R1 \leftarrow -C(R2)$
Load Positive Register	LPR R1,R2	$R1 \leftarrow |C(R2)|$
Load Negative Register	LNR R1,R2	$R1 \leftarrow -|C(R2)|$
Load and Test Register	LTR R1,R2	See Chapter 9
Load	L R1,S2	$R1 \leftarrow C(S2)$
Store	ST R1,S2	$S2 \leftarrow C(R1)$
Load Multiple	LM R1,R3,S2	See text
Store Multiple	STM R1,R3,S2	See text
Half-word		
Load Half-word	LH R1,S2	See Topic 1
Store Half-word	STH R1,S2	See Topic 1

Register to Register (RR Type) Instructions. The general form of the *Load Register* instruction is:

LR   R1,R2

The action of Load Register instruction is:

R1 ← C(R2)

Example 6.1

LR   3,7

Before execution	*After execution*
C(Reg 3) is immaterial	C(Reg 3) = 000000A1
C(Reg 7) = 000000A1	C(Reg 7) is unchanged

The general form of the *Load Complement Register* instruction is:

LCR   R1,R2

The action of the Load Complement Register instruction is:

$$R1 \leftarrow -C(R2)$$

Example 6.2

LCR   5,7

Before execution	*After execution*
C(Reg 5) is immaterial	C(Reg 5) = FFFFFFE9
C(Reg 7) = 00000017	C(Reg 7) is unchanged

Surprise! Did you remember that negative integers are stored in two's complement? All the CPU had to do was to copy the value of register 7 into register 5, complement each bit, and add one.

The general form of the *Load Negative Register* instruction is:

LNR   R1,R2

The action of this instruction is:

$$R1 \leftarrow -|C(R2)|$$

The negative of the absolute value of the C(R2) is placed into R1.

Example 6.3

LNR   2,3

Before execution	*After execution*
C(Reg 2) is immaterial	C(Reg 2) = FFFFFFFE
C(Reg 3) = FFFFFFFE	C(Reg 3) is unchanged

The CPU checked the sign bit in register 3. Since the sign bit was 1, the contents of register 3 was copied into register 2. If the sign bit had been positive, then the two's complement of C(Reg 3) would have been placed into register 2.

The general form for the *Load Positive Register* instruction is:

  LPR   R1,R2

The action of this instruction is:

  R1 ← |C(R2)|

The absolute value of C(R2) is placed into R1.

Example 6.4

LPR   12,11

Before execution   *After execution*
C(Reg 11) = 00000040   C(Reg 11) is unchanged
C(Reg 12) is immaterial   C(Reg 12) = 00000040

If the C(Reg 11) = FFFFFF12 before execution, then what will be the content of register 12 after execution?

Register to Storage (RX Type) Instructions.   The general form of the *Load* instruction is:

  L   R1,S2

The action of this instruction is:

  R1 ← C(S2)

Example 6.5

L   5,SAM

Before execution   *After execution*
C(Reg 5) is immaterial   C(Reg 5) = 0000A01B
C(SAM) = 0000A01B   C(SAM) is unchanged

Example 6.6

Load the complement of the C(BLUE) into register 6.
Solution 1:

  L   7,BLUE
  LCR   6,7

Solution 2:

  L   6,BLUE
  LCR   6,6

The general form of the *Store* instruction is:

    ST   R1,S2

The action of this instruction is:

    S2 ← C(R1)

Example 6.7

ST   8,GREEN

Before execution   *After execution*
C(Reg 8) = 000000AB   C(Reg 8) is unchanged
C(GREEN) is immaterial   C(GREEN) = 000000AB

Register to Storage (RS Type) Instructions.   The general form of the *Load Multiple* instruction is:

    LM   R1,R3,S2

The action of this instruction is:

    R1   ← C(S2)
    R1 + 1 ← C(S2+4)
    R1 + 2 ← C(S2+8)
        ⋮
    R3   ← C(S2+k)

If R1 is less than R3, then registers R1, R1 + 1, . . . , R3 are loaded from consecutive full-word locations. If R1 is greater than R3, then we have "wrap around." R1, R1 + 1, . . . , Reg 15, Reg 0, . . . , R3 are loaded from consecutive full-word locations.

Example 6.8

LM   5,8,DATA

Before execution
1. Contents of the registers are immaterial.
2. See Figure 6.1 for contents of the storage locations involved.

FIGURE 6.1

DATA   DATA+4   DATA+8   DATA+12
 ↓   ↓   ↓   ↓

| 00 | 0A | 00 | 5F | 00 | AB | CD | EF | 00 | 00 | 00 | 1A | 00 | 00 | 00 | 00 |

The action of this instruction is:

Register 5 ← C(DATA)
Register 6 ← C(DATA+4)
Register 7 ← C(DATA+8)
Register 8 ← C(DATA+12)

After execution
C(Reg 5) = 000A005F
C(Reg 6) = 00ABCDEF
C(Reg 7) = 0000001A
C(Reg 8) = 00000000

Four consecutive full-word binary integers are loaded into registers 5, 6, 7, and 8.

The general form of the *Store Multiple* instruction is:

STM   R1,R3,S2

The action of this instruction is:

S2   ← C(R1)
S2+4 ← C(R1 + 1)
S2+8 ← C(R1 + 2)
      ⋮
S2+k ← C(R3)

If R1 is less than R3, then registers R1, R1 + 1, R1 + 2, . . . , R3 are stored into consecutive full-word locations starting at S2. If R1 is greater than R3, then we have "wrap around." R1, . . . , Reg 15, Reg 0, . . . , R3 are stored into consecutive full-word locations starting at S2.

Example 6.9

STM   14,3,SAM

Before execution	*After execution*	
C(Reg 14) = 0000011A	C(SAM)	= 0000011A
C(Reg 15) = FFFFFFED	C(SAM+4)	= FFFFFFED
C(Reg 0) = 00000000	C(SAM+8)	= 00000000
C(Reg 1) = 0000000A	C(SAM+12)	= 0000000A
C(Reg 2) = 0000001A	C(SAM+16)	= 0000001A
C(Reg 3) = 000000FF	C(SAM+20)	= 000000FF

6.2 Full-word Binary Arithmetic Instructions

The binary arithmetic instructions appear in Table 6.3. We restrict discussion in this section to the full-word binary arithmetic instructions. The reader will find a discussion of the half-word arithmetic instructions in Topic 1. Note that there is no half-word divide instruction.

TABLE 6.3 Full-word Arithmetic Instructions

Instruction	Mnemonic		Action
Full-word (RR type)			
Add Register	AR	R1,R2	R1 ← C(R1) + C(R2)
Subtract Register	SR	R1,R2	R1 ← C(R1) − C(R2)
Multiply Register	MR	R1,R2	See text
Divide Register	DR	R1,R2	See text
Full-word (RX type)			
Add	A	R1,S2	R1 ← C(R1) + C(S2)
Subtract	S	R1,S2	R1 ← C(R1) − C(S2)
Divide	D	R1,S2	See text
Multiply	M	R1,S2	See text
Half-word (RX type)			
Add Half-word	AH	R1,S2	See Topic 1
Subtract Half-word	SH	R1,S2	See Topic 1
Multiply Half-word	MH	R1,S2	See Topic 1

Register to Register Binary Arithmetic Instructions. The general form of the *Add Register* instruction is:

    AR   R1,R2

The action of this instruction is:

$$R1 \leftarrow C(R1) + C(R2)$$

Example 6.10

    AR   3,4

The action of this instruction is:

    Reg 3 ← C(Reg 3) + C(Reg 4)

Before execution	*After execution*
C(Reg 3) = 0000000A	C(Reg 3) = 00000001
C(Reg 4) = FFFFFFF7	C(Reg 4) is unchanged

    AR   5,6

Before execution	*After execution*
C(Reg 5) = 00000009	C(Reg 5) = 00000012
C(Reg 6) = 00000009	C(Reg 6) is unchanged

The general form of the *Subtract Register* instruction is:

    SR   R1,R2

The action of this instruction is:

$$R1 \leftarrow C(R1) - C(R2)$$

Example 6.11

SR   3,9

Before execution   *After execution*
C(Reg 3) = 00000014   C(Reg 3) = FFFFFFFC
C(Reg 9) = 00000018   C(Reg 9) is unchanged

The general form of the *Multiply Register* instruction is:

MR   R1,R2

The action of this instruction is:

$$[R1, R1 + 1] \leftarrow C(R1 + 1) * C(R2)$$

Multiply Register uses an *even-odd pair*. R1 must be even. The multiplicand must be in the odd register, R1 + 1. The product will be placed into the concatenation of the two registers—[R1, R1 + 1]. No overflow can occur. The product will always be contained in the 64 bit register [R1, R1 + 1].

The sign bit of the product is bit 0 of R1. If the product is entirely "contained" in R1 + 1, then the sign bit, bit 0, of R1 + 1 has the correct sign of the product. We say "multiplication readies the even-odd pair for division." The sign bit is extended throughout the even register when the odd register contains the product. In this text, we will always assume that the product is contained in the odd register.

Example 6.12

MR   4,7

Before execution   *After execution*
C(Reg 4) is immaterial   C(Reg 4) = 00000000
C(Reg 5) = 00000010   C(Reg 5) = 000000A0
C(Reg 7) = 0000000A   C(Reg 7) is unchanged

The sign, 0, is extended throughout all bits in register 4. Since the product is contained in bits 1–31 of register 5, the sign bit, bit 0, of register 5 reflects the correct sign.

Example 6.13

MR   2,9

Before execution   *After execution*
C(Reg 2) is immaterial   C(Reg 2) = FFFFFFFF
C(Reg 3) = 00000005   C(Reg 3) = FFFFFFEC
C(Reg 9) = FFFFFFFC   C(Reg 9) is unchanged

The product is negative. The negative sign bit is extended throughout all bits in register 2. Since the product is contained in bits 1–31 of register 3, then 1 in bit position 0 in register 3 reflects the correct sign.

Exercise 5 at the end of the chapter has an example of a product which cannot be contained in the odd register of the even-odd pair. When this occurs, the 0 bit of the odd register does *not* reflect the correct sign of the product.

The general form of the *Divide Register* instruction is:

DR   R1,R2

The first operand is an even-odd pair of registers. R1 must be even. CONTROL assumes the dividend is in the 64 bit register, the concatenation of registers R1 and R1 + 1, [R1, R1 + 1]. If the dividend is contained in bits 1–31 of R1 + 1, the sign bit must be extended into all bits of R1. The extension of these bits is the programmer's responsibility. An even-odd pair of registers is "ready" for division immediately after a multiplication instruction which involves the pair is given.

The action of the Divide Register instruction is:

Quotient of $C([R1,R1 + 1])/C(R2) \rightarrow R1 + 1$
Remainder of $C([R1,R1 + 1])/C(R2) \rightarrow R1$

The algebraic sign of the division will be the sign of the quotient. The sign of a nonzero remainder will reflect the sign of the dividend. If the remainder is 0, then every bit in R1 will be zero.

Example 6.14

① MR   2,7
② DR   2,5

Before execution of ①	*After execution of* ①
C(Reg 2) is immaterial	C(Reg 2) = 00000000
C(Reg 3) = 00000100	C(Reg 3) = 00001000
C(Reg 7) = 00000010	C(Reg 5) is unchanged
C(Reg 5) = 00000005	C(Reg 7) is unchanged

The even-odd pair—registers 2 and 3—is ready for division after the execution of ①. The sign bit has been extended into all bits of register 2.

Before execution of ②	*After execution of* ②
C(Reg 2) = 00000000	C(Reg 2) = 00000001
C(Reg 3) = 00001000	C(Reg 3) = 00000333
C(Reg 5) = 00000005	C(Reg 5) is unchanged

The remainder is in register 2 with the original sign of the dividend. The quotient is in register 3 with the algebraic sign of the division.

Shift Right Double Arithmetic. What if we do not perform multiplication before we issue a divide instruction? That is, how does the programmer extend the sign bit of the dividend into the even register of the concatenated pair?

Suppose, for example, we want to divide the contents of register 3 by the contents of register 7. We do not know the contents of register 2. Before we issue the instruction DR 2,7, we must extend the sign bit of the dividend into all bits of register 2.

If the dividend is positive and we know it is positive, then we can set register 2 to zero by a simple SR 2,2. Register 2 ← C(Reg 2) − C(Reg 2). Since every bit of register 2 is now zero, we have extended the sign bit throughout register 2.

But this is not a general technique. Suppose we do not know the sign of the dividend, or worse, suppose the dividend is negative; if we clear register 2, set each bit to zero, then the result of the division would be completely erroneous. It would be very difficult to determine what relationship the quotient thus obtained has to the true quotient of the desired division.

There is a second technique which uses the fact that multiplication "readies" the even-odd pair of registers for division. Suppose, for instance, that we wish to divide C(SAM) by C(BLUE). Then we load C(SAM) into the odd register. We multiply the dividend (which is in the odd register) by a *positive* one. The multiplication extends the sign bit—be it negative or positive—into all bits of the even register. The register pair is now ready for division.

Example 6.15

```
        L    3,SAM      Dividend → odd register
        M    2,ONE      Sign bit extended
        D    2,BLUE     Division accomplished
                :
ONE  DC  F'1'
        :
```

The trouble with this technique is that multiplication is one of the slower instructions. In other words, this technique is the *slowest* way to extend the sign bit. Let us now turn to the fastest way to extend the sign bit.

The best way to extend the sign bit is to use the Shift Right Double Arithmetic instruction. The shift instruction executes rapidly. And we get a bonus when we use it. We do not have to be concerned about the sign of the dividend.

The mnemonic for Shift Right Double Arithmetic is

SRDA   R1,nn[1]

1. nn is any positive decimal integer not greater than 63.
2. R1 must be even. An even-odd pair is involved in the shift.

The contents of the concatenation [R1, R1 + 1] is shifted to the right nn times. The sign bit in R1 is regenerated for each shift. Bit 31 of R1 + 1 is lost in each shift. Lost bits are referred to as being in a bit bucket.

Example 6.16

a. SRDA   4,1

   Before execution (in bits)
   C(Reg 4) = 1011 1111 0000 1111 0000 1111 0000 1111
   C(Reg 5) = 0000 0000 1111 0000 1111 0000 1111 1010
   bit bucket is empty

   After execution
   C(Reg 4) = 1101 1111 1000 0111 1000 0111 1000 0111
   C(Reg 5) = 1000 0000 0111 1000 0111 1000 0111 1101
   C(bit bucket) = 0

b. SRDA   6,5

   Before execution (in bits)
   C(Reg 6) = 0000 0111 1111 0000 1010 0000 1111 0000
   C(Reg 7) = 1111 1111 1111 1111 1111 0000 1111 0000
   bit bucket is empty

   After execution
   C(Reg 6) = 0000 0000 0011 1111 1000 0101 0000 0111
   C(Reg 7) = 1000 0111 1111 1111 1111 1111 1000 0111
   C(bit bucket) = 10000

Note that five bits from register 6, 10000, have been shifted into bit positions 0–4 of register 7. The sign bit in register 6 has been regenerated five times.

c. SRDA   4,32

Before execution	*After execution*
C(Reg 4) = FE001234	C(Reg 4) = FFFFFFFF
C(Reg 5) is immaterial	C(Reg 5) = FE001234

---

[1] SRDA is actually an RS type of instruction. Its general form is:

   SRDA   R1,D2(B2)

We have used "nn" as the second operand in the present instance to simplify our discussion. A complete discussion of all shift operations appears in Chapter 8.

The original contents of register 4 have been shifted into register 5. The sign bit of register 4 has been extended into all of its 32 bits.

Be sure to provide a bit bucket for your computer center whenever you use this instruction. Stray bits, falling from the right end of the odd numbered register, have been known to foul many programs which follow in the queue.

Example 6.17

Divide the contents of register 9 by the contents of register 4. The sign of the dividend in register 9 is not known.

Solution:

    ① LR 8,9
    ② SRDA 8,32
    ③ DR 8,4

The dividend is loaded into register 8 by the instruction in ①. The sign bit is extended into all bits of register 8 by ②. The quotient is in register 9 with the correct algebraic sign. The remainder is in register 8 with the sign of the dividend.

Binary Arithmetic Instructions (RX Type). The general form of the *Add* instruction is:

    A R1,S2

The action of this instruction is:

    R1 ← C(R1) + C(S2)

Example 6.18

    A 3,SAM

Before execution	*After execution*
C(Reg 3) = 000000A0	C(Reg 3) = 00000096
C(SAM) = FFFFFFF6	C(SAM) is unchanged

The general form of the *Subtract* instruction is:

    S R1,S2

The action of this instruction is:

    R1 ← C(R1) − C(S2)

Example 6.19

S   7,GREEN

Before execution   *After execution*
C(Reg 7) = FFFFFFF2   C(Reg 7) = FFFFFFE4
C(GREEN) = 0000000E   C(GREEN) is unchanged

The general form of the *Multiply* instruction is:

M   R1,S2

R1 must be even. The multiplicand must be in R1 + 1. The product will be placed in the concatenation of R1, R1 + 1. (Review the Multiply Register instruction.)

The action of the Multiply instruction is:

[R1,R1 + 1] ← C(R1 + 1) * C(S2)

Example 6.20

a. M   2,BLUM

The action of this instruction is:

[Reg 2,Reg 3] ← C(Reg 3) * C(BLUM)

Before execution   *After execution*
C(Reg 2) is immaterial   C(Reg 2) = FFFFFFFF
C(Reg 3) = FFFFFFF6   C(Reg 3) = FFFFFF9C
C(BLUM) = 0000000A   C(BLUM) is unchanged

We have caused the multiplication of +10 and −10. The magnitude of the product is in register 3. The negative sign is extended into all bits of register 2.

b. M   4,BLUE

The action of this instruction is:

[Reg 4,Reg 5] ← C(Reg 5) * C(BLUE)

Before execution   *After execution*
C(Reg 4) is immaterial   C(Reg 4) = 00000000
C(Reg 5) = 0000001A   C(Reg 5) = 000001A0
C(BLUE) = 00000010   C(BLUE) is unchanged

The general form of the *Divide* instruction is:

D   4,SAM

The action of the Divide instruction is:

Quotient of C([Reg 4,Reg 5])/C(SAM) → Reg 5
Remainder of C([Reg 4,Reg 5])/C(SAM) → Reg 4

The comments made in the discussion of Divide Register are pertinent here; therefore, we repeat many of those comments. However, we suggest the student review the Divide Register discussion.

The sign of the quotient is the algebraic sign of the division. The sign of a nonzero remainder is the sign of the dividend. R1 must be even. It is the programmer's responsibility to extend the sign of the dividend into all bits of R1.

Example 6.21

Divide C(SAM) by C(DATA).

Solution:

     ① L   6,SAM
     ② SRDA 6,32
     ③ D   6,DATA

Note that:

     ① C(SAM) was loaded into the even register of the even-odd pair.
     ② The sign of the dividend has been extended in all bits of register 6. The dividend, itself, is now in register 7. We are ready for division.
     ③ The quotient goes to register 7. The remainder is in register 6.

Before execution of ①	*After execution of* ①
C(Reg 6) is immaterial	C(Reg 6) = 0000000A
C(Reg 7) is immaterial	C(Reg 7) is unchanged
C(SAM) = 0000000A	C(SAM) is unchanged
C(DATA) = 00000003	C(DATA) is unchanged

After execution of ②	*After execution of* ③
C(Reg 6) = 00000000	C(Reg 6) = 00000001
C(Reg 7) = 0000000A	C(Reg 7) = 00000003
C(SAM) is immaterial	C(SAM) is immaterial
C(DATA) is unchanged	C(DATA) is unchanged

6.3   Some Storage to Storage Instructions

The registers, four bytes long, determine, in general, the length of the operands which use them. The storage to storage instructions execute without referencing the registers. How, then, does CONTROL know the length of the operands when an SS type instruction is issued?

In the implicit mode, the only mode discussed in this chapter, the length of the SS operand is determined by its implied length attribute. If the length subfield of the instruction's location field is omitted, the Assembler will pass the implied length associated with the symbolic name to CONTROL.

The programmer can, of course, override the implied length of a symbolic name by inserting a decimal integer into the length subfield. In that case, the Assembler will pass this designated length to CONTROL. In any case, the maximum length which an SS type operand may assume is 256 bytes. The minimum is one.

We realize that, at the moment, the student's understanding of much of the above discussion may be vague. However, a careful perusal of the following material will clarify many points.

The Move Character Instruction. The general form of the *Move Character* instruction is:

MVC S1,S2

The action of this instruction is:

$$S1 \quad \leftarrow C(S2)$$
$$S1+1 \leftarrow C(S2+1)$$
$$S1+2 \leftarrow C(S2+2)$$
$$\vdots$$
$$S1+k \leftarrow C(S2+k)$$

where $k + 1$ is either the implied length of the operand S1 or the length specified by the programmer in the length subfield.

1. $k + 1$ bytes will be moved.
2. One byte is moved at a time. $C(S2) \rightarrow S1$, then $C(S2+1) \rightarrow S1+1$, etc.
3. The maximum number of bytes which can be moved by one instruction is 256.

Example 6.22

MVC OUTPUT,NAME

We assume that the implied length of OUTPUT is five. The implied length of NAME is immaterial.

Before execution

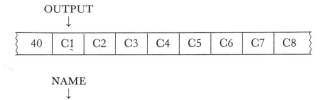

After execution

OUTPUT
↓

| 40 | D2 | D3 | D4 | D5 | D6 | C6 | C7 | C8 |

1. After execution, the contents of the bytes at NAME are unchanged.
2. The contents of five bytes starting at NAME have been copied into the five bytes starting at OUTPUT.

Example 6.23

The implied length of BLUE is 5. Move 7 bytes of data starting at SAM to BLUE, BLUE+1, BLUE+2, . . . , BLUE+6.

Solution:

```
MVC  BLUE(7),SAM
```

Before execution

BLUE
↓

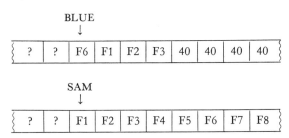

| ? | ? | F6 | F1 | F2 | F3 | 40 | 40 | 40 | 40 |

SAM
↓

| ? | ? | F1 | F2 | F3 | F4 | F5 | F6 | F7 | F8 |

After execution

BLUE
↓

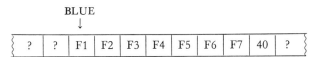

| ? | ? | F1 | F2 | F3 | F4 | F5 | F6 | F7 | 40 | ? |

1. The contents of the bytes starting at SAM are unchanged.
2. When the first operand is written in symbolic form, its implied length can be overridden by the juxtaposition of (integer) and the symbolic name. BLUE(7) overrides the implied length of BLUE. CONTROL will use 7 for the number of bytes involved in the instruction.

Example 6.24

BALANCE is the beginning of a block of storage 50 bytes long. The length attribute of BALANCE, in other words, is 50. Put blanks into each byte of BALANCE. The EBCDIC for a blank is 40 in hex.

Partial solution: consider the *Move Immediate* instruction (MVI).

    MVI S1,I2

The action of this instruction is:

    S1 ← I2

The term written as the second operand is an immediate operand. It is a one-byte self-defining term which is copied into the location S1. (See Topic 2 of the Computer Notebook.)

If we issue the instruction:

    MVI SAM,X'00'

hex 00 will be placed in location SAM.

To solve our problem here, we will move a blank into location BALANCE. Then we will move that blank into all locations which belong to BALANCE.

    ① MVI BALANCE,X'40'
    ② MVC BALANCE+1,BALANCE

Before execution of ①

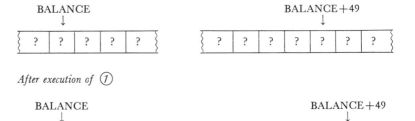

After execution of ①

A blank has been moved into location BALANCE.

After execution of ②

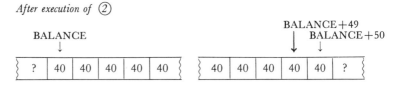

The move is made byte by byte. The blank in BALANCE, placed there by MVI, is copied into BALANCE+1. So before the character in BALANCE+1 is copied into BALANCE+2, that character is a blank. When the character in BALANCE+2 is copied into BALANCE+3, BALANCE+2 is by then a blank. The move instruction proceeds in this fashion until 50 bytes are moved.

The entire field, BALANCE, is blanked out. Problem? Yes. We blanked out BALANCE+50 which is one byte beyond the limits of our field. Why did this occur?

The implied length of the first operand in ②, BALANCE+1, is 50. The rule to remember is: If an operand is an arithmetic expression involving a symbolic name, the symbolic name passes its length attribute to that operand.

Exercise 7 at the end of the chapter asks the student to modify our code so that exactly 50 bytes beginning at BALANCE will be blanked out.

The Move Numeric Instruction.   The general form of the *Move Numeric* instruction is:

MVN   S1,S2

A byte can be divided into two parts, the left nibble and the right nibble. The left nibble is the zone portion. The right nibble is the numeric part of the byte. The diagram in Figure 6.2 illustrates the concept.

The action of the Move Numeric instruction is:

$$S1_{numeric} \leftarrow C(S2)_{numeric}$$
$$S1+1_{numeric} \leftarrow C(S2+1)_{numeric}$$
$$\vdots$$
$$S1+k_{numeric} \leftarrow C(S2+k)_{numeric}$$

where $k + 1$ is the length attribute of S1.

FIGURE 6.2

0	1	2	3	4	5	6	7
1	1	1	1	0	1	0	1

zone   numeric

Example 6.25

MVN   BLACK,RED

Assume that the implied length of BLACK is 3. The implied length of RED is immaterial.

Before execution

BLACK
↓

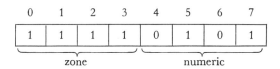

?	46	F2	00	40	40

RED
↓

?	F0	40	D1	40	40

After execution

BLACK
↓

?	40	F0	01	40	40

The number of bytes affected is equal to the length attribute associated with the first operand of the instruction.

We emphasize: Even if the implied length of RED were one, three bytes would be moved. CONTROL would go into the area beyond that which belongs to RED, if necessary, to get the bytes needed to satisfy the requirements of the instruction.

The Move Zone Instruction. The general form of the *Move Zone* instruction is:

MVZ   S1,S2

The action of the Move Zone instruction is:

$$S1_{zone} \quad \leftarrow C(S2)_{zone}$$
$$S1+1_{zone} \leftarrow C(S2+1)_{zone}$$
$$\vdots$$
$$S1+k_{zone} \leftarrow C(S2+k)_{zone}$$

Move Zone is similar to Move Numeric, the difference being that MVZ copies the zone portion of the bytes starting at S2 into the zone portion of the bytes starting at S1. MVN, of course, deals with the numeric portion of a byte.

Example 6.26

MVZ   BLACK,RED

Assume that the implied length of BLACK is 3.

Before execution

BLACK
↓

?	46	F2	00	40	40

RED
↓

?	F0	40	D1	40	40

After execution

BLACK
↓

?	F6	42	D0	40	40

The contents of the bytes at RED are unchanged.

Example 6.27

Write a sequence of two SS type instructions which will accomplish the equivalent of MVC BLACK,RED.

Solution:

```
MVN   BLACK,RED
MVZ   BLACK,RED
```

6.4 Some Sample Programs

The Area of a Circle.   The program in Table 6.4 finds the area of a circle. PI has been defined 10,000 times too large by the DS in ⑧. Therefore, in ④, we have divided "Pi-r-squared" by 10,000. This division places the integral part of our desired area into register 5, while the fractional part goes into register 4.

Instructions ⑤ and ⑥ convert those parts, integral and fractional, into packed decimal form. The Convert to Decimal instruction[2] converts a register operand to a 15 digit packed decimal number with sign.

The QDump is shown in Table 6.4 immediately after the program. Note the leading zeros in each packed decimal numeral. What is the area of our circle? 314.16.

Evaluation of a Polynomial by Horner's Method.   Table 6.5 shows the program we use to evaluate the polynomial

$$y = 3x^3 - 2x^2 - 6x + 7$$

for y using Horner's method. The polynomial has been nested (Horner's form) in order to reduce the number of multiplications during evaluation.

---

[2] A complete discussion of Convert to Decimal (CVD) appears in Chapter 8, Section 8.1.

TABLE 6.4 The Area of a Circle

Program

		INIT		
①		L	5,RADIUS	RADIUS TO ODD REGISTER
②		M	4,RADIUS	RADIUS SQUARED
③		M	4,PI	PI-R-SQUARED→REG 5
④		D	4,T10000	SCALED
⑤		CVD	5,AREA1	INTEGRAL PART→AREA1
⑥		CVD	4,AREA2	FRACTIONAL PART→AREA2
⑦		QDUMP	STORAGE=(AREA1,AREA2+7)	
		GOBACK		
⑧	PI	DC	F'31416'	
	RADIUS	DC	F'10'	
	AREA1	DS	D	
	AREA2	DS	D	
	T10000	DC	F'10000'	SCALING FACTOR
		END		

The QDump

0071C0	0000000A	0000711C	00000000	0000314C
	00000000	0001600C		

Address of first byte in dump   fractional part   integral part

---

When nested, our polynomial has the form

$$y = ((3x - 2)x - 6)x + 7.$$

This form reduces the number of multiplications to three. In general, the evaluation of a polynomial written in Horner's form requires n multiplications, where n is the degree of the polynomial.

Another advantage of the nested form is that it can easily be programmed in a loop. The body of the loop consists merely of one multiplication instruction and one addition instruction.

Assembler Language Code for a Fortran Assignment Statement. Table 6.6 gives the Assembler Language code which is equivalent to the Fortran statement, $X = (X/Y) + (A * B)/C - D$.

The Case of the Hidden Proverb. A proverb written by Joshua Steinberg (1839–1908) is jumbled in the declarative section of the program in Table

TABLE 6.5   Horner's Method

The Program

```
      INIT
      L       5,A      REG 5 ← A
      M       4,X      MULTIPLY BY X
      S       5,B      SUBTRACT B
      M       4,X      MULTIPLY BY X
      S       5,C      SUBTRACT C
      M       4,X      MULTIPLY BY X
      A       5,D      ADD D
      CVD     5,Y      CONVERT Y
      QDUMP   STORAGE = (Y,Y+7)
      GOBACK
Y     DS      D
X     DC      F'3'
A     DC      F'3'
B     DC      F'2'
C     DC      F'6'
D     DC      F'7'
      END
```

The QDump

0071C0   D00C07FE   0000711C   00000000   0000052C
$$\underbrace{}$$
Y = 52 when X = 3

6.7. The program itself unravels the proverb, and the result can be read in the EBCDIC dump which is next to the hex dump. Our program requests a QDump but we have not shown the dump in Table 6.7.

Computer Notebook

TOPIC 1   Half-word Binary Integer Arithmetic Instructions

The half-word binary integer arithmetic operation is useful when we have a great many data items, each of which is not very large in magnitude. If, for example, we have 1000 pieces of data, and if we decide to employ full-word binary arithmetic instructions to process them, then we will need 4000 bytes of storage.

If, however, we decide to process these items using half-word arithmetic operations, we can store the data items in 1000 half-words or 2000 bytes. Our storage needs will be cut by one-half. We would expect, though, that none of our values will exceed $2^{15}-1$ or $32,767_{10}$.

These half-word instructions may, of course, appear along with the full-word instructions in any program. CONTROL insists only that all data

TABLE 6.6 A Fortran Statement in Assembler Language

	INIT		
	L	4,X	X TO EVEN REGISTER
	SRDA	4,32	THE SIGN BIT EXTENDED
	D	4,Y	REG 5 ← QUOTIENT
	L	7,A	A TO ODD REGISTER
	M	6,B	A*B → REG 7
	D	6,C	READY FOR DIVISION
	S	7,D	SUBTRACT D
	AR	5,7	ADD 2 TERMS
	ST	5,X	X ← VALUE
	CVD	5,XPRIME	
	QDUMP	STORAGE = (XPRIME,XPRIME+7)	
	GOBACK		
XPRIME	DS	D	
X	DC	F'17'	
Y	DC	F'−6'	
A	DC	F'13'	
B	DC	F'16'	
C	DC	F'−12'	
D	DC	F'1'	
	END		

The QDump

0071D0   00000000   0000020D

$$\underbrace{\hspace{5cm}}$$

C(XPRIME) = −20

---

items used as operands in half-word instructions be aligned on half-word boundaries.

The Load Half-word Instruction.   The general form of the *Load Half-word* instruction is:

   LH   R1,S2

The action of this instruction is:

$$R1_{16-31} \leftarrow C(S2)_{0-15}$$

The value of bit position 0 of S2 is copied into bits 0–15 of R1.

1. Bit 0 of S2 is the sign bit of the data item stored in S2. Thus, the sign bit of our half-word data item is extended throughout the high order bits of R1.
2. The extension of the sign bit means that the value in R1 can now be considered as either a full-word or half-word binary integer.

TABLE 6.7 A Proverb by Joshua Steinberg

	PRINT	ON,DATA,NOGEN	
	INIT		
	MVI	PROVERB,C' '	BLANK OUT PROVERB
	MVC	PROVERB+1(51),PROVERB	AREA
	MVC	PROVERB(6),WORD1	
	MVC	PROVERB+7(2),WORD3+6	
	MVC	PROVERB+10(8),WORD4+3	
	MVC	PROVERB+18(1),PUNC+1	
	MVC	PROVERB+20(5),WORD1+5	
	MVC	PROVERB+26(6),WORD2+7	
	MVC	PROVERB+32(1),PUNC+1	
	MVC	PROVERB+34(3),WORD4	
	MVC	PROVERB+38(7),WORD2	
	MVC	PROVERB+46(6),WORD3	
	MVC	PROVERB+52(1),PUNC	
	QDUMP	STORAGE=(PROVERB,PROVERB+52)	
	GOBACK		
WORD1	DC	C'WEALTHONOR'	
WORD2	DC	C'CHARITYWINGED'	
WORD3	DC	C'ABIDESIS'	
WORD4	DC	C'BUTFLEETING'	
PUNC	DC	C'.,'	
	DS	0D	
PROVERB	DS	CL52	
	END		

Example 6.28

a. LH   3,ABC

Before execution	*After execution*
C(Reg 3) is immaterial	C(Reg 3) = FFFFFF7
C(ABC) = FFF7	C(ABC) is unchanged

b. LH   2,CDE

Before execution	*After execution*
C(Reg 2) is immaterial	C(Reg 2) = 00000006
C(CDE) = 0006	C(CDE) is unchanged

The Store Half-word Instruction. The general form of the *Store Half-word* instruction is:

STH   R1,S2

The action of this instruction is:

$$S2_{0-15} \leftarrow C(R1)_{16-31}$$

The contents of bits 16–31 of R1 are copied into bit positions 0–15 of S2.

Example 6.29

STH   5,RED

Before execution	*After execution*
C(Reg 5) = FFFFFFED	C(Reg 5) is unchanged
C(RED) is immaterial	C(RED) = FFED

The Add Half-word Instruction.   The general form of the *Add Half-word* instruction is:

AH   R1,S2

The action of this instruction is:

$$R1 \leftarrow C(R1) + C(S2)_{0-15}$$

Note that the entire content of R1 participates as an addend.

EXAMPLE 6.30

AH   7,GREEN

Before execution	*After execution*
C(Reg 7) = 00004623	C(Reg 7) = 00007835
C(GREEN) = 3212	C(GREEN) is unchanged

The Subtract Half-word Instruction.   The general form of the *Subtract Half-word* instruction is:

SH   R1,S2

The action of this instruction is:

$$R1 \leftarrow C(R1) - C(S2)_{0-15}$$

Example 6.31

SH   3,ABLE

Before execution	*After execution*
C(Reg 3) = 00004623	C(Reg 3) = 00004624
C(ABLE) = FFFF	C(ABLE) is unchanged

The correct half-word difference is in bits 16–31 of register 3. The full register, bits 0–31, may not reflect the correct result of the arithmetic operation.

The Multiply Half-word Instruction.   The general form of the *Multiply Half-word* instruction is:

   MH   R1,S2

The action of this instruction is:

   $C(S2)_{0-15} * C(R1) \rightarrow R1$
   Bits 16–47 of the 48 bit product replace the multiplicand.

The 16 bit multiplier in S2 is multiplied by the 32 bit multiplicand in R1. Hence, the product is 48 bits long (leading 0's included). Only bits 16–48 of the product are saved. They replace the multiplicand in R1.

We would usually expect the truncated bits, bits 0–15, of the product to consist of leading 0's. The programmer, however, must be aware that the product may have been truncated on the left.

Example 6.32

a. MH   1,DATA

   Before execution   *After execution*
   C(Reg 1) = 00000003   C(Reg 1) = 0000D233
   C(DATA) = 4611   C(DATA) is unchanged

b. MH   3,SAM

   Before execution
   C(DATA) = 6001
   C(Reg 3) = 60000000

The multiplication (in hex) is:

```
              60000000
           ×      6001
              60000000
              00000000
              00000000
            240000000
            240060000000
```

truncated
         in register 3

After execution
C(DATA) is unchanged
C(Reg 3) = 60000000

TOPIC 2 A Short Note on Operands

We now discuss two types of operands which often appear in the location field of an instruction.

Self-defining Terms. Any term which contains its own value is called a *self-defining term*. Decimal self-defining terms, which need no type designators, are unsigned integers such as 128, 12, 42. The integers 5 and 6 in LR 5,6 are both examples of such decimal type terms.

Hexadecimal, binary, and character self-defining terms must be preceded by a type designator. The value of the term must be enclosed in apostrophes. X'Cl', C'A', and B'11000001' are examples of hexadecimal, character, and binary terms, respectively.

All three of the above constants are equivalent. The binary type will be copied directly into the instruction. The Assembler will convert both X'Cl' and C'A' into their binary values before placing them into the machine language instruction. Since both X'Cl' and C'A' convert to 11000001_2, all three terms express the same value.

Some uses of the self-defining terms are illustrated in Example 6.32. The self-defining terms are italicized.

Example 6.33

a. decimal

```
L   5,DATA
ST  6,0(1,2)
AR  9,5
```

b. hexadecimal

```
MVI  DATA,X'FO'
```

c. character

```
MVI  SAM,C'A'
```

d. binary

```
BC  B'1110',BLUE
```

Note that B'1110' is an example of a four–bit binary mask. (See Section 10.1 for a complete discussion of the four-bit binary mask.)

Self-defining terms are used to specify registers, the displacements in addresses written in the explicit mode, immediate operands, and, as we have seen, the values of the constants in DC pseudo instructions.

A desired value can usually be expressed in many ways. The value 12, for instance, might be expressed by B'1100' or X'C'. The programmer should, we feel, pick the type which expresses the desired value in the most direct and natural way. It would be, in our opinion, quite outlandish to write LR X'C', B'1010' for LR 12,10.

The self-defining terms X'60', B'01100000', C'—', and 150 are all equivalent. If a user wishes to move a minus sign into location DATA, then surely MVI DATA,C'—' is the most direct and natural way of expressing the value that is to be moved.

One last word. Self-defining terms are limited to a maximum of three bytes. If a programmer chooses a value for a self-defining term which fails to fill the associated field in the machine language instruction, the Assembler will fill this field with high order binary zeros.

Literals. A literal is a constant preceded by an equal sign. Table 6.8 lists most types of constants which can be written in the literal mode.

TABLE 6.8 Table of Literals

Type	Example	Storage value	Alignment
F	=F'12'	0000000C	full-word
H	=H'12'	000C	half-word
C	=C'AF'	C1C6	byte
X	=X'2221'	2221	byte
B	=B'0001'	01	byte
D	=D'12'	41C0000000000000	double-word
E	=E'12'	41C00000	full-word
Z	=Z'23'	F2C3	byte
A	=A(DATA)	00007002	full-word
V	=V(SUB)	00000000	full-word

We assume that the address of DATA is 007002. The Assembler is unable to fill in the address of SUB, since it is on external address. The actual address will be filled in during the link-edit job step. The details of this are beyond the scope of our discussion.

Is there an advantage to using a literal? We believe there is. When a programmer needs a constant he may, of course, ask the Assembler to generate the required value and type of constant into the location allocated by his Define Constant pseudo instruction. In that case he must choose a name for his constant. And whenever he wants to use that particular constant, he must either remember the name of his constant or take the time and trouble to look it up in his coding.

On the other hand, if the programmer uses a literal, then the Assembler takes care of all the details. The Assembler will set aside the location, name it, and generate the constant into that location. The programmer need not remember anything. All he has to do is specify the type and value of the literal he wants in his instruction. The Assembler does the work.

The literal does not give the programmer any additional "power," but it does give him a lot of convenience. So we suggest that the student get in the habit of using literals. The advantage you gain will be convenience. Be sure, however, that you read about the Ltorg assembly control statement near the end of this discussion.

The Assembler maintains a literal table somewhat similar to the symbol table. Each time the programmer uses a literal, the Assembler searches this table. If the literal is "new," that is, it has not been previously defined in the program, then the Assembler will generate the value specified in the enclosed apostrophes. It will place this value, properly aligned, in an area known as the literal pool.[3]

If the Assembler finds that a literal it encounters in the program has already been defined, then it will not generate a second one. However, two literals are equal only if they have the same value and they are of the same type. For instance, =X'0000000A' and =F'10' are of equal value, but since they are different types, the Assembler would, if they were encountered in the program, generate both of them.

In the second pass, the Assembler will insert the address where the value of the literal was placed into the machine language instruction.

We stated that the literal pool will be placed near the end of the program in an area convenient to the Assembler. This area, however, may not be convenient to the programmer. In fact, if there is more than one control section in the program, the area where the literal pool is organized is important.

Hence, we suggest that the programmer use the assembly control statement —LTORG—to inform the Assembler where he wants the literal pool placed.

LTORG has no operand field, but a symbolic name may appear in the name field. This will associate the first byte in the literal pool with a symbolic name.

The programmer tells the Assembler via LTORG, "If the LOCATION COUNTER is pointing to a double-word boundary, don't move it. If not, advance it to the first double-word boundary. Now, I want you to organize the literal pool for all literals generated up to this time in this spot."

The Assembler will respond by organizing the literal pool at the point designated. We suggest that LTORG be placed just before the END control statement. This insures that the literal pool is organized in the user's control section.

It is possible to have more than one LTORG statement. The first LTORG encountered by the Assembler will result in the pool of all literals generated since the start of the program. The second LTORG will result in a literal pool of all literals generated since the first LTORG. Each subsequent

[3] This literal pool belongs to the program and usually appears, unless otherwise stipulated, after the last pseudo instruction. In the printout, the literal pool appears after the END control statement if the programmer does not specify that the literal pool must be placed elsewhere.

LTORG creates a pool for all literals generated since the previous LTORG was encountered.

Students will find that one LTORG statement is sufficient. It should appear at a point so that the literal pool it organizes contains all the literals used in the program. Putting the LTORG just before the END statement will insure this result.

TABLE 6.9

	PRINT	NOGEN	
	INIT		
	L	4,=F'−412'	NEGATIVE 412 TO REG 4
	SRDA	4,32	REGS 4,5 READY FOR DIVISION
	D	4,=F'25'	QUOTIENT IN REG 5
	CVD	4,REM	REMAINDER TO REM
	CVD	5,QUOT	QUOTIENT TO QUOT
	A	5,=F'10'	ADD 10
	S	5,=F'42'	SUBTRACT 42
	M	4,=F'12'	MULTIPLY BY 12
	CVD	5,RESULT	RESULT TO LOCATION RESULT
	QDUMP	STORAGE=(REM,RESULT+7),ID=1	
	GOBACK		
REM	DS	D	
QUOT	DS	D	
RESULT	DS	D	
	LTORG		
		=F'−412'	
		=F'25'	
		=F'10'	Literal pool
		=F'42'	
		=F'12'	
		=V(RDUMP)	
	END		

Table 6.9 is a short program in which several instructions use literals. The LTORG statement appeared just before the END statement. In the program the Assembler caused the printing of the literals in the literal pool which we see just before the END statement.

Example 6.34 has several other illustrations of literals.

Example 6.34

a. L   3,=F'12'

The Assembler will generate a full-word binary integer equal to decimal 12. At execution time, this constant, which has been aligned a full-word boundary, is loaded into register 3.

b. AH   5,=H'16'

A half-word constant equal to decimal 16 is generated. At execution time, this value is added to register 5.

c. MVC DATA(5),=C'ABCDE'

The character string ABCDE is generated. It will be moved into the five bytes which start at DATA.

d. L 15,=A(SUBA)

The address of SUBA is generated into a full-word. At execution time, this address is loaded into register 15. Register 15 now points to SUBA.

EXERCISES

1. Before execution of the following code, the C(Reg 3) was 00000003. What is the C(Reg 7) after execution of the code?

```
LCR   7,3
A     7,=F'-3'
LPR   3,7
A     3,=F'7'
LNR   7,3
A     7,=F'7'
LPR   3,7
LNR   7,3
```

2. Write the Assembler Language code for the following Fortran statement. Assume that all locations have been defined.

$$X = A + (B / X) - X * A + (C * X) / Y$$

3. Give the contents of the first operand after execution of each of the following instructions. The contents of the second operand are in the remarks field. Give all eight bytes in hex.

```
LPR   3,5      C(Reg 5) = FFFFF123
LNR   1,7      C(Reg 7) = 00000467
L     5,SAM    C(SAM)   = FFFFFFFF
LCR   4,5      C(Reg 5) = FFFFFFFF
```

4. a. Define two full-word binary integers, X and Y. Find the sum, the difference, the product, and the quotient of X and Y. Use the Store Multiple instruction to store the results of the four arithmetic operations into consecutive storage locations.

   b. Now find SUM $= (x + y) + (x - y) + (x * y) + (x / y)$ where x is the value in X and y is the value in Y.

5. Suppose C(Reg 7) = 70000000 and C(SAM) = 00000004. After execution of M 6,SAM, the contents of the concatenation of registers 6 and 7 will be 00000001 C0000000. If the programmer knows that his product is too large for the odd number register, how might he store the result of his multiplication?

40	00	40	40	00	00	40	40	40	00	00	00	40	40	40	40	etc.

FIGURE 6.3

6. Let A, B, and C be half-word binary integers. Let X, Y, and Z be full-word binary integers. Write the Assembler Language code for the following Fortran statements. Store the results into the specified locations.

$$X = A * B + C - (Y / Z) * (B / X)$$
$$X = (X / Y) + (A * Z) - (B - X)$$

7. a. Consider Example 6.24. Write the code so that only the BALANCE is blanked out.

   b. Let BALANCE be a field with an implied length of 50. Write the code so that BALANCE has the configuration depicted in Figure 6.3. Define all constants needed for your program. (40 is the EBCDIC for a blank.)

8. The only Ltorg statement in a program appears just before the End control statement. When the Assembler encounters LTORG, the LOCATION COUNTER points to 007202. The programmer has used four literals in his program in the following order:

   $= X'OF'$, $= D'1.2'$, $= C'ABC'$, $= F'10'$.

   Give the address into which the Assembler will place each literal.

9. Write a complete program of your own choice which uses each of the arithmetic operations at least once. The program must use at least three literals. Get a QDump of the literal pool. Get a second QDump which includes the results of your arithmetic operations.

10. Find the value of

$$y = 3x^4 - 2x^3 + x^2 - 6x + 7 \quad \text{for} \quad x = 7.$$

   Write the polynomial in Horner's form. Define all constants. Convert y to pack decimal by CVD. (See Section 6.4.)

11. Give the value stored in location A after execution of the following code:

```
        L       7,A
        LCR     7,7
        L       9,A+4
        A       9,=F'12'
        AR      7,9
        LNR     7,7
        S       7,A+8
        ST      7,A
        GOBACK
A       DC      F'10'
B       DC      F'-10'
C       DC      F'-3'
```

12. Let $x = 127$. Let $y = .061767$. Write a program which will find the product of x times y. Convert the integral part of the product into packed decimal in the double-word INTEGER. Convert the fractional part into packed decimal in the double-word FRACTION. See the program in Table 6.4.

13. Write the instruction which will accomplish the following:
    a. Load registers 0, 1, 2, and 3 from consecutive full-word locations starting at DATA.
    b. Load registers 14, 15, 0, 1, 2, 3, 4, 5, 6, 7, 8, 9, 10, 11, and 12 from consecutive full-word locations starting at SAVE.
    c. Add 17 to register 6.
    d. Multiply the contents of register 7 by 181.
    e. Move a blank to location BLUE.
    f. Clear register 9.
    g. Guarantee that C(Reg 7) is nonnegative.
    h. Store registers 3, 4, and 5 into consecutive full-word locations starting at SAM.
    i. Move exactly five bytes starting at the third byte in BLACK to the fifth, sixth, seventh, eighth, and ninth bytes of GREEN.

14. Pick any computer not in the 360 family. Find out how your chosen computer determines the length of various data fields defined by the programmer.

7 | Elements of Machine Language

In this chapter we discuss some complex concepts of System/360 machine language. Quite a few of the concepts discussed are interdependent. We suggest, therefore, that the student go through the chapter at least twice. Pay strict attention to the details in the second reading.

7.1 Base Registers and Displacement

Every instruction which references a MEMORY location must specify a general purpose register, whose address the Assembler will pass to CONTROL. CONTROL will use the contents of this register, called the *implied base register* for the instruction, as an aid in determining the effective address of the machine language operand.

The programmer may specify this base register explicitly in the instruction, in which case we say the register is an *explicit base register*. He may choose not to mention a base register in the instruction. Then he is specifying, by default, that the address of the implied base register be passed to CONTROL.

If the user gives the address of the base register explicitly, then he must also specify a twelve-bit quantity called the *displacement*. Both the explicit base register and the displacement will be passed to CONTROL via the machine language format.

If the programmer does not designate the base register in the instruction, then the Assembler will calculate the displacement. Again, both the address of the implied base register, a four-bit quantity, and the displacement will be passed to CONTROL.

What is an implied base register? Every user must establish a register pointer to a *base-location* which is somewhere in the beginning of his program. He must inform the Assembler which one of 15 general purpose registers he has chosen for this purpose. (Register 0 cannot be used as a base register.) He must then also pass the address of the base-location to the Assembler. Establishing the implied base register, informing the Assembler of its address, and passing the base-location address are accomplished by a single assembly control statement. (See Chapter 10.)

Figure 7.1 illustrates this concept. The Assembler stores the address of the implied base register into a location named BASE. The value of the two high order digits in the implicit base register are immaterial, so we have designated them by question marks.

We can use the INIT or the SETUP macro to establish the implied base register and to designate the base-location for our program. (Both macros—INIT and SETUP—should not, of course, be used in the same program.) These macros also initialize the base register in the beginning of the program so that during execution the base register points to the base-location. We will continue to use one or the other of these macros in our sample programs to establish the base register and to do the other "housekeeping" which is necessary before a program can be executed on a System/360 or System/370 computer.

If, however, the student wishes to establish his own base register and wishes to do his own "housekeeping," we suggest he turn to Chapter 10 where we pursue this subject further.

Figure 7.1 also illustrates how to find the displacement of a machine language operand. The definition of RED occurs at location 007240_x. The base-location is 007000_x. The displacement of an operand is the difference between these two values. Hence the displacement of RED is $007240_x - 007000_x = 240_x$, which is the 12 bit quantity 001001000000_2.

We now turn to a discussion of how the Assembler passes the displacement and the base register associated with an operand to CONTROL. We will also show how CONTROL then determines the effective address of the machine language operand from this information. We will, at times, substitute AL and ML for Assembly Language and Machine Language, respectively, since these words occur so frequently.

FIGURE 7.1

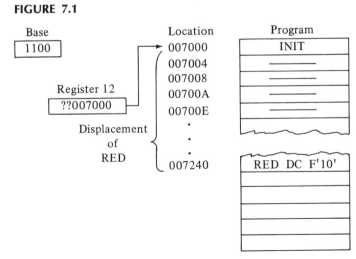

Note: Register 12 points to base-location.

7.2 Machine Language Operand Addressing

An address in System/360 is 24 bits long. This address is usually represented by six hex digits, leading zeros included. In our discussion which follows, we will, therefore, use hex digits, not decimal. We will henceforth attach a subscript to a numeral only when it is not clear from the context to which number base the numeral belongs. Since all addresses belong to base 16, no address will be subscripted.

Example 7.1

The 24 bit address of location BLACK is 0000 0000 1110 0000 0000 1111. BLACK's equivalent hex address is 00E00F.

Do you recall what happens when the FINAC Assembler encounters a symbolic address in the assembly code? In the first pass, the Assembler builds the program's symbol table. Each symbolic name used in the name field is associated with a numeric value.

In the second pass, the Assembler searches the symbol table for any symbol encountered in the operand field. If found, the numeric value associated with that symbolic name is copied from the table into the operand field of the ML instruction. This numeric address is, in general, the effective address of the ML operand. (This is the effective address unless it is modified by an index register.)

The System/360 Assembler, however, does not pass the numeric address associated with the symbolic name to CONTROL. Instead, the Assembler uses this value to determine the displacement of the operand. Let us see how the Assembler does this.

The user, as we know, must designate an implied base register for his program. This base register cannot be overridden when an operand is expressed symbolically. If the programmer uses a symbolic name in the operand field of an AL instruction, then this implied base register is, by default, the base register for that instruction.

Now when the Assembler encounters a symbolic name, say BLUE, in the operand field in the second pass, it will search the symbol table for BLUE. If BLUE has been defined, then the Assembler will find its associated relative address in the table.

The displacement of BLUE will be calculated by subtracting the numeric value (address) of the base-location from the numeric address associated with BLUE. The Assembler will pass this displacement to CONTROL by placing it into bits 20–31 of the ML instruction. There are two storage operands in an SS type instruction. (If BLUE is the second operand of an SS type instruction, its displacement will be placed in bits 36–47 of the ML instruction. In all other cases the displacement will be passed by bits 20–31.)

CONTROL, at execution time, determines the effective address of an operand by using one of the two formulas given in Table 7.1. (EF in the table represents effective address.)

TABLE 7.1   Effective Address Formulas

Formula I   (Index register designated)
EF = C(base register) + displacement + C(index register)
Formula II   (No index register designated)
EF = C(base register) + displacement

Formula I indicates that an index register may be used in determining an effective address. Since up to this point we have made no mention of an index register, let us discuss index registers and indexing so that Formula I will have more meaning.

Certain instructions (the RX type—see next section) in the BAL repertoire are said to be "indexable." A programmer may specify an index register when he uses these instructions. The Assembler will pass the address of the index register to CONTROL. CONTROL will use the contents of such a designated index register to modify the effective address of an operand.

The programmer generally uses an index register to modify the address of an operand which appears in a loop. The index register is initialized so that the effective address referenced will be the location of the first of several contiguous data items. After each pass through the loop, the index is incremented by an appropriate amount so that the next data item in sequence will be referenced when the loop is reentered. This technique, called address modification by changing the contents of an index register, is covered thoroughly in Chapter 9.

Any general purpose register except register 0 may be used as an index. However, registers 13, 14, 15, and 1 have special functions to perform in subroutine linkages; therefore, it is a good idea to avoid designating these registers as index registers. (Their use as base registers should also be avoided for the same reason.)

It will be most instructive if, at this time, we look at the individual roles of CONTROL and the Assembler in developing the effective address for an ML operand.

Example 7.2

Let us assume that:

1. the implied base register is 12
2. C(LOCATION COUNTER) = 007120
3. C(Reg 12) = 40007000
4. base-location = 007000

In the first pass the Assembler encounters the pseudo

GREEN   DC   F'5'

The Assembler builds the symbol table in the first pass. Any symbol which it encounters in the name field will be entered into the table if it has not been previously defined and it satisfies the three criteria for a symbol.

Do you recall what the three criteria are? GREEN has not been previously defined, so the Assembler will enter it right along with its type and length, which are F and 4, respectively. Now the Assembler must copy the contents of the LOCATION COUNTER. This is the numeric address which will be associated with GREEN in this assembly. Did you note the value? 007120.

The Assembler encounters the instruction L 5,GREEN in the second pass. The Assembler's first concern in the second pass is: Has GREEN been defined? If it hasn't been defined, then there is no way by which the Assembler can determine its displacement.

GREEN's numeric address is 007120. Now the Assembler must determine the displacement. What is the base-location? It is 007000. The difference between GREEN's address and the base-location is the displacement. That value is 120, which is in hex, of course.

The Assembler must pass this value to CONTROL by placing it into the displacement field, bits 20–31, of the ML instruction the Assembler is building.

By the way, the Assembler is working on an RX type instruction. Since the programmer did not designate any index register, the Assembler must put 0000_2 in the index field, bits 12–15, of the format.

The last item that the Assembler must pass to CONTROL is the address of the base register. You have learned already that the implied base register cannot be overridden for an operand which is specified by a symbolic name. The Assembler must, therefore, pass the address of the implied base register to CONTROL. The contents of the pointer, BASE, are copied into bits 16–19 of the ML instruction.

The Assembler is done. The operation code is in bits 0–7. The address of the first operand, register 5, is in bits 8–11. Bits 12–15 point to the index, bits 16–19 point to the base register, and bits 20–31 contain the displacement.

The machine language instruction for L 5,GREEN is depicted in Figure 7.2. The contents of the fields are given in hex.

At execution time, CONTROL determines that this instruction may designate an index register. Hence, CONTROL must use Formula I,

$$EF = C(base\ register) + displacement + C(index\ register)$$

to determine the effective address.

Figure 7.2

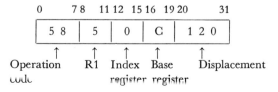

The index field points to register 0, but register 0 cannot be used as an index register. Therefore, CONTROL will substitute the value 0 for the contents of the index register.

The base field points to register 12. CONTROL is interested only in the first 6 hex digits in register 12. They are 007000.

CONTROL will copy the displacement directly from the ML format. It is 120. Now, EF = 007000 + 120 + 0 = 007120. CONTROL will see that the contents of location 007120 are copied into register 5.

Example 7.3

Let us assume that:

1. the implied base register is 10
2. C(Reg 10) = 00007200
3. BLUE's displacement is FF0
4. the index register is 4
5. C(Reg 4) = 00000044

What is the effective address of BLUE in

A   5,BLUE(4)

Using Formula I, we find

$$EF = C(\text{base register}) + \text{displacement} + C(\text{index register})$$
$$= C(\text{Reg } 10) + FF0 + C(\text{Reg } 4) = 007200 + FF0 + 000044$$
$$= 008234$$

Example 7.4

Let us assume that:

1. C(Reg 12) = 40007200
2. C(Reg 4) = 00000044

What is the effective address of the second operand in the Subtract instruction if the ML format is as given in the diagram below?

0	7 8	11 12	15 16	19 20	31
5 B	6	4	C	2 4 0	

Again using Formula I, we find

$$EF = C(\text{base register}) + \text{displacement} + C(\text{index register})$$
$$= C(\text{Reg } 12) + 240 + C(\text{Reg } 4) = 007200 + 240 + 000044$$
$$= 007484$$

Note that bits 12–15, the index field, point to register 4, and bits 16–19, the base register field, point to register 12.

Although we write C(base register), only the first 6 hex digits in the register are pertinent. The sum, however, will be correct if we add the entire contents of both registers, 12 and 4, to EF. It is understood, of course, that the two high order hex digits will be truncated. Consider

$$EF = C(\text{Reg } 12) + \text{displacement} + C(\text{index register})$$
$$= 40007200 + 240 + 00000044 = 40007484 = 007484.$$

(The high order digits, 40, are truncated.)

Example 7.5

Let us assume that:

1. C(base register) = 40007214
2. displacement = 016
3. no index is allowed

What is the effective address?
Using Formula II, we find

$$EF = C(\text{base register}) + \text{displacement} = 007214 + 016$$
$$= 00722A$$

Example 7.6

Let us assume that:

1. C(base register) = 40FFFF16
2. C(displacement) = FFF
3. no index is allowed

What is the effective address?
Again using Formula II, we find

$$EF = C(\text{base register}) + \text{displacement} = \text{FFFF16} + \text{FFF}$$
$$= \quad \text{①} \quad 000\text{F15} = 000\text{F15}.$$
$$\uparrow$$
$$\text{truncated}$$

Note that the effective address is 000F15. The overflow is disregarded. Remember that an address is 6 hex digits long.

7.3 Machine Language Format

There are five types of ML instructions. Our procedure will be to discuss each type in considerable detail. We will first give the machine language format in general form. Then we will present a specific Assembler instruction of the type under discussion. Finally, we will diagram the ML format for the given Assembler instruction.

In our discussion, we will take the opportunity to present additional Assembler Language instructions. The new mnemonics we introduce will be covered thoroughly. We will use such AL instructions without explanation in later portions of this text. This practice, however, should not work any hardship on the student. Appendix B has a complete list of the AL instructions presented in this text. If a mnemonic seems strange, refer to this appendix.

RR-Type Instruction. The register to register type instruction is two bytes long. Since both operands are register operands, no base register, no index register, and no displacement is involved. The Assembler passes the address of the first operand to CONTROL in bits 8–11 of the ML instruction. The address of the second register operand is placed in bits 12–15.

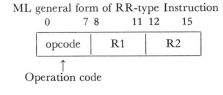

ML general form of RR-type Instruction

Operation code

Example 7.7 Or Register

OR   3,7

The action of OR is a Boolean operation. If bit i in register 7 is 1, then bit i in register 3 will be set to 1. If bit i in register 7 is 0, then bit i in register 3 will be unchanged.

> *Before execution*
> C(Reg 3) = 1111 0110 0011 1110 0111 1110 1111 0000
> C(Reg 7) = 0100 1001 1000 0001 1000 0000 1000 1001
>
> *After execution*
> C(Reg 3) = 1111 1111 1011 1111 1111 1110 1111 1001
> C(Reg 7) is unchanged

The Assembler will, in the second pass, search the Operation Table for the numeric code associated with the Boolean *Or*. It will place this value in bits 0–7 of the ML instruction. 0011 and 0111 are placed into bits 8–11 and 12–15, respectively. The definitions of the Boolean operations appear in the next chapter, Section 8.3.

The ML Instruction

0	7 8	11 12	15
0001 0110	0011	0111	
1	6	3	7

RX-Type Instruction.   The RX type is four bytes long. It is the only type in which an index register may be specified.

ML General Format of RX-type Instruction

0	7 8	11 12	15 16	19 20	31
opcode	R1	X2	B2	D2	

Note that:

1. CONTROL will use Formula I to determine the effective address:

   EF = C(base register) + displacement + C(index register)

2. Bits 12–15 point to the index register, bits 16–19 point to the base register, bits 20–31 are the displacement of the operand.
3. If bits 12–15 contain 0000, then since register 0 cannot be used as an index register, the value zero will be used in the formula instead of the C(Reg 0).

Example 7.8

Let us assume that:

1. C(Reg 5) = 00000008
2. C(Reg 12) = 40007000
3. the numeric address associated with SAM is 007120
4. the displacement of SAM is 120

   L   8,SAM(5)

The ML Instruction

0	7 8	11 12	15 16	19 20	31
0101 1000	1000	0101	1100	0001 0010 0000	
5 8	8	5	C	1 2 0	

Note that:

EF = C(base register) + displacement + C(index register)
   = C(Reg 12) + 120 + C(Reg 5) = 007000 + 120 + 000008
   = 007128

Figure 7.3 illustrates how the index register has modified the effective address.

FIGURE 7.3

The contents of location 007128 are loaded into register 8.

Example 7.9

L   8,SAM

Let us use the same assumptions that we used in Example 7.8.

The ML Instructions

0	7 8	11 12	15 16	19 20	31
0101 1000	1000	0000	1100	0001 0010 0000	
5 8	8	0	C	1 2 0	

1. No index is specified in the AL instruction. Hence, the Assembler puts 0000 into bits 12–15.
2. EF = C(base register) + displacement + C(index register)
   = C(Reg 12) + 120 + 0
   = 007000 + 120 + 0
   = 007120.
3. Note that the effective address is the numeric value associated with the symbolic name SAM.
4. The contents of location 007120 are loaded into register 8.

Example 7.10

A   12,0(10,6)

The second operand has been written in the *explicit mode*; that is, we have explicitly stated the address of the base register for this instruction. The general form of the explicit mode for an RX type instruction is D2(X2,B2). Thus, we see that the displacement is zero, the index is register 10, and the base register is 6. See Section 7.4. We assume that C(Reg 10) = 00000004 and C(Reg 6) = 00007000.

The ML Instruction

0	7 8	11 12	15 16	19 20	31
0101 1010	1100	1010	0110	0000 0000 0000	
5 A	C	A	6	0 0 0	

With regard to our assumptions which are depicted in the above diagram:

1. EF = C(base register) + displacement + C(index register)
   = C(Reg 6) + 000 + C(Reg 10)
   = 007000 + 000004
   = 007004.
2. The contents of location 007004 are added to register 12.

RS-Type Instruction.   The abbreviation RS stands for Register to Storage. These instructions are four bytes long. The RS type differs from the RX type (Register Indexable) in that no index register can be designated to modify the effective address of an operand. The effective address of an RS type operand can be modified by techniques which we will discuss in Chapter 9.

Some RS instructions do not have an R3 operand. In that case, CONTROL will ignore bits 12–15 of the ML format.

ML General Format of RS-type Instruction

0	7 8	11 12	15 16	19 20	31
opcode	R1	R3	B2	D2	

Example 7.11

LM   5,7,DATA

The ML Instruction

0	7 8	11 12	15 16	19 20	31
1001 1000	0101	0111	1001	0100 0000 0000	
9 8	5	7	9	4 0 0	

Questions

The answers to these and subsequent questions can be found on pages 160–61.

Set I
1. What is the base register used in the instruction?
2. Is this base register the implied base register?
3. What is the displacement of DATA?
4. If the contents of the base register are 007210, what is the effective address of the second operand?
5. Explain the action of the instruction.

Example 7.12   Shift Right Logical

A complete discussion of the shift operations appears in Chapter 8.

SRL   3,12

The contents of register 3 are shifted to the right 12 bits. The bits shifted through bit position 31 are lost. Zeros are shifted into bit position 0.

Before execution
C(Reg 3) = 1000 0110 0001 1000 1111 0000 1010 0111
C(bit bucket) is empty

After execution
C(Reg 3) = 0000 0000 0000 1000 0110 0001 1000 1111
C(bit bucket) = 0000 1010 0111

SRL 3,12 has been written in the explicit mode. The general form of the explicit mode for the second operand in the RS type is D2(B2). If B2 equals zero, then D2(0) and D2 are equivalent forms. Hence, 12 in the instruction is a displacement, and register 0 has been designated as the base register. Since register 0 cannot serve as a base register, CONTROL will substitute the value zero for the contents of register 0.

We note that the second operand is not used to reference data in MEMORY. CONTROL uses the last six binary digits of the effective address (see Formula II of Table 7.1) to determine the number of bits to shift. This six-digit binary field is always regarded as a nonnegative quantity. (See the discussion of the shift instructions in Section 8.4.)

The ML Instruction

0	7 8	11 12	15 16	19 20	31
1000 1000	0011	0000	0000	0000 0000 1100	
8 8	3	0	0	0 0 C	

Note that:

1. SRL has no R3 operand. The Assembler places zeros into bits 16–19. These are, however, ignored by CONTROL.
2. Number of bits shifted = C(base register) + displacement
$$= 0 + 00C = 0 + 00C_x = 0000\ 0000\ \underbrace{1100_2}_{\substack{\text{Digits}\\\text{used}}}$$

SI-Type Instruction. The Storage Immediate-type instruction is four bytes long. The first operand is in MEMORY. The second is an *immediate* operand; that is, the operand is part of the instruction. The example will make this clear.

ML Format of SI-Type Instruction

0	7 8	15 16	19 20	31
opcode	I2	B1	D1	

Note that even if I2 is the second operand, it appears in the ML instruction before the first operand.

Example 7.13

OI SAM,B'10110111'

Or Immediate is a Boolean operation. A one-to-one correspondence is established between the contents of SAM and the binary mask, B'10110111'. Bit i in SAM is associated with bit i in the mask. The bits in SAM are then modified by the following rule:

    a. If bit i in the mask is 1, then bit i in SAM is set to 1.
    b. If bit j in the mask is 0, then bit j in SAM is unchanged.

Before execution   *After execution*
C(SAM) = 11001100   C(SAM) = 11111111

The ML Instruction

0 7 8	15 16	19 20	31
1001 0110	1011 0111	1100	0000 1000 0111
9 6	B 7	C	0 8 7

Questions

Set II

1. What is the base register for the first operand?
2. What is the displacement of SAM?
3. If C(base register) = 007200, what is the numeric value associated with SAM?

The mask, 10110111, which is the second operand, is part of the ML instruction; hence its name, immediate operand.

SS-Type Instruction. The Storage to Storage type instruction is six bytes long. The length attributes of the operands are used by CONTROL to monitor the amount of the action caused by the instruction.

There are two classes of the SS type instruction. In the first class, which we label Class I, the implied length of the first operand, if not overridden by the programmer, "monitors" the action. In the second, Class II, the implied length of both operands govern the action of the instruction. One, none, or both implied lengths may be overridden by the programmer.

ML Format of SS-type Instruction (Class I)

0 7 8	15 16 19 20	31 32 35 36	47

opcode	L	B1	D1	B2	D2

Note that both operands are in MEMORY. The Assembler places the value of the implied length of the first operand *minus one* into bits 8–15. If, for example, the implied length of the first operand is 8, then the value 7 will be placed into bits 8–15. If the length is supplied by the programmer, it is treated in a like manner.

The "amount" of action will, however, be equal to the implied length or to the length supplied by the programmer, since CONTROL will always add 1 to the value of the L field during execution.

B1 and D1 are the base register and displacement associated with the first operand. B2 and D2 belong to the second operand.

Example 7.14

MVC   DATA,SAM

Let us assume that:

1. the implied length of DATA is five
2. the contents of the implied base register are 007200
3. C(SAM) = 471727374767
4. the displacement of DATA is 420
5. the displacement of SAM is 177

The ML Instruction

0	7 8	15	16 19	20	31	32 35	36	47
1101 0010	0000 0100	1100	0100 0010 0000	1100	0001 0111 0111			
D 2	0 4	C	4 2 0	C	1 7 7			

Questions

Set III

1. What is the base register for the first operand?
2. What is the effective address of the first operand? The second operand?
3. What are the contents of DATA after execution?
4. How many bytes will be moved?

Example 7.15

MVC   BLUE(4),12(10)

Here, the second operand is in the explicit mode. The general form of the explicit mode for the second operand in the SS type is D2(B2).

The ML Instruction

0	7 8	15	16 19	20	31	32 35	36	47
1101 0010	0000 0011	1100	0001 0100 0000	1010	0000 0000 1100			
D 2	0 3	C	1 4 0	A	0 0 C			

Questions

Set IV

1. If C(Reg 10) = 00007214, what is the effective address of the second operand?
2. If C(Reg 12) = 00007200, what is the effective address of the first operand?
3. What is the implied base register in the program?
4. Do we know the implied length of BLUE?
5. How many bytes will be moved?

ML Format of SS-type Instruction (Class II)

opcode	L1	L2	B1	D1	B2	D2

0 7 8 11 12 15 16 19 20 31 32 35 36 47

Note that the L1 and L2 fields contain the number of bytes associated with the first and second operands, respectively.

Example 7.16

PACK   RED,BLACK

C(BLACK) is converted to a packed decimal and placed into location RED.

The ML Instruction

0 7 8 11 12 15 16 19 20 31 32 35 36 47

1111 0010	0100	0011	1100	0001 0010 0011	1100	0001 1111 1111
F 2	4	3	C	1 2 3	C	1 F F

A diagram of the action produced by this instruction is:

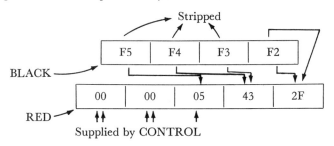

Supplied by CONTROL

The hardware (CONTROL) does not check the contents of BLACK. The action proceeds as depicted in the action diagram. If the contents of BLACK is an EBCDIC field or a Z-type constant, then, after execution, the contents of RED will be a packed decimal number.

If the contents of BLACK is neither an EBCDIC nor a Z-type constant, the action proceeds as depicted anyway. However, the contents of RED will not, in general, be a packed decimal number after execution.

Note that:

1. The contents of BLACK is unchanged by the instruction.
2. RED is a nine-digit packed decimal number.
3. If the recipient field is too small to hold all the digits from the source field then high order digits will be truncated.

7.4 Main Storage Specification Forms

Table 7.2 lists the various forms storage operands may take when written in the implicit mode. Note that S1 and S2 are symbolic names or arithmetic expressions which contain symbolic names.

An assembly error will occur if an operand in the implicit mode does not assume one of the forms in the table.

TABLE 7.2 Implicit Mode Address Specification Forms

Type	Form	Comment
RX	S2(X2)	index designated
RX	S2	no index designated
RS	S2	no index allowed
SI	S1	first operand
SS (Class I)	S1(L)	implied length overridden
SS (Class I)	S1	implied length used
SS (Class I)	S2	second operand
SS (Class II)	S1(L1)	implied length overridden
SS (Class II)	S1	implied length used
SS (Class II)	S2(L2)	implied length overridden
SS (Class II)	S2	implied length used

Example 7.17

Consider the instructions below. Then try to answer the following questions.

1. What is the type of each instruction?
2. Find the form in Table 7.2 which is equivalent to each of the storage operands in each instruction.

1	L	3,SAM+4(6)
2	S	5,BLUE
3	MVI	DATE,X'FF'
4	MVC	DATA(8),DATE
5	MVC	SAM(8),BLUE(6)
6	PACK	DOUBLE,X(5)
7	MVC	BLOCK,ABLE
8	LM	3,4,YET+8(6)
9	MVC	GREEN+4,BLACK+12
10	LR	5,9

Check your answers with the following ones.

1	RX type	SAM+4(6) is S2(X2)
2	RX type	BLUE is S2
3	SI type	DATE is S1
4	SS type—class I	DATA(8) is S1(L), DATE is S2
5	SS type—class I	SAM(8) is S1(L), BLUE(6) is in error
6	SS type—class II	DOUBLE is S1, X(5) is S2(L2)
7	SS type—class I	BLOCK is S1, ABLE is S2
8	RS type	YET+8(6) is in error
9	SS type—class I	GREEN+4 is S1, BLACK+12 is S2
10	RR type	No storage operands present

Table 7.3 lists the various forms which storage operands may take when written in the explicit mode. Note that when an operand is written in the explicit mode, all information pertinent to the ML instruction must be given in the AL instruction to the Assembler. The Assembler does not use the symbol table as a reference when an operand is written in the explicit mode.

The displacement and the base register, even if it is the implied base register, must be given for each storage operand. The length, which is a pertinent item in SS type instructions, must be explicitly stated in AL instructions.

TABLE 7.3 Explicit Mode Address Specification Forms

Type	Form	Comment
RX	D2(X2,B2)	index designated
RX	D2(B2)	no index designated
RS	D2(B2)	no index allowed
SI	D1(B1)	first operand
SS (Class I)	D1(L,B1)	first operand
SS (Class I)	D2(B2)	second operand
SS (Class II)	D1(L1,B1)	first operand
SS (Class II)	D2(L2,B2)	second operand

Example 7.18

Write each of the operands in the following instructions in the explicit mode.

1	L	5,SAM+8(6)
2	A	4,BLUE+4
3	S	3,DATA
4	LM	3,5,BLOCK
5	MVI	ALICE,X'FF'
6	PACK	DOUBLE,X(5)

```
7   MVC    BLOCK,ABLE
8   PACK   DOUBLE(4),X(5)
9   MVC    GREEN+4,BLACK+12
10  MVC    GREEN+4(5),BLACK+12
```

We must create register pointers to storage operands. We do this using the Load Address instruction. See Section 7.5 for a discussion of Load Address.

```
1   LA    7,SAM          register 7 points to SAM
    L     5,8(6,7)
2   LA    6,BLUE         register 6 points to BLUE
    A     4,4(6)
3   LA    8,DATA         register 8 points to DATA
    S     3,0(8)
4   LA    9,BLOCK        register 9 points to BLOCK
    LM    3,5,0(9)
5   LA    3,ALICE
    MVI   0(3),X'FF'
6   We assume that the implied length of DOUBLE is 8.
    LA    3,DOUBLE
    LA    4,X
    PACK  0(8,3),0(5,4)
7   We assume that the implied length of BLOCK is 6.
    LA    3,BLOCK
    LA    7,ABLE
    MVC   0(6,3),0(7)
8   LA    8,DOUBLE
    LA    9,X
    PACK  0(4,8),0(5,9)
9   We assume that the implied length of GREEN is 4.
    LA    4,GREEN
    LA    5,BLACK+12     register 5 points to BLACK+12
    MVC   4(4,4),0(5)
10  LA    3,GREEN
    LA    5,BLACK
    MVC   4(5,3),12(5)
```

7.5 The Load Address Instruction

The general form of the *Load Address* instruction in the implicit mode is:

LA   R1,S2

The action of this instruction is:

bits 0–7 of R1 ← 00_x
bits 8–31 of R1 ← the *address* S2

Example 7.19

LA   5,DATA

Let us assume that the numeric address associated with DATA is 007268.

Before execution   *After execution*
C(Reg 5) is immaterial   C(Reg 5) = 00007268

The address DATA is loaded in bits 8–31. We say that register 5 points to DATA. The implicit mode of LA is quite straightforward. The numeric value associated with the symbolic name is loaded into R1.

LA is, however, an RX type instruction. The programmer may, if he desires, designate an index register for the instruction. In that case, the effective address will be modified by the contents of this index. This modified address is then loaded into bits 8–31 of the first operand, R1.

Example 7.20

LA   5,GREEN(4)

Let us assume that:

1. C(Reg 4) = 00000004
2. the numeric value associated with the symbolic name GREEN is 007404
3. C(Reg 12) = 007200

The ML Instruction

0	7 8	11 12	15 16	19 20	31
4 1	5	4	C	2 0 4	

The effective address = C(base register) + displacement + C(index register) = C(Reg 12) + 204 + C(Reg 4) = 007200 + 204 + 000004 = 007408.

Before execution   *After execution*
C(Reg 5) is immaterial   C(Reg 5) = 00007408

1. Register 5 points to the location four bytes beyond GREEN.
2. A word of caution: It is easy to forget that bits 0–7 of the first operand are set to 00_x by the instruction.

The Load Address instruction, when written in the explicit mode, is a very handy way of setting a register counter or an index to an initial value. LA is also the fastest way to increment the contents of any register, be it an index, a base, or a counter.

Example 7.21 illustrates how the explicit mode establishes a pointer. Examples 7.22 and 7.23 illustrate the initialization of a counter or index register to zero and the incrementation of an index register by four.

Example 7.21

LA   5,3(4,6)

Let us assume that:

1. C(Reg 4) = 00000008
2. C(Reg 6) = 00007200

The ML Instruction

0		7 8	11 12	15 16	19 20	31
4 1		5	4	6	0 0 3	

The second operand is written as D2(X2,B2) in the explicit mode of the LA instruction. In this form, D2 is the displacement, X2 is the index, and B2 is the base register.

In our example, D2 = 3, X2 = 4, and B2 = 6. Therefore, the index field in the ML instruction points to register 4 and the base field points to register 6. The Assembler has converted 3 to a 12 bit quantity which is reflected as a three-digit hex numeral in bits 20–31.

The effective address = C(base register) + displacement + C(index) = C (Reg 6) + 003 + C(Reg 4) = 007200 + 003 + 000008 = 00720B.

Before execution   *After execution*
C(Reg 5) is immaterial   C(Reg 5) = 0000720B

Note that register 5 points to location 00720B after the execution of Load Address.

Example 7.22

LA   5,0

The ML Instruction

0		7 8	11 12	15 16	19 20	31
4 1		5	0	0	0 0 0	

If no index register is designated and the user desires CONTROL to use the value zero instead of the contents of a base register, then he might code the second operand in the form D2(0,0). However, D2(0,0) "reduces" to D2.

The Assembler, therefore, when it encounters LA   5,0 will place zero into the index field and zero into the base field of the ML instruction. Since D2 = 0, the Assembler will insert a three-digit hex zero into bits 20–31.

The effective address = C(base register) + displacement + C(index register) = 0 + 000 + 0 = 000000. Hence, 000000_x → register 5 (bits 8–31).

Before execution   *After execution*
C(Reg 5) is immaterial   C(Reg 5) = 00000000

Example 7.23

LA   4,4(4)

Let us assume that

C(Reg 4) = 00000004.

The ML Instruction

0	7 8	11 12	15 16	19 20	31
4 1	4	4	0	0 0 4	

If no base register is specified in the explicit mode, then D2(X2,B2) "reduces" to D2(X2,0). However, D2(X2,0) and D2(X2) are equivalent forms. (The comma signifies to the Assembler that a parameter is omitted. An omitted parameter in this case is zero by default.) If only one decimal self-defining term appears within the parentheses, then the Assembler will, by convention, take it to be the address of the index register.

The base field of the ML instruction points to register 0 while the index field points to register 4.

EF = 0 + 004 + C(Reg 4) = 004 + 000004 = 000008.

The content of register 4 has been incremented by 4.

Before execution   *After execution*
C(Reg 4) = 00000004   C(Reg 4) = 00000008

Computer Notebook

TOPIC 1   Why Base Registers?

What is the purpose of a base register? Why do System/360 and System/370 use the base-displacement addressing approach? Why not specify the effective address in the instruction? If these and other similar questions come to your mind, read this section. We provide some of the answers here.

There are two important reasons why System/360 uses the base-displacement approach instead of specifying the effective address in the instruction proper. The first reason we look at is the saving in instruction length. The saving is quite impressive.

Recall that an address in System/360 and System/370 is 24 bits long. These 24 bits enable the programmer to reference 16,777,216 bytes. And if we allow the programmer to reference any and all of those bytes by having him specify the effective address in the instruction, then 24 bits of that instruction must be reserved for the address.

The RX type instruction which specifies an effective address by Formula I—EF = C(base register) + displacement + C(index register)—needs only 20 bits to reference any one of those 16,777,216 bytes. Let us check this. The

RX type requires 4 bits for specifying the base register, 4 bits for specifying the index register, and 12 bits for the displacement—a total of 20 bits. The saving (in bits) for each indexable instruction is 16.67 per cent.

The saving for the nonindexable instructions—RX, SI, and SS—is still greater. We need to specify the base register—4 bits—and the displacement —12 bits, which give us a total of 16 bits. This is a saving of 33.33 percent.

Now suppose we have a program which has 1000 instructions using about 4000 bytes of MEMORY when we use the base-displacement method of specifying the effective address. The program will need about 5000 bytes of MEMORY if the effective address is specified in the instruction. The little extra trouble of learning base-displacement addressing is worth the saving.

The second reason for using the base-displacement addressing technique involves *relocation*.

Almost all programs written for modern computers are assembled so that the addresses of all instructions and all data are relative to some starting address, usually 0. For example, when we issue the assembly control statement, START 0, we request that the LOCATION COUNTER be set to zero. Our program is then assembled relative to location 0.

Let us define a *relocatable program* as a program which has been assembled with all its addresses relative to its starting point. This program can then be executed from any MEMORY location provided the Loader adds the *relocation factor* to all addresses. That is, the Loader must add the difference between the *relative* (assembled) starting location and the *actual* (execution) starting location to all addresses in the program.

When we use the base-displacement method of determining the effective address of an operand, we minimize the problem of adding a relocation factor to each relative assembled address. Recall that in our discussion about establishing base registers we said that USING *,R1 designates the address to which the LOCATION COUNTER points right now as the base-location. In addition, USING specifies that R1 is the implied base register for the program. (See Chapter 10.)

Note that the address specified by * (asterisk) is a relative one. The displacement of any operand address determined by the Assembler using that relative base-location address is, however, an absolute value.

The displacement of an operand is the "distance" of the operand from the base-location. It doesn't matter where the program is relocated; the distance between the address of the relocated base-location and the relocated operand address will not change. Hence, the value of this distance—the displacement— can be determined and placed into the displacement field of the ML instruction during assembly.

We also said when discussing the Using instruction that USING does *not* put the address of the base-location into the base register. We also said that the implied base register has to point to the actual base-location at execution time. It is, we stated, a programmer's responsibility to put that address into the base register. This, recall, is easily done by issuing the instruction BALR R1,0. (See Chapter 10.)

But what has happened? When BALR   R1,0 is executed, the actual address (the execution time address) of the base-location is put into the implied base register. And with respect to the effective addresses of the operands of the instructions, we have relocated the entire program! The effective address determined by CONTROL, using Formula I or Formula II, will be the actual (relocated) address of the operand. There are, of course, other problems involved when a program is relocated. For instance, the Loader must add the relocation factor to the contents of all address constants. The discussion of these items is, however, beyond the scope of this section.

TOPIC 2   Elementary Data Structure

We have deferred this discussion until the reader had an opportunity to use the Move Character instruction. The worth of the type of data structure we plan to discuss is best appreciated when used in conjunction with MVC.

A review of the duplication subfield of the DS pseudo instruction might be useful. (Chapter 5, Section 5.4.) If the concept of implied length is not thoroughly understood, we suggest that the reader also review Section 5.2 before going on.

Example 7.24

Suppose we have a file of 500 records in MEMORY. Each record consists of the names and addresses of people who buy stocks and bonds. Each record is 50 bytes long. The name field takes 20 bytes. The remaining 30 bytes represent the address field.

Now suppose that sometimes we want to print the entire record, sometimes we want to print just the name field, and at other times we want to print just the addresses.

Define a data structure which will facilitate the implementation of each of the above three procedures.

	Location	Name	Operation	Operand
①	007200	NAMEADD	DS	0CL50
②	007200	NAME	DS	CL20
③	007214	ADDRESS	DS	CL30

We assumed that LOCATION COUNTER was pointing to 007200 when the Assembler encountered NAMEADD.

The zero in the duplication subfield tells the Assembler, "Do not change the value in the LOCATION COUNTER regardless of the length attribute you find in the length subfield of this instruction." The Assembler will, of course, heed this injunction. The Assembler will enter NAMEADD, along with its numeric address of 007200 and its length attribute of 50, into the symbol table. The LOCATION COUNTER, however, will continue to point to 007200.

The Assembler will proceed to the next DS. The symbolic address, NAME, will be associated with the same numeric address as NAMEADD. Location 007200 will have two symbolic names associated with it. However, the length attribute of NAME will be only 20. In other words, 50 bytes, starting at 007200, belong to NAMEADD, while only 20 bytes, starting at the same address, belong to NAME.

The LOCATION COUNTER will be moved 20 bytes in the process of assembling ② . ADDRESS will be associated with hex address 007214.

a. What instruction will move the entire first record from the file to the NAME-ADD storage location?

    MVC   NAMEADD,RECORD

A record in the file is 50 bytes long. NAMEADD has an implied length of 50. Hence MVC will move the entire first record to NAMEADD.

b. What instructions will "blank out" the entire NAMEADD field and then move just the name field of the first record in the file to the name field of our data structure?

    ① MVI   NAMEADD,X'40'
    ② MVC   NAMEADD+1(49),NAMEADD
    ③ MVC   NAME,RECORD

① The MVI instruction will put a blank into location NAMEADD.

② MVC will blank out the entire NAMEADD field. The implied length of NAMEADD has been overridden, so only 49 bytes will be moved. The last byte moved will be NAMEADD+48. It will be copied into NAMEADD+49.

③ The implied length of NAME is 20. MVC will, therefore, move just the first 20 bytes in the first record.

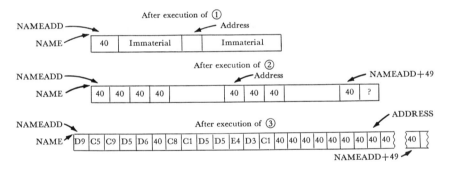

c. What instructions will "blank out" the entire NAMEADD field and move just the address portion of the first record into the ADDRESS field?

    ① MVI   NAMEADD,X'40'
    ② MVC   NAMEADD+1(49),NAMEADD
    ③ MVC   ADDRESS,RECORD+20

The move in ③ starts at RECORD+20, which is the first byte of the address portion of the record. How many bytes will be moved? Why?

Example 7.25

Table 7.4 is a slightly more complicated data structure. The structure purports to be a partial record of a bank customer file.

TABLE 7.4

Location	Name	Opcode	Operand	Remarks
007200	BANKSTA	DS	0CL80	CUSTOMER BANK RECORD
007200		DS	C	CONTROL FOR PRINTING
007201	ACCOUNT	DS	0CL40	CUSTOMER FIELD
007201	NAME	DS	CL20	CUSTOMER NAME
007215	ADDRESS	DS	CL20	CUSTOMER ADDRESS
007229	BALANCE	DS	0CL14	BALANCE FIELD
007229	OLDBAL	DS	CL7	OLD BALANCE
007230	NEWBAL	DS	CL7	NEW BALANCE
007237	ACTION	DS	0CL14	ACTIVITY FIELD
007237	DEPNUM	DS	CL7	NO. DEPOSITS MADE
00723E	CHECKS	DS	CL7	NO. CHECKS ISSUED
007245	ACCTNUM	DS	CL11	ACCOUNT NUMBER

Figure 7.4 is a diagram of the data structure described in Table 7.4.

We might define elements in our data structure as follows:

1. *Group item:* a symbolic name which is associated with a zero duplication factor.

2. *Elementary item:* all symbolic names which are not group names.

We immediately see that a group item is composed of group items and/or elementary items.

How many group items are there in the structure depicted in Table 7.4?

FIGURE 7.4

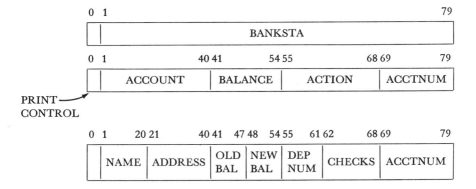

Consider the following problems. Assume a file of bank records has been read into MEMORY. The first record is located at symbolic address BLUE. The records in the file have the same form as BANKSTA.

Blank out the entire BANKSTA field. Move the following items from BLUE to BANKSTA:

1. the group item ACCOUNT
2. the elementary item NEWBAL
3. the elementary item ACCTNUM

The solution is:

```
MVI     BANKSTA,X'40'
MVC     BANKSTA+1(79),BANKSTA
MVC     ACCOUNT,BLUE+1
MVC     NEWBAL,BLUE+48
MVC     ACCTNUM,BLUE+69
```

Answers to Questions

Set I

1. The address of the base register is in bits 16–19. It is register 9.
2. None was specified in the instruction so the implied base register was used. The answer is yes.
3. The displacement of DATA is in bits 20–31. The answer is 400. That is in hex, of course.
4. Formula II applies.
   Effective address = C(base register) + displacement = C(Reg 9) + 400 = 007210 + 400 = 007610.
5. See Chapter 6 where Load Multiple is covered quite thoroughly.

Set II

1. Bits 16–19 point to the base register for the first operand. It is register 12.
2. The displacement of SAM is 087.
3. The numeric value associated with SAM is the effective address for Or Immediate. Formula I applies: EF = C(base register) + displacement = C(Reg 12) + 087 = 007200 + 087 = 007287.

Set III

1. The base register is 12. It is the implied base register used in the program.
2. The effective address of DATA, the first operand, is 007200 + 420 = 007620. The effective address of the second operand is 007200 + 177 = 007377.
3. Five bytes will be moved from SAM to DATA.
   C(DATA) = 4717273747.

4. Five bytes. The implied length of DATA "monitors" the number of bytes moved.

Set IV

1. Add C_x to 007214.
2. The effective address of the first operand is equal to C(Reg 12) + 140 = 007340.
3. No base register was stated explicitly by the user for the first operand. But the Assembler put 1100 into bits 16–19. So register 12 must be the implied base register.
4. No, we don't. The implied length of BLUE has been overridden by the programmer.
5. Four bytes will be moved as requested by the programmer.

EXERCISES

1. What is the effective address for each of the storage operands in the following code?

```
L       5,GREEN(6)
A       4,BLUE
S       3,WHITE(9)
MVC     WHITE,GREEN
ST      4,WHITE(6)
A       5,8(9,8)
MVC     0(2,7),4(9)
```

Assume that:

a. the implied base register is 12
b. the displacements and register contents are as given below
c. the implied length of WHITE is 9

Register	Contents	Name	Displacement
0	00004000	GREEN	120
6	00000120	WHITE	644
7	00007400	BLUE	440
8	00007200		
9	00000FF0		
12	40007000		

2. Write the machine language instructions for each of the assembly instructions in Exercise 1.

3. Give the contents of the first operand after execution of each of the following instructions. Draw an "action" diagram similar to the one in Example 7.16.

a. PACK   BLACK,EBCDIC
b. PACK   RED,EBCDIC
c. PACK   DATA,SAM

Assume that:

Name	Implied length	Contents
BLACK	8	immaterial
EBCDIC	6	F1F2F3F4F5F0
RED	3	immaterial
DATA	2	immaterial
SAM	2	F12D

4. Play the Assembler game. Be the System/360 Assembler for the following code. In the first pass, build the symbol table and generate the constants. Associate both the implied length and numeric address with each symbolic name in the table.

   In the second pass, use the symbol table as an aid in assembling the machine language instruction.

```
            L      5,R1
            S      5,R2
            M      4, = F'10'
            D      4, = F'100'
            CVD    5,DOLLARS
            CVD    4,CENTS
            STM    14,12,12(13)
            BR     14
R1          DC     F'1000'
R2          DC     F'680'
DOLLARS     DS     D
CENTS       DS     D
            END
```

Assume that:

   1. register 12 is the implied base register
   2. the address of the base-location is 007000
   3. the LOCATION COUNTER points to 007200 when L   5,R1 is encountered
   4. the machine language instruction for BR   14 is 07FE

5. Write the following instructions in the explicit mode so that each storage operand has a nonzero displacement.

   a. L   5,RED
   b. A   6,GREEN
   c. S   7,DATA

6. Consider the illustration of the water bill in Figure 2.3. Use the Define Storage pseudo to define a data structure which will be "equivalent" to this diagram.

7. Find the form in Table 7.2 or Table 7.3 which is equivalent to each of the storage operands in the following instructions.

      a. L   5,DATE(6)
      b. MVC   4(2,1),BLUE
      c. PACK 0(4,4),RED(2)
      d. LM   2,3,0(4)
      e. A   7,12(0,2)

8 | Data Conversions and the Shift Instructions

8.1 Data Conversion

When data is punched into a punch card, it is in a code named after Herman Hollerith, the inventor of the card. The CARDREADER has a device which converts the Hollerith code into EBCDIC. Hence, data, which has been read into MEMORY via the CARDREADER, is stored in EBCDIC form.

The CPU does not perform arithmetic operations on EBCDIC data fields. The user must convert this data to packed decimal. (The CPU can perform all four arithmetic operations on packed decimal fields. See Chapter 13.) If the programmer desires to use full-word binary integer arithmetic instructions on his data, then he must convert the packed decimal fields to binary integer form.

The diagram in Figure 8.1 depicts the steps necessary to convert the input data to full-word binary integer form.

Any data that we wish to print must be converted to EBCDIC form before the user initiates the write routine. The diagram in Figure 8.2 depicts the conversion procedure which we might follow to get a readable output.

The Unpack instruction (UNPK) converts a packed decimal field to zone decimal. UNPK preserves the sign of the original packed decimal number. If the packed decimal field is positive, the right nibble in the rightmost byte will be a hex "C." This "C" will be copied into the left nibble of the rightmost byte of the new field. If we now print the data field, without changing the "C" to an "F," one of the letters A through I will be printed. In our example in the flowchart of Figure 8.2, our output will be 0012G since hex "C7" is the EBCDIC form for the letter G.

Suppose we convert a negative binary integer to packed decimal. The CPU will generate a hex "D" as the sign of the packed decimal field. UNPK will preserve the hex "D." The last byte in the printed line will now be one of the letters J through R.

If we know that the original contents of the packed decimal field were positive, then we can *Or* the rightmost byte in the unpacked field with the immediate operand X'F0'. This will change the contents of this byte to a

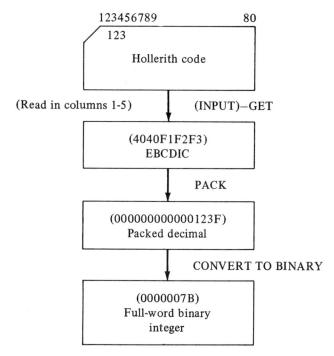

123456789   80

123

Hollerith code

(Read in columns 1-5)   (INPUT)–GET

(4040F1F2F3)
EBCDIC

PACK

(000000000000123F)
Packed decimal

CONVERT TO BINARY

(0000007B)
Full-word binary
integer

FIGURE 8.1

printable digit as depicted in the flowchart of Figure 8.2. We are, we might say, merely changing from a positive to an unsigned field.

If we do not know the sign of the original contents of our packed decimal field, then our solution is not so easy. We certainly do not want to *Or* a negative field with the immediate operand X'F0'. That would change the data item from negative to positive.

To simplify matters in this chapter, we will assume that our desired output is positive. We will discuss the general case in Chapter 13.

Table 8.1 lists the conversion instructions.

TABLE 8.1   Conversion Instructions

Instruction	*Action*
PACK	Converts EBCDIC to packed decimal
UNPK	Converts packed decimal to EBCDIC
CVB	Converts packed decimal to binary
CVD	Converts binary to packed decimal

Convert to Binary.   *Convert to Binary* is an RX type instruction. Its general form is:

CVB   R1,S2

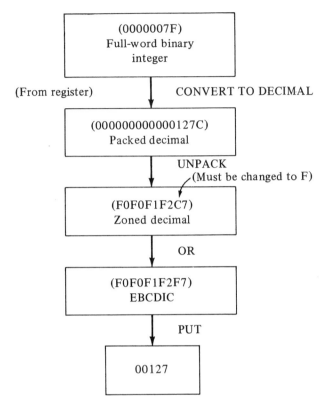

FIGURE 8.2

When this instruction is executed, the contents of S2 are converted to a full-word binary integer. The result of the conversion is copied into R1. Note that S2 must be a double-word.

Example 8.1

a.   CVB   3,DOUBLE

Before execution
C(Reg 3) is immaterial
C(DOUBLE) = 000000000000016C

After execution
C(Reg 3) = 00000010
C(DOUBLE) is unchanged

b.   CVB   5,GREEN

Before execution
C(Reg 5) is immaterial
C(GREEN) = 000000000000017D

After execution
C(Reg 5) = FFFFFFEF
C(GREEN) is unchanged

In part (b) of this example, the contents of GREEN are equivalent to -17_{10}. CONTROL put the two's complement form of -17_{10} into register 5.

Convert to Decimal. The general form of *Convert to Decimal* is:

CVD   R1,S2

When CVD is executed, the full-word binary integer in R1 is converted to a 15 digit packed decimal number with a sign. The converted number is copied into location S2. Note that S2 must be a double-word.

Example 8.2

a.   CVD   3,BLUE

Before execution   *After execution*
C(Reg 3) = 00000045   C(Reg 3) is unchanged
C(BLUE) is immaterial   C(BLUE) = 000000000000069C

b.   CVD   5,DOUBLE

Before execution   *After execution*
C(Reg 3) = FFFFFF12   C(Reg 3) is unchanged
C(DOUBLE) is immaterial C(DOUBLE) = 000000000000238D

Pack. The general form of *Pack* is:

PACK   S1,S2

When this instruction is executed, the contents of S2, assumed to be an EBCDIC data field, are converted to a packed decimal field. The converted field is the new contents of S1.

Note that S1 is the recipient field, while S2 is the source field.

The Pack instruction may be partitioned into three cases. We list the cases below. We discuss case 1 and case 2 in Examples 8.3 and 8.4, respectively. Case 3 is discussed in section 7.3 of Chapter 7 under the SS type machine language format.

The Three Pack Cases. In case 1, the source field and the recipient field are "compatible." The recipient field is large enough to hold all of the digits of the source field, and the digits from the source field fill the recipient field.

In case 2, the recipient field is too small to hold all the digits of the source.

In case 3, the source field does not contain enough digits to fill the recipient field. (See Example 7.16 in Section 7.3, Chapter 7.)

Example 8.3   Case 1

The action for case 1 is:

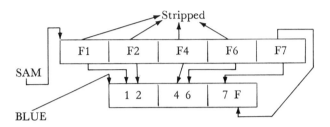

We assumed that the implied length of BLUE and SAM are 3 and 5, respectively.

Example 8.4   Case 2

The action for case 2 is:

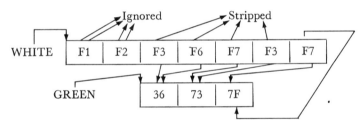

Note that the high order digits of WHITE are truncated; the recipient is too small. In addition, CONTROL expects the source to be an EBCDIC numeric field. No check is made. The stripping of the zone bits and the transfer of the sign are made as depicted in the action diagram. If the source is not an EBCDIC numeric field, a data exception will occur if the user attempts to convert the recipient field to binary.

Unpack.   The general form of *Unpack* is:

UNPK   S1,S2

When this instruction is executed, the contents of S2, the source field, are converted to zoned decimal. The converted value is the new contents of S1, the recipient field.

Unpack is an SS type instruction, class II. Since the implied length of each operand "monitors" the amount of action of its associated field, we again have the three cases which we listed above.

Example 8.5 Case 1

UNPK BLUE,DATA

The action for case 1 is:

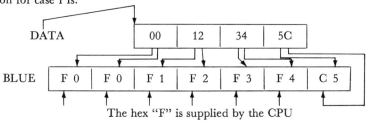

The hex "F" is supplied by the CPU

Note that if we print the contents of BLUE, our output will be 001234E. If we perform a Boolean *Or* operation on location BLUE+6 by OI BLUE+6,X'F0', our output will be 0012345.

Example 8.6 Case 2

The action for case 2 is:

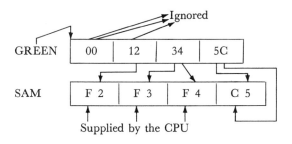

Supplied by the CPU

Example 8.7 Case 3

The action for case 3 is:

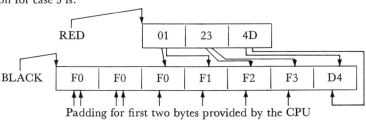

Padding for first two bytes provided by the CPU

8.2 A Sample Program—The Sum of X + Y

The numbered instructions in the sample program are discussed in considerable detail in the comments following the code. In the program itself, we trace the conversion of the data by giving, in the remarks field, the contents of the recipient location after the execution of each instruction.

We urge the reader to pay close attention to the steps which convert X and Y from EBCDIC to binary and, then, to the conversion of the sum of X + Y from binary to its printed value.

Figure 8.3 shows the contents of the card which will be read into the location AREAIN by the Operating System macro GET in instruction 3. We might say that the data structure set up by the Define Storage pseudos in the program describe the fields of the input card as well.

Compare the four pseudo instructions which comprise (14) in the sample program with the punch card in Figure 8.3.

Note that both X and Y are right justified on the punch card. Leading zeros may be omitted.

```
(14) AREAIN  DS    0CL9    NINE BYTES WILL BE READ IN
     X        DS    CL3     X FIELD, THREE BYTES LONG
              DS    CL3     BLANK FIELD
     Y        DS    CL3     Y FIELD, THREE BYTES LONG
```

Note the following points about the instructions:

(1) INIT is a macro which establishes register 12 as the implicit base register for the program. INIT also performs several other housekeeping functions.

(2) PROLOG has three operands of which only END=label is required. EPI is the symbolic address to which the computer will branch if the end-of-file (/*) card is read.

FIGURE 8.3 The Input Data Card

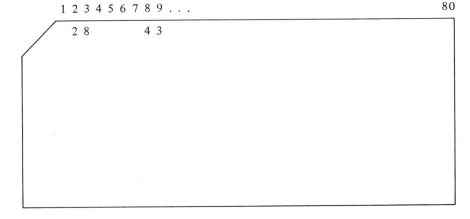

TABLE 8.2 Sample Program

		TITLE	ꞮTHE SUM OF X + YꞮ	
		PRINT	NOGEN,DATA	
①		INIT		
②		PRØLØG	END = EPI,CSIZE = 9,LSIZE = 24	
③		GET	CARDIN,AREAIN	C(AREAIN) = 40F2F840404040F4F3
④		PACK	DØUBLE,X	C(DØUBLE) = 000000000000028F
⑤		CVB	3,DØUBLE	C(REG 3) = 0000001C
⑥		PACK	DØUBLE,Y	C(DOUBLE) = 000000000000043F
⑦		CVB	4,DØUBLE	C(REG 4) = 0000002B
⑧		AR	3,4	C(REG 3) = 00000047
⑨		CVD	3,DØUBLE	C(DØUBLE) = 000000000000071C
⑩		UNPK	SUM,DØUBLE	C(SUM) = F0F0F7C1
⑪		ØI	SUM+3,XꞮF0Ꞽ	C(SUM) = F0F0F7F1
⑫		PUT	LINEOUT,AREAØUT	THE PRINTED LINE WILL READ:
	*		THE SUM OF X+Y IS 0071.	
⑬	EPI	GØBACK		
⑭	AREAIN	DS	0CL9	
	X	DS	CL3	
		DS	CL3	
	Y	DS	CL3	
⑮	AREAØUT	DS	0CL24	
	PRØSE	DC	CꞮ THE SUM OF X+Y IS Ꞽ	
	SUM	DS	CL4	
	PERIØD	DC	Cꞽ.Ꞽ	
	DØUBLE	DS	D	
		END		

CSIZE=9 limits the number of bytes read from the punch card to nine. CSIZE is a keyword. If omitted, the default value of 80 will be assigned to the record length. LSIZE=24 limits the length of the record which will be printed. The record will be 133 bytes long if this keywood is omitted. (See the discussion of these macros in Appendix C. Remember these are not IBM macros.)

③ The GET macro causes 9 bytes of our data card to be read and moved into location AREAIN.

④ The implied length of X is 3 and that of DOUBLE is 8. The action of PACK is illustrated in Figure 8.4.

⑤ CVB converts the packed decimal field, DOUBLE, to binary. Note that CONTROL interprets hex "F" in the rightmost nibble of DOUBLE as a positive sign.

FIGURE 8.4

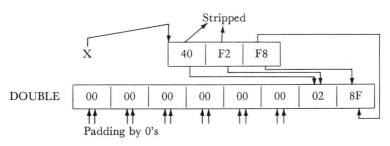

(6) The implied lengths of Y and DOUBLE "monitor" the action of the instruction. The action in (6) is, therefore, quite similar to the action of (4).
(7) CVB converts the packed decimal field into a binary field.
(8) The sum of X + Y is in register 3.
(9) The sum is converted by CVD to a 15 digit signed packed decimal number. Note that the CPU generates a hex "C" as the positive sign indicator for the field.
(10) The implied lengths of DOUBLE and SUM are 8 and 4, respectively. The 15 digit packed decimal number in DOUBLE is converted to a 4 digit zoned decimal type numeral.
(11) If we print SUM in the form it has after execution of (10), our output will read: THE SUM OF X + Y IS 007A. OI replaces the hex "C" in the left nibble of SUM+3 by hex "F."

$$\begin{aligned} C(SUM+3) &= 1100\ 0001 \\ \text{binary mask} &= \underline{1111\ 0000} \\ \text{Boolean } Or \text{ result} &= 1111\ 0001 \end{aligned}$$

(12) PUT moves 24 bytes (as designated by LSIZE=24) from AREAOUT (the second operand of the macro) to a buffer. The contents of this buffer, which include the prose, the sum, and the period, will be printed.

Suppose we issue the instruction PUT   LINEOUT,AREAIN immediately after instruction (12). What will be the printed result?

Twenty-four bytes starting at AREAIN will be moved to a buffer. Eventually these 24 bytes will be printed. Figure 8.5 gives the contents of these bytes.

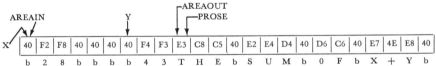

Note: The printed result is depicted beneath the diagram of the bytes. The lowercase b represents a blank.

FIGURE 8.5

8.3 The Boolean Instructions

Three Boolean functions are implemented in System/360. These are *AND*, *INCLUSIVE-OR*, and *EXCLUSIVE-OR*. We define these functions in Figure 8.6. Note that all three functions are commutative, so that the order in which the operands appear does not affect the result. However, when a Boolean instruction is issued, the contents of the first operand are always replaced by the result of the Boolean operation.

The Boolean functions are used in the manipulation of individual bits. Although the byte is the smallest set of addressable bits, it is possible, using

AND	0	1
0	0	0
1	0	1

OR	0	1
0	0	1
1	1	1

(inclusive)

OR	0	1
0	0	1
1	1	0

(exclusive)

FIGURE 8.6 The Boolean Functions

the Boolean operations, to change the value of any bit in a byte. A natural one-to-one correspondence is made between the bits of operand 1 and operand 2 of a Boolean instruction. Bit i of the first operand is associated with bit i of the second operand. Bit i of operand 1 is then affected according to the schedule given in Figure 8.6.

TABLE 8.3 The Boolean Instructions

Type	AND	OR(incl.)	OR(excl.)
RX	N	Ø	X
RR	NR	ØR	XR
SS	NC	ØC	XC
SI	NI	ØI	XI

Example 8.8 The AND Instructions

The result, usually called a product, of the Boolean AND of the contents of operand 1 and operand 2 replaces the former contents of operand 1.

a. NR   3,5

Before execution	*After execution*
C(Reg 3) = 00FF00FF	C(Reg 3) = 00770077
C(Reg 5) = 77777777	C(Reg 5) is unchanged

b. N   3,SAM

Before execution	*After execution*
C(Reg 3) = 01234567	C(Reg 3) = 00000000
C(SAM) = 76543210	C(SAM) is unchanged

c. NC   BLUE,SAM

The implied length of BLUE determines how many bytes enter the AND operation. We assume that BLUE has an implied length of 2.

Before execution	*After execution*
C(BLUE) = FF0F	C(BLUE) = 1204
C(SAM) = 1234	C(SAM) is unchanged

d. NI BLUE,B'11010111'

The implied length of BLUE is immaterial in this case. Only one byte of the storage operand participates in an SI type instruction.

> *Before execution* *After execution*
> C(BLUE) = FF C(BLUE) = D7

Example 8.9 The INCLUSIVE-OR Instructions

The result of the logical operation performed by INCLUSIVE-OR on the contents of operand 1 and operand 2 replaces the former contents of operand 1.

a. Give the code which will make bit position 25 in register 3 reflect the value in bit position 25 in register 5. All other bits in both registers 3 and 5 must be unchanged.

The solution is:

①	SR	4,4	clear register 4
②	Ø	4,=F'64'	bit position 25 of register 4 equals 1
③	LCR	6,4	C(Reg 6) = FFFFFFC0
④	S	6,=F'1'	bit position 25 of register 6 set to 0
⑤	NR	6,3	bit position 25 of register 6 still equals 0
⑥	LR	3,6	bit position 25 of register 3 set to 0
⑦	NR	4,5	bit position 25 of register 4 reflects desired value
⑧	ØR	3,4	done

After execution of ②, C(Reg 4) = 00000040. L 4,=F'64' might be substituted for ① and ②. ③ and ④ set bit position 25 of register 6 to zero. All other bits in register 6 are set to one. We might accomplish this phase by

> L 6,=F'−1'
> XR 6,4

⑤ and ⑥ set bit position 25 of register 3 to zero. All other bits in register 3 retain their original values. ⑦ and ⑧ finally cause bit position 25 of register 3 to reflect the desired value. No other bits in register 3 are changed.

b. Ø 4,SAM

> *Before execution* *After execution*
> C(Reg 4) = 00000000 C(Reg 4) = 12345670
> C(SAM) = 12345670 C(SAM) is unchanged

c. ØC BLUE,DATA

ØC is an SS type instruction of class I. Only the implied length of the first operand "monitors" the amount of action. We assume that the implied length of BLUE is three.

Before execution   *After execution*
  C(BLUE) = 0F0F0F   C(BLUE) = 1F3F5F
  C(DATA) = 123456   C(DATA) is unchanged

d. ØI   SUM+3,X'F0'

See the sample program in Table 8.2.

Example 8.10   EXCLUSIVE-OR Instructions

a. Let us change every bit in register 4. We accomplish this with the following instructions:

    L   5,=F'−1'   C(Reg 5) = FFFFFFFF
    XR   4,5

The solution to this problem is the Boolean function NOT. The definition of NOT is given in Figure 8.7.

b. X   5,GREEN

Before execution   *After execution*
C(Reg 5) = 0014F6F7   C(Reg 5) = FEC84C6F
C(GREEN) = FEDCBA98   C(GREEN) is unchanged

c. Consider the data structure defined by the following code.

    AREA   DS   0CL10
    A   DS   CL4
            DS   CL2
    B   DS   CL4

Set all bytes which belong to AREA to 00_x.
The solution is:

    XC   AREA,AREA

d. XI   SAM,B'11101111'

Before execution   *After execution*
  C(SAM) = 34   C(SAM) = DB

FIGURE 8.7

Operand	NOT Value
0	1
1	0

8.4   The Shift Instructions

There are eight shift instructions. We list them in Table 8.4.

TABLE 8.4   The Shift Instructions

SLL	Shift Left Logical
SLA	Shift Left Arithmetic
SRL	Shift Right Logical
SRA	Shift Right Arithmetic
SLDL	Shift Left Double Logical
SLDA	Shift Left Double Arithmetic
SRDL	Shift Right Double Logical
SRDA	Shift Right Double Arithmetic

We can partition the set of shift instructions in three different ways: (1) direction of shift (see Table 8.5), (2) number of registers involved (see Table 8.6, and (3) type of shift—logical or arithmetic (see Table 8.7).

TABLE 8.5   Partition 1 (Direction)

Left shift	Right shift
SLA	SRA
SLL	SRL
SLDL	SRDL
SLDA	SRDA

An arithmetic shift of the contents of a register one bit to the left is equivalent to a multiplication of the contents by two. An arithmetic shift to the right is equivalent to a division by two.

TABLE 8.6   Partition 2 (Number of Registers)

1 Register	2 Registers
SLA	SLDA
SLL	SLDL
SRL	SRDL
SRA	SRDA

The first operand, R1, of a double register shift instruction must be an even numbered register. The two registers involved in the shift are often called the "even-odd" pair.

The logical shifts disregard the sign bit. A left logical shift moves bit 1 into bit 0. The former bit 0 is lost. A right logical shift moves the sign from

TABLE 8.7   Partition 3 (Mode)

Logical	Arithmetic
SLL	SLA
SRL	SRA
SLDL	SLDA
SRDL	SRDA

bit 0 to bit 1. CONTROL generates a zero to replace the former value in bit 0. The diagram in Figure 8.8 illustrates this action.

The left arithmetic shift "protects" the sign bit. The sign bit does not participate in the shift. The bit in bit position 1 falls into the bit bucket. CONTROL regenerates the sign bit in the right arithmetic shift. Bit 0, the sign bit, moves into bit 1. However, the regenerated bit replaces the old value in bit 0. Hence the sign of the contents is unchanged. The schemata in Figure 8.9 illustrates our discussion.

The shifts are RS type instructions. Since R3 is not needed, the R3 field of the ML code is ignored by CONTROL. The Assembler, however, fills the field with binary zeros.

FIGURE 8.8

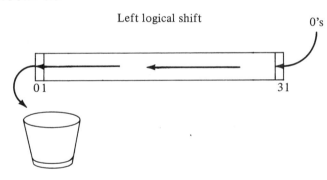

Left logical shift   0's

0 1   31

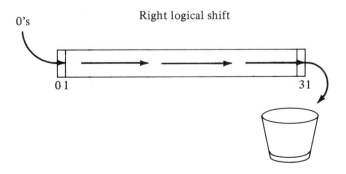

0's   Right logical shift

0 1   31

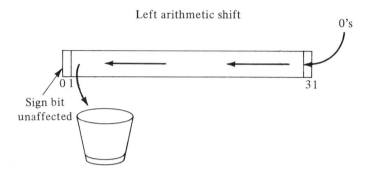

Left arithmetic shift

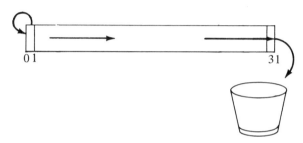

Right arithmetic shift

FIGURE 8.9

The first operand, R1, designates the register (or the even register of the even-odd pair) which will participate in the shift. The second operand has the general form D2(B2) where D2 is displacement and B2 is the designated base register. Now CONTROL will find the effective address, EF, by Formula II. EF = C(base register) + displacement. However, only the low order 6 binary digits of EF are used to determine the number of bits to shift.

The programmer usually specifies register 0 as the explicit base for the instruction. Since D2 is equivalent to D2(0), the usual practice is to give the shift as a decimal integer. For example, when we write SRDA   6,32, we are using the general form SRDA   R1,D2(B2) where B2 has been omitted because it is zero.

Example 8.11   The Logical Shifts

a. SLL   3,12

> *Before execution*   *After execution*
> C(Reg 3) = 80804123   C(Reg 3) = 04123000
> bit bucket is empty   C(bit bucket) = 808

b. SRL   4,7

Before execution (in binary)
C(Reg 4) = 1011 1000 1111 0000 1010 1010 1111 0110
bit bucket is empty

After execution
C(bit bucket) = 111 0110
What is the contents of register 4?

c. SLDL   4,28

The action of this instruction is:

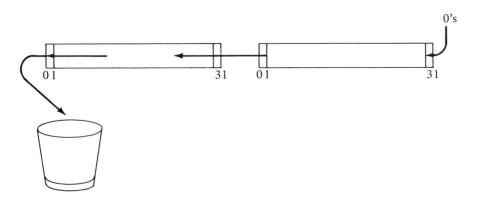

Before execution
C(Reg 4) = 01234567
C(Reg 5) = 89ABCDEF
bit bucket is empty

After execution
C(Reg 4) = 789ABCDE
C(Reg 5) = F0000000
C(bit bucket) = 0123456_x

d. SRDL   6,11

The action of this instruction is:

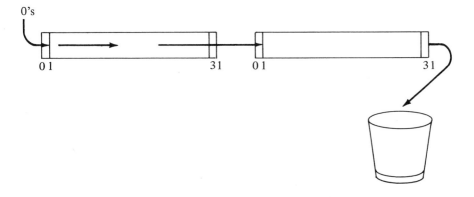

Before execution	*After execution*
C(Reg 6) = 40404040	C(Reg 6) = 00080808
C(Reg 7) = 6789ABCD	C(Reg 7) = 080CF135
bit bucket is empty	C(bit bucket) = 011 1100 1101$_2$

Check our result by using the following procedure. Convert the hex dump to binary. Shift the binary digits 11 places to the right. Convert the binary to hex.

Example 8.12   The Arithmetic Shifts

a. SLA   3,12

Before execution	*After execution*
C(Reg 3) = 80804123	C(Reg 3) = 84123000
bit bucket is empty	C(bit bucket) = 0000 0001 0000$_2$

Compare this result with SLL in Example 8.11a.

b. SRA   4,7

Before execution (*in binary*)
C(Reg 4) = 1011 1000 1111 0000 1010 1010 1111 0110
bit bucket is empty

After execution (*in binary*)
C(Reg 4) = 1111 1111 0111 0001 1110 0001 0101 0101
C(bit bucket) = 1110110

Compare this result with SRL in Example 8.11b.

c. SRDA   4,32

Shift Right Double Arithmetic is the "shift before division" instruction which was discussed in Chapter 6. (See Page 111.)

What will be the contents of register 4 after execution of SRDA   4,32?

d. SLDA   4,28

The action of the instruction is:

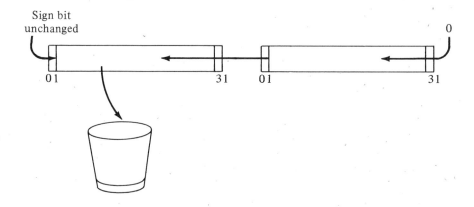

Sign bit unchanged

Before execution	*After execution*
C(Reg 4) = 01234567	C(Reg 4) = 789ABCDE
C(Reg 5) = 89ABCDEF	C(Reg 5) = F0000000
bit bucket is empty	C(bit bucket) = $02468AC_x$

Compare this result with Example 8.11c.

8.5 The Byte Transfer Instructions

In this section, the shortest section in the text, we discuss the byte transfer instructions—Insert Character and Store Character. Both instructions are of the RX type.

The general form of *Insert Character* is:

IC   R1,S2

The action of this instruction is:

$$R1_{24-31} \leftarrow C(S2)_{\text{one byte}}$$

Note that bit positions 0–23 of R1 are unchanged. Moreover, S2 need not be aligned on any particular boundary.

Example 8.13

IC   3,RED

Before execution	*After execution*
C(Reg 3) = 0708090A	C(Reg 3) = 070809F1
C(RED) = F1	C(RED) is unchanged

The general form of *Store Character* is:

STC   R1,S2

The action of this instruction is:

$$S2_{0-7} \leftarrow C(R1)_{24-31}$$

Note that S2 need not be aligned on any particular boundary.

Example 8.14

STC   8,BLUE+7

Before execution	*After execution*
C(Reg 4) = 0F0F0F12	C(Reg 4) is unchanged
C(BLUE+7) is immaterial	C(BLUE+7) = 12

Example 8.15

Consider the following problem. A character string, ABCD, is stored at location BLUE. It is not known whether BLUE is aligned on a word-boundary. Reverse this character string.

The solution without using a loop is:

IC	3,BLUE+3	'D' is in Register 3
SLL	3,8	
IC	3,BLUE+2	'DC' is in register 3
SLL	3,8	
IC	3,BLUE+1	'DCB' is in register 3
SLL	3,8	
IC	3,BLUE	'DCBA' is in register 3
SLDL	2,8	'D' is in register 2
STC	2,BLUE	
SLDL	2,8	'C' is in register 2
STC	2,BLUE+1	
SLDL	2,8	'B' is in register 2
STC	2,BLUE+2	
SLDL	2,8	'A' is in register 2
STC	2,BLUE+3	

Can you write a more efficient code which will reverse the character string? Consider exercise 3 of the problem section of Chapter 9 after you complete the study of that chapter.

Computer Notebook

TOPIC 1 Three-address, Two-address, One-address, and Zero-address Computers

It is possible to classify computers by the number of addresses specified in the location field of the assembly language arithmetic instructions. A computer whose assembly language instructions usually specify three addresses in the operand field belongs to the class of three-address computers. The assembly language instructions of two-address, one-address, and zero-address computers specify two, one, and zero addresses, respectively, in the operand field.

We shall present the assembly language code for the Fortran statement $A = A*(B + C*(D - E)) + (A/B)$ for each class of computer. We shall assume that all variables are full-word binary integers and that all of them have been defined.

It will be worthwhile to see how the change in the instruction format forces a modification of the program. The examples will not only point out the differences in the programming techniques but will also illustrate the methodology of assembly language programming in general.

Three-address Computers.   Table 8.8 lists the arithmetic instructions which we will need to write the assembly code for a three-address computer.

Note that since CONTROL places the result of an arithmetic operation into the location designated by the third operand in the instruction, there is no need to give the programmer access to any registers in the CPU. We do not need a Load or a Store operation.

TABLE 8.8   Three-address Optable

Instruction	Action
ADD X,Y,Z	$Z \leftarrow C(X) + C(Y)$
SUB X,Y,Z	$Z \leftarrow C(X) - C(Y)$
MUL X,Y,Z	$Z \leftarrow C(X) * C(Y)$
DIV X,Y,Z	$Z \leftarrow C(X) / C(Y)$

Our assembly code for the Fortran statement is given in Table 8.9. We use a temporary storage location to hold the interim result $C(A)/C(B)$. The symbolic name TEMP is this location. We assume TEMP has been defined.

TABLE 8.9   Three-address Code

DIV A,B,TEMP	$TEMP \leftarrow C(A) / C(B)$
SUB D,E,D	$D \leftarrow C(D) - C(E)$
MUL C,D,C	$C \leftarrow C(C) * C(D)$
ADD B,C,B	$B \leftarrow C(B) + C(C)$
MUL A,B,A	$A \leftarrow C(A) * C(B)$
ADD A,TEMP,A	$A \leftarrow C(A) + C(TEMP)$

We have destroyed the original values of D, C, and B. The intermediate results, except for A/B, have been lost. Table 8.10 has a modified code in which all original values except A have been saved. We have assumed, of course, that all temporary storage locations have been defined.

TABLE 8.10   Modified Code

DIV A,B,TEMP1	$TEMP1 \leftarrow C(A) / C(B)$
SUB D,E,TEMP2	$TEMP2 \leftarrow C(D) - C(E)$
MUL TEMP2,C,TEMP2	$TEMP2 \leftarrow C(TEMP2) * C(C)$
ADD TEMP2,B,TEMP2	$TEMP2 \leftarrow C(TEMP2) + C(B)$
MUL A,TEMP2,A	$A \leftarrow C(TEMP2) * C(A)$
ADD A,TEMP1,A	$A \leftarrow C(TEMP1) + C(A)$

Two-address Computers. Four arithmetic instructions of a two-address computer are listed in Table 8.11.

TABLE 8.11 Two-address Optable

Instruction	Action
ADD X,Y	X ← C(X) + C(Y)
SUB X,Y	X ← C(X) − C(Y)
MUL X,Y	X ← C(X) * C(Y)
DIV X,Y	X ← C(X) / C(Y)

However, when we write the assembly code for our Fortran statement, we hit a snag. Let's try to write it.

①	DIV	A,B	A ← C(A) / C(B)
②	SUB	D,E	D ← C(D) − C(E)
③	MUL	C,D	C ← C(C) * C(D)
④	ADD	B,C	B ← C(B) + C(C)
⑤	MUL	A,B	? ? ?

The original contents of A were destroyed when ① was executed. In ⑤, we are multiplying A/B—the new contents of location A—by B. We must augment our set of instructions by a Move command, say MOVE X,Y, which will move the contents of location Y into location X. With this new instruction added to our repertoire, we are able to complete our program. The assembly code for our Fortran statement appears in Table 8.12.

TABLE 8.12 Two-address Code

MOVE	A,TEMP	SAVE A
DIV	TEMP,B	TEMP ← C(TEMP) / C(B)
SUB	D,E	D ← C(D) − C(E)
MUL	C,D	C ← C(C) * C(D)
ADD	B,C	B ← C(B) + C(C)
MUL	A,B	A ← C(A) * C(B)
ADD	A,TEMP	A ← C(A) + C(TEMP)

If we want the sum of X and Y placed into location Y, all we have to do is transpose the two operands. Thus, ADD Y,X C(Y) + C(X) → Y. If, however, we want the quotient of X/Y placed into location Y, we have a problem.

Is it possible to write some code using just the instructions from our list in Table 8.11 augmented by MOVE which will accomplish this? Yes. But then we will have the quotient in two locations—in X and in Y. We could also, when designing the hardware, put in a sort of inverse division instruction:

DIVD   X,Y   C(X) / C(Y) → Y

Now consider multiplication. If we want to specify that the product of X and Y be stored in location Y, then all we have to do is transpose the operands. MUL X,Y puts the product into location X, while MUL Y,X stores it in location Y. We can do this because multiplication is a commutative operation.

How about subtraction? What shall we do if we want the difference, X − Y, placed into location Y. Or, to ask a more general question: Since subtraction is not commutative, how do we get the difference of a subtrahend and a minuend into the minuend's location?

One-address Computers.   FINAC is a one-address computer. Chapters 2 and 3, where we introduced FINAC, contain a great deal of information about one-address computers. Hence we need not tarry very long in this part of our discussion.

We note, however, that the CPU must store the results of its arithmetic operations into registers or accumulators. Since these cells hold the intermediate or the final results, they must be made available to the programmer.

Table 8.13 reflects the need to access the registers in the CPU. Two new instructions have been added. MOVE, however, is no longer needed, so it has been dropped.

TABLE 8.13   One-address Optable

LOAD	X	ACC ← C(X)
STORE	X	X ← C(ACC)
ADD	X	ACC ← C(ACC) + C(X)
SUB	X	ACC ← C(ACC) − C(X)
MUL	X	ACC ← C(ACC) * C(X)
DIV	X	ACC ← C(ACC) / C(X)

We present in Table 8.14 the one-address AL code for our Fortran statement, A = A*(B + C*(D − E)) + (A/B), without comment.

Zero-address Computers.   Our discussion of the zero-address machine is necessarily simplified. A detailed technical presentation of zero-address computers is beyond the scope of this text. The reader should bear in mind that our discussion and our diagrams show how the zero-address machine appears to work, not how it actually works.

The zero-address machine has registers in the CPU where the operands for and the results of the arithmetic operations are stored. These registers are,

TABLE 8.14 One-address Code

LOAD	A	$ACC \leftarrow C(A)$
DIV	B	$ACC \leftarrow C(ACC) / C(B)$
STORE	TEMP	$TEMP \leftarrow C(ACC)$
LOAD	D	$ACC \leftarrow C(D)$
SUB	E	$ACC \leftarrow C(ACC) - C(E)$
MUL	C	$ACC \leftarrow C(ACC) * C(C)$
ADD	B	$ACC \leftarrow C(ACC) + C(B)$
MUL	A	$ACC \leftarrow C(ACC) * C(A)$
ADD	TEMP	$ACC \leftarrow C(ACC) + C(TEMP)$
STORE	A	$A \leftarrow C(ACC)$

however, in a *stack*. We depict this stack, also known as LIFO (Last In, First Out), push-down list, or the cellar, in Figure 8.10.

The programmer has access to the top level register. The instruction LOAD X (one of the few instructions where an address appears in the operand field) will copy the contents of location X into the top level register of the stack. The previous contents of the top level will be "pushed down" into the second level. In general, the load instruction will "push" the contents of level k to level k + 1.

FIGURE 8.10

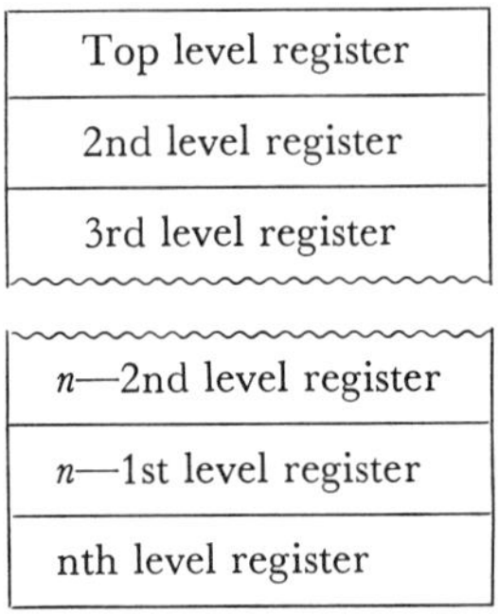

Example 8.16

LOAD A
LOAD B
LOAD C

We assume that:

$C(A) = 10_{10}$
$C(B) = 137_{10}$
$C(C) = 43_{10}$

Before execution		After execution	
Stack		Stack	
17_{10}	L1	43_{10}	L1
29_{10}	L2	137_{10}	L2
3_{10}	L3	10_{10}	L3
?	L4	17_{10}	L4
?	L5	29_{10}	L5
?	L6	3_{10}	L6
?	.	?	.
?	.	?	.

While LOAD is said to "push," STORE "pops" the stack. If we issue the command STORE A, then the contents of the top level register will be copied into location A. The value in the second level register will replace the value in the top level. We might say the contents of the stack "move up 1 register." In general, the contents of the $k + 1$st level register is moved to the kth level.

Example 8.17

STORE A

Before execution		After execution	
Stack		Stack	
17_{10}	L1	10_{10}	L1
10_{10}	L2	8_{10}	L2
8_{10}	L3	16_{10}	L3
16_{10}	L4	14_{10}	L4
14_{10}	L5	?	L5
?		?	

Table 8.15 gives the zero-address repertoire which we need to write the assembly language code for our Fortran statement.

TABLE 8.15   Zero-address Optable

Instruction	Action	Type
LOAD X	$L1 \leftarrow C(X)$	PUSH
STORE X	$X \leftarrow C(L1)$	POP
ADD	$L1 \leftarrow C(L1) + C(L2)$	POP
SUB	$L1 \leftarrow C(L2) - C(L1)$	POP
MUL	$L1 \leftarrow C(L2) * C(L1)$	POP
DIV	$L1 \leftarrow C(L2) / C(L1)$	POP

When the contents of the level 1 and level 2 registers are the operands of an arithmetic operation, both operands are destroyed. The result of the arithmetic instruction is placed into the top level register (level 1). The contents of all registers (except level 2) "pop" to a higher level.

Example 8.18

①	LOAD	B	push
②	LOAD	C	push
③	LOAD	D	push
④	ADD		pop
⑤	MUL		pop
⑥	STORE	A	pop

FIGURE 8.11

Snap 1		Snap 2		Snap 3		Snap 4	
5	L1	17	L1	170	L1	?	L1
12	L2	10	L2	?	L2	?	L2
10	L3	?	L3	?	L3	?	L3
?	L4	?	L4	?	L4	?	L4
?	L5	?	L5	?	L5	?	L5

TABLE 8.16   Zero-address Code

		Type
LOAD	A	push
LOAD	B	push
DIV		pop
LOAD	D	push
LOAD	E	push
SUB		pop
LOAD	C	push
MUL		pop
LOAD	B	push
ADD		pop
LOAD	A	push
MUL		pop
ADD		pop
STORE	A	pop

1. Snapshot 1 in Figure 8.11 is after the execution of ①, ②, and ③.
2. Snapshot 2 is after the execution of ④.
3. Snapshot 3 is after ⑤.
4. Snapshot 4 is after ⑥.

Table 8.16 lists the zero-address assembly language code for our Fortran statement. Note that there is only one Store instruction in the program segment.

TOPIC 2 Interrupts and Debugging

The CPU, during the execution of a user's program, is constantly watching for unusual or abnormal conditions. If such a condition should occur, then the CPU interrupts the program by transferring control of the computer to the Supervisor. (The Supervisor is a monitor program of the Operating System.)

What happens? Well, the Operating System maintains a 64 bit register called the PROGRAM STATUS WORD. This register contains a good deal of information concerning the status of the user program being executed.

When the interrupt takes place, an Operating System routine will save the contents of this 64 bit register by storing it into a special MEMORY location dedicated to this purpose. (The contents of the PROGRAM STATUS WORD register are called the program status word. Confusing? In this text, when we abbreviate the register, we write PSWR. When we refer to the contents, we either write the full name—program status word—in lowercase letters or we abbreviate, thus, PSW.) All bits in this PSW are the same as they were before the interrupt except bits 16–31 which have been set to a code indicating the reason for the interrupt.

A "new" PSW is loaded into the register. This "new" PSW will direct the Supervisor to the error subroutine which will attempt to rectify the cause of the interrupt. (The user may, in some cases, have the Supervisor transfer control to a user written error subroutine.) If the error subroutine is able to resolve the interrupt in a satisfactory manner, then the "old" PSW will be reloaded into the PROGRAM STATUS WORD register. The contents of the general purpose registers, which were saved by the Supervisor prior to passing control to the error subroutine, will be restored. Control of the computer is returned to the user's program at the point where it was interrupted. It is interesting to note that if the Operating System is able to resolve the exception, then neither the user nor his program will have any knowledge of the interrupt.

The CPU will once again execute the user's instructions. The user's program will remain in control of the computer until normal termination or until another interrupt takes place.

Interrupts generally—at least those we have knowledge about—end in an abnormal termination. The Supervisor will cause a routine to give an *indicative dump* which will contain the reason for the termination.

Figure 8.12 is a reproduction of an indicative dump. We will discuss only those aspects of the dump which should be readily understood by the reader at this time.

The second line of the dump gives the completion code. (For additional information with respect to debugging, we suggest the reader refer to the IBM manuals: *IBM System/360 Operating System Messages and Codes,* and *IBM System/360 Operating System Programmers Guide to Debugging.*) The interpretation of the code is given in line 3. For example, in Figure 8.12, the completion code is 0C7. The third digit in the completion code is the interrupt code, which is interpreted on the third line as a data exception.[1] Line 3 also gives the address of the instruction which was being executed when the exception took place. (The cause of an interrupt is called an *exception.*)

The address in line 3 is an absolute address in MEMORY. The addresses of the instructions in the printout of the program are relative addresses. How, then, do we find the instruction which was associated with the interrupt in the printout?

If the macro INIT was used to establish a base register, then the relative address can be found by subtracting the contents of register 12 from the location given in line 3.

Example 8.19

Consider the indicative dump in Figure 8.12. Find the relative address of the instruction which was being executed when the interrupt occurred.

The solution is:

address given in line 3	007176
address in register 12	007108
relative address	00006E

If the macro SETUP was used, then add six to the difference between the address given in line 3 and the address in the base register. The result is the relative interrupt address.

The address thus obtained can be checked by using the instruction image in line 7 of the dump. The last instruction in this image is the one which was being executed at the time of the interrupt. The relative address of the last instruction in this image should then be equal to the address obtained by the methods described above.

Lines 5 and 6 of the indicative dump give the contents of the general purpose registers. The contents of these registers should be quite useful in debugging since they show what the program had accomplished before the exception occurred. In all cases, the contents of the implied base register should be checked by the user. If the implied base register does not point to the base-location, then the technique given to find the relative address of the interrupted instruction will not work.

---

[1] If the completion code is not interpreted on line 3, consult the Messages and Codes manual.

FIGURE 8.12

CONTROL BYTE = C0   TCB FLAGS = A1   NO. ACTIVE RB = 2   NO. LOAD RB = 0
COMPLETION CODE—SYSTEM = 0C7   USER = 0000
PROGRAM INTERRUPTION (DATA) AT LOCATION 007176
REGISTER SET 1
GPR 0–7   00002B00 0001D308 000000E4 00000181 00004D78 0001FE88 000028C8 00000000
GPR 8–15   00000000 6001214A 0001FE70 000028C8 00007108 A000711C 00002918 00007108
INSTRUCTION IMAGE   18CFF272C088C0844F30C088
FPR 0–4   01000000 00000002 01000088 00070002 40419076 62FF2B11 C1679CB4 5F1FA72D
ACTIVE RB LIST
PROGRAM ID = O < 301C   RB TYPE = D0   ENTRY POINT = 001FB8
RESUME PSW   SM = 00   K = 0   AMWP = 4   IC = 0007   IL + CC = 7   PM = 0   IA = 001FB8
PROGRAM ID = ASMFAST   RB TYPE = 00   ENTRY POINT = 007020
RESUME PSW   SM = FF   K = 1   AMWP = 5   IC = 000D   IL + CC = 8   PM = 0   IA = 00717A
IEF242I ALLOC. FOR DECK   ASM   AT ABEND

We conclude this section with a detailed discussion of the more common completion codes.

Operation Exception   Code 0C1. The operation in the opcode field of the machine language instruction is not recognized by CONTROL. Or, an attempt has been made to use an operation which is not available in the particular model.

The operation exceptions in students' programs are quite often the result of an inadvertent modification of the opcode field of an ML instruction by a storage command. Look for an improperly indexed operand which appears in a loop.

Protection Exception   Code 0C4. The System/360 was designed for multiprogramming, which means that there might be several programs in MEMORY at any particular moment. To prevent one program from affecting the others which share CORE, MEMORY is divided into 2048 byte blocks. Each block is assigned a four bit mask called its *storage key*.

Bits 8–11 of the user's PSW are a mask called the *protection key*. If the user desires to access a particular block of MEMORY, his protection key is matched against the storage key for that block. If the keys do not match, then a protection interrupt will occur.

1. Look for an improperly indexed operand in a loop when you debug the program.
2. Check the effective address of the storage operands. Either the contents of the index register, if one is used, or the contents of the base register may have been inadvertently modified.

Addressing Exception   Code 0C5. The effective address of one of the operands referenced by the interrupted instruction is beyond the limits of the available storage on the particular computer.

1. Look for an improperly indexed operand in a loop when you debug the program.
2. Check the effective address of the storage operands. Either the contents of the index register, if one is used, has been improperly incremented or the contents of the implied base register has been inadvertently modified.

Specification Exception   Code 0C6. Specification exceptions are usually alignment errors. Full-word binary integer instructions require storage operands which are aligned on word boundaries. If we write, for instance, L 5,DATA(3), and the effective address of the second operand is not divisible by four, then a specification exception will cause an interrupt.

Half-word instructions require operands with half-word alignment. Double-precision floating point instructions require operands which must be aligned on a double-word boundary. Convert to Binary (CVB) and Convert to Decimal (CVD) expect the second operand to be a double word.

A branch instruction may cause a specification exception if the address to which control is passed is not divisible by two.

If the R1 field of a machine language instruction which uses an even-odd pair of registers does not contain an even nonnegative binary integer less than 16, then a specification exception will cause an interrupt.

If an interrupt occurs, check the effective address of the second operand. Is the operand properly aligned for the kind of instruction used?

Data Exception Code 0C7. Convert to Binary (CVB) expects the second operand to be a packed decimal number. If, inadvertently or otherwise, the digits in the packed decimal operand are not from the set $\{0,1,2,3,4,5,6,7,8,9\}$, or if the sign of the field is not from the set $\{A,B,C,D,E,F\}$, then a data exception will cause a program interrupt.

Data exceptions can also occur when the CPU executes instructions from the packed decimal repertoire. See the discussion of packed decimal arithmetic instructions in Chapter 13.

Example 8.20

① PACK X,BLUE
② CVB 3,X

Let us assume that:

1. C(BLUE) = F1F240
2. X is a double word

After execution of ①, C(X) = 0000000000001204. Recall that PACK does not check the contents of the bytes of the second operand.

Since CVB encounters a decimal 4 in the sign field, a data exception will occur when ② is executed. The exception will result in a program interrupt.

Fixed-point Overflow Exception Code 0C8. A fixed-point overflow exception will occur if the sum or difference of an add or subtract instruction is too large for a 32 bit register. The following arithmetic instructions can generate a fixed-point overflow exception:

S,SH,SR,A,AH,AR

Load Complement Register (LCR) and Load Positive Register (LPR) can also generate a fixed-point exception.

The fixed-point overflow exception is one of the four exceptions which may be masked by the user. Bits 36–69 of the user's program status word is called the *program mask*. If the value of bit position 36 is zero, then no interrupt will be given even though a fixed-point overflow exception occurs. If the value in bit position 36 is one, then the interrupt will be issued. A more detailed discussion of the program mask and its related exceptions appears in Chapter 17.

Fixed-point Divide Exception   Code 0C9.   A fixed-point divide exception will occur when the divisor of the division instruction is 0 or when the quotient of the division is too large to be contained in 32 bits.

If an interrupt occurs, check the dividend in the concatenated even-odd pair of registers. Has the pair been readied for division by a Shift Right Double Arithmetic operation which extended the sign bit of the dividend into all positions of the even register?

EXERCISES

1. Assume:
   a. C(BLUE) = F0F0F1F2
   b. L'DOUBLE = 8
   (Note: Read L'DOUBLE as "the implied length of DOUBLE.")
   Write a trace of the code in Figure 8.13. That is, give the contents of the recipient location after the execution of each instruction. (Use the remarks field of the sample program of Table 8.2 as a model.)

   FIGURE 8.13

   ```
   PACK    DOUBLE,BLUE
   CVB     3,DOUBLE
   M       2,=F'10'
   CVD     3,DOUBLE
   UNPK    BLUE,DOUBLE
   ```

2. a. A record, 15 bytes long, consists of 4 subfields—A,B,C, and D. The record will be read into MEMORY. Use the DS pseudo to define an area in MEMORY for the record. The lengths of the subfields A,B,C, and D are 2,5,5, and 3, respectively.
   b. If the first record has A = 17, B = 21, C = 137, and D = 22, show how to punch the IBM card.

3. Submit a program which reads in 3 positive values. Find the average of the values using binary integer arithmetic. Print the average. (Get a QDump of the area in MEMORY pertinent to the instruction after the execution of each instruction. Underline, in the printout of each dump, the value which appears in the recipient location after execution of the associated instruction.

4. Let C(BLUE) = F1F2F3C4
   Let L'SAM = 8

Give the action diagram for

    PACK   SAM,BLUE

(Use Figure 8.4 as a model.)

5. Let C(GREEN) = 0000067C
   Let L'RED = 5
   Give the action diagram of

    UNPK   RED,GREEN

6. Is it possible to find two implied lengths and a data item such that the contents of POSS are unchanged after execution of

    PACK   RED,POSS
    UNPK   POSS,RED

7. Some computers have a circular shift. Bits which leave bit position 0 enter bit position 31. Write the code which will accomplish a circular shift for a System/360 computer. (Hint: use a Boolean operation in conjunction with a shift.)

8. Write the AL code for A = (A + B) / (C * D)) − (A * B) + C + D for a three-address, two-address, and zero-address computer. The code for the zero-address machine should have exactly one Store instruction.

9. Write a sequence of instructions that will complement bit positions 7–12 of register 3 and leave the other bit positions unchanged.

10. Write the code that will accomplish the equivalent of

    IC   3,BLUE

if the alignment and implied length of BLUE is unknown. Define additional storage locations if necessary.

11. The sequence of instructions

    L   3, = F'128'
    SLL   3,20
    SPM 3

will set the program mask so that a fixed-point overflow exception will result in an interrupt. Insert the sequence in a program. Now create a fixed-point overflow. The interrupt will result in abnormal termination. Use the technique given in Topic 2 to find the address of the "interrupted" instruction.

12. L'BLUE = 8. Write a sequence of instructions which will reverse the bits of all eight bytes of BLUE. Bit 0 replaces bit 63, bit 1 replaces bit 62, etc. BLUE is aligned on a word boundary.

13. Write a sequence of instructions involving the Boolean operations which will exchange the contents of registers 5 and 9.

14. L'SAM = 5. Write a sequence of instructions which will accomplish the equivalent of

    STC 3,SAM

15. L'GREEN = 5, L'DATA = 3, and C(GREEN) = F1F2F3F4F5. Write a series of instructions that will accomplish the equivalent of

    PACK DATA,GREEN

9 | Loops and Address Modification

Suppose we want to add ten data items which occupy ten consecutive full-word MEMORY locations. The first item in the set is located at SAM. (See Figure 9.1.)

Any problem? No. The sequence of instructions in Figure 9.2 will do the job.

The sum of the 10 data items is in register 4. But somehow we are uneasy. Everything is so inelegant. There is too much writing and too much key punching. And each instruction takes four bytes of MEMORY; that means it takes 40 bytes of MEMORY to add 10 data items.

Suppose we had 1000 data items. That would mean 4000 bytes of MEMORY for the add instructions. And, don't forget, 1000 cards must be punched! There is a better approach to this problem—write a loop.

FIGURE 9.1

SAM	0000000A
SAM+4	00001000
SAM+8	0000010A
SAM+12	FFFFFFE1
SAM+16	00000000
SAM+20	00000012
SAM+24	FFFFFFED
SAM+28	FFFFFFF1
SAM+32	FFFFF1FF
SAM+36	0000000A

```
SR   4,4              SUM SET TO 0
A    4,SAM
A    4,SAM+4
A    4,SAM+8
A    4,SAM+12
A    4,SAM+16
A    4,SAM+20
A    4,SAM+24
A    4,SAM+28
A    4,SAM+32
A    4,SAM+36
```

FIGURE 9.2

9.1 The Programmer's Effective Address Pointer

In this section we develop a most useful concept which we call EFP—*the programmer's effective address pointer*. We will find this pointer quite helpful, not only in the analysis of loops, but also in the writing of them.

If a program needs more than one effective address pointer, we merely subscript them—EFP1, EFP2, EFP3, etc. When we write $\overrightarrow{EFP}$ we mean the location to which EFP points. If we write $(\overrightarrow{EFP})$, then we mean the contents of the location to which EFP points. For example, suppose EFP equals 007200, then $(\overrightarrow{EFP})$ is equal to C(location 007200). Note that EFP equals the value to which it points.

EFP is calculated in exactly the same way as CONTROL calculates the effective address of an operand. If EFP is moved by changing the contents of an index register, then

$$EFP = C(\text{base register}) + \text{displacement} + C(\text{index register})$$

If the pointer is "moved" by changing the contents of an explicit base register, then

$$EFP = C(\text{base register}) + \text{displacement}$$

We shall refer to the first equation as Formula I and the second as Formula II. These formulas were discussed in Section 7.2.

Now let us return to the program segment in Figure 9.2. Let us write our Add instruction in a more general form:

```
A   4,EFP
```

The computer science notation for the action of this instruction is:

$$\text{Register 4} \leftarrow C(\text{Reg 4}) + (\overrightarrow{EFP})$$

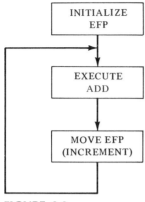

FIGURE 9.3

We might read this as "the sum of the contents of register 4 and the contents of the location pointed to by EFP is placed into register 4."

Remember, in the discussion which follows, that EFP is not a MEMORY location. It is a programmer's pointer to a MEMORY location. Before we are done, we must find a way to express EFP as an operand in the Add instruction.

If we set EFP so that it initially points to SAM, execute the instruction, "move" the pointer so that it points to SAM+4, execute the instruction, "move" EFP to SAM+8, . . . , "move" EFP so that it points to SAM+36, and execute the instruction, we will have succeeded in adding all ten data items with exactly one instruction. The flowchart in Figure 9.3 recapitulates our discussion.

How do we initialize EFP? ADD is an RX type instruction, so Formula I applies:

$$EFP = C(base\ register) + displacement + C(index\ register)$$

We will "move" the pointer, EFP, by changing the value in the index register. To simplify matters, let us choose register 5 as the index. The symbolic address SAM is equal to the contents of the base register plus the displacement.[1] That is, SAM = C(base register) + displacement. So Formula I reduces to:

$$EFP = SAM + C(Reg\ 5)$$

Hence, the initialization of EFP can be done by merely setting the contents of register 5 to 0. This can be accomplished in many ways; the simplest, perhaps, is SR 5,5, which we label as instruction   3

The formula now is:

$$EFP = SAM + C(Reg\ 5) = SAM + 0 = SAM$$

---

[1] See Section 7.1. The Assembler determined the displacement by subtracting the value of the base-location from the numeric address associated with SAM.

How is EFP expressed as an operand in an instruction? Recall that whenever a symbolic name is used in an operand, the programmer is restricted to the implicit mode. Table 7.2 lists the general form of an indexed RX type operand as S2(X2). Hence EFP = SAM + C(Reg 5) = SAM(5). The instruction becomes A 4,SAM(5). We label this instruction as ④.

The pointer is "moved" by incrementing the contents of the index register. This is done quite handily with the Load Address instruction LA 5,4(5).[2] We label this instruction as ⑤. (See Section 7.5 for a discussion of the Load Address instruction.)

We combine ③, ④, and ⑤ into a single program segment:

	SR	4,4	SET SUM TO 0
③	SR	5,5	INITIALIZE INDEX
④	A	4,SAM(5)	C(REG 4) + $\overrightarrow{(EFP)}$ → REG 4
⑤	LA	5,4(5)	INCREMENT INDEX

Two questions should immediately come to mind:

1. How do we make a loop so that we execute ④ exactly ten times?
2. How do we exit from a loop when the addition has been completed?

The Branch on Count instruction will solve the problems posed by our two questions.

The general form of *Branch on Count* is:

BCT   R1,S2

The action of this instruction is:

R1 ← C(R1) − 1

If C(R1) ≠ 0, then control is transferred to location S2; otherwise RNI from P + 1. (Read RNI as "read next instruction.")

Note that R1 is a counter. If BCT is used in a loop, then the initial value of R1 will be the maximum number of passes that will be made through the loop. The initial value in R1 should be positive.

Example 9.1

a. BCT   6,LOOP

Before execution	*After execution*
C(Reg 6) = 00000043	C(Reg 6) = 00000042

The next instruction to be executed by the computer will be taken from symbolic address LOOP.

[2] Register 5 ← C (Reg 5) + 4

b. BCT   7,LOOP

Before execution   *After execution*
C(Reg 7) = 00000001   C(Reg 7) = 00000000

The next instruction in sequence (P + 1 where P is the present instruction) will be executed by the computer. The program has exited from a loop.

Suppose we pick register 6 to be the counter or BCT register to monitor the loop. We must initialize register 6 to decimal 10 before entering the loop proper. We must also label the first instruction in the loop proper by a symbolic name, say BLUE. The first instruction in the loop is ④.

Finally, we put BCT 6,BLUE as the last instruction in the loop. Our loop is complete. The program segment adds the 10 integers. The loop appears in Figure 9.4, and Figure 9.5 shows the flowchart for the loop.

FIGURE 9.4

	① LA	6,10	BCT REGISTER
	② SR	4,4	SET SUM TO 0
	③ SR	5,5	INDEX
BLUE	④ A	4,SAM(5)	C(REG 4) + $\overrightarrow{(EFP)}$ → REG 4
	⑤ LA	5,4(5)	MOVE POINTER
	⑥ BCT	6,BLUE	EXIT IF DONE

FIGURE 9.5

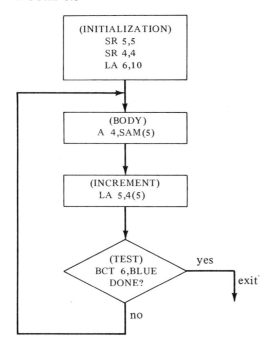

9.2 The Structure of a Loop

A loop can take many forms, and the diversity of System/360 branch instructions is such that we can devise a loop for a particular task in a great number of ways. Still, there are only four basic elements or steps in a loop. They are *initialization, body, test-for-exit,* and *increment.*

The initialization, while an integral part of a loop, will be executed only once. It must be the first step of the loop. The other three elements may appear in any order; hence we might say that there are six basic general loop structures. But since we can break up the body into several sections, scatter increment steps throughout the loop, and have more than one test-for-exit, the number of loop designs is immense.

Figure 9.6 depicts two of the six basic structures.

Initialization.   All controls used in the loop are set to their initial values in the initialization step. An index register is set to the particular value which will ensure that EFP points to the correct address in the first pass through the loop. A counter or BCT register which will count the number of passes made through the loop must be set to the proper value. The register or counter which monitors the loop should be set with some care. Quite often programs pass through a loop one time more than necessary or one time less than necessary.

If the loop is to be used more than once in a program, then the reentry into the loop should be made in the initialization step. The increment, the

FIGURE 9.6

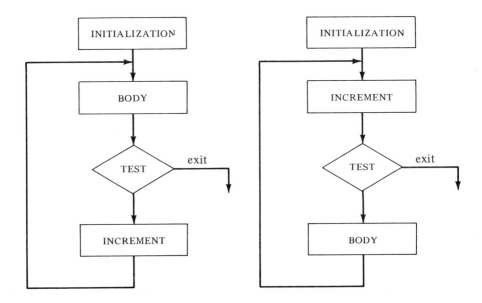

body, and/or the test-for-exit steps will undoubtedly have changed the initial values of the parameters used in the loop. Reentry into the loop via the initialization step will guarantee that these parameters are reset to the correct initial values. The loop, then, will function a second time in the manner intended.

Body.   The body is the *raison d'être* of the loop. The initialization, the increment, and the test-for-exit have all been designed to expedite the work of the body.

Since each instruction in the body will be executed many times, and since we usually have many instructions to choose from, we should pick the most efficient ones. The fastest loops are the most elegant.

A loop parameter whose value remains constant in each pass should always be set in the initialization step. For example, suppose the programmer wants to multiply the contents of register 5 by 10 in each pass through the loop. In the program segment given below, ① should not appear in the body.

    ① LA   7,10
    ② M   4,7

LA   7,10 should be placed in the initialization step. The time saved in executing unnecessary instructions may be insignificant in a student program, but it may be considerable in other circumstances.

Test-for-Exit.   The test-for-exit checks to see if all of the conditions for the completion of the loop have been satisfied. There may be several tests such that each test must be satisfactorily completed in order to exit from the loop. Or, the satisfactory completion of any one of several tests might lead to an exit. Usually, however, there is only one test-for-exit.

The important point, however, is that each test must provide a switch which will lead to an entry back into the loop if the specified conditions are not met or the switch will lead to an exit from the loop otherwise. A loop cannot exist if this choice is not provided.

Increment Step.   The increment step has two functions:

    1. to "move" the pointers by increasing or decreasing the contents of the index register(s) and/or the explicit base register(s);
    2. to count the number of passes through the loop by adding or by subtracting the "count value" [3] from the counter register. The BCT register is decremented automatically.

The programmer should be cautious about the increment (or decrement) to the index register(s). If EFP is a pointer to a full-word data item, then the increment or decrement is 4. The increment or decrement is 1, 2, or 8 if EFP

---

[3] Not everyone counts by one!

points to a data item aligned on a byte, half-word, or double-word, respectively. If the pointer is in the explicit mode, then the size of the record being processed in the loop will determine the increment or decrement. In this case our increment or decrement will be added to an explicit base register.

9.3 Address Modification by Changing the Value in an Index Register (I)

Our first example, Figure 9.7, is a program which stores the sum of $Ai + Bi$ into location Ci. We need 3 pointers, one for each block. But since we traverse each block at the same rate, all pointers are able to use the same index register.

Let us choose register 4 as the index. Our pointers, then, to the A, B, and C blocks are, respectively: EFPI = A(4), EFP2 = B(4), EFP3 = C(4).

In the second example, Figure 9.8, we use Branch on Count to Register (BCTR) instead of Branch on Count to monitor the loop. The only difference between BCTR and BCT is that the transfer of control address is placed in a register when BCTR is used. The general form of *Branch on Count to Register* is:

BCTR   R1,R2

The action of this instruction is:

R1 ← C(R1) − 1

If $C(R1) \neq 0$, then control is transferred to the address in R2; otherwise, RNI from $P + 1$.

It is the programmer's responsibility to load the branch address into R2.

The only difference between the two programs in Figures 9.7 and 9.8 is that the BCTR instruction forced us to load the address LOOP into register 8.

FIGURE 9.7

	LA	5,20	BCT REGISTER
	LA	4,0	INDEX REG SET TO 0
LOOP	L	6,A(4)	(EFP1) → REG 6
	A	6,B(4)	C(REG 6) + (EFP2) → REG 6
	ST	6,C(4)	A(I) + B(I) → EFP3
	LA	4,4(4)	MOVE POINTERS
	BCT	5,LOOP	BRANCH TO LOOP IF NOT DONE

Example 9.2

Let us assume that GREEN is a block of 100 full-word integers. We wish to convert each integer to packed decimal and store the packed decimal numbers in consecutive locations starting at BLUE.

```
        LA      5,20        R1 OF BCTR
        LA      4,0         INDEX SET TO 0
        LA      8,LOOP      R2 POINTS TO LOOP
*
*   THE TRANSFER ADDRESS IS IN R2
*
LOOP    L       6,A(4)      (EFP1) → REG 6
        A       6,B(4)      C(REG 6) + (EFP2) → REG 6
        ST      6,C(4)      A(I) + B(I) → EFP3
        LA      4,4(4)      MOVE POINTERS
        BCTR    5,8         BRANCH ADDRESS IN REG 8
```

FIGURE 9.8

We will need two index registers. The pointer to the full-word binary integer field will be incremented by four and the pointer to the packed decimal field will be incremented by eight.

Let EFP1 = GREEN(4) and EFP2 = BLUE(5)

The solution appears in Figure 9.9.

```
        LA      4,0          INDEX FOR EFP1
        LA      5,0          INDEX FOR EFP2
        LA      6,LOOP       R2 FOR BCTR
        LA      7,100        R1 FOR BCTR
LOOP    L       3,GREEN(4)   (EFP1) → REG 3
        CVD     3,BLUE(5)    CONVERTED
        LA      4,4(4)       MOVE EFP1
        LA      5,8(5)       MOVE EFP2
        BCTR    7,6          TEST AND INCREMENT
```

FIGURE 9.9

9.4 The Arithmetic Extended Mnemonics

Bits 34 and 35 of the program status word are a two-digit binary number called the *condition code*. Since this code is set by most instructions, we have listed in Table 9.1 the instructions studied to this point which do *not* set the condition code.

TABLE 9.1 Instructions Which Do Not Set Condition Code

LR	L	ST	LH	STH
MR	M	MH	DR	D
MVC	MVI	LM	STM	LA
PACK	UNPK	CVB	CVD	

(1) L   5, = F'1'
(2) A   5, = F' − 1'
(3) L   6, = F'0'
(4) A   6, = F'1'
(5) L   7, = F'0'
(6) A   7, = F' − 1'
(7) L   8, = F' − 2147483648'
(8) A   8, = F' − 1'

FIGURE 9.10

The condition code (often abbreviated to CC) is set to zero, one, or two if the value in the recipient after the execution of an instruction is equal to zero, less than zero, or greater than zero, respectively. The condition code is set to three if the recipient overflows.

For example, consider the program segment in Figure 9.10. The condition code is set to $00_2 = 0_{10}$ after execution of (2) since the value in the recipient, register 5, equals 0.

After execution of (4) in Figure 9.10, the value in the recipient, register 6, is greater than 0. The condition code will reflect this by being set to $10_2 = 2_{10}$. After execution of (6), the condition code will equal $01_2 = 1_{10}$. An overflow will occur when (8)[4] is executed. The condition code will be set to $11_2 = 3_{10}$.

Table 9.2 summarizes our discussion.

TABLE 9.2

C (recipient)	Value of CC
= 0	00_2
< 0	01_2
> 0	10_2
Overflow	11_2

The set of arithmetic extended mnemonics listed in Table 9.3 provides the programmer with the means for making a two-way decision based on the status of the condition code. In all cases, if the condition code does not satisfy the requirements for the branch, the program follows the normal sequence—the next instruction to be executed will be P + 1.

---

[4] The "largest" negative integer which can be held in a register is −2,147,483,648. Adding −1 to this value will cause an overflow.

TABLE 9.3   Arithmetic Extended Mnemonics

Extended mnemonic	Instruction		Action
Branch on Zero	BZ	S2	branch if CC = 0
Branch on Minus	BM	S2	branch if CC = 1
Branch on Plus	BP	S2	branch if CC = 2
Branch not Zero	BNZ	S2	branch if CC ≠ 0
Branch not Minus	BNM	S2	branch if CC ≠ 1
Branch not Plus	BNP	S2	branch if CC ≠ 2
Branch on Overflow	BØ	S2	branch if CC = 3
Branch not Overflow	BNØ	S2	branch if CC ≠ 3

Example 9.3

a. L   5, = F'6'
   A   5, = F' − 5'
   BP   LOOP   Branch if positive to LOOP.

Control will be transferred to location LOOP since the value of the condition code is 2 which reflects the positive contents of register 5.

b. ① S   5, = F'17'
   ② BNP   DATA

Note that if the C(Reg 5), after execution of ①, is not greater than zero, then ② will transfer control to location DATA.

If C(Reg 5) > 0, then CC = 2. No branch will be made. The next instruction in the normal sequence will be executed.

c. Write a sequence of instructions which will cause a branch to DATA if the contents of ABLE are not less than 0.
   The sequence of instructions is:

       L   5,ABLE
       LTR   5,5
       BNM   DATA

Note that Load does not set the condition code, but LTR (Load and Test Register) does. The general form of *Load and Test Register* is:

       LTR   R1,R2

The action of LTR is:

       R1 ← C(R2)

The condition code is set according to the criteria given in Table 9.2.

Load Register (LR) and Load and Test Register (LTR) are equivalent, but the programmer should not use LTR unless he expects to check the status of the condition code. We also note that R1 may equal R2.

d. S   5,BLUE
  BNP   GREEN

Under what conditions will the computer branch to GREEN?

9.5 The Compare Extended Mnemonics

Compare, an RX type, and Compare Register, an RR type, are two instructions whose only function is to set the condition code. The general form of *Compare* is:

    C R1,S2

The action of this instruction is [note that we write op1 (operand 1) for the contents of R1 and op2 (operand 2) for the contents of S2]:

     If op1 $=$ op2, CC is set to 00_2.
     If op1 $<$ op2, CC is set to 01_2.
     If op1 $>$ op2, CC is set to 10_2.

Neither Compare nor Compare Register can set the condition code to $11_2 = 3_{10}$.

The general form of *Compare Register* is:

    CR R1,R2

The action for the Compare Register instruction is the same as that for the Compare instruction (see above).

The only difference between Compare and Compare Register is that the former compares the contents of a register with a full-word binary integer stored in MEMORY, while the latter compares two register operands.

The Compare instructions have their own set of extended mnemonics which we list in Table 9.4. These mnemonics can be used to make a two-way decision based on the setting of the condition code by a Compare instruction. Example 9.4 should help clarify our discussion.

TABLE 9.4 Compare Extended Mnemonics

Extended mnemonic	Instruction		Branch (with respect to CC)	Branch (with respect to Compare)
Branch Equal	BE	S2	If CC $= 0$	If op1 $=$ op2
Branch Low	BL	S2	If CC $= 1$	If op1 $<$ op2
Branch High	BH	S2	If CC $= 2$	If op1 $>$ op2
Branch not Equal	BNE	S2	If CC $\neq 0$	If op1 $\neq$ op2
Branch not Low	BNL	S2	If CC $\neq 1$	If op1 $\not< $ op2
Branch not High	BNH	S2	If CC $\neq 2$	If op1 $\not> $ op2

Example 9.4

a. ① L   5, = F'4'
   ② L   6, = F'0'
   ③ CR   5,6
   ④ BH   LOOP

Control will be transferred to location LOOP since operand 1 is greater than operand 2. The condition code is set to 10_2 by ③.

b. Write a program segment which will transfer control to BLUE if the contents of register 7 are not less than the contents of DATA.
   The program segment is:

       C   7,DATA
       BNL BLUE

c. Write a sequence of instructions which

   1. will cause a branch to BLUE if C(Reg 5) = C(DATA).
   2. will cause a branch to GREEN if C(REG 5) < C(DATA).

   The sequence of instructions is:

       C   5,DATA
       BE   BLUE
       BL   GREEN

d. Write a program segment which will cause a branch to SAM1 if C(DATA) = 0. If no branch is made, then compare the contents of DATA to the contents of BLUE. If the absolute value of the contents of BLUE is less than the contents of DATA, branch to SAM2.
   The program segment is:

       L   5, = F'0'   REGISTER 5 ← 0
       C   5,DATA   C(DATA) = 0?
       BE   SAM1   BRANCH IF EQUAL
       L   5,BLUE   REGISTER 5 ← C(BLUE)
       LPR 5,5 |C(BLUE)| ARE IN REG 5
       C   5,DATA   OP1 < OP2?
       BL   SAM2   BRANCH IF S0

Table 9.5 lists four extended mnemonics which cannot be classified as belonging to either the compare or the arithmetic set. Two of the instructions are unconditional branch instructions, while the remaining two are No Operation instructions.[5] We note that Branch Register and No Operation Register are two RR type extended mnemonics recognized by the Assembler.

[5] The No Operation instructions are mentioned here for completeness. We do not discuss them in this chapter.

TABLE 9.5 Miscellaneous Extended Mnemonics

Instruction	Opcode		Action
Branch	B	S2	unconditional branch
Branch Register	BR	R2	unconditional branch
No Operation	NOP	S2	no operation
No Operation Register	NOPR	R2	no operation

Example 9.5

a. B LOOP

The next instruction to be executed by the computer will be at location LOOP.

b.   ⋮

  ① BCT 5,LOOP

  ② B EXIT

If $C(\text{Reg } 5) \neq 0$, then the next instruction to be executed will be at location LOOP. However, if $C(\text{Reg } 5) = 0$, then the computer will execute ②. B EXIT is an unconditional branch to location EXIT.

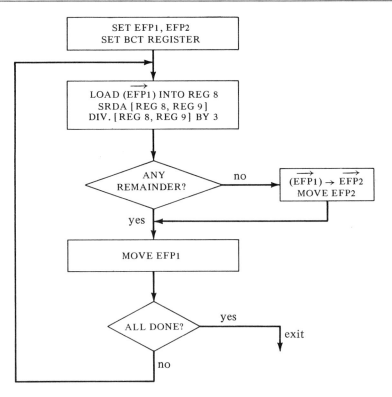

FIGURE 9.11

9.6 Address Modification by Changing the Value in an Index Register (II)

Example 9.6

Let us assume that location BLUE is the beginning of 50 full-word data items. We wish to store all integers divisible by three into a file named ABLE.

To solve this problem:

1. We need 2 effective address pointers. EFP1 will point to the BLUE file. EFP2 will point to the ABLE file. We let EFP1 = BLUE(5) and EFP2 = ABLE(6).
2. Register 7, the BCT register, will be initialized to 50.
3. All division will be done in the concatenation of registers 8 and 9.
4. We assume that the block of storage at ABLE has been defined.
5. Figure 9.11 is a flowchart of the solution to this problem.

We have the comments on page 212 to make about the program in Figure 9.12:

①		SR	5,5	BLUE(5) POINTS TO BLUE
②		SR	6,6	ABLE(6) POINTS TO ABLE
③		LA	7,50	BCT REGISTER SET TO 50
	*			
	*	END OF INITIALIZATION		
	*			
④	LOOP1	L	8,BLUE(5)	$\overrightarrow{(EFP1)} \rightarrow$ REG 8
⑤		SRDA	8,32	READY FOR DIVISION
⑥		D	8,=F'3'	DIVIDE BY 3
⑦		C	8,=F'0'	ANY REMAINDER?
⑧		BE	STORE	BRANCH IF NO REMAINDER
	*			
⑨	LOOP2	LA	5,4(5)	MOVE EFP1
⑩		BCT	7,LOOP1	ALL DONE?
⑪		B	EXIT	IF SO, EXIT
	*			
⑫	STORE	L	9,BLUE(5)	RELOAD $\overrightarrow{(EFP1)}$
⑬		ST	9,ABLE(6)	STORE IN $\overrightarrow{EFP2}$
⑭		LA	6,4(6)	MOVE EFP2
⑮		B	LOOP2	TO INCREMENT STEP
	*			
	*	TWO QUESTIONS		
	*	1. CAN YOU DO THIS PROBLEM BY SHIFTING?		
	*	2. CAN WE ELIMINATE THE NEED TO LOAD BLUE(5) TWICE?		
	*			

FIGURE 9.12

1. The circled numbers are not part of the program. We will use them as reference numbers in the discussion.
2. The initialization step consists of the first three instructions: ①, ②, and ③.
3. The body is split into three parts. Part A is comprised of instructions ④ through ⑧. Part A will be executed in each pass through the loop. Part B consists of ⑫ and ⑬. Part C is just one instruction— ⑮. Parts B and C of the body are executed only if a data item is divisible by three.
4. The increment step has two parts, each consisting of one instruction. ⑨ moves EFP1 in each pass through the loop while ⑭ increments EFP2 only after an integer divisible by three has been stored in ABLE.
5. ⑪ is not part of the loop. It is the first instruction to be executed when the work of the loop is done.

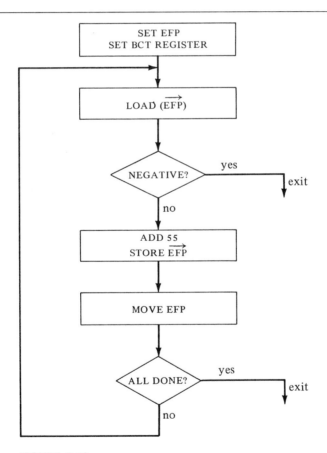

FIGURE 9.13

Example 9.7

Let us assume that there are 100 data items in a file named GREEN. We wish to add 55 to each data item. It is assumed that all data items are nonnegative. However, we should test this assumption before the addition of 55. If a negative number is found, we will exit from the loop.

To solve this problem, we must write a loop which has two test-for-exit steps.

We initialize register 9 to 0 and register 10 to 55 since CR 8,9 is faster than C 8,=F'0' and AR 8,10 is faster than A 8,=F'55'.

Figure 9.13 has the flowchart which describes the solution to our problem. Figure 9.14 is the program segment which solves our problem.

FIGURE 9.14

	L	9,=F'0'	0 → REG 9
	L	5,=F'100'	BCT REGISTER
	SR	4,4	INDEX SET TO 0
	L	10,=F'55'	ADDEND TO REG 10
LOOP	L	8,GREEN(4)	$\overrightarrow{(EFP)}$ → REG 8
	CR	8,9	LESS THAN ZERO?
	BL	NOMORE	EXIT IF LESS
	AR	8,10	ADD 55
	ST	8,GREEN(4)	STORE NEW ITEM
	LA	4,4(4)	MOVE EFP
	BCT	5,LOOP	SECOND EXIT

Example 9.8

Assume that we have a file named ABLE with 100 data items. We wish to store all negative items *not* divisible by three into a file named BLUE and to store all items divisible by three into a file named SAM.

To solve this problem, we need three pointers: EFP1 = ABLE(4), EFP2 = BLUE (5), and EFP3 = SAM(6). Note that we can divide by three before testing for negativity, since if the data item is not divisible by three, then the sign of the remainder will have the sign of the original data item.

Figure 9.15 has the program segment which is a solution to our problem.

9.7 The Branch on Index Instructions

All loops have three basic parameters: (1) the *initial value* of an index register, or a counter in the first pass through the loop; (2) the *increment value*, the amount by which the index on counter is increased (or decreased) in

```
              SR    4,4        EFP1 INDEX
              SR    5,5        EFP2 INDEX
              SR    6,6        EFP3 INDEX
              LA    7,100      BCT REGISTER
                                ⟶
LOOP          L     8,ABLE(4)  (EFP1) → REG 8
              LR    10,8       SAVE ITEM
              SRDA  8,32       READY FOR DIVISION
              D     8,=F'3'    DIVIDE BY 3
              C     8,=F'0'    DIVISIBLE?
              BE    STORE1     IF SO, GO TO SAM FILE
              BL    STORE2     IF NOT AND NEGATIVE
*                             PUT IN BLUE FILE
INCRE         LA    4,4(4)     MOVE EFP1
              BCT   7,LOOP     ALL DONE?
              B     EXIT       EXIT FROM LOOP
                                ⟶
STORE1   ST   10,SAM(6)   ITEM → EFP3
              LA    6,4(6)     MOVE EFP3
              B     INCRE      BACK TO MAIN LOOP
                                 ⟶
STORE2   ST   10,BLUE(5)  ITEM → EFP2
              LA    5,4(5)     MOVE EFP2
              B     INCRE      BACK TO MAIN LOOP
```

FIGURE 9.15

each pass through the loop; and (3) the *test value,* the value to which the index or counter is compared to determine if the work of the loop has been completed.

Branch on Index High and Branch on Index Less than or Equal are two RS type instructions which have been provided in the System/360 repertoire to facilitate the programmer's use of the loop parameters. Both instructions not only increment a designated index register but also test for completion of the loop.

The general form of *Branch on Index Less than or Equal* is:

BXLE   R1,R3,S2

The action of BXLE is:

1. If R3 is even:

$$R1 \leftarrow C(R1) + C(R3)$$

If $C(R1) \leq C(R3 + 1)$, then a branch is made to location S2; otherwise RNI (Read next instruction) from P + 1.

2. If R3 is odd:

$$R1 \leftarrow C(R1) + C(R3)$$

If $C(R1) \leq C(R3)$, then a branch is made to location S2; otherwise RNI from $P + 1$.

Note that:

1. If R3 is even, then the instruction has four operands—R1, R3, R3 + 1, and S2.
2. R1 is an index register. It is generally used to modify the effective address of an RX type instruction operand.
3. R3 contains the increment value.
4. R3 + 1, the odd numbered register of the even-odd pair (R3,R3 + 1), contains the test value. In each pass through the loop, the contents of R1 will be incremented by the amount in R3. This augmented value will be compared to the test value in R3 + 1. If the contents of R1 exceed this test value, then an exit will be made from the loop. The work of the loop has been completed. If the contents of R1 are less than or equal to the test value, then the program will branch again into the loop proper.
5. All three registers, R1, R3, and R3 + 1, must be set to their appropriate values in the initialization step.

Example 9.9

a. We wish to add ten consecutive data items, the first of which is at SAM.

FIGURE 9.16

①	L	3, = F'0'	R1 OF BXLE
②	L	4, = F'4'	R3 OF BXLE
③	LA	5,36	R3 + 1 OF BXLE
	SR	6,6	SUM ← 0
LOOP	A	6,SAM(3)	C(REG 6) + (EFP⃗) → REG 6
	BXLE	3,4,LOOP	ALL DONE?

The index, the increment, and the test value registers are set by ①, ②, and ③.

BXLE will add the contents of register 4 to register 3 in each pass through the loop. BXLE will then compare the value in register 3 with the test value.

If $C(\text{Reg } 3) \leq C(\text{Reg } 5)$, then a branch will be made to LOOP. If $C(\text{Reg } 3) > C(\text{Reg } 5)$, then the work of the loop is done. The program will exit from the loop.

b. Assume that BLACK is a file of 100 data items. We wish to move all even data items to a file named EVEN and to move all odd data items to a file named ODD. To solve this problem:

1. We need three effective address pointers. We associate the index register of BXLE with EFP1. EFP2 = EVEN(8) and EFP3 = ODD(9).
2. The last data item in the BLACK file is located at BLACK+396. Our test value is 396.
3. Figure 9.17 is a solution to our problem

```
          LA    8,0          EFP2 = EVEN(8)
          LA    9,0          EFP3 = ODD(9)
          LA    7,0          EFP1 = R1 OF BXLE
          LA    10,4         R3 OF BXLE
          LA    11,396       R3 + 1 OF BXLE
LOOP      SR    5,5          TEST REG − EVEN OR ODD?
          L     4,BLACK(7)   (EFP1) → REG 4
          LR    3,4          SAVE ITEM
          SRDA  4,1          SHIFT UNIT DIGIT TO 5
          LTR   5,5          SET CONDITION CODE
          BZ    DIV2         IF EVEN BRANCH
          ST    3,ODD(9)     STORE IN EFP3
          LA    9,4(9)       MOVE EFP3
          BXLE  7,10,LOOP    FIRST BXLE
          B     EXIT         ALL DONE
DIV2      ST    3,EVEN(8)    STORE IN EFP2
          LA    8,4(8)       MOVE EFP2
          BXLE  7,10,LOOP    SECOND BXLE
```

FIGURE 9.17

Note that there are two BXLE instructions in the loop. Only one will be executed in each pass through the loop.

Branch on Index High.   Branch on Index High is useful when the programmer intends to reference a block of storage "backwards." The high order address in the block will be referenced first; the low order address will be referenced last. The index register will, of course, be decremented in each pass through the loop.

The general form of *Branch on Index High* is:

BXH   R1,R3,S2

The action of BXH is:

1. If R3 is even: R1 ← C(R1) + C(R3)
   If C(R1) > C(R3 + 1), then a branch will be made to location S2; otherwise RNI (Read next instruction) from P + 1.
2. If R3 is odd: R1 ← C(R1) + C(R3)
   If C(R1) > C(R3), then a branch will be made to location S2; otherwise RNI from P + 1.

Example 9.10

We wish to add the ten data items which are stored in consecutive locations start-ing at SAM. Use **BXH**.

FIGURE 9.18

	L	5,=F'36'	R1 OF BXH
	L	6,=F'−4'	R3 OF BXH
	L	7,=F'−4'	R3 + 1 OF BXH
	SR	4,4	SUM SET TO 0
LOOP	A	4,SAM(5)	C(REG 4) + $\overrightarrow{(\text{EFP1})}$ → REG 4
	BXH	5,6,LOOP	DONE

The first data item added to register 4 is SAM + 36. The last is SAM. Note that we do not need both R3 and R3 + 1. We can use register 7 in both roles—the decrement register and the test value register. Figure 9.19 illustrates our point.

FIGURE 9.19

	L	5,=F'36'	R1 OF BXH
	L	7,=F'−4'	R3 OF BXH
	SR	4,4	SUM SET TO 0
	A	4,SAM(5)	C(REG 4) + $\overrightarrow{(\text{EFP})}$ → REG 4
⑤	BXH	5,7,LOOP	DONE

BXH, in ⑤, decrements the value in the index by the contents of register 7. Then BXH tests the value in register 5 against the value in register 7.

If C(Reg 5) > −4, then a branch is made to LOOP. If C(Reg 5) ≤ −4, then the data items have been added. The work of the loop is done. The program exists to P + 1.

The names of the instructions Branch on Index High and Branch on Index Less than or Equal seem to imply that an index register must be used in conjunction with the instructions. Such is *not* the case.

We will see in the next section that an explicit base register, used to modify an effective address of a loop operand, may be the so-called "index" register of a BXH or BXLE instruction. In fact, both BXH and BXLE can be used very effectively in loops where the operands must be written in the explicit mode. The important point to remember is the programmer may use any Assembler Language instruction for any purpose which suits his needs.

9.8 Address Modification by Changing the Value in a Base Register

Perhaps the best way to modify the effective address of a loop operand is by changing the value in an index register. The foremost advantage is the natural appearance of the operand in the implicit mode. For instance, when we write L 5,DATA(3), we see immediately that: (1) DATA is the first of a set of records being referenced, and (2) the index register which moves the effective address pointer is register 3.

But not all instructions allow the programmer to use an index register. If the programmer must modify the effective address of an operand in an RS, SI, or SS type instruction, then he is forced to write the operand in the explicit mode.

This means that an explicit base register must be chosen for the instruction. The address of the MEMORY location which will be referenced in the first pass through the loop must be loaded into this explicit base register in the initialization step. This base register is said to point to the effective address.

The increment step must move this pointer in each pass through the loop. This is done quite simply with the Load Address instruction. For instance, if register 5 is the pointer, then we move the pointer 11 bytes by LA 5,11(5).

The contents of the base register may also be used in a comparison test to determine if the work of the loop is done. However, any of the tests discussed in this chapter may be used in the test-for-exit step of the loop. We suggest that the programmer, at all times, pick a test for completion which is natural to his loop.

There is nothing difficult about address modification by changing the contents of an explicit base register. There is, however, considerable difference in the appearance of an operand written in the explicit mode from one written in the implicit mode. Although a casual reader may readily grasp the significance of L 5,DATA(3), the meaning of MVC 0(4,9),0(5) is no longer so apparent. This suggests, of course, that the programmer must, when using the explicit mode, provide a good deal of documentation for his program.

Example 9.11

a. A file named PROBE consists of 25 records, each 63 bytes in length. Each record has its own key in bytes 3–6. Search the file for a record whose key matches a key which has been placed into register 10. If a match is found, move the record to OUTPUT. (The implied length of OUTPUT is 80.) If the search is unsuccessful, branch to NOMATCH.

The key of each record will not always be aligned on a full-word boundary. Therefore, we assume that TEST, a full-word MEMORY location, has been defined. We will move the record key to TEST before comparing it to the key in register 10.

The solution to this problem, using BCT, is:

FIGURE 9.20

①		LA	7,PRØBE	EFP = 0(7)
②		LA	5,25	BCT REGISTER
③	LØØP	MVC	TEST,3(7)	KEY → TEST
④		C	10,TEST	MATCH
⑤		BE	SUCCESS	IF SØ GØ TØ SUCCESS
⑥		LA	7,63(7)	MØVE EFP
⑦		BCT	5,LØØP	DØNE
⑧		B	NØMATCH	FAILURE
⑨	SUCCESS	MVI	ØUTPUT,C' '	BLANK TØ ØUTPUT
⑩		MVC	ØUTPUT+1(79),ØUTPUT	BLANK AREA
⑪		MVC	ØUTPUT+1(63),0(7)	MØVE RECØRD

Note that:

In ①, the address of the first record is loaded into register 7.

In ③, TEST has a length attribute of four, so four bytes will be moved. Notice the displacement of the second operand. Register 7 points to the first byte of the record. We want to move four bytes starting at the fourth byte (byte 3); therefore, we gave the second operand a displacement of three.

In ⑥, the pointer, EFP, is moved 63 bytes. It now points to the next record. ⑨ and ⑩ blank out the OUTPUT area. ⑪ moves the 63 byte record into the 80 byte field.

The solution to this problem, using BXLE, is:

FIGURE 9.21

	LA	7,PROBE	R1 OF BXLE
	LA	4,63	R3 OF BXLE
	LA	5,PROBE+1512	R3 + 1 OF BXLE
LOOP	MVC	TEST,3(7)	KEY → TEST
	C	10,TEST	MATCH
	BE	SUCCESS	IF SO, GO TO SUCCESS
	BXLE	7,4,LOOP	DONE
	B	NOMATCH	FAILURE
SUCCESS	MVI	OUTPUT,C' '	BLANK TO OUTPUT
	MVC	OUTPUT+1(79),OUTPUT	BLANK AREA
	MVC	OUTPUT+1(63),0(7)	MOVE RECORD
	PUT	LINEOUT,OUTPUT	

Note that register 7 is an explicit base register, but it works well as the "index" register for BXLE.

b. We have 100 full-word binary integers stored in a data set named BLUE. We wish to move all negative integers to GREEN. (Use the explicit mode.)

EFP1 will point to BLUE in the first pass through the loop. We will use register 2 as the pointer. Since we are told to use the explicit mode, register 2 will be an index register. Hence EFPI = 0(2).

EFP2 will point to the first available byte in the GREEN file. Our pointer will be the first operand of Move Character, an SS type instruction. EFP2 must also utilize an explicit base register. Let us choose register 3.

The first operand of MVC designates the number of bytes involved in the move. We are required to state explicitly the number of bytes to move. Since our records are full-word binary, we will move four bytes each time we encounter a negative integer. We, therefore, must incorporate decimal four into our pointer. Hence EFP2 = 0(4,3) where zero is the displacement, four is the number of bytes involved in the move, and register 3 is the pointer to the first byte in the recipient.

FIGURE 9.22

	LA	2,BLUE	EFP1 = 0(2)
	LA	4,4	R3 OF BXLE
	LA	5,BLUE+396	R1 + 1 OF BXLE
	LA	3,GREEN	EFP2 = 0(4,3)
LOOP	L	6,0(2)	$\overrightarrow{(EFP1)}$ → REG 6
	LTR	6,6	SET CONDITION CODE
	BM	NEGATIVE	IF NEGATIVE, MOVE
	BXLE	2,4,LOOP	FIRST BXLE
	B	EXIT	FAILURE
NEGATIVE	MVC	0(4,3),0(2)	$\overrightarrow{(EFP1)}$ → EFP2
	LA	3,4(3)	MOVE EFP2
	BXLE	2,4,LOOP	SECOND BXLE

9.9 Logical Compares

The *logical compare* instructions, which are listed in Table 9.6, are not concerned with the type of data in the fields being compared. Starting at the leftmost bit positions of each operand, these instructions make a bit-by-bit comparison. Bit i of operand 1 is compared with its corresponding bit, bit i of operand 2.

TABLE 9.6 The Logical Compares

Instruction	Mnemonic	Type
Compare Logical	CL	RX
Compare Logical Character	CLC	SS
Compare Logical Register	CLR	RR
Compare Logical Immediate	CLI	SI

This comparison, which is called a logical comparison, terminates as soon as an inequality is detected between two corresponding bits. The condition code is then set according to the schedule in Table 9.7 (op1 and op2 stand for operand 1 and operand 2).

TABLE 9.7 Schedule A

Value of bit i		Setting of condition code	Remarks
op1	op2		
1	0	2	op1 is logically greater than op2
0	1	1	op1 is logically less than op2

If all corresponding bits are equal, then the condition code is set to zero. In this case, the two fields being compared are logically equal even if the data of operand 1 is of a different type than that of operand 2.

We now discuss each instruction in greater detail.

Compare Logical Register. The general form of *Compare Logical Register* is:

    CLR R1,R2

When CLR is executed, the contents of R1 are logically compared to the contents of R2. If the operands are logically equal, the condition code is set to 0. If the operands are logically unequal, the condition code is set according to the schedule in Table 9.7.

Example 9.12

    CLR   3,5
    BL   BLUE

We assume that:

    C(Reg 5) = 0000000A
    C(Reg 3) = FFFFFFF6

An inequality is immediately detected. Bit position zero of register 3 is one, while bit position zero of register 5 is zero; hence the contents of register 3 are logically greater than the contents of register 5. The condition code will be set to two. No branch will be made.

Note that in this case even though $C(Reg\ 3) = -10_{10}$ and $C(Reg\ 5) = +10_{10}$, the content of register 3 is logically greater than the content of register 5.

Compare Logical. *Compare Logical* is an RX type instruction. Its syntax has the form

    CL R1,S2

When this instruction is executed, C(R1) is logically compared to C(S2). If the two operands are logically equal, the condition code is set to zero; otherwise the condition code is set according to Schedule A of Table 9.7.

Example 9.13

CL 5,BLUE
BL DATA

We assume that:

C(Reg 5) = 00000001
C(BLUE) = 01000004

The first seven corresponding pairs of bits are equal. But bit position seven of register 5 is zero, while bit position seven of BLUE is one; hence, the condition code is set to one, which reflects the fact that C(Reg 5) is logically less than C(BLUE). A branch will be made to DATA.

Compare Logical Immediate. The syntax of *Compare Logical Immediate,* an SI type instruction, has the form

CLI S1,I2

When CLI is executed, an immediate operand one byte in length is compared logically to S1. If the immediate operand is logically equal to S1, the condition code is set to zero; otherwise, the condition code is set according to Schedule A in Table 9.7.

Example 9.14

A block of 80 bytes has been read from a card into AREAIN. The entire block may consist of blanks. We wish to find the address of the first nonblank character, if there is one.

FIGURE 9.23

①		LA	6,AREAIN−1	EFP POINTS TO BYTE
②	LOOP	LA	6,1(6)	INCREMENT POINTER
③		C	6,=A(AREAIN+80)	DONE?
④		BNL	ALLDONE	IF SO BRANCH OUT
⑤		CLI	0(6),C' '	IS BYTE BLANK?
⑥		BE	LOOP	YES, TEST NEXT BYTE
⑦		B	SUCCESS	

EFP, the effective address pointer, is equal to 0(6), which is the first operand in ⑤. EFP points to each byte in turn until all 80 bytes of the block have been tested or until a nonblank character is found.

The test for a nonblank character is instruction ⑤, CLI 0(6),C' '. If 0(6) is pointing to a nonblank character, the condition will be set to 1 or 2. In either case, the program will drop to instruction ⑦.

The address, if the program is successful in finding a nonblank character, is passed to the routine at SUCCESS by register 6.

Compare Logical Character. *Compare Logical Character* is an SS type instruction, Class I. Its general form is:

CLC   S1,S2

When CLC is executed, the contents of locations S1 and S2 are compared logically. If equal, the condition code is set to zero. If unequal, the condition code is set according to the schedule in Table 9.7.

The number of bytes involved in the test is determined by the implied length of S1 or by the length given by the programmer in the instruction.

Example 9.15

a. We wish to compare the record at location SAM with the record at location BLUE. (Both records have the same implied length.) If they are logically unequal, we want to branch to PROCESS.

The solution is:

```
CLC   SAM,BLUE
BNE   PROCESS
```

b. We have a file named SAM which consists of 100 records, each 80 bytes long. The record key is in bytes 9–13 of each record. Find, if possible, a record whose key matches a key which has been placed into location MASTER. If a match is found, branch to SUCCESS. If no match is found, branch to NORECORD.

FIGURE 9.24

```
        LA    10,100         BCT REGISTER
        LA    6,SAM          REG 6 POINTS TO SAM
LOOP    CLC   9(5,6),MASTER  EQUAL?
        BE    SUCCESS
        LA    6,80(6)         MOVE POINTER
        BCT   10,LOOP        ALL DONE
        B     NORECORD
```

EFP, the effective address pointer, is 9(5,6). The key is 9 bytes beyond the location to which register 6 points; hence EFP has a displacement of 9.

Computer Notebook

TOPIC 1 Absolute and Relocatable Terms

The numeric values which the Assembler associates with the symbolic addresses it encounters in the first pass are not absolute. The values it assigns to these symbolic names are relative to some initial value of the LOCATION COUNTER. We will see (Chapter 10) that if we issue the assembly control statement START 0 as the first instruction, then we insure that this initial value is 000000_x.

The lower portion of MEMORY is reserved for the Supervisor, which is a subroutine of the Operating System. Thus, when our program is loaded into MEMORY just prior to execution, the actual origin will not be 000000_x. The difference between the actual value of the location of our first instruction and its initial relative value is called the *relocation factor*.

Suppose the relative address of the base-location of our program was 000006_x. If the relocation factor is 007200, then the actual address (relocated address) of the base-location is 007206. If the relative address of the symbolic name BLACK was 000126, then its actual address for this run is 007326. Notice, however, that the displacement of BLACK is the same in both cases. The difference between the relative address of the base-location and the relative address of BLACK is—000126 minus 000006—120_x. The difference between the actual addresses is also 120_x (007326 minus 007206).

Terms such as the displacement whose values are independent of the relocation factor are called *absolute terms*. Other absolute terms are the register addresses, most constants, and all self-defining terms. If a symbolic name is defined by the assembly control statement EQU, which equates it to an absolute term, then that symbolic name is also an absolute term.

TOPIC 2 Expressions for Operands

An expression which is to be used as an assembly instruction operand is an arithmetic combination of absolute or relocatable terms. The arithmetic operations of addition, subtraction, multiplication, and division are given by the symbols +, −, *, and /, respectively.

We list the rules which govern the formation of these expressions below.

Arithmetic Expression Rules

1. An expression may not have more than 16 terms.
2. Parentheses must be paired.
3. No more than five levels of parentheses may appear at any point.
4. An expression may not begin with an arithmetic operator.

Not allowed	*Allowed*
$-15+A$	$0-15+A$
$+15-A$	$15-A$

5. An expression may not contain two successive arithmetic operators.

Not allowed   *Allowed*
14*−A   14*(0−A)

6. An expression may not contain two successive terms. If ABLE and SAM−16 are two terms, then ABLE(SAM−16) is not allowed. ABLE*(SAM−16) is allowed.

7. Any expression which contains more than one term may not contain a literal.

Not allowed   *Allowed*
=F'14'+SAM   =F'14'
=F'19'+6   =F'19'

8. Relocatable terms may not enter a multiply or divide operation.

(Let SAM and DATA be relocatable.)

Not allowed   *Allowed*
5*SAM   (SAM−DATA)/15
SAM/9   5/(SAM−DATA)

9. The result of division is always an integer. The remainder is disregarded. Division by zero is allowed; the result is zero.

10. Expressions are evaluated from left to right following the rules of algebra.

11. The final result of an evaluation may not exceed $2^{24} - 1$ (6 hex digits). An intermediate result may not exceed $2^{31} - 1$ (8 hex digits).

12. If the LOCATION COUNTER reference is used in an expression, then it must be the first term. For example,

*+7*SAM

There is no confusion. The first asterisk is the LOCATION COUNTER reference. The second is the multiplication operator.

13. Relocatable terms may enter an absolute expression only if they are paired. That is, for each relocatable term which is added to an expression, one relocatable term must be subtracted.

14. A relocatable expression may have only one unpaired relocatable term. It must be added to the expression. All other relocatable terms which enter the expression must be paired—one added, the other subtracted.

15. The addition of an absolute term to a relocatable expression results in a relocatable expression.

We have listed a fairly complete list of rules which govern the formation of the expressions which can be used as operand in an assembly language instruction. We have, however, no intention of using complicated operands in this text. We feel that addresses are in most cases simple expressions. (We do not recall writing an address more complicated than SAM+24 in this text.)

TOPIC 3   Miscellaneous Items

When the shift and the Boolean instructions were presented, we did not mention how they set the condition code. Since the effect they have on the code is not obvious, we return to a discussion of them in this topic. Now that the reader has a background knowledge of the code, we will, when presenting a new instruction, note how it sets the condition code.

Equate, an assembly control statement unrelated to the condition code, is the third item we discuss in this topic. We will use Equate in Topic 4 where we give a program which illustrates a *bubble sort*.

The Shift Instructions and the Condition Code.   The logical shift instructions do not set the condition code, but the arithmetic ones do. The right arithmetic shifts, however, cannot set the code to three, which is the overflow condition. Both left arithmetic shifts will set the code to three if a single significant digit is shifted out of the high order digit position, bit position one.

The first bit which differs in value from the sign bit is the first significant digit in any full-word binary integer. All digits which follow it are also significant. The first significant digit in register 3 in Figure 9.25 is in bit position seven. Bit position 23 of register 2 holds the first significant digit of that register.

If no overflow occurs when Shift Left Arithmetic or Shift Left Double Arithmetic is issued, then the condition code is set according to the same schedule as that followed by Shift Right Arithmetic and Shift Right Double Arithmetic. This schedule is given in Table 9.8. We emphasize that this schedule is always followed by SRA and SRDA. This schedule holds for

TABLE 9.8   Schedule B

Contents of operand	Setting of condition code
= 0	0
< 0	1
> 0	2

FIGURE 9.25

0	7 8	15 16	23 24	31	0	7 8	15 16	23 24	31
0	0000000	00000000	00000001	00100010	1	1111110	10000000	00001000	00000000

Register 2   Register 3

SLA and SLDA only if no overflow has occurred. (Note: The operand is 63 bits long in a double shift.)

Let us work through an example. Give the value of the condition code after the execution of each instruction. The initial value of R1 before the execution of each instruction is given in Figure 9.25.

```
 1. SRA    3,31
 2. SRA    2,31
 3. SRDA   2,10
 4. SLDA   2,10
 5. SLA    3,5
 6. SLA    3,8
 7. SLDL   2,32
 8. SLL    3,12
 9. SLA    2,10
10. SLA    2,25
```

The solution is:

```
 1. CC = 1   since C(Reg 3) < 0 and no overflow
 2. CC = 0   since C(Reg 2) = 0 and no overflow
 3. CC = 2   since C([Reg 2, Reg 3]) > 0 and no overflow
 4. CC = 2   since C([Reg 2, Reg 3]) > 0 and no overflow
 5. CC = 1   since C(Reg 3) < 0 and no overflow
 6. CC = 3   since register 3 overflowed
 7. CC is not set by logical shifts
 8. CC is not set by logical shifts
 9. CC = 2   since C(Reg 2) > 0 and no overflow
10. CC = 3   since register 2 overflowed
```

The Boolean Operations and the CC.   All 12 Boolean operations set the condition code to either 0 or 1. The code is set to zero if all bits in the recipient are turned off. Or, to say it another way, if all bits in the recipient are zero after completion of the Boolean operation, then the condition code is set to zero. If at least one bit in the recipient is not turned off by the Boolean operation, then the condition code is set to one. For the convenience of the reader, we have listed this information in Table 9.9.

TABLE 9.9

Status of bits in recipient	Value in recipient	Condition code
All bits turned off	= 0	0
At least one bit on	<0, >0	1

The Equate Assembly Control Statement. The programmer may associate a symbolic label with an absolute or relocatable value by using the Equate assembly control statement. The general form of *Equate* is:

　　label　EQU　value

The statement requests the Assembler to associate the label with the value given in the operand field. The programmer may refer to this value by using the associated symbolic label in the operand field of any instruction. The Equate statement may appear anywhere in the user's program.

Example 9.16

FIGURE 9.26

RED	EQU	4
R1	EQU	1
REG3	EQU	3
DISPLACE	EQU	16

The code given below illustrates how these Equate names might be used.

FIGURE 9.27

L	RED,DATA	C(DATA) → REG 4
LR	R1,REG3	C(REG 3) → REG 1
MVC	ABLE,DISPLACE(6)	$\overrightarrow{(16(6))}$ → ABLE

Note that DISPLACE(6), the second operand in MVC, is in the explicit mode.

TOPIC 4　A Bubble Sort

There are a large number of sorting techniques scattered throughout the literature of computer science. We have picked one to present here which belongs to the class called *bubble sort*. We will assume that we have a file of 40 80-byte long records which our bubble sort will alphabetize. It will alphabetize this file with respect to the key which is the NAME field, bytes 0–19, of each record. We say that the file is sorted in the ascending order of the EBCDIC collating sequence.

We will use three effective address pointers in our program: X, Y, and Z. All three pointers will point to the key in the first record when we start. Then Y, which will traverse the entire unsorted part of the file many times, will be moved so that it points to the next record key. The key that Y now points to will be compared to the X-key.

If the Y-key is logically less than the X-key, then X will be moved so that it points to the Y-key. Then Y will be moved to the next record key.

If, in the comparison, the Y-key is found to be greater than or equal to the X-key, then no action will be taken with respect to the X-pointer. The Y-pointer, however, will be moved so that it points to the next record key.

The X-keys and the Y-keys will be compared in this manner as Y traverses the entire unalphabetized file. When all comparisons have been made, X will be pointing to the logically smallest record in the data set. Now we want to exchange the X-record and the Z-record. We do so by moving the Z-record to a temporary location which we will call SAVEZ. The X-record is then moved to Z (to the location to which Z points). And finally we move the old Z-record from SAVEZ to X.

The logically smallest record is now the first record in the file. We reinitialize by moving Z so that it points to the next key. Then we move X and Y so that they point to the same key as Z does.

If we now repeat this process 39 times, our entire data set will be alphabetized.

The algorithm for our bubble sort is given below. One of the exercises at the end of this chapter suggests that the student submit a flowchart of the algorithm. The code for our bubble sort is given in Figure 9.28. Note that we use the Equate assembly control statement so that we might retain the names X, Y, and Z for our pointers. LASTREC has been equated with register 10, which will contain the address of the last record.

We assume that our file begins at location NAMEFILE. We also assume that SAVEZ has been defined.

Bubble Sort Algorithm

Step 1: Let Z point to the key of the first record.
Step 2: Let X and Y point to the same key that Z points to.
Step 3: Move Y so that Y points to the key of the next record in sequence.
Step 4: Compare Y-key with X-key.
Step 5: If Y-key < X-key, go to step 14; otherwise, continue in normal sequence.
Step 6: Compare Y with LASTREC.
Step 7: If Y < LASTREC, go to step 3; otherwise, continue in normal sequence.
Step 8: Move Z-record to SAVEZ.
Step 9: Move X-record to location pointed to by Z.
Step 10: Move C(SAVEZ) to location pointed to by X.
Step 11: Move Z so that Z points to the next record in sequence.
Step 12: Compare Z with LASTREC.
Step 13: If Z < LASTREC, go to step 2; otherwise, go to step 16.
Step 14: Move X so that it points to the same record as Y.
Step 15: Go to step 6.
Step 16: Stop.

FIGURE 9.28

```
LIMIT       EQU   10                    LIMIT = 10
X           EQU   3                     X = 3
Y           EQU   4                     Y = 4
Z           EQU   5                     Z = 5
            LA    10,NAMEFILE+3120      LIMIT ESTABLISHED
            LA    Z,NAMEFILE            Z POINTS TO 1ST KEY
LOOP2       LR    X,Z                   X POINTS TO Z-KEY
            LR    Y,Z                   Y POINTS TO Z-KEY
LOOP1       LA    Y,80(Y)               MOVE Y
            CLC   0(20,Y),0(X)          COMPARE X-KEY AND Y-KEY
            BL    EXCHANGE              IF Y-KEY LESS, BRANCH
LOOP3       CR    Y,LIMIT               ALL RECORDS COMPARED?
            BL    LOOP1                 IF NOT GO TO LOOP1
            MVC   SAVEZ,0(Z)            MOVE Z-RECORD TO SAVEZ
            MVC   0(80,Z),0(X)          MOVE X-RECORD TO Z
            MVC   0(80,X),SAVEZ         MOVE SAVEZ TO X
            LA    Z,80(Z)               MOVE Z
            CR    Z,LIMIT               ALL DONE?
            BL    LOOP2                 NO GO TO LOOP2
            B     WRITE                 YES GO TO WRITE ROUTINE
EXCHANGE    LR    X,Y                   LET X POINT TO Y-RECORD
            B     LOOP3                 GO TO LOOP3
NAMEFILE    DS    40CL80
SAVEZ       DS    CL80
```

EXERCISES

1. Write a program segment which finds the sum of the first 1000 positive integers. $\left(\text{You are not allowed to use Gauss' formula } S_n = \dfrac{n(n + 1)}{2}.\right)$ Use a BCT register to monitor the loop.

2. Define a storage block consisting of 50 full words by, say, BLACK DS 50F. (Each word in BLACK contains an integer.) Move all integers in BLACK which are divisible by 121 to a new storage block which has been defined by RED DS 50F. (Set up two effective address pointers—EFP1 and EFP2. Let EFP1 point to BLACK and EFP2 to RED. Use a BCT register to monitor the loop.) Submit an algorithm and a flowchart with the program.

3. Consider Example 8.15 in the last chapter. IC and STC are RX type instructions. The code, therefore, can be shortened by using an index register. Show how to do this. Submit a flowchart with your solution.

4. Consider the following diagram:

$$\text{ABLE} \rightarrow \text{STUBBS} \rightarrow \text{WEBRE} \rightarrow \text{BLUE}$$

Write a short program segment which gains control at location ABLE. Let the segment starting at ABLE cause a branch to location STUBBS because the condition code equals zero. Let the STUBBS module cause a branch to WEBRE because the setting of the condition code is one. And, finally, let WEBRE cause a branch to BLUE because the condition code is two.

5. Define ten packed decimal numbers in a block named WELTY. Define ten full-word binary integers in a block named BOHLE. Write a single loop in which each data item in WELTY is converted to binary and added to a data item in BOHLE. (The ith item in WELTY should be added to the ith item in BOHLE.) Submit an algorithm and a flowchart with your solution.

6. Use Move Character and address modification by changing the value in a base register in this problem.

   Let HSU be a block of records such that each record is 80 bytes long. The number of records in the block is not known. The last record in the block is, however, a dummy record which has a negative key. The key is in bytes 0–3 of each record.

   Move all records in HSU which have keys divisible by two to a new block named WU. Move all other records to SAM. Put dummy records as the last entry in both WU and SAM. Submit a flowchart with your solution.

7. (The condition code and the Boolean operations.) Define a one-byte location TANIA by TANIA DS C. *AND* the contents of TANIA by the binary number 01010101. Use the setting of the condition code to accomplish the following:
   a. Move blanks into TANIA if the result of the Boolean operation is all zeros.
   b. Move ones into location TANIA otherwise.
   Submit a flowchart with your solution.

8. Define your name into location NAME by the Define Constant pseudo. Remove all vowels from your name. Compress the result and pad with blanks on the right.

   Example
   ```
   Name   DC   C'CAROL YOUNG'
   ```
   After execution of program
   ```
   C(NAME) = CRLbYNGbbbb where b is a blank.
   ```

   a. Try to do this without moving any character out of the NAME location.
   b. You will have a loop nested within a loop. Use BCT registers to monitor both loops.

9. Figure 9.6 of this chapter depicted two of the six possible basic loop structures. Sketch the other four basic structures.

10. Submit a program which determines the first 100 primes. Submit an algorithm and flowchart with your program.

11. a. Let each member of the class punch several punch cards using the following format:

    Columns 1–20 name (left justified with last name first)
    Columns 21–40 address (left justified)
    Columns 41–80 any information

    b. Distribute these cards so that each student has a data set which consists of one record for each member of the class.
    Write a program which:
    1. reads the records into a matrix
    2. sorts the records in ascending order with respect to the name field
    3. prints the sorted data set
    Hints: (1) The matrix is defined by

    DATA   DS   35CL80

    (We have a 35 × 80 matrix.) (2) Recall that PROLOG uses the first byte of an output record as a carriage control character. The first byte of an output record, if you use PROLOG, should be blank. Take this factor into consideration as you write the program. Submit an algorithm and a flowchart with your solution.

12. Write a program which will print one A, two B's, three C's, four D's, . . . , twenty-six Z's. You must generate your character strings from the following constant:

    ANNE   DC   C'ABCDEFGHIJKLMNOPQRSTUVWXYZ'

13. Pick any 100 full-word storage locations at random. (Use BLUE DS 100F in the declarative section of your program.) Count the number of integers in this block that are divisible by seven. Use BXLE to monitor the loop.

14. Consider exercise 13. Find the smallest positive integer in the 100-word block. Use BXH to monitor the loop.

15. Consider the computer chosen in exercise 14 of Chapter 6. Discuss the looping and indexing techniques used in the assembly language of that computer.

16. Submit a flowchart for the bubble sort in Topic 4 of this chapter.

10 | Transfer of Control

In Chapter 9 we learned how to use the "arithmetic" and the "compare" extended mnemonics in making a two-way decision based on the status of the condition code. If the condition code had been set to an appropriate value, then we were able to cause a branch (reentry) into the body of our loop. If the condition code reflected the fact that the work of the loop was done, then the program was able to exit to instruction $P + 1$.

In Section 10.1 we will study in detail Branch on Condition (BC) and Branch on Condition to Register (BCR), the two Basic Assembler Language instructions from which the extended mnemonics are derived. In Section 10.2 we will discuss the two linkage instructions, Branch and Link (BAL) and Branch and Link Register (BALR), which "tie together" (link) two or more independent programs or modules. Then, finally, after we have developed sufficient background material, we will show how to establish an implied base register for an assembly language program.

10.1 The Branch on Condition Instructions

The general form for the *Branch on Condition* instruction is:

    BC   M1,S2

If M1 is an appropriate mask for the status of the condition code at the time the ML equivalent of BC M1,S2 is executed, then the program will branch to location S2. Otherwise the program will continue in the normal sequence.

Branch on Condition to Register (BCR) is similar to BC. Its general form is:

    BCR   M1,R2

If M1 masks the status of the condition code when BCR is executed, then a branch is made to the address in R2. Otherwise the program continues in the normal sequence.

The only difference between BC and BCR is that R2, the second operand of BCR, is a pointer to the branch address, while S2 of BC is the branch address. It is, of course, the programmer's responsibility to put the branch address into R2.

The examples which illustrate the action of BC and BCR will be deferred until after we have given a detailed explanation of the first operand, the four-bit binary mask.

The Condition Code and the Binary Mask. We have seen that the condition code, bits 34 and 35 of the PROGRAM STATUS WORD register, can assume any one of four possible values. (See Section 9.4, Chapter 9.) Table 10.1 lists these values in both binary and decimal.

TABLE 10.1 The Condition Code Values

Bit 34	Bit 35	Binary	Decimal
0	0	00	0
0	1	01	1
1	0	10	2
1	1	11	3

The mask, M1, is a four-digit binary number. Let us label the digits in this number as follows: d0d1d2d3. For instance, if M1 = 1011; then d0 = 1, d1 = 0, d2 = 1, and d3 = 1. Now consider the natural one-to-one correspondence which has been established between the four digits of the mask and the four decimal values which the condition code may assume, which appears in Table 10.2.

TABLE 10.2 The Correspondence Table

Value of CC	0	1	2	3
	$\updownarrow$	$\updownarrow$	$\updownarrow$	$\updownarrow$
Digit in mask	d0	d1	d2	d3

If di of the mask, M1, is equal to one, then the decimal value i of the condition code which is associated with it in the correspondence table is said to be masked. Suppose, for example, M1 = 1000; then d0 = 1, d1 = 0, d2 = 0, and d3 = 0. The only value of the condition code which is masked is the value zero.

If, when we issue the command BC   M1,S2, the condition code contains a value which is masked by M1, then the program will branch to location S2. Or, to say it another way, the program will branch to S2 if the condition masked by M1 is *on*.

Similarly, the mask in BCR   M1,R2 also acts as a switch. If M1 masks the condition code value when BCR is executed, then control will be passed to the instruction whose address is in R2; otherwise, the next instruction in the normal sequence will be executed.

Example 10.1

List the values of the condition code which are masked (or covered) by the following masks:

a. M1 = 1100
b. M1 = 1101
c. M1 = 1111
d. M1 = 0000
e. M1 = 0101

The solutions are:

a. d0 = 1 and d1 = 1; hence the values 0 and 1 of the condition code are masked.
b. The values 0, 1, and 3 of the condition code are masked or covered.
c. All values which the condition code can assume are covered.
d. No values are masked.
e. The values 1 and 3 are masked.

Example 10.2

a. ① C   3,SAM
   ② BC   B'0110',GREEN

We assume that:

C(Reg 3) = 00000009
C(SAM) = 00000008

① sets the condition code to 2 because opl > op2. M1 in ② masks the values 1 and 2 of the condition code. A condition masked by M1 is on; hence the program will branch to location GREEN.

b. ① A   3,DATA
   ② BC   B'1111',SAM

The contents of register 3 and the contents of DATA are immaterial since all states of the condition code are masked. ② is an unconditional branch.

c. C   4,BLUE
   BC   B'1100',BLACK

We assume that:

C(Reg 4) = FFFFFFFE
C(BLUE) = 00000000

Will control be transferred to location BLACK?

d. ① S   6,BLUE
   ② BCR   B'1000',5

If C(Reg 6) = 0 after the execution of ①, then the program will branch to the address in register 5. Otherwise the next instruction in the normal sequence, P + 1, will be executed.

The mask, M1, is a self-defining term. It may be written in decimal, hexadecimal, or binary. For instance, BC 15,GREEN and BC B'1111',GREEN are equivalent. The mask is also an immediate operand. The Assembler will convert a decimal or hex term into a four-digit binary number. This four-digit binary number will then be placed into bits 8–11 of the machine language instruction.

Table 10.3 lists all 16 binary masks along with the corresponding values of the condition code that each will cover.

TABLE 10.3   The Branch on Condition Masks

Decimal mask	Binary mask	CC values masked
0	0000	0 NONE
1	0001	3
2	0010	2
3	0011	2,3
4	0100	1
5	0101	1,3
6	0110	1,2
7	0111	1,2,3
8	1000	0
9	1001	0,3
10	1010	0,2
11	1011	0,2,3
12	1100	0,1
13	1101	0,1,3
14	1110	0,1,2
15	1111	0,1,2,3

Since there are 16 possible masks, we might say that each Branch on Condition instruction (BC or BCR) is a set with 16 elements. Each time we change the mask, M1, we get a different element of the set. For instance, ① and ② in Figure 10.1 are different elements from the set BC.

Each of the extended mnemonics which we discussed in Chapter 9 is equivalent to exactly one element in the BC set. However, a one-to-one correspondence does not exist between the elements of Branch on Condition and the set of extended mnemonics since an element in the set of BC instructions may be associated with more than one extended mnemonic.

FIGURE 10.1

① BC   B'1000',SAM
② BC   B'1011',SAM

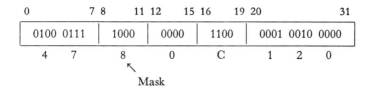

FIGURE 10.2

Branch Equal and Branch Zero, for example, are both equivalent to the Branch on Condition instruction which has a mask equal to 1000_2. If the displacement of BLUE is 120_x, and if the designated implied base register is 12, then the two instructions BZ BLUE and BE BLUE will encode into the machine language instruction in Figure 10.2. This is the machine language instruction associated with the Assembler Language instruction BC B'1000',BLUE.

Table 10.4 lists all 16 elements of the set BC along with the "compare" and "arithmetic" extended mnemonics associated with each element. Note that several elements of BC do not have an associated extended mnemonic

TABLE 10.4 The Elements of BC

Element	Compare equivalent	Arithmetic equivalent	CC covered
BC B'0000',S2	NOP	NOP	None
BC B'0001',S2	None	BO S2	3
BC '0010',S2	BH S2	BP S2	2
BC '0011',S2	None	None	2,3
BC '0100',S2	BL S2	BM S2	1
BC '0101',S2	None	None	1,3
BC '0110',S2	None	None	1,2
BC '0111',S2	BNE S2	BNZ S2	1,2,3
BC '1000',S2	BE S2	BZ S2	0
BC '1001',S2	None	None	0,3
BC '1010',S2	None	None	0,2
BC '1011',S2	BNL S2	BNM S2	0,2,3
BC '1100',S2	None	None	0,1
BC '1101',S2	BNH S2	BNP S2	0,1,3
BC '1110',S2	None	BNO S2	0,1,2
BC B'1111',S2	B S2	B S2	0,1,2,3

10.2 Branch and Link

Suppose that we have a program which repeats a sequence of instructions many times. The flowchart in Figure 10.3 illustrates the type of situation we are thinking about.

It is, of course, not necessary for the code in SEQA to appear at every point where it is executed. We can put SEQA into some convenient spot in our program. Then we can cause a branch from the appropriate points in segments I, II, and III into SEQA whenever necessary. When SEQA has finished its task, it can then return control to the proper segment.

But several questions immediately come to mind. How does SEQA know where it should transfer control? How does SEQA know that it should branch to segment II when segment I passes control to it?

Consider the flowchart in Figure 10.4 When the program entered SEQA

FIGURE 10.3

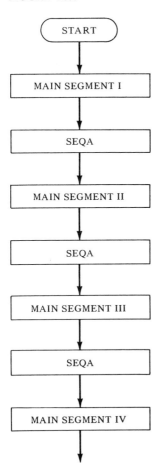

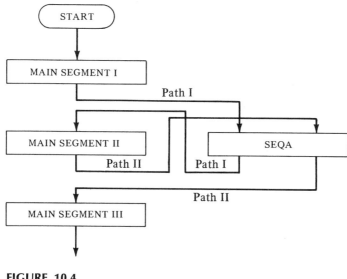

FIGURE 10.4

via path I, what knowledge did the program possess so that it exited via the same path? What, in other words, keeps the program from exiting along path II instead of path I? What keeps it from exiting along path I instead of path II when it enters SEQA via path II?

The answer to our question is that we must pass the return address to SEQA whenever we give control to that subroutine. When we branch from MAIN SEGMENT I to SEQA, then we give SEQA the address of MAIN SEGMENT II. When we enter SEQA from MAIN SEGMENT II, the return address that we pass to SEQA is MAIN SEGMENT III.

Both the branch and the passing of the return address are accomplished by Branch and Link (BAL), an RX type instruction, or by Branch and Link Register (BALR), an RR type instruction.

Branch and Link has the general form:

(P)   BAL   R1,S2
(P + 1) --- ---

When Branch and Link is executed, bits 32–63 of the PROGRAM STATUS WORD register are copied into R1. The program then branches to location S2. See Chapter 17 for a discussion of the program status word.

Note that we use (P) as the address of the present instruction; (P + 1) is the address of the next instruction in the normal sequence. The action of the instruction (P + 1) is not pertinent to our discussion.

Bits 40–63 of the PROGRAM STATUS WORD are the INSTRUCTION COUNTER CELL of a 360 computer. (IBM and many programmers refer to those bit positions as the INSTRUCTION ADDRESS REGISTER.

Henceforth we will use ICC and IAR interchangeably.) These bit positions always point to the next instruction to be executed. When instruction Ⓟ —BAL   R1,S2—is being executed, this INSTRUCTION ADDRESS REGISTER points to the address of the instruction (P + 1). Hence when bits 32–63 of the PROGRAM STATUS WORD are copied into R1, the address of (P + 1) gets into bit positions 8–31 of R1. This is the return address that is being passed to the subroutine.

However, it should be noted that R1 contains more information than just the return address since BAL also copies the information contained in bit positions 32–37 of the PSW register into bit positions 0–7 of R1. It is not our intention to discuss these bits at this time. Here we only wish to point out that the programmer should not expect bits 0–7 of R1 to be 00_x after execution of either Branch and Link or Branch and Link Register.

Example 10.3

a.   Ⓟ   BAL   14,SEQA
   (P + 1)   --- ---

Ⓟ is the last instruction in MAIN SEGMENT I. Control is passed to SEQA by this instruction. The return address, (P + 1), the first instruction in MAIN SEGMENT II, is placed into register 14. The last instruction in SEQA will be BR 14 which will be an unconditional branch to MAIN SEGMENT II.

b.   Ⓢ   BAL   14,SEQA
   (S + 1)   --- ---

Ⓢ is the last instruction in MAIN SEGMENT II. (S + 1) is the first address in MAIN SEGMENT III. Since BAL puts the address (S + 1) into register 14 before transferring control, SEQA will transfer control to MAIN SEGMENT III when it issues BR 14 at the completion of its task.

Figure 10.5 illustrates the linkage which has been created between the main program and SEQA by (a) and (b) of Example 10.3. We have detached the last instruction in each segment and the last instruction of SEQA from their respective blocks so that the action of BAL in establishing linkage is clearly demonstrated.

Branch and Link Register is an RR type instruction which is also used to create linkage between 2 programs. Its general form is:

   BALR   R1,R2

When Branch and Link Register is executed, the contents of bit positions 32–63 of the PSW register is copied into R1. The program then branches to the address in R2.

Our earlier remarks about Branch and Link are also pertinent here. The important point to remember is that the return address is in R1 after the

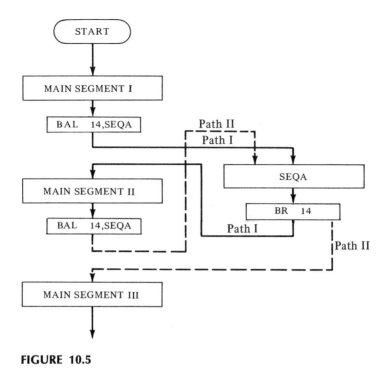

FIGURE 10.5

execution of both BALR and BAL. It is, of course, the programmer's responsibility to put the branch address into R2 when he uses the BALR instruction.

Example 10.4

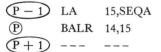

	LA	15,SEQA
	BALR	14,15
	---	---

$(P - 1)$ loaded the address of the entry point of the subroutine SEQA into register 15. (This could have been done anywhere in the main program.) The return address, $(P + 1)$, is put into register 14 by BALR. Then the program branches to SEQA, which is the address in register 15.

10.3 Establishing an Implied Base Register

The first items in this section are intended to provide additional background material about the establishment of an implied base register. We suggest that all of it be read carefully; it is pertinent to the main purpose of this section.

Special Uses of Register 0. We have seen that if register 0 is designated as the index or base register for the operand of an instruction, then when the effective address is determined by CONTROL, the value 0 will be substituted for the contents of register 0.

This convention has additional extensions. One of the extensions is that register 0 cannot be used as a pointer. Consider the extended mnemonic Branch Register (BR), which is an unconditional branch. BR has one operand, a register that points to the branch address. However, if R2 of BR R2 is register 0, then the convention applies. No branch will be made since register 0 cannot be used as a pointer. The instruction reduces to a no operation instruction equivalent to BCR 0,R2 or to the register no operation instruction NOPR R2.

The convention that register 0 cannot be used as a pointer provides some interesting and useful results when used with Branch and Link Register.

BALR R1,R2—as we learned in the last section—will cause a branch to the address pointed to by R2. Now suppose R2 is register 0. Since register 0 cannot serve as a pointer, no branch will be made.

The address of the instruction P + 1 , however, will be placed into R1. Example 10.5 will help clarify our discussion.

Example 10.5

a. ⓟ   BALR 12,0
   (P + 1)   – – –   – – –

The address of the instruction (P + 1) is put into register 12. No branch is made because register 0 cannot be used as a pointer. The next instruction to be executed will be (P + 1).

b. Suppose that the symbolic name of (P + 1) is BLUE. Are the codes (i) and (ii) then equivalent?

    i.   BALR 12,0   ii.   LA   12,BLUE
    BLUE – – –   – – –   BLUE – – –   – – –

Not quite. We can say that register 12 points to BLUE after execution of both (i) and (ii). However, bit positions 0–7 of register 12 will all be set to 0 by Load Address in code (ii). After execution of (i), bits 0–7 of register 12 will reflect the contents of bit positions 32–39 of the PSW register at the time BALR 12,0 was executed.

We might say that the address BLUE got into register 12 in code (ii) via the symbol table. In code (i), the address BLUE got into register 12 via the PSW register. In both cases, however, the second instruction to be executed will be at the address BLUE.

c. BCTR 10,0

The contents of register 10 will be decremented by 1. No branch will be made even though the contents of register 10 are not equal to 0 since register 0 cannot serve as a pointer. (See Example 13.13 for an application of BCTR R1,0.)

The Location Counter Reference. The LOCATION COUNTER is, as we have indicated in previous chapters, a pointer maintained by the Assembler. This register points to the first MEMORY location, relative to zero, which is available to the program being assembled. The programmer may refer to the contents of the LOCATION COUNTER, the address to which it points, by using an asterisk (*) in the operand field of most instructions. When the asterisk is used in this manner it is called the *location counter reference*.

Example 10.6

a. *Location*   *Instruction*
  ① 007200   B   *+6
  ② 007204   AR   3,4
  ③ 007206   S   3,=F'5'

The LOCATION COUNTER is pointing to 007200 when ① is being assembled. Hence the effective address of the operand in ① is 007206 = C(LOCATION COUNTER) + 6. At execution time the computer branches to ③. ② is never executed.

b. *Location*   *Instruction*
  ① 007200   SR   4,4
  ② 007202   A   4,=F'5'
  ③ 007206   C   4,=F'50'
  ④ 00720A   BC   B'0010',GREEN
  ⑤ 00720E   B   *−14

⑤, B   *−14, is an unconditional branch to 007200. The LOCATION COUN-TER is pointing to 00720E at the time ⑤ is being assembled. Hence instruction ⑤ is equivalent to B   X'007200'.

The location counter reference is an effective programming aid which is very easy to use with assembly languages whose instructions are of a fixed length. If, for instance, we want to branch back four instructions as we did in Example 10.6b, all we need to do is to write B   *−4.

The instructions, however, in the Basic Assembler Language of System/360 are of variable length. (See Chapter 7.) In order to branch back four instructions we must count the number of bytes occupied by each of the 4 instructions that we wish to jump. If we know the instruction type, then of course, we know its length. Table 10.5 illustrates our counting technique. The count shows that to branch back four instructions to ①, we must write B *−14.

TABLE 10.5

Instruction	Type	Length
BC	RX	4
C	RX	4
A	RX	4
SR	RR	2
Total		14

The Using Assembly Control Statement. The declaration of an implied base register and base-location is accomplished by the Using assembly control statement. The simple form of *USING* is:

USING V1,R2

The programmer passes two pieces of information to the Assembler via the Using statement. The first operand, V1, informs the Assembler of the address of the base-location. The second piece of information given to the Assembler is that R2 will be the implied base register for the program.

Example 10.7

① USING DATA,12

① informs the Assembler that register 12 is the implied base register for the program. ① also informs the Assembler that the symbolic name of the base-location is DATA. The Assembler can find the numeric value associated with DATA in the symbol table. Recall that the Assembler will calculate the displacement of all symbolic names using the base-location DATA as the reference point. Bear in mind that the base-location is not necessarily the entry point into the program or control section. (See Section 7.1, Chapter 7.)

The numeric value associated with DATA must be in register 12, the implied base register, before any symbolically named operand is referenced during the execution of the program. In other words, it is the programmer's responsibility to see that register 12 does point to the actual base-location during the execution of the program.

Perhaps the easiest way to establish both the implied base register and the base-location and to make the implied base register point to the designated base-location is given in Example 10.8.

Example 10.8

Reference number	Location	Instruction	
① P	007200	BALR	12,0
②	007202	USING	*,12
③ P + 1	007202	– – –	– – –

BALR in ① puts the address of the next instruction, P + 1, which is 007202, into register 12 prior to the branch, which is never made since register 0 is designated as the pointer to the branch address.

After ① has been assembled, the LOCATION COUNTER points to the address 007202 which is the next available address in MEMORY for the program. The location counter reference, *, which is the first operand in ②, informs the Assembler that the address to which the LOCATION COUNTER is pointing right now is the base-location for the program. The Assembler will, therefore, use 007202 as the base-location when it calculates displacements.

② also informs the Assembler that register 12 will be the implied base register for the program. Note that register 12 will point to the base-location when the program is executed. The BALR in ① ensures this.

How can ② and ③ have the same address in MEMORY? Can two instructions reside in the same location? The answers are: they don't and they can't.

② is an assembly control statement by which we passed some information to the Assembler. When the Assembler has received this information, the work of ② is done. It is not needed at execution time; hence the Assembler does not "move" the LOCATION COUNTER when it encounters USING. ③ is the second executable instruction in our program.

The programmer may designate more than one implied base register. In fact, since the largest possible displacement is $4095_{10} = \text{FFF}_x$, he may be forced to do so if his program is very long, since if only one implied base register is designated, then all locations more than 4095 bytes beyond the base-location are not addressable.

Additional implied base registers may be designated at any point in the program by issuing another Using statement. The base-locations which are to be used by these additional base registers must be stipulated at the same time. And, of course, the user must be sure that at execution time these "new" implied base registers point to their associated base-locations.

If a programmer wishes, he may declare all implied base registers in one Using statement at the beginning of the program. To see how this is done, consider the general form of USING:

    USING   V1,R2,R3,. . .,RN

Up to 16 operands may appear after R2. The Assembler will assume that base-location V1 is associated with R2, base-location V1 + 4096 will be associated with R3, and base-location V1 + 8192 will be associated with R4, etc. The programmer, however, must make sure that these implied base registers point to the proper base-locations during execution of the program. Example 10.9 gives one technique to accomplish this.

Example 10.9

```
①          BALR    12,0
②          USING   BLUE,12,6,7,8
③ BLUE     LM      6,8,ADCON
           ⋮
           GOBACK
④ ADCON    DC      A(BLUE+4096,BLUE+8192,BLUE+12288)
           ⋮
```

① puts the address of P + 1, BLUE, into register 12.

The Using statement, ②, designates registers 12, 6, 7, and 8 as the implied base registers. The Assembler will assume that:

  a. base-location BLUE is associated with register 12
  b. base-location BLUE+4096 is associated with register 6
  c. base-location BLUE+8192 is associated with register 7
  d. base-location BLUE+12288 is associated with register 8

④ in the declarative part of the program created the block of base-location addresses. LM in ③ will load each of these base-location addresses into its associated implied base register.

Suppose a program has more than one designated base-location. How does the Assembler know which base-location to choose when calculating the displacement of an operand?

The base-location chosen by the Assembler to calculate the displacement will be the one which will result in the smallest nonnegative displacement for the operand. (All displacements must be nonnegative integers.)

10.4   The Housekeeping Instructions

The macros INIT and SETUP do more than just establish a base register. Both of these macros perform all of the housekeeping duties required of a program to which control is transferred by the 360 Operating System. In this section we intend to discuss each of these housekeeping instructions and the rationale behind it in some detail. Then we will present as the last item in this chapter a complete program in which we, the user, not INIT nor SETUP, establish the implied base register and in which we perform all of the necessary housekeeping duties.

The START, CSECT, and ORG Control Statements.   The Start assembly control statement has the general form:

       label   START   blank or self-defining term

The operand field, when not left blank, specifies the tentative starting point for the program. If the operand field is left blank, then the Assembler uses the default value of zero.

All locations specified in the operand field are tentative. One of two Operating System subroutines, the Linkage Editor or the Loader may relocate any program if necessary. That is, either one of these programs can override any starting point specified by the user.

The Supervisor, another subroutine of the Operating System, occupies from 4,000 to 15,000 bytes in the low order part of MEMORY. The Supervisor, which handles all interrupts and I/O requests in addition to numerous other chores, has priority over all programs. Hence if the user specifies a location occupied by the Supervisor, Program Fetch will relocate the program by placing it in CORE immediately following the Supervisor.

Now a definition. A *control section* is the *smallest segment* of a program which can be relocated independently of other sections in the program. That is, a control section is an independent routine which can perform its function no matter where it is relocated during load time.

A program is composed of one or more control sections, only one of which may be unnamed. If the label field of the Start statement is left blank, then the Assembler will assume that the control section defined by START is unnamed. If the label field is nonblank, or to be more specific, if the control section has been named BLUE, then the programmer should use BLUE in the operand field of the End statement.

Example 10.10

```
BLUE   START   X'7200'
         :
       END     BLUE
```

The Start statement must precede any statement which refers to the LOCATION COUNTER. Only one may be used in a program. We suggest that the Start statement be the first statement of the program. (Both the INIT and the SETUP macro use START; so *do not use* both INIT or SETUP and START.)

The CSECT assembly control statement defines a control section for the program. The CSECT assembly control statement has the general form:

       label   CSECT   blank

There can be only one unnamed control section in a program. If the label field is left blank, then that control section defined by CSECT is the unnamed control section in the program. We note that student programs usually consist of one control section.

The ORG assembly control statement has the general form:

blank   ORG   symbolic name or self-defining term

The LOCATION COUNTER is referenced by ORG. The value in that register is reset to the value specified by the symbolic name or to the value of the self-defining term which appears in the operand field.

The Start control statement is equivalent to ORG followed by CSECT. For instance, the code

BLUE   START   X'7200'

is equivalent to

ORG   X'7200'
BLUE   CSECT

The Save Area. Every program is expected to define an 18 word block of storage which will be known as that program's *save area*. All subroutines called by the program are expected, if the subroutines use the registers, to "save" the contents of the calling program's registers in this block of storage. When the subroutine has finished its task, it is expected to restore these registers to their original values before returning control to the calling program.

If the calling program, let us call it program A, invokes an Operating System macro, and if that macro uses the registers, then the Operating System will expect to be able to save program A's registers in the save area set up by A itself. If program A calls an installation macro or subroutine, then undoubtedly that macro too will expect, if necessary, to be able to "save A's registers" in the save area.

The save area is defined easily by a simple Define Storage pseudo in the declarative part of program A. For instance, the declarative SAVE DS 18F accomplishes this task.

The calling program is expected to make register 13 a pointer to this save area. By convention, all program macros, all Operating System subroutines, "know" that register 13 points to program A's save area when A transfers control to them. Creating this pointer is one of the housekeeping instructions which every user must perform when given control by the Operating System.

The Instruction STM 14,12,12(13). The first executable instruction which should be issued by the user when he receives control from the Operating System is STM 14,12,12(13). Let us look at the rationale behind this instruction. (We will, at times, substitute the programmer's colloquialism OS for the Operating System in the discussion that follows.)

Register 13	──→	SAVE	?
		SAVE+4	?
		SAVE+8	?
		SAVE+12	C(Reg14)
		SAVE+16	C(Reg15)
		SAVE+20	C(Reg0)
		SAVE+24	C(Reg1)
		SAVE+28	C(Reg2)
		SAVE+32	C(Reg3)
		SAVE+36	C(Reg4)
		SAVE+40	C(Reg5)
		SAVE+44	C(Reg6)
		SAVE+48	C(Reg7)
		SAVE+52	C(Reg8)
		SAVE+56	C(Reg9)
		SAVE+60	C(Reg10)
		SAVE+64	C(Reg11)
		SAVE+68	C(Reg12)

FIGURE 10.6

The Operating System transfers control to the user's program by issuing BALR 14,15. Register 15 contains the address of the first instruction in the user's program. (This address has been loaded in register 15 by one of the OS subroutines.) OS expects the user to return control to the address which has been placed into register 14 by BALR. In a sense, then, the user's program is a subroutine called by the Operating System.

Does this mean then that the user is expected to save the contents of the OS registers? Yes. Register 13, as stipulated by our convention, is a pointer to the save area set up by OS. The programmer is expected to use this save area pointer, register 13, to "save the registers" before using them in his own program.

The usual practice followed by many programmers is to issue the instruction STM 14,12,12(13) immediately after receiving control. Figure 10.6 depicts the OS save area after execution of Store Multiple. Notice that the first three words of the save area have not been affected by the action. In the discussion that follows in this section and in the next chapter, we will see what role these three words play in the transfer of control. There is a system macro, SAVE (14,12), which can be used instead of STM 14,12,12(13) to save the registers for OS or for any calling program which has set register 13 as a pointer to its save area.)

Linking the Save Area. A block of four instructions, issued after the user has established an implied base register, completes the housekeeping needed in the beginning of a program. Table 10.6 lists a typical sequence of instructions which might appear in the beginning of a program.

TABLE 10.6

①	BLUE	START	0
②		PRINT	NOGEN,DATA
③		STM	14,12,12(13)
④		BALR	12,0
⑤		USING	*,12
⑥		LA	11,SAVE
⑦		ST	11,8(13)
⑧		ST	13,SAVE+4
⑨		LR	13,11

The instructions ⑥, ⑦, ⑧, and ⑨, must come after the implied base register has been established because both ⑥ and ⑧ reference SAVE, the symbolic address of the user's save area. SAVE is addressable only after an implied base register has been established.

⑥ loads the address of the user's save area into register 11. ⑦ stores this address into the third word of the OS save area. The OS save area now has a pointer to the user's save area. ⑧ stores the pointer to the OS save area into the second word of the user's save area. This is called *chaining the save areas.* (Chaining the save areas is useful in debugging large programs. The details of this process are not within the scope of this text.)

After the execution of ⑨, register 13 is a pointer to the user's save area. The initial housekeeping has been accomplished. The user may now proceed with his own work.

The Terminal Instructions. The last imperative (executable) instructions in a user program restore the registers for the Operating System before returning control. We list a feasible set of such instructions in Table 10.7.

TABLE 10.7

①	L	13,SAVE+4
②	LM	14,12,12(13)
③	BR	14

① restores register 13 as a pointer to the OS save area, ② restores the registers, and ③ causes a branch to the return address in register 14.

The macro GOBACK consisted of the instructions ①, ②, and ③.

There is a system macro, RETURN, which restores the registers before returning control to OS. RETURN assumes, however, that register 13 points to the OS save area. Hence register 13 must be restored before RETURN is invoked. The normal sequence using RETURN is:

```
L        13,SAVE+4
RETURN   (14,12)
```

10.5 A Complete Program

In this section we present a complete program in which the user has established his own base register and performed his own housekeeping. We have included the first ten instructions in the INIT macro. The three terminal instructions are shown as part of the GOBACK macro.

The program itself is an *exchange sort*. A file of 20 records is sorted in an ascending order. The key to each of the 80 byte long records is in bytes 0–19. We suggest that the reader use the Exchange Sort Algorithm as a guide to the flow of the program logic in Figure 10.7.

We assume that the reader has considered the material on the bubble sort in Topic 4 of the Computer Notebook in Chapter 9, and the information given about Equate, the assembly control statement, in Topic 3 of the same chapter. Both these items are prerequisites for an understanding of this exchange sort program. We assume that the defined storage location FILEA contains the records to be sorted by our program.

The Exchange Sort Algorithm

Step 1: Let X point to the key of the first record.
Step 2: Move Y so that Y points to the same record that X points to.
Step 3: Move Y so that Y points to the next record in sequence.
Step 4: Compare the Y-key with the X-key.
Step 5: If the Y-key is less than the X-key, go to step 7.
Step 6: If Y is pointing to the last record in the file, go to step 11; otherwise go to step 3.
Step 7: Move the X-record to SAVEX.
Step 8: Move the Y-record to X (to the location pointed to by X).
Step 9: Move C(SAVEX) to Y.
Step 10: Go to step 6.
Step 11: Move X so that it is pointing to the next record in sequence.
Step 12: If X is pointing to the last record in the file, proceed in the normal sequence; otherwise go to step 2.
Step 13: Stop.

```
          PRINT  NOGEN
BLUE      CSECT
          STM    14,12,12(13)     SAVE OS REGISTERS
          BALR   12,0             REG 12 POINTS TO BASE-LOCATION
          USING  *,12             IMPLIED BASE REGISTER ESTABLISHED
          LA     11,SAVE          HOUSEKEEPING
          ST     11,8(13)         HOUSEKEEPING
          ST     13,SAVE+4        HOUSEKEEPING
          LR     13,11            HOUSEKEEPING
RED       B      START            BRANCH OVER SAVE AREA
SAVE      DS     18F              SAVE AREA
*    END OF HOUSEKEEPING.
*    THE EXCHANGE SORT.
X         EQU    2
Y         EQU    3
*    THE DECLARATIVES
LIMIT     DC     A(FILEA+1520)
SAVEX     DS     CL80
FILEA     DS     20CL80
START     LA     X,FILEA          X POINTS TO FIRST RECORD
LOOP1     LR     Y,X              Y POINTS TO SAME RECORD AS X
LOOP2     LA     Y,80(Y)          MOVE Y
          CLC    0(20,Y),0(X)     Y-KEY < X-KEY
          BL     MOVE             IF SO, BRANCH
CHECK     C      Y,LIMIT          IS Y POINTING TO LAST RECORD?
          BL     LOOP2            NO, GO TO LOOP2
          LA     X,80(X)          IF SO, MOVE X
          C      X,LIMIT          DONE?
          BL     LOOP1            IF NOT GO TO LOOP1
          B      STOP             YES, STOP
MOVE      MVC    SAVEX,0(X)       SAVE X-RECORD
          MVC    0(80,X),0(Y)     Y-RECORD → X
          MVC    0(80,Y),SAVEX    SAVEX → Y
          B      CHECK
STOP      L      13,SAVE+4        RESTORE OS SAVEAREA POINTER.
          LM     14,12,12(13)     RESTORE OS REGISTERS
          BR     14
          END    BLUE
```

FIGURE 10.7

Computer Notebook

TOPIC 1   Linked Lists

A file or data set whose members are stored in consecutive locations in MEMORY are called *sequential lists*. All of the files we have used in our discussions to this point have been sequentially organized. In this topic we introduce the concept of a *linked list*. However, before we study the structure of data sets organized as linked lists, let us consider a few situations in which the structure of a sequential data set is a definite liability to the programmer.

Suppose we have a sequentially organized data set. Suppose further that in our processing of this file we must frequently delete old records and/or insert new records into particular points in the file.

When we delete a record from our list, we must decide what is to be done with the released storage locations. Suppose each record in our file is stored in ten words and we release, say, record 5. These ten words which no longer contain information pertinent to our data set are in the "middle" of the data set. We might put blanks or some other character into the locations which held our deleted record and call the locations "empty." Or we might *collapse* the entire file so that all of our "empty" or released storage locations are at the end of the file.

One way to collapse our data set is as follows. Let the kth record be deleted. Move record $k + 1$ to the storage location which held record k. Move record $k + 2$ to $k + 1$, record $k + 3$ to $k + 2$, etc. That is, all records j, where $j > k$, are moved to $j - 1$. It should be clear that if we have a large file with many deletions, then a large portion of the data processing will be consumed in moving records. It also should be clear that our data set structure is not the most efficient one for our needs.

The insertion of a record into the "middle" of a sequential list presents the user with a problem somewhat similar to the deletion one. If, for instance, we want to insert a record between data item 16 and data item 17 in our file, then all records from data item 17 to the last record in the data set must be moved "back" to make room for the new entry.

The amount of moving can soon become quite exorbitant. Suppose we have a sequential list which consists of 1000 records such that each record is 10 words in length. Imagine the amount of moving that will be required to insert a new record between, say, item 25 and item 26. There are, of course, better ways to organize a file in which there are a great many insertions and deletions. Let us now consider one of them, a structure called a *linked list*.

A record, often called a *node* or a *cell*, is divided into at least two fields in a linked list. One of these fields is a *pointer* which points to the next node (record) in the linked list. The other field is the information field which contains the data that belongs to the record. The record key, which may or may not be pertinent data, is included in the information field.

Figure 10.8 is a schema of three "consecutive" nodes in a linked list. Each node is four bytes long. The pointer is in the first word of each cell. The key to each record is in bytes eight and nine of the node. We note that the pointer and the key may be placed anywhere in the node. A programmer must, of course, know the location of both fields. Note that these consecutive records (nodes) in the linked list do not occupy consecutive storage locations.

The first element of a linked list is a pointer which we will call the LISTHEAD. The LISTHEAD is not part of the data set. It contains no data. It

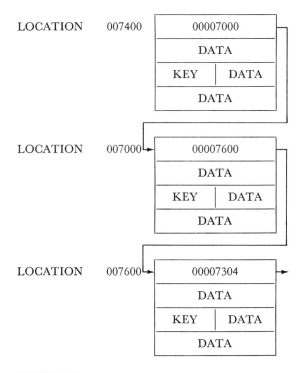

FIGURE 10.8

always occupies the same physical location in MEMORY. The LISTHEAD has one job—to point to the first node in the linked list. Figure 10.9 illustrates our concept. (Recall that an address is six hex digits long.)

The last node in a linked list will have some type of null character in the pointer field. This null character signifies that this node is the last cell in the list. We shall assume in the discussion that follows that 000000_x in the last cell signifies the end of the list. If LISTHEAD points to 000000_x, then

FIGURE 10.9

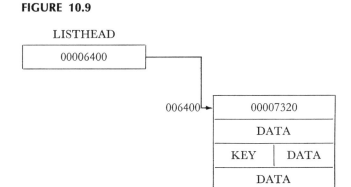

the entire data set is empty. Either the file has not been organized yet or the number of deletions has reduced the file to an empty status.

We now consider the problem of insertion of nodes into the linked list. We leave the problem of deletion as an exercise for the reader.

Example 10.11

a. LISTHEAD points to the first node of a linked list. Register 10 points to the address of a new node which is to be inserted into the list immediately following the node whose key matches the key which has been placed into register 5. Write the program segment which does the insertion. Put the new node at the end of the list if there is no key-match.

We assume that the linked list has been organized as given in Figure 10.8:

1. The pointer is in the first word of each node.
2. The key to each node is in bytes 8 and 9.
3. Each node is four words long.

The notation POINTER(X) is read, "The pointer in the node that X points to." The reader should be sure that he understands this notation. Do *not* take X as a subscript.

Consider Figure 10.8. What is the value of POINTER(X) if X points to location 007000? POINTER(X) = 007600 since X points to location 007000 and the value of the pointer in that node is 007600.

KEY(X) refers to the key of the node that X points to.

We offer two algorithms. Insertion Algorithm A uses the language familiar to us. Insertion Algorithm B introduces the new link list notation described above.

The last node of a linked list is often called the *tail* of the list. Neither algorithm checks for a key-match with the tail since even if there is a match, the new mode will be the new tail of the list anyway.

The word KEY in both algorithms refers to the key in register 5.

Insertion Algorithm A

Step 1: Let X point to the first node in the linked list.
Step 2: Let Y point to the same node as X.
Step 3: Move Y so that Y points to the next node in sequence.
Step 4: If the X-key matches the KEY, go to step 8.
Step 5: If the Y-pointer equals zero, go to step 11.
Step 6: Move X so that X points to the same node as Y.
Step 7: Go to step 3.
Step 8: Store the address in register 10 into the pointer field of the X-node.
Step 9: Store Y into the pointer field of the new node.
Step 10: Go to step 13.
Step 11: Store the address in register 10 into the pointer field of the Y-node.
Step 12: Move zero into the pointer field of the new node.
Step 13: Stop.

Insertion Algorithm B

Step 1: Set X = LISTHEAD.
Step 2: Set Y = POINTER(X).
Step 3: If KEY(X) = KEY, go to step 7.
Step 4: If POINTER(Y) = 0, go to step 10.
Step 5: Set X = Y.
Step 6: Go to step 2.
Step 7: Set POINTER(X) = C(Reg 10).
Step 8: Set pointer in new node equal to Y.
Step 9: Go to step 12.
Step 10: Set POINTER(Y) = C(Reg 10).
Step 11: Set pointer of new node to 0.
Step 12: Stop.

If we had equated register 10 to Z, we might write steps 7 through 11 in Insertion Algorithm B as:

Step 7: Set POINTER(X) = Z.
Step 8: Set POINTER(Z) = Y.
Step 9: Go to step 12.
Step 10: Set POINTER(Y) = Z.
Step 11: Set POINTER(Z) = 0.

The solution to our problem appears in Figure 10.10.

FIGURE 10.10

```
X        EQU  4
Y        EQU  6
Z        EQU  10
KEY      EQU  5
         L    X,LISTHEAD    SET X = LISTHEAD
LOOP     L    Y,0(X)        SET Y = POINTER(X)
         CH   KEY,8(X)      COMPARE HALF-WORD
         BE   INSERT
         CLC  0(4,Y),=F'0'  POINTER(Y) = 0?
         BE   BLUE          GO TO BLUE, IF SO
         LR   X,Y           SET X = Y
         B    LOOP          TRY NEXT LINK
INSERT   ST   Z,0(X)        POINTER(X) = Z
         ST   Y,0(Z)        POINTER(Z) = Y
         B    DONE
BLUE     ST   Z,0(Y)        POINTER(Y) = Z
         MVC  0(4,Z),=X'00000000'  POINTER(Z) = 0
```

EXERCISES

1. Which instruction sets the condition code used by the BC in ③ ?
   a.   SR   3,3   b.   C   5,ANDY
         L   3,VIOLA   SR   3,3
         LPR   3,3   ③ BC   B'1010',SAM
   ③ BC   B'1010',BLUE

2. We do not discuss Subtract Logical and Add Logical in this text. Look up those instructions in the *Principles of Operation* manual. Find the answers to the following questions:
   a. What is the general form of both instructions?
   b. What action is caused by both instructions?
   c. Give an example of the use of each instruction.
   d. How is the condition code set by the instructions?

3. Suppose that C(Reg 2) = 04040404 and C(STUBBS) = 76432ABC. What is the value of the condition code after the execution of
   a. AL   2,STUBBS   b. SL   2,STUBBS
   (See exercise 2.)

4. What will be the setting of the condition code if C(Reg 3) = 00004000 and C(Reg 2) = FFFFFFFF after the execution of the following instructions. The instruction in part (b) is Compare Logical Register. (See Section 9.9, Chapter 9.)
   a. CR   3,2   b. CLR   3,2

5. Define two blocks of 200 full-word locations by EMIL DS 200F and PAT DS 200F. Add EMIL(i) and PAT(i) from $i = 0$ to $i = 199$. Count the numbers of negative, positive, and zero sums. Count also the number of times that the sum overflows. Use the condition code to determine if the sum is negative, positive, zero, or overflow.

   Issue the following two instructions before you begin the addition loop to ensure that any overflow will not cause a program interrupt. (See Section 17.1, Chapter 17.)

   L   2, = F'0'
   SPM   2

6. Test under Mask (TM) is an SI type instruction. Its general form is:

   TM   S1,I2

   A one-to-one natural correspondence is made between the bits of S1 and the bits of the immediate operand I2.

When this instruction is executed, the 1 bits in the immediate operand test their associated bits in S1. The condition code is set as follows:

CC = 0 if all tested bits are zeros.
CC = 1 if tested bits are mixed.
CC = 2 if all tested bits are ones.

Define a 500-byte block of storage by CONVERSE DS 500C. Count the number of ones in bit position three of each byte in the CONVERSE block.

7. Suppose that we have a linked list such that LISTHEAD points to the first node in the list. Assume that the list has the structure depicted in Figure 10.8. Assume further that register 5 has a key which may match one of the keys for a node.

   Delete the node whose key matches the key in register 5. If there is no key-match, branch to an error subroutine. Figure 10.11 shows how to set up an assembly language linked list for this problem.

8. Consider exercise 7. What happens to the deleted nodes? They may be needed for data in later insertions, but these cells which now contain "garbage," will be scattered throughout MEMORY. It may be difficult to retrieve them. The usual practice is to attach deleted nodes to another linked list which consists of nodes available to the programmer.

   Assume that AVAIL points to the first element of a linked list of available nodes. Write a complete routine which deletes and adds nodes to a linked list which we will call LIST. All deleted nodes must be attached to the AVAIL list. (Each deleted node becomes the new head of the AVAIL list.) Nodes that are inserted into LIST must be detached from the AVAIL list. (Be sure to put data into the inserted nodes before attaching them to LIST.)

FIGURE 10.11   A Linked Structure

LISTHEAD	DC	A(A)
C	DC	F'0'
	DS	F
	DC	H'4'
	DS	3H
A	DC	A(B)
	DS	F
	DC	H'18'
	DS	3H
B	DC	A(C)
	DS	F
	DC	H'17'
	DS	3H

9. Consider the DROP assembly control statement. Suppose a user specifies that register 11 shall be the implied base register. He issues the pseudo instruction DROP 11, and then he issues USING *,10.

What restrictions, if any, are placed on the symbolic names defined when register 11 was the implied base? Consider the code below. Will ③ compile? Will it execute?

```
        BALR    11,0
        USING   *,11
        B       *+8
RED     DC      F'10'
        DROP    11
        BALR    10,0
        USING   *,10
③   L       3,RED
```

Test your assertions by running a program. Use the *Assembler Language* manual as your reference.

10. Consider the location counter reference in the two program segments A and B.

	A			B	
L	3,RED		① B	*+8	
A	3,BLUE		L	3,RED	
ST	3,WHITE		AR	3,5	
① B	*−8		ST	3,WHITE	

a. Will both parts A and B execute?
b. Where will control be transferred in each segment when ① is executed?

11. Consider the bubble sort of Figure 9.28 and the exchange sort of Figure 10.7. In the bubble sort, the X-record and Z-record were exchanged by the sequence of instructions:

① MVC SAVEZ,0(Z)
② MVC 0(80,Z),0(X)
③ MVC 0(80,X),SAVEZ

In the exchange sort the X-record and the Y-record were exchanged by ④, ⑤, and ⑥ which are repeated below:

④ MVC SAVEX,0(X)
⑤ MVC 0(80,X),0(Y)
⑥ MVC 0(80,Y),SAVEX

We can accomplish the swap (without the use of an auxiliary storage location such as SAVEX or SAVEZ) by ⑦, ⑧, and ⑨ which are given below. (Our example refers to the bubble sort.) We assume that each record is unique.

⑦ XC 0(80,X),0(Z)
⑧ XC 0(80,Z),0(X)
⑨ XC 0(80,X),0(Z)

Test the validity of our assertion by running the bubble sort using ⑦, ⑧, and ⑨. What will happen if two records are exactly equal?

11 | Subroutine Conventions

Many programs are written in phases. One programmer may have written part of the program in a high level language, while another has written part of it in Assembler Language. It may be that both parts are in the same language but were assembled separately; that is, each part is an independent control section. Or it may be that one part is the main program, and the other is a subroutine. But whatever the reason for the existence of the program modules, all parts must be able to communicate with each other. This communication between modules is known as *linkage.*

To simplify the discussion that follows, we will name the program which transfers control to another module as the *calling program,* the *main program,* or *program A.* The program to which control is transferred will be the *called program,* the *subprogram,* or *program B.*

We have already seen in Chapter 10 that BAL and BALR (the branch and link instructions) are used to provide some linkage between two programs. However, if program B, the subroutine, is expected to perform some functions for program A, then, in addition to the return address, the address of the input parameters must also be passed to B. When subroutine B has finished its processing, the results of this processing must somehow be returned to the main program A.

We have already noted that the calling program is expected to provide a *save* area where the called program may store the registers before processing the input parameters. The called program, in fact, expects the main program to pass a pointer to this save area. Program B, the called program, uses this pointer when it stores the registers before processing the input parameters. It uses this pointer again when it restores the original contents to the main program.

In this chapter we study the conventions set up for the System/360 which regulate the programming of all such linkages. These conventions not only list the responsibilities of both the calling and the called programs, but they also designate a set of linkage registers. Each of the registers in this set has a specific role to perform in the linkage procedure.

If a user deviates from these conventions, he does so at the risk of a program interrupt since these conventions are followed by the Operating System, including the compilers of the high level languages. For instance, suppose a program consists of a Fortran segment which calls an Assembler subprogram. The linkage for the Fortran load module will be prepared according to the rules set up by the conventions discussed in this chapter. We also point out that if an Assembler program calls a Fortran subroutine, the Fortran compiler will assume when it compiles the object module that the linkage in the Assembler program followed the established convention procedures.

In Section 11.1 we discuss the register assignments. In Sections 10.2 and 10.3 we discuss the responsibilities of the calling program and the called program, respectively.

11.1   The Linkage Registers

Table 11.1 lists the set of linkage registers and their assigned roles with respect to the linkage conventions.

TABLE 11.1   The Register Assignments

---

1. Register 15 contains the address of the subroutine's entry point.
2. Register 14 passes the calling program's return address to the subroutine.
3. Register 13 passes the address of the calling program's save area to the subroutine.
4. Register 0 may return an integer result from the subroutine to the main program.
5. Register 1 passes the address of the parameter address block to the subroutine.

Register 15 will contain the address of the entry point to the subroutine. If this entry point address is specified by a symbolic name which is external to the calling program, the Assembler cannot determine the actual numeric address associated with the label. Hence to get the address into register 15, the programmer usually defines a V-type constant in the declarative section of his assembly language coding or, what amounts to the same thing, he loads register 15 with a V-type literal which contains the address of the entry point. (In either case, one of the Operating System subroutines—the Loader or the Linkage Editor—will find the actual address associated with the external name when the program is loaded just prior to execution.) We will give examples of both methods when we discuss the responsibilities of the calling program.

Register 14 passes the main program's return address to the subroutine. This address is usually loaded into register 14 by BALR 14,15 (see Section 10.2, Chapter 10).

We note, however, that there is nothing built into the hardware that forbids a user to modify the return address in the subroutine. In fact, many student programs "bomb" because the return address has been inadvertently changed in the subprogram. The contents of register 14 have been unwittingly changed. Hence control is transferred to an inappropriate location instead of the main program. The program most likely had an interrupt caused by one of the exceptions discussed in Topic 2 of the Computer Notebook in Chapter 8.

The programmer may use the contents of register 14 as a switch. If the value, for instance, of some output parameter exceeds some predetermined limit, then the user might modify the address in register 14 so that the return to the main program is made at some other point than the one inserted into register 14 by BALR.

Remember, though, that there is no definite convention in the System/360 which provides for the type of usage just described. No provision has been made that will allow the user to pass the information that such a switch is desired. Hence, either the programmer must write both the main program and its subroutine, or he must personally inform his colleague, who is writing the subroutine, that such a switch is desired. Then he must also inform him how and when the contents of register 14 will be modified in the subroutine. No provision has been made in the established conventions for passing such information. With respect to these established conventions, the return address in register 14 is "inviolable."

Register 13 passes the address of the calling program's save area to the subroutine and program B will, after saving A's registers, store the contents of this pointer in the second word of its own save area. This may be done for one or both of the following two reasons: (1) it frees register 13 so that this register is available to help in the work of the subroutine, and (2) it enables the subprogram to load the address of its own save area into the register before the subprogram branches to another subroutine or before it uses a system or installation macro.

If program B branches to a new subroutine when register 13 is still pointing to A's save area, the results may be unpredictable. When the return from the "new" subroutine is made, control is passed to A, not B. If this is what the user intended, fine. If not, then, of course, the results will be, as stated, unpredictable.

The important fact to remember with respect to register 13 is that all called programs which use the established register linkage conventions assume that register 13 points to the save area of the program that called it.

Register 0 is used frequently to return an integer result from the subroutine to the main program. A floating-point result is usually returned via floating-point register 0. All Fortran integer function subroutines will return their values to the main program via register 0. Integer function calls in PL/I also return their values in the same register.

The manner in which the contents of the registers are restored by the called program—prior to the return of control—is affected by register 0's role in the linkage. We will discuss this further in Section 11.3.

Register 1 has perhaps the most interesting role to play in the System/360 linkage conventions. And perhaps its role is the most difficult to understand since it carries the address of the parameter address block to the subroutine.

Suppose, for example, that program A wants to pass two input parameters,

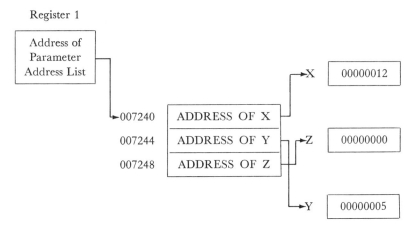

Register 1

C(Reg 1) = 00007240

FIGURE 11.1   The Structure of the Parameter Address List

X and Y, to subroutine B. Suppose further that one output parameter, Z, will be returned to A by B. The main program, in order to pass the input parameters to B and to receive the output parameter from B, will create a block of storage such that each word in the block will be a pointer to one of the parameters. Program A will also put the address of the first word in this block into register 1. Figure 11.1 depicts a typical structure created by A to pass and to receive parameters from B.

How does the main program create this parameter address list structure? Very simply. All the pointers in the structure in Figure 11.1 can be created by issuing the single instruction

    ① LA   1, = A(X,Y,Z)

We might interpret ① as telling the Assembler, "Create a block of three consecutive pointers such that the first pointer has the address of X, the second points to Y, and the third points to Z. Then when this has been done, load the address of the first pointer, the pointer to X, into register 1."

If ① appears in a program which has more than one independent control section, it is important to use the assembly control statement LTORG so that the literal pool which will contain the address block will be placed into the control section that belongs to A.

How does the subroutine B access the variable X? When control is transferred to B, register 1 is pointing to the first word in the parameter address block. (In our case, this happens to be the address of X.) B can, with this pointer, make its own pointer to X by loading the contents of the X-pointer into some register. The instruction L 2,0(1) does this. Now register

2 points to X. The contents of X may be loaded into, for example, register 5 by L 5,0(2).

The address of Y is four bytes beyond the address of X in the parameter address block. Hence if we add a displacement of four to the contents of register 1 as in L 2,4(1); then register 2 will point to Y. The instruction A 5,0(2) adds the contents of Y to register 5.

Example 11.1 should help to clarify most questions concerning this programming technique.

Example 11.1

Let us assume that a subprogram B has received via register 1 the address of the parameter address block as depicted in Figure 11.1. We want to write a sequence of instructions for the subroutine B so that B stores the product of X and Y into Z.

We let the addresses of X, Y, and Z be 007100, 007050, and 007150, respectively. (The actual addresses of the three parameters are immaterial. It might, however, be helpful to the student if he uses these addresses to follow the "action.")

According to the information given in Figure 11.1, C(Reg 1) = 00007240.

We give two solutions. The first solution appears in Figure 11.2.

Note that register 1 always points to the first word in the parameter address list. It is never moved. In order to reference the addresses of Y and Z in ③ and ⑤, we change the value of the displacement of the second operand. We did not change the value in register 1.

The second solution appears in Figure 11.3.

Load Multiple created three pointers. After execution of ①, register 2 points to X, register 3 points to Y, and register 4 points to Z. The LM instruction reduced the number of instructions by two.

FIGURE 11.2

①	L	2,0(1)	REGISTER 2 POINTS TO X
②	L	5,0(2)	C(X) → REGISTER 5
③	L	2,4(1)	REGISTER 2 POINTS TO Y
④	M	4,0(2)	C(REG 5) * C(Y) → [REG 4, REG 5]
⑤	L	2,8(1)	REGISTER 2 POINTS TO Z
⑥	ST	5,0(2)	C(REG 5) → Z

FIGURE 11.3

①	LM	2,4,0(1)	THREE POINTERS ARE CREATED
②	L	7,0(2)	C(X) → REGISTER 7
③	M	6,0(3)	C(REG 7) * C(Y) → [REG 6, REG 7]
④	ST	7,0(4)	C(REG 7) → Z

11.2   The Main Program's Responsibilities

Table 11.2 lists the responsibilities of the main program with respect to the linkage conventions. Many of the entries in the table should look familiar since we have referred to them in other contexts. We shall include a short synopsis of the familiar entries along with a more lengthy interpretation of the others in the discussion that follows the table.

TABLE 11.2   Responsibilities of the Main Program

1. Prepare the input parameters.
2. Allocate storage for all output parameters which will not be returned via register 0.
3. Set up the pointers in the parameter address block.
4. Put the address of the parameter address block into register 1.
5. Allocate storage for an eighteen-word save area.
6. Put the address of the save area into register 13.
7. Put the branch address into register 15.
8. Put the return address into register 14.
9. Cause a branch to the subroutine.

The Input Parameters.   The input parameters are data items which belong to the main program. They may have been read in, they may have been generated by the Define Constant pseudo, or they may be the result of some processing done by the main program.

The Output Parameters.   The storage space for the output parameters must be provided by the main program. The amount of space allocated should exactly "fit" the requirements of the results to be stored.

The Parameter Address Block.   The parameter address block is handily set up and its address put into register 1 by LA 1,=A(S1,S2, . . . ,Sn). A complete discussion of this entry appeared in Section 11.1.

The Save Area.   The eighteen-word save area is defined by the user as part of his housekeeping chores when the Operating System transfers control to his program. Register 13 should always point to this area when a branch to a subroutine is made.

Register 15 and the Branch Address.   The address of a subroutine which is local to the main program may be put into register 15 by LA 15,SUBPGM where SUBPGM is the subprogram address. See Example 10.4 in the last chapter. If the branch address is external, then it may be loaded into register 15 by using an external address type literal such as the second operand in L 15,=V(SUBPGM), or an external address constant may be defined in the declarative section of the program and the constant can then be loaded into register 15 just prior to the branch. Figure 11.4 illustrates the concept.

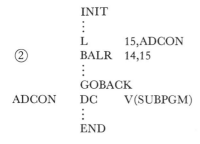

```
          INIT
          ⋮
          L      15,ADCON
    ②     BALR   14,15
          ⋮
          GOBACK
ADCON     DC     V(SUBPGM)
          ⋮
          END
```

FIGURE 11.4

Register 14 and the Return Address.   The return address is put into register 14 by the instruction which causes the branch to the subroutine. This is accomplished in the example in Figure 11.4 by ②, (BALR 14,15). We have covered this instruction quite thoroughly in Chapter 10.

11.3   The Responsibilities of the Subroutine

Table 11.3 lists the responsibilities of the called program with respect to the linkage conventions. Most of the entries in the table have been discussed in other sections of the text. We will, therefore, keep our comments about the entries to a minimum.

TABLE 11.3   Responsibilities of the Subroutine

1. Save the registers for the main program.
2. Retrieve the input parameters.
3. Store any results in the output parameter storage location.
4. Restore the registers.
5. Transfer control to the main program.

Save the Registers.   The called program should "save the registers" for the calling program. Program B should issue the instruction STM 14,12,12(13) at the entry point to the subroutine, since register 13 points to the main program's save area when control is transferred. (A thorough discussion of this entry appears in Chapter 10, Section 10.4.)

The Input and Output Parameters.   The techniques by which the input parameters are retrieved by the subroutine and how the results are stored in the output parameter locations are given in Section 11.1.

Restoring the Registers.   The diagram of a calling program's save area appeared in the last chapter. (See Figure 10.6.) Note carefully where the contents of each register are stored.

The triplet of instructions given below will restore the registers and return control to the main program. It is assumed that register 0 does not return a result to the main program.

```
        L    13,SAVE+4
        LM   14,12,12(13)
        BR   14
```

If, however, register 0 is returning a result to the calling program, then its former contents must *NOT* be restored. This means that two Load Multiple instructions must be given to restore the other registers. Care must be taken to assure that the registers are loaded from the correct locations in the save area.

The sequence of instructions given below restores all registers except register 0. Note that location SAVE+20 is "skipped" when the registers are restored in the sequence.

```
        L    13,SAVE+4
        LM   14,15,12(13)
        LM   1,12,24(13)
        BR   14
```

Example 11.2 illustrates how a main program and its subroutine pass parameters using the techniques discussed in this chapter. The main program passes two input parameters, X and Y, and the location for one output parameter, Z.

Example 11.2

FIGURE 11.5 The Main Program

```
RED    CSECT
       STM    14,12,12(13)      SAVE REGS
       BALR   12,0
       USING  *,12
       ⋮
       LA     13,SAVE           POINTER TO SAVE AREA
       LA     1,=A(X,Y,Z)       PARAMETER ADDR BLOCK
       L      15,=V(BLUE)       EXTERNAL ADDRESS
       BALR   14,15             BRANCH TO BLUE
*      ⋮                        RETURN ADDR IN REG 14
       L      13,SAVE+4
       LM     14,12,12(13)
       BR     14
SAVE   DS     18F
X      DC     F'10'
Y      DC     F'26'
Z      DS     F
       ⋮
       LTORG
              =A(X,Y,Z)
              =V(BLUE)
       END    RED
```

```
BLUE   CSECT
       STM   14,12,12(13)    SAVE RED'S REGISTERS
       LR    12,15
       USING BLUE,12
       LA    11,SAVE
       ST    11,8(13)        CHAIN SAVE AREA
       ST    13,SAVE+4       POINTER → BLUE SAVE AREA
       LR    13,11           13 POINTS TO NEW SAVE
       L     2,0(1)          ADDR OF X → REG 2
       L     5,0(2)          X → REG 5
       LR    10,5            SAVE X
       L     2,4(1)          ADDR OF Y → REG 2
       A     10,0(2)         X + Y → REG 10
       M     4,0(2)          X * Y → REG 5
       L     2,8(1)          ADDR OF Z → REG 2
       ST    5,0(2)          X * Y → LOCATION Z
       LR    0,10            X + Y → REG 0
       L     13,SAVE+4       RESTORE POINTER
       LM    14,15,12(13)    RESTORE 14 AND 15
       LM    1,12,24(13)     RESTORE ALL BUT REG 0
       BR    14              GOBACK
SAVE   DS    18F             BLUE'S SAVE AREA
       END   BLUE
```

FIGURE 11.6 The Subroutine

The subroutine multiplies X by Y and stores the product in Z. The subroutine also returns the sum of X and Y via register 0. All of the conventions discussed in this chapter are followed by both, modules.

In Topic 1 of the Computer Notebook, An Introduction to Job Control Language, we list the job control cards which may be necessary to execute our two modules on the level we have indicated.

In Section 11.4, we present two lower level subroutines which can be executed with their calling programs as a single unified module. The level-3 subroutine in that section, however, requires an Assembler which will code the two independent control sections in one job step. If the student's installation does not have such an Assembler, then the job control given in Topic 1 may be necessary.

11.4 Types of Subroutines

Some types or levels of assembly language subroutines do not need to use the extensive subroutine linkage conventions that we have presented. In other words, there are several ways a subroutine can be incorporated into a program. No particular names or labels have been given to these methods. So to differentiate one type from another, we have attached level numbers to them. A level-1 type subroutine will be the simplest, and level-3, the most complex.

The complexity of the code in the subroutine does not determine its class or level number. A subroutine belongs to a particular class depending on how it is linked to the main program. A subroutine with an extremely complex code may belong to level-1, while another composed of a simple sequence of instructions may be in level-3.

Level-1. A subroutine which resides in the same control section as the main program belongs to the level-1 class. Both the main sequence and the subsequence reference the same variables. That is, all variables in the program are available to both parts. Hence there is no need to pass the address of a parameter address list. Nor is there any particular need to save the registers.

We note, however, that when the branch is made, if not enough registers are available to the subroutine for its work, then the subroutine may store the contents of some or all of the registers. We suggest that these registers be stored in a location especially allocated for that purpose. They should not be stored in the program's save area. In general, the main program's save area should be used only when control is transferred to an independent module.

At this point we consider some information about level-1 subroutines which is useful to know when debugging programs. In addition, our discussion will provide some insight about the Operating System.

Suppose a programmer issues BAL 14,PRINT to branch to his own level-1 print subroutine. In this subroutine he calls the PUT macro to print some records. After the printing has been done he wants control returned to his main sequence. The print subroutine, however, may not be able to do this.

Why not? One fact, often forgotten when one is writing level-1 subroutines, is that invoking PUT, GET, or some other system macro instruction is equivalent to calling a high level subroutine. These macro instructions use registers 0, 1, 14, and 15 for linkage between the user program and the Operating System. The original contents of these registers—the contents pertinent to the user program—will not be restored.

Although the programmer very carefully placed the return address to the main sequence into register 14 by BAL 14,PRINT, the PUT macro instruction in the print subroutine destroyed that address. Hence, the instruction BR 14 at the end of the print subroutine will not transfer control back to the main sequence.

The following example gives a method which might be used by our print subroutine to assure successful transfer of control back to the main sequence.

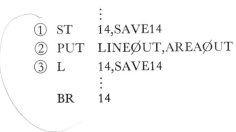

```
          ⋮
①  ST    14,SAVE14
②  PUT   LINEØUT,AREAØUT
③  L     14,SAVE14
          ⋮
    BR    14
```

We note that ② might be the call of any system macro. The location SAVE14, used by ① and ③, must be defined, of course. We further note that the programmer might save himself the above coding if he uses register 7 (or some other register not used by the macro instruction) for linkage between his main sequence and his level-1 subroutine.

It is a good idea to learn which registers are used by a system macro before calling it. This information is available in the IBM manual, Data Management and Supervisor Macros. Another way to gain this information is to look at the macro expansion of the macro call in the program printout.

The example of a level-1 subroutine which is given in Figure 11.7 does the same job as that done by the subprogram in Example 11.2. The product of $C(X)$ times $C(Y)$ is stored in location Z. This same job is also done by the other types of subroutines, level-2 and level-3, in this chapter.

Level-2. A subroutine will belong to level-2 if it and the main program are assembled together but each belongs to a different control section. (Usually both the subroutine and the main program are written by a single programmer.) Communication between the two parts is accomplished by the use of A-type address constants; hence there is no need to define a parameter address block.

The Assembler maintains only one symbol table, even though each control section maintains its own implied base register and its own base-location. This means that the programmer may not use duplicate symbolic names. If, for example, SAM is defined in the main program's control section, then SAM must not be defined again by appearing in the label field of any assembly statement in any other control section.

Again we note that the control section which contains the subroutine does

FIGURE 11.7

```
            LA     15,SUBA
            ST     3,X
            ST     4,Y
            BALR   14,15
            L      3,Z
            ⋮
SUBA        L      5,X   ⎤
            M      4,Y   ⎟   level-1
            ST     5,Z   ⎟   subroutine
            BR     14    ⎦
            ⋮
EXIT        GOBACK
SAVE        DS     18F
X           DC     F'10'
Y           DC     F'26'
Z           DS     F
            END
```

not have to save the registers, although it may do so if necessary. Notice also that although the system is able to generate the addresses of the constants X, Y, and Z in the subroutine, the subroutine itself cannot reference X, Y, or Z directly. The subprogram must use the retrieval techniques introduced in Section 11.1.

The program in Figure 11.8 illustrates the method by which the program and its subroutine communicate with each other.

FIGURE 11.8

```
RED       CSECT
          BALR    12,0
          USING   *,12
            ⋮
          L       15,=A(BLUE)
          ST      3,X
          ST      4,Y
          BALR    14,15
            ⋮
          GOBACK
            ⋮
X         DS      F
Y         DS      F
Z         DS      F
          LTORG
                  =A(BLUE)
            ⋮
BLUE      CSECT
          BALR    10,0
          USING   *,10
            ⋮
          L       3,=A(X)
          L       4,=A(Y)
          L       7,0(3)
          M       6,0(4)
          L       3,=A(Z)
          ST      7,0(3)
          BR      14
          LTORG
                  =A(X)
                  =A(Y)
                  =A(Z)
          END     RED
```

Level-3—Explicit Passing of Parameters.   If a subroutine and a main program are in different control sections which are assembled separately, then the subroutine belongs to level-3. We can use the methods developed in the first two sections on subroutine linkage conventions to pass the necessary information from one part of the program to the other. However, we can also, if both the main sequence and its subroutine know the names of the parameters involved, pass the information explicitly.

We introduce at this point two new assembly control statements, ENTRY and EXTRN, which give the Assembler the names of the parameters which are to be passed explicitly from one program to the other. (See Figures 11.9 and 11.10.) The syntax of the general form of ENTRY is:

ENTRY   symbol1,symbol2, . . . ,symboln

```
RED     CSECT
        BALR    12,0
        USING   *,12
        EXTRN   BLUE
        ENTRY   X,Y,Z
        .
        .
        L       15, = A(BLUE)
        .
        .
        BALR    14,15
        .
        .
        GOBACK
X       DC      F'10'
Y       DC      F'20'
Z       DS      F
        .
        .
        LTORG
        END     RED
```

FIGURE 11.9 The Main Program

```
BLUE    CSECT
        BALR    10,0
        USING   *,10
        EXTRN   X,Y,Z
        ENTRY   BLUE
        .
        .
        L       3, = A(X)
        L       5,0(3)
        L       3, = A(Y)
        M       4,0(3)
        L       3, = A(Z)
        ST      5,0(3)
        BR      14
        LTORG
        END     BLUE
```

FIGURE 11.10 The Subroutine

The symbolic names listed in the operand field must be defined in the program in which the Entry statement appears.

ENTRY informs the Assembler that the symbolic names which appear in the operand field will be referenced by another module (another program). The Assembler will respond by placing these symbolic names into the *External Symbol Dictionary* (ESD).[1]

Each symbolic name in the operand field of an Entry statement must also appear in the operand field of some External statement.

The syntax of the general form of the External statement is:

EXTRN   symbol1,symbol2, . . . ,symboln

EXTRN informs the Assembler that the module in which EXTRN appears will refer to the external symbolic names which appear in the operand field. The Assembler replies by placing these names into the External Symbol Dictionary also. Thus, the ESD of each module has two types of entries:
1. symbolic names local to the program but which will be referred to by other modules
2. external symbolic names which will be referenced by the program

Then at load time, the Linkage Editor or the Loader will obtain the necessary information from these dictionaries to determine the actual addresses of the passed parameters.

None of the generalized linkage conventions need to be followed since both the main program and the subroutine are usually written by the same person. However, if the programmer wishes to follow the conventions, he may. We have not used any of the standard conventions in our examples in Figures 11.9 and 11.10. Our purpose in these examples is to show explicitly how to pass the parameters between two modules.

Computer Notebook

TOPIC 1   Introduction to Job Control Language

The programmer communicates with the IBM/360 Operating System via Job Control Language. When he submits a program the first card in his deck is a *job card*. This job card is one of several types of Job Control Language (JCL) cards. We list them in Table 11.4.

We will discuss the JOB, EXEC, DD, and delimiter cards in this topic. Information concerning the other four types of JCL cards (and further information about the ones we cover in this topic) can be found in the IBM manual, *Job Control Language User's Guide, GC 28-6703.*

All JCL cards except the delimiter card must have a double slash (//) in columns 1 and 2. These slashes are followed by a name field, an operation field, and an operand field. The name field must start in column 3. Just as

---

[1] The External Symbol Dictionary is part of the object deck produced by the Assembler.

TABLE 11.4   JCL Cards

1. JOB card
2. EXEC card
3. DD (Data Definition) card
4. Delimiter (/*) card
5. Null statement card
6. Comment card
7. PROC statement card
8. Command statement card

in Basic Assembler Language, one or more blanks must separate all the fields. The usual practice is, however, to start the operation field in column 10 and the operand field in column 16. (An optional comment field, preceded by at least one blank, may follow the operand field.)

The name field, if not omitted, identifies the JCL card so that other JCL cards and certain Assembler Language statements can refer to it. (See Chapter 14.) The name is limited to eight characters. Any alphabetic character from A through Z, any digit from 0 to 9, or any national character (#, $, @) may appear in the name. The first character, however, must be alphabetic.

The operand field specifies the type of JCL statement. We will study the ones that specify JOB, EXEC, or DD in the operand field.

The operand field of a JCL card is composed of positional and keyword parameters. All positional parameters must precede the keyword parameters. Positional parameters must, as the name implies, appear in a designated order. Omitted positional parameters must be noted by commas. Keyword parameters may appear in any order. Our discussion of the JOB card, which we turn to now, should help make these points clear.

The general form of the JOB card is:

//jobname   JOB   (acct information),username,keywords

A typical example is:

//CSC221   JOB   (1432,6,100),KENSKEWES

Both the accounting information and the user name are positional parameters. *Accounting information* is composed of subparameters which happen to be positional also.

A general rule is, if more than one positional subparameter is coded, then the set must be enclosed in parentheses.

Example 11.3

a. //CSC222   JOB   (3432,,100),GARYNUNES

The extra comma between 3432 and 100 designates that a positional subparameter has been omitted. Notice that no blanks appear in the programmer's name.

If any special character except a period appears in the name, then the entire name must be enclosed in apostrophes.

b. //CSC221   JOB   3432,JAMESTURCH

Only one subparameter appears in the accounting information field; hence the parentheses may be dropped.

We have by no means exhausted the rules which govern the coding of the JOB card. We note that the accounting information parameter is defined by the installation. Additional information should be requested from the computer center.

The JOB Card Keyword Parameters.   There is one keyword parameter which we feel the student should code on the JOB card. This is the message level keyword MSGLEVEL. When MSGLEVEL=1 is coded on the JOB card, all the JCL statements used by the Operating System in executing the job will be on the printout. If MSGLEVEL=2 is coded, then only the JCL statements the user has included in his source deck will be listed on the printout. The student will find this JCL listing quite useful when debugging the job control language for the suggested exercises for this chapter and for those input/output routines given in Chapter 14. We suggest MSGLEVEL=1 be coded on all jobs submitted as solutions to exercises in this and the chapters that follow. Figure 11.11 depicts a JOB card in which the message level parameter has been coded.

FIGURE 11.11

//CSC221   JOB   (3462,6,100),MATOZA,MSGLEVEL=1

EXEC Card.   The EXEC card has two functions. First, it denotes the end of a job step and the beginning of a new one. (We note here that a computer job consists of one or more job steps.) The EXEC card, as its name implies, *may* also specify the name of a program to be executed by the computer in that job step.

Usually, however, matters are not that simple. The EXEC card in most jobs will specify a *procedure* in the operand field. Let us see what this means before we consider the format of the EXEC card in detail.

Every program—remember the Assembler, the Fortran, and other language compilers are computer programs—needs at least one computer resource such as the CARDREADER, the PRINTER, a disk pack, etc. All requests for these computer resources are passed to the Operating System by Job Control Language. (A more detailed discussion on how to define data sets and request computer resources for these data sets is given in Chapter 14.)

Since so many programs require the same data sets and the same resources each time they are executed, the JCL (Job Control Language) associated with these programs has been grouped into several sets called *procedures*. These procedures are stored on a disk pack in an Operating System library called SYS1.PRØCLIB (or procedure library). Since these procedures are *catalogued,* they are quite often also referred to as *catalogued procedures.*

The EXEC card may call one of these catalogued procedures. The call consists of a request for a program such as the Assembler along with all the standard JCL needed to execute that program.

We note that one or more procedures may be called in each job. Each procedure may consist of one or more job steps.

Exercise 10 in the problem section of this chapter suggests one way to get a listing of the JCL cards that constitute a procedure. Another way has been given earlier in this topic—code MSGLEVEL=1 on the JOB card.

We now turn to a discussion of the format of the EXEC card.

The general form of EXEC is:

//stepname   EXEC   procedure name

We might, for instance, want to execute the ASMFCLG procedure. Then we code

//STEP1   EXEC   ASMFCLG

ASMFCLG is a three jobstep procedure. It consists of a compile step in which the Assembler encodes the Assembler Language of the source deck into the machine language of the object deck.

The second step in this ASMFCLG procedure is the link-edit one in which the Linkage Editor processes the object deck (or object module) into a load module that can be executed. The Linkage Editor places the load module into a partitioned data set named &GOSET. The load module has the name GO.

The third step in this procedure is called the GO step. The user's program, which is now a load module named GO, is executed. The Linkage Editor will write the following message when it completes its processing: "**** GO DOES NOT EXIST BUT HAS BEEN ADDED TO THE DATA SET." This cryptic message means that the program is now a load module. It is all set to execute.

The DD Card.   The third JCL card we discuss is the DD card (data definition card). A DD card must be included after the EXEC card for each data set used in the step. The Operating System must allocate a computer resource for each data set. In the "compile" step, the Assembler reads and processes our source deck. We are expected to provide one DD card [1] which gives the

---

[1] The other data sets needed by the Assembler are described in the catalogued procedure ASMFCLG.

Operating System the information it needs about this data set—our source deck. This DD card is quite simple:

//ASM.SYSIN   DD   *

The asterisk (*) in this statement is a positional parameter. It signifies to the System that the data set associated with the name in the label field of the DD card follows immediately. In our example, this asterisk, *, informs the System that the data set associated with the SYSIN DD card follows immediately. Our program is "data" to the Assembler.

If our program reads in data cards via the CARDREADER, then those cards are a data set. That means we must include in the GO step a DD card which describes this data set to the Operating System. If our program prints any results of its processing, then each line is a record of a print data set. Hence we must include a DD card which also describes this data set to the Operating System.

These two types of data sets are so common in the GO step that the DD cards which describe them are quite simple. The first DD card in Figure 11.12 refers to a print file (a data set that will utilize the printer). The second DD card refers to a data set that will be read in by the CARDREADER. Note that they must be in the order listed when the user's deck is submitted to the computer. We point out that the names SYSPRINT and SYSIN are arbitrary. See Chapter 14.

The user must also describe the data set in his program by using the data management macro instruction DCB (Data Control Block). He must, in this instruction, name the DD card which is associated with his data set. If we used the two DD cards of Figure 11.12 in our object deck, then our program would specify both SYSPRINT and SYSIN in the Data Control Block macro instructions of their respective data sets. (Data control blocks are considered in some depth in Chapter 14.)

The last JCL card we cover is the delimiter card, or, as it is commonly known, the slash-asterisk card (/*). This card is used to mark the end of a data set. It is used to mark the end of our object program, which is a data set used by the Assembler. It is used to mark the end of our data cards, which is a data set used by our program.

We now present the JCL cards which are necessary to execute the main program and its subroutine from Section 11.3. (The JCL may differ slightly in some installations.)

The JCL format given in Figure 11.13 can be used to link any two independent modules. The EXEC statement STEP1 (see ①) invokes the ASMC

FIGURE 11.12

//GO.SYSPRINT   DD   SYSOUT=A
//GO.SYSIN   DD   *

procedure. In this procedure, the main program is encoded and stored as an object program. We note that ASMC is a one-step procedure. It is independent of the ASMFCLG discussed above. See exercise 10.

The EXEC statement in ② invokes the ASMFCLG procedure. The //LKED.SYSIN DD * (see ③) specifies a data set for the link-edit step of this procedure. There is one record in this data set. It is a message telling the Linkage Editor to give initial control of the CPU to the main program at location RED at execution time (see ④). Location RED is the entry point in the main program.

These JCL cards are intended for the main program and its subroutine of Figure 11.5 and Figure 11.6 in Section 11.3.

Example 11.4

FIGURE 11.13

```
     //EXAMPLE      JOB       2311,ATTALA,MSGLEVEL=1
 ①  //STEP1        EXEC      ASMC
     //ASM.SYSIN    DD        *

     Main program

     /*
 ②  //STEP2        EXEC      ASMFCLG
     //ASM.SYSIN    DD        *

     Subprogram

     /*
 ③  //LKED.SYSIN   DD         *
 ④                 ENTRY     RED
     /*
     //GO.SYSPRINT  DD        SYSOUT=A
     //GO.SYSIN     DD        *

     Data if any

     /*
```

EXERCISES

1. Suppose a branch is made to a subroutine by

        L   15,=V(SUB)
        BALR   14,15

Register 15 points to SUB, the first byte in the subroutine's control section, when the subroutine is entered.

a. Can register 15 be designated as the implied base register?

b. Can SUB be designated as the base-location?

c. What will happen if a base register is established by coding the pair of instructions as in (i) instead of as in (ii)?

   i. USING *,12
      BALR   12,0
  ii. BALR   12,0
      USING *,12

2. a. What is wrong with establishing a base register in a subroutine (or main program, for that matter) by

   ① LR   12,15
   ② USING *,12

b. Keep ① of part a. Write ② so that the base register and base-locations are established correctly.

3. Is it possible to save the registers before branching and restore them after returning from the subroutine? Give reasons for your answers.

4. Write the code (without reference to the text or any manual) that will divide C(X) by C(Y) and that will store the quotient into location A and the remainder into location B. Let the parameters be passed to the subroutine by

   LA 1,=A(A,B,X,Y)

5. A student turned in the code in Figure 11.14 as his solution to the following problem in an exam. Although his program "ran," he was marked off for his solution. Why?

   The problem given to the student was: Show how a main program defines and passes the addresses to a subroutine. Show how the subroutine retrieves these parameters.

(Hint: read the pertinent part of Section 11.1 again. The program ran because of a fortunate or contrived arrangement in the main program.)

FIGURE 11.14 The Student's Solution

Main program		Subroutine	
	⋮		⋮
	LA 1,=A(A,B,C)	L	2,0(1)
	⋮	L	3,0(2)
A	DC F'10'	A	3,4(2)
B	DC F'12'	ST	3,8(2)
C	DS F		⋮
	⋮	END	
	LTORG		
	END		

6. Describe the format of the External Symbol Dictionary (ESD). Use the *OS Assembler (F) Programmer's Guide* as your reference.

7. Write a main program and a subroutine. Let these programs be on a high enough level so that the linkage described in this chapter and the job control described in the Computer Notebook are used.

   Let the main program pass the parameters which include a random integer and ten contiguous full-word locations, the first being named PRIME.

   Let the subroutine return the prime factors in the ten full-word locations. If the random integer is a prime itself, then set register 0 to zero. If the integer has more than ten prime factors, then register 0 should be set to minus one.

8. Write a main program and a subroutine in which the parameters are passed explicitly.

   Let the main program pass bridge hands to the subroutine. Let the subroutine count the number of *points* in the hand. (Ace equals 4; King, Queen, and Jack are equal to 3, 2, and 1, respectively.)

9. Pick a computer of some make other than IBM. Contrast the linkage conventions of System/360 Basic Assembler Language with the linkage conventions used by the computer of your choice.

10. The JCL procedures are stored in the SYS1.PRØCLIB. One may get a listing of the JCL statements in a procedure by executing a utility program named IEBPTPCH. Research the IBM *Utilities* manual to determine how this is done. Then get a listing of the ASMC and ASMFCLG procedures.

12 | Floating-point Instructions

We begin this chapter with a ten question quiz. If the reader fails to get a 100 per cent score on this quiz, we strongly urge that he review the material on floating-point constants in Topic 4 of the Computer Notebook in Chapter 4 and in Section 5.3 of Chapter 5. The answers to our questions can be found on page 307.

Except for the length of the fractions involved, the action of the single-precision and the double-precision arithmetic instructions are exactly the same. We will, therefore, present both types together. In our discussion, however, we will tend to go into greater detail about the single-precision or short form. The reader should bear in mind that the comments made concerning the short form apply also to the double-precision or long form.

Our chapter is divided into four sections: load and store instructions, normalized arithmetic operations, unnormalized add and subtract instructions, and finally a discussion of two conversion routines. The first conversion routine converts a binary integer to a normalized floating-point constant. The second converts a normalized floating-point constant to a full-word binary integer.

Now the quiz.

The Floating-point Quiz

1. What is the difference between a normalized and an unnormalized floating-point constant?
2. List the three fields of both types of floating-point constants.
3. Give the field length and the bit positions occupied by each part of a floating-point constant.
4. What is the bias value of the exponent in a System/360 floating-point constant?
5. Use the Define Constant pseudo to define a single-precision floating-point constant equal to 3.14_{10}.
6. Use the Define Constant pseudo to define a double-precision floating-point constant equal to 14.76_{10}.
7. An exponent is always attached to a base. For instance, in 7^8, the exponent 8 is attached to the base 7. Give the base of a BAL floating-point number.
8. Which statement is correct?

    a. A negative number expressed as a floating-point constant is in sign-absolute value form.

    b. A negative number expressed as a floating-point constant is in two's complement form.

9. Find the decimal equivalent of BLUE if C(BLUE) = 41110000.

10. How many floating-point registers are there? Give their names, or addresses.

12.1   Load and Store Instructions

Table 12.1 lists the floating-point load and store instructions. Note first that all floating-point instructions are either RX or RR type. Then note how easy it is to distinguish between the short and long forms. The mnemonics of the short form end in E or ER, while their long form counterparts end in D or DR. (The instruction is type RR if the mnemonic ends in R; otherwise it is type RX.)

Recall that the effective address of an operand referenced in an RX type instruction may be modified by an index register. Hence, all of the information given in Chapter 9 concerning address modification by changing the value in an index register is applicable to floating-point operands.

The programmer does not need to restrict himself to floating-point instructions when working with floating-point constants. He may use any instruction which he feels is appropriate to his purposes. He can, for instance, move floating-point constants from one location in MEMORY to another by MVC (Move Character). If, to give another example, location BLUE contains a floating-point number, and if the programmer wants to be sure that the content of BLUE is negative, he may issue ØI BLUE,X'80'. (We accomplish the same result in Example 12.1g by using three instructions from the floating-point repertoire.)

As we discussed earlier in this chapter, the only difference between a single-precision instruction and its double-precision counterpart is the length of the fraction involved in the "action." Each of the four floating-point registers is 64 bits long; only 32 bits, however, are involved in the single-precision instructions. All 64 bits take part in the double-precision operation. The storage operand, S2, may be written in either the implicit or explicit mode. If S2 is the second operand of a long form instruction, it must be on a double-word boundary. Otherwise S2 must be on a full-word boundary.

We designate the registers, in the syntax of the general form of the floating-point instructions, by FLP1 and FLP2. FLP1 stands for the floating-point register which is the first operand of the operation, while FLP2 is the second register operand. CONTROL will consider both FLP1 and FLP2 as 32-bit registers when a short form instruction is involved.

Each single-precision load and store operation is illustrated in Example 12.1. The syntax of the general form of both the long and short forms appears in Table 12.1. This general form will not be repeated in the examples.

TABLE 12.1 Load and Store Operations

Mnemonic		Action	Condition code set	Mode
LE	FLP1,S2	$FLP1 \leftarrow C(S2)_{1\ word}$	No	Single
LD	FLP1,S2	$FLP1 \leftarrow C(S2)_{double\ word}$	No	Double
LER	FLP1,FLP2	$FLP1 \leftarrow C(FLP2)_{0-31}$	No	Single
LDR	FLP1,FLP2	$FLP1 \leftarrow C(FLP2)_{0-63}$	No	Double
LPER	FLP1,FLP2	$FLP1 \leftarrow |C(FLP2)|_{0-31}$	Yes	Single
LPDR	FLP1,FLP2	$FLP1 \leftarrow |C(FLP2)|_{0-63}$	Yes	Double
LNER	FLP1,FLP2	$FLP1 \leftarrow -|C(FLP2)|_{0-31}$	Yes	Single
LNDR	FLP1,FLP2	$FLP1 \leftarrow -|C(FLP2)|_{0-63}$	Yes	Double
LTER	FLP1,FLP2	$FLP1 \leftarrow C(FLP2)_{0-31}$	Yes	Single
LTDR	FLP1,FLP2	$FLP1 \leftarrow C(FLP2)_{0-63}$	Yes	Double
LCER	FLP1,FLP2	$FLP1 \leftarrow -C(FLP2)_{0-31}$	Yes	Single
LCDR	FLP1,FLP2	$FLP1 \leftarrow -C(FLP2)_{0-63}$	Yes	Double
STE	FLP1,S2	$S2 \leftarrow C(FLP1)_{0-31}$	No	Single
STD	FLP1,S2	$S2 \leftarrow C(FLP1)_{0-63}$	No	Double

All the load instructions except those noted in Table 12.1 set the condition code according to the value of the contents of the recipient which is FLP1 in each case. Table 12.2 gives the correspondence between the status of the condition code and the value of the recipient.

TABLE 12.2 Schedule D

Value in recipient	Status of code
$= 0$	0
< 0	1
> 0	2

The load instructions cannot set the condition code to three, since no overflow can occur.

Example 12.1 The Single-precision Instructions

a. Load

LE   4,BLUE

Before execution	After execution
	Unchanged ↓
C(Flreg 4) = 41100000 00000000	C(Flreg 4) = 42010000 00000000
C(BLUE) = 42010000	C(BLUE) is unchanged

Bits 32–63 of floating-point register 0 do not participate in single-precision operations.

b. Load Positive Register

LPER   2,4

Before execution   *After execution*

Unchanged
↓

C(Flreg 2) = 41164312 FFFFFFFF   C(Flreg 2) = 42121212 FFFFFFFF
C(Flreg 4) = C2121212 00000000   C(Flreg 4) is unchanged

CONTROL sets the sign bit of Flreg 2 to zero. Then bits 1–31 of Flreg 4 are copied into bit positions 1–31 of Flreg 2. The condition code is set to two.

c. Load Negative Register

LNER   0,2

Before execution   *After execution*

Unchanged
↓

C(Flreg 0) = 40121000 00000000   C(Flreg 0) = C1112121 00000000
C(Flreg 2) = 41112121 FFFFFFFF   C(Flreg 2) is unchanged

CONTROL sets the sign bit of Flreg 0 to one. Then bits 1–31 of Flreg 2 are copied into bit positions 1–31 of Flreg 0. The condition code is set to one.

d. Load Complement Register

LCER   4,6

Before execution   *After execution*

Unchanged
↓

C(Flreg 4) = 41010111 12111111   C(Flreg 4) = 4012111F 12111111
C(Flreg 6) = C012111F FEDFEDFE   C(Flreg 6) is unchanged

The second operand with its sign changed is copied into Flreg 4. The condition code is set to two.

e. Load and Test Register

LTER   4,4

Before execution   *After execution*
C(Flreg 4) = C1212222 13131313   C(Flreg 4) is unchanged

The action of LTER and LER are the same except LTER sets the condition code according to Schedule D in Table 12.2. In this example, we are setting the condition code by testing the value in Flreg 4. What is the value of the condition code after execution of the instruction?

f. Store

STE   4,BLUE

	Before execution	*After execution*

Before execution   *After execution*
C(Flreg 4) = 41123467 FFFFFFFF   C(Flreg 4) is unchanged
C(BLUE) is immaterial   C(BLUE) = 41123467

Bits 32–63 of Flreg 4 are not involved in the action. The status of the condition code is not affected by the execution of the instruction.

g. The content of BLUE is a floating-point number. Write a sequence of load and store operations which will ensure that the value in BLUE is negative.
The solution is:

```
LE     2,BLUE
LNER   2,2
STE    2,BLUE
```

Double-precision. The action of each double-precision load and store instruction is exactly the same as its short form counterpart except for the length of the fraction referenced. We have, therefore, grouped the examples of the long form instructions into one set which is given in Figure 12.2. The initial contents of each storage location and each floating-point register are given in Figure 12.1.

Example 12.2 The Double-precision Instructions

We assume the information given in Figure 12.1.

FIGURE 12.1

C(BLUE) = 43164789 23164719
C(SAM) is immaterial
C(Flreg 0) = 41654321 012489AB
C(Flreg 2) = 43126422 AFFFFFFF
C(Flreg 4) = BC98126B 00000000
C(Flreg 6) = C3461233 53453453

FIGURE 12.2

Reference number	*Instruction*		*Contents after ececution*
①	LD	0,BLUE	C(Flreg 0) = 43164789 23164719
②	LPDR	0,4	C(Flreg 0) = 3C98126B 00000000
③	LNDR	4,2	C(Flreg 4) = C3126422 AFFFFFFF
④	LCDR	0,2	C(Flreg 0) = C3126422 AFFFFFFF
⑤	LTDR	0,6	C(Flreg 0) = C3461233 53453453
⑥	STD	6,SAM	C(SAM) = C3461233 53453453

What is the value of the condition code after the execution of each instruction listed in Figure 12.2?

The condition code is not affected by the execution of 1 and ⑥. The status of the code equals one after execution of ③, ④, and ⑤. After the execution of ②, the condition code equals two.

12.2 Normalized Arithmetic Instructions

A real number may have many representations in floating-point form. For instance, the real number 1 can be represented in System/360 by 41100000_x, 42010000_x, 43001000_x, and by several other hex patterns. (Note that a shift of the fractional part of a floating-point number one hex digit (4 bits) to the right is equivalent to a division of the number by 16. If we increase the exponent by one for each hex digit shift to the right, the value of the real number represented is unchanged.)

The first representation, 41100000, is the normalized floating-point representation of the quantity 1. Since the normalized form is so important in this section, we recall for the convenience of the reader the definition of a normalized number: *The first hex digit of the fractional part of a normalized floating-point number is nonzero.* The second two representations of 1, 42010000 and 43001000, are said to be unnormalized.

Most operands of the arithmetic operations we discuss in this section are, if necessary, normalized before being used in the arithmetic process. Normalization again takes place when an unnormalized intermediate result is put into final form. The former function is called *prenormalization,* and the latter is referred to as *postnormalization.*

There are two more concepts we must consider before we present the arithmetic instructions. The first is *true zero.* A *true zero* is a number with a zero fraction, zero characteristic, and a plus sign. We note that a short form floating-point true zero is indistinguishable from a full-word binary integer zero.

If the fractional part of the sum, difference, product, or quotient of a floating-point arithmetic operation is zero, then CONTROL *forces* a true zero into the recipient. Since all significant digits have been lost, forcing the true zero into the recipient ensures that further computation, which may be meaningless or which may result in serious errors, cannot be continued with this intermediate value.

Although a significance exception has occurred, it may not necessarily lead to a program interrupt. Topic 1 of the Computer Notebook is devoted to floating-point arithmetic exceptions. A detailed explanation is given there of the circumstances which cause the significance exception to lead to a program interrupt. We assume, in all forthcoming examples and algorithms, that no exception of any kind occurs.

All arithmetic operations are performed with the help of special registers which are not available to the programmer. The final result which is copied into the regular floating-point registers has a precision of six hex digits and fourteen hex digits for the short and long forms, respectively. The intermediate results in the special registers, however, have a precision of seven and fifteen hex digits. The extra digit of precision is provided by a *guard digit*.

At the beginning of an arithmetic operation, the guard digit of both operands is zero. If it is necessary to shift the fractional part of an operand to the right, the shift is through the guard position. A shift of one hex digit to the right will move the low order digit into the guard position. A shift of two hex digits to the right will move the low order or "last" digit through the guard position into the bit bucket. The "penultimate" digit will become the new guard digit. Example 12.3 should help clarify our discussion.

Example 12.3

We assume that the contents of the special register and the guard position before the designated shift in examples (a) and (b) are 421644AB [0]

guard digit

a. Right shift one hex digit.

Result: 4201644A [B]

0 into bit bucket

b. Right shift two hex digits.

Result: 42001644 [A]

B into bit bucket

We assume that the contents of the special register and the guard position are as in the result obtained in (b).

c. Left shift one hex digit.

Result: 4201644A [0]

guard digit

Table 12.3 lists the floating-point arithmetic instructions. Schedule D of Table 12.2 gives the status of the condition code with respect to the value in the recipient after execution of those instructions which affect the code. Note that Add and Subtract cannot set the condition code to three. Multiply and Divide do not affect the status of the code.

Addition. The first step in the addition of two floating-point operands is a comparison of their characteristics. If the characteristics are equal, then the fractions are added algebraically without further ado. If the characteristics are unequal, then the fraction of the operand with the smaller characteristics

TABLE 12.3

Mnemonic		Action	Condition code set	Mode
ADD				
AE	FLP1,S2	FLP1 ← C(FLP1) + C(S2)	YES	SINGLE
AER	FLP1,FLP2	FLP1 ← C(FLP1) + C(FLP2)	YES	SINGLE
AD	FLP1,S2	FLP1 ← C(FLP1) + C(S2)	YES	DOUBLE
ADR	FLP1,FLP2	FLP1 ← C(FLP1) + C(FLP2)	YES	DOUBLE
SUBTRACT				
SE	FLP1,S2	FLP1 ← C(FLP1) − C(S2)	YES	SINGLE
SER	FLP1,FLP2	FLP1 ← C(FLP1) − C(FLP2)	YES	SINGLE
SD	FLP1,S2	FLP1 ← C(FLP1) − C(S2)	YES	DOUBLE
SDR	FLP1,FLP2	FLP1 ← C(FLP1) − C(FLP2)	YES	DOUBLE
MULTIPLY				
ME	FLP1,S2	$FLP1_{0-63}$ ← C(FLP1) * C(S2)	NO	SINGLE
MER	FLP1,FLP2	$FLP1_{0-63}$ ← C(FLP1) * C(FLP2)	NO	SINGLE
MD	FLP1,S2	$FLP1_{0-63}$ ← C(FLP1) * C(S2)	NO	DOUBLE
MDR	FLP1,FLP2	$FLP1_{0-63}$ ← C(FLP1) * C(FLP2)	NO	DOUBLE
DIVIDE				
DE	FLP1,S2	FLP1 ← C(FLP1) / C(S2)	NO	SINGLE
DER	FLP1,FLP2	FLP1 ← C(FLP1) / C(FLP2)	NO	SINGLE
DD	FLP1,S2	FLP1 ← C(FLP1) / C(S2)	NO	DOUBLE
DDR	FLP1,FLP2	FLP1 ← C(FLP1) / C(FLP2)	NO	DOUBLE

Note: The recipient, FLP1, in single-precision multiply instructions, ME and MER, is 64 bits long.

is shifted to the right. For each hex digit shift to the right, the characteristic is increased by one. This alignment step will continue until the characteristics agree; then the fractions are added algebraically.

The intermediate sum will be shifted one hex digit to the right if an overflow carry occurs. The characteristic will be increased by one to compensate for this shift. No postnormalization is needed in this case. The first hex digit of the normalized sum will be one.

If no overflow carry occurs, then CONTROL must make a normalization test since an unnormalized intermediate sum must be normalized. Postnormalization, if necessary, is accomplished by shifting the fraction of the intermediate sum to the left a sufficient number of hex digits so that the first digit in the fraction is nonzero. The characteristic is decreased by one for each hex digit shift to the left. The normalized sum is then copied into the recipient.

CONTROL might follow the Addition Algorithm below in the process of adding two floating-point numbers. This algorithm and the examples which follow should clarify most of our previous discussion. We note, however, that our explanation is general. The Addition Algorithm assumes that no exceptions will occur. However, Topic 1 of the Computer Notebook discusses all floating-point exceptions in some detail. The algorithm given there takes into account the possibility of the occurrence of exceptions.

The Addition Algorithm

Step 1: If both operands have equal characteristics, go to step 5.

Step 2: Shift the fraction of the operand with the smaller characteristic one hex digit to the right.

Step 3: Add one to the characteristic of the operand whose fraction was shifted.

Step 4: Go to step 1.

Step 5: Add the fractions algebraically.

Step 6: If the sum overflowed, go to step 11.

Step 7: If the sum is normalized, go to step 13.

Step 8: Shift the fraction of the sum one hex digit to the left.

Step 9: Subtract one from the characteristic of the sum.

Step 10: Go to step 7.

Step 11: Shift the fraction of the sum (including overflow) one hex digit to the right.

Step 12: Add one to the characteristic of the sum.

Step 13: Copy the sum into the recipient.

Step 14: Stop.

Example 12.4

The steps in the solution of the problems in this example refer to the steps in the Addition Algorithm.

a. Add 411267AB and 41371ABC.

The solution is:

Step 1: The characteristics agree.

Step 5: Add the fractions algebraically.

```
41   1267AB  [0]
41   371ABC  [0]  ──→ guard digits
─────────────────
41   498267  [0]
```

Step 6: The sum did not overflow.

Step 7: The sum is normalized.

Step 13: Copy 41498267 into the recipient.

b. Add 40ABC123 and 40712345.

Step 1: The characteristics agree.

Step 5: Add the fractions algebraically.

overflow
$$\begin{array}{l} 40 \quad \text{ABC123} \ [0] \\ 40 \quad 712345 \ [0] \\ \hline 40 \quad ①\text{CE468} \ [0] \end{array}$$

Step 6: The sum overflowed.

Step 11: Shift the fraction of the sum one hex digit to the right.

40 11CE46 [8]

0

↘

Step 12: Add one to the characteristic of the sum.

41 11CE46 [8]

Step 13: Copy 4111CE46 into the recipient.

c. Add C10B1234 and 40126432.

Step 1: The characteristics do not agree.

Step 2: Shift the fraction of operand 2 one hex digit to the right.

40 012643 [2]

0

↘

Step 3: Add one to the characteristic of the second operand.

41 012643 [2]

Step 1: The characteristics agree.

Step 5: Add the fraction algebraically.

$$\begin{array}{l} \text{C1} \quad \text{0B1234} \ [0] \\ 41 \quad 012643 \ [2] \\ \hline \text{C1} \quad \text{09EBF0} \ [E] \end{array}$$

Since the signs differ, the fraction with the smaller magnitude is subtracted from the fraction of the other operand. The sign of the operand with the larger magnitude is attached to the "sum." Notice that the guard digits participate in this arithmetic process.

Step 6: The sum did not overflow.

Step 7: The sum is unnormalized.

Step 8: Shift the fraction of the sum one hex digit to the left.

C1 9EBF0E [0] ← supplied by
CONTROL

Step 9: Subtract one from the characteristic of the sum.

C0 9EBF0E [0]

Step 7: The sum is normalized.

Step 13: Copy C09EBF0E into the recipient.

Example 12.5

Consider the following sequence of instructions:

        AER   0,2
        AE   4,SAM
        ADR   2,6
        AD   6,SAM

Before execution   *After execution*
C(Flreg 0) = 41124367 01010101   C(Flreg 0) = 40820209 01010101
C(Flreg 2) = C0A23467 FFFFFFFF   C(Flreg 2) = C0A22053 AAAAAAA9
C(Flreg 4) = C2436718 12345612   C(Flreg 4) = C24366F5 12345612
C(Flreg 6) = 3F014145 55555555   C(Flreg 6) = 3E364850 50504F50
C(SAM)   = 40002233 FAFAFAFA   C(SAM) is unchanged

Not rounded

We suggest that the reader check his understanding of the floating-point addition operation by verifying the results listed in the *after execution* column.

Subtraction.   The normalized subtract operation is exactly the same as the normalized add operation, except subtract inverts the sign of the second operand, the subtrahend. In other words, subtract inverts the sign of the subtrahend and then follows the normalized add procedure.

Let step 0 be "Invert the sign of the subtrahend." If we now attach this step to the addition algorithm so that it is the first step in that procedure, then we have a feasible subtraction algorithm. We dispense with examples of the subtraction instruction since it and the addition instruction follow such similar procedures. We suggest, however, that the student test our assertions on the computer. Work out some examples by hand, using the subtraction algorithm we have developed as a guide. Let the computer verify the results.

Multiplication.   The short form intermediate product has 14 hex digits. Since both operands, the multiplier and the multiplicand, have only 6 hex digits in their fractions, their product will be only 12 hex digits long. Hence the two low order hex digits in the fraction of the intermediate product will be set to zero. All 14 digits participate in the left shift if postnormalization is necessary.

The long form intermediate product is truncated from 28 hex digits to 15. Only these 15 digits participate in the postnormalization. If a left shift of one or more hex digits is required in the postnormalization, then hex zeros will enter the guard position which held the low order digit of the truncated product.

The Multiplication Algorithm below will find the product of two floating-point operands. We note, however, that this algorithm does not consider any of the floating-point operation exceptions that can occur. These, as in the case of addition and subtraction, are covered in Topic 1 of the Computer Notebook.

A true zero will be placed into the recipient if the fraction of the product of two floating-point operands is zero. No significance exception will occur. Since this is different from the addition case, we have included a check for a zero fraction in the algorithm.

Part of the process of multiplying two floating-point numbers is finding the characteristic of the product. This is equal to the sum of the true exponents of the multiplier and the multiplicand plus the bias value of 64_{10}. In step 4 of the algorithm, we find the sum of the two characteristics. This sum, however, includes the bias value of both factors and is, therefore, 64_{10} too large. In step 5, we rectify this. The adjusted quantity, consisting of the sum of the true exponents of both operands and a bias value of 64_{10}, is the correct characteristic for the product.

Finally, we issue two reminders. First, multiplication does not affect the status of the condition code. Second, the fraction of the product, even in single-precision, is 56 bits long. Hence, all 64 bits of the floating-point register which is the first operand in the instruction will be changed when the final product is copied into the recipient.

The Multiplication Algorithm

Step 1 : Prenormalize the operands if necessary.
Step 2 : Multiply the fraction of the multiplicand by the fraction of the multiplier.
Step 3 : If the fraction of the intermediate product equals zero, go to step 11.
Step 4 : Add the characteristics of the multiplicand and the multiplier.
Step 5 : Subtract 64_{10} from the sum of the characteristics.
Step 6 : Find the algebraic sign of the product.
Step 7 : If the product is normalized, go to step 13.
Step 8 : Shift the fraction of the product one hex digit to the left.
Step 9 : Subtract one from the characteristic of the product.
Step 10 : Go to step 13.
Step 11 : Set recipient to a true zero.
Step 12 : Go to step 14.
Step 13 : Copy product into recipient.
Step 14 : Stop.

Example 12.6

The steps in the solutions to the problems in this example refer to the steps in the Multiplication Algorithm. The hex point is analogous to the decimal point.

a. Multiply 41900000 and 42020000

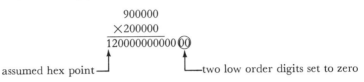

assumed hex point

Step 1: Operand 1 is already normalized. The second operand after pre-normalization is 41200000.

Step 2: Multiply fractions.

$$\begin{array}{r} 900000 \\ \times 200000 \\ \hline 120000000000\,\text{00} \end{array}$$

assumed hex point ——————— ⎿— two low order digits set to zero

Step 3: The fraction is nonzero.

Step 4: The sum of the characteristics is 82 (41 + 41 = 82).

Step 5: The characteristic of the product is 42 (82 − 40 = 42).

Step 6: The sign of the product is plus.

Step 7: The product is normalized: 42120000 00000000.

Step 13: 42120000 00000000 is copied into the recipient.

b. Multiply 42111111 11111111 by C3222222 00000000

⎿—assumed hex point—⎤

Step 1: No prenormalization is necessary.

Step 2: The product truncated to 15 hex digits is

02468ACC CCCCCCCC [C]

assumed hex point —⎤   ⎿—guard digit

Step 3: The fraction is nonzero.

Step 4: The sum of the characteristics is 85 (42 + 43 = 85).

Step 5: The characteristic of the product is 45 (85 − 40 = 45).

Step 6: The sign of the product is negative.

Step 7: The product is unnormalized.

C502468A CCCCCCCC [C]

Step 8: Shift the fraction of the product one hex digit to the left.

C52468AC CCCCCCCC [0]

Step 9: Subtract one from the characteristic of the product.

C42468AC CCCCCCCC [0]

Step 7: The product is normalized.

Step 13: C42468AC CCCCCCCC is copied into the recipient.

Where did the leading zero come from in step 2? If the student is unsure, we suggest he consider the product of $.11_{10}$ and $.22_{10}$, which is $.0242_{10}$.

Example 12.7

Consider the following sequence of instructions.

```
MER    0,2
ME     4,SAM
MDR    2,6
MD     6,SAM
```

Before execution	*After execution*
C(Flreg 0) = 4 1 2 0 0 0 0 0 00000000	C(Flreg 0) = C2 1 5 5 5 5 5 40000000
C(Flreg 2) = C1AAAAAA 00000000	C(Flreg 2) = C16AAAAA 40000000
C(Flreg 4) = C3 0 0 A 0 0 0 00000000	C(Flreg 4) = C1 6 4 0 0 0 0 00000000
C(Flreg 6) = 4 0 A 0 0 0 0 0 00000000	C(Flreg 6) = 4 0 6 4 0 0 0 0 00000000
C(SAM) = 4 1 0 A 0 0 0 0 00000000	C(SAM) is unchanged

We suggest that the student verify the results of Example 12.7 by hand, using the Multiplication Algorithm. The results might be verified again by running a computer program.

Division.   The first operand in the floating-point division instruction is divided by the second operand. The quotient replaces the first operand. Only 24 bits (6 hex digits) participate in the short form division, whereas 56 bits (14 hex digits) participate in the long form. No guard digits are used since the prenormalization insures that postnormalization will not be required.

Although postnormalization is not required, it may be necessary to have a right shift of the fractional part of the intermediate quotient. This right shift is necessary only if the fraction of the divisor is less than the fraction of the dividend. We will explain why this right shift is necessary.

Consider the division of A by B, where A and B are written in scientific notation. Let $A = .50 \times 10^4$. Let $B = .2 \times 10^2$. (Although these numerals are not in scientific notation standard form, they both are expressed in a form analogous to the normal form of a floating-point number.)

The division process which involves operands written in scientific notation consists of a division of the mantissas and a subtraction of the exponents. Thus:

$$.50 \div .2 = 2.5$$
$$4 - 2 = 2$$

The result is 2.5×10^2.

If we want to express the mantissa of the quotient as a decimal fraction—which was the original form of our operands A and B—we must shift the digits one decimal place to the left. Our shifted result is $.25 \times 10^3$. (The exponent was increased by one so that the numeral would still express the same quotient.) We will refer to this phenomenon as quotient overflow.

Step 3 of the division algorithm is a subtraction of the characteristic of the divisor from the characteristic of the dividend. The difference we obtain is the true exponent of the quotient. The sum of 64_{10}, the bias value, and this true exponent is the characteristic of the quotient. Hence, in step 4, we add 64_{10} to the true exponent.

Again we remind the reader that our algorithm does not take into account any exceptions that may occur. We leave these considerations to Topic 1 of the Computer Notebook. Remember, too, that division does not affect the status of the condition code.

The Division Algorithm

Step 1: Prenormalize both operands if necessary.

Step 2: Divide the fraction of the dividend by the fraction of the divisor.

Step 3: Subtract the characteristic of the divisor from the characteristic of the dividend.

Step 4: Add 64_{10}, the bias value, to the difference between the characteristics.

Step 5: Determine the sign of the quotient.

Step 6: If the intermediate quotient did not overflow, go to step 9; otherwise, proceed in the normal sequence.

Step 7: Shift the intermediate quotient one hex digit to the right.

Step 8: Add one to the characteristic of the quotient.

Step 9: Copy the quotient into the recipient.

Step 10: Stop.

Example 12.8

a. Divide 42600000 by 41025000.

Step 1: 42600000 is normalized. The divisor, after normalization, is 40250000.

Step 2: The fraction of the intermediate quotient is 2,983759.

└─assumed hex point

Step 3: The difference between the characteristics is 2 (42 − 40 = 2).

Step 4: The characteristic of the intermediate quotient is 42 (2 + 40 = 42).

Step 5: The sign of the quotient is plus.

Step 6: The intermediate quotient overflowed.

Step 7: Shift the fraction of the quotient one hex digit to the right.

42298375 [9]←guard digit

└─hex point

Step 8:   Add one to the characteristic of the quotient: 43298375 [9].

└─guard
digit

Step 9:   Copy 43298375 into the recipient.

b. Divide 44055000 by 40006000.

Step 1:   The dividend, after normalization, is 43550000. The divisor, after normalization, is 3E600000.
Step 2:   The fraction of the intermediate quotient is E2AAAA.

└─assumed hex point

Step 3:   The difference between the characteristics is 5 (43 − 3E = 5).
Step 4:   The characteristic of the intermediate quotient is 45 (5 + 40 = 45).
Step 5:   The sign of the quotient is plus.
Step 6:   The intermediate quotient did not overflow.
Step 9:   Copy 45E2AAAA into the recipient.

Example 12.9

Consider the following sequence of instructions:

```
DER   0,2
DE    4,SAM
DDR   2.6
DD    6,SAM
```

Before execution
C(Flreg 0) = 41200000 00000000
C(Flreg 2) = C1A00000 00000000
C(Flreg 4) = C3005000 00000000
C(Flreg 6) = 40500000 00000000
C(SAM)   = 410A0000 00000000

After execution
C(Flreg 0) = C0333333 00000000
C(Flreg 2) = C2200000 00000000
C(Flreg 4) = C1800000 00000000
C(Flreg 6) = 40800000 00000000
C(SAM) is unchanged

Again we urge the reader to verify the results listed in the *after execution* column.

12.3   Conversion of Data

In Chapter 9 we studied several instructions which readily converted data from one form to another. The programmer must remember a few rules about alignment and implied length, but otherwise the instructions are quite easy to use. Conversion to floating-point, however, is another matter. There is no single instruction which will do the job. If the programmer wants to convert a binary integer into a floating-point number, he must write a short program segment. The conversion from floating-point to binary integer is equally demanding.

We present two program segments in this section which convert data to floating-point. One routine converts a packed decimal integer, the other converts a decimal fraction. We discuss the integer to floating-point conversion first. We will refer to the integer as X.

To simplify matters, we make the following assumptions:

1. X is in a double-word location.
2. X is less than or equal to $2^{31} - 1$ (2,147,483,647).

The first Conversion Algorithm, which gives the logic of our program segment, is not generalized. In order to make it easier to follow our procedure, we specified the registers that will be used in the routine.

Conversion Algorithm: Integer to Floating-point

Step 0: Convert packed decimal X to binary. (Binary X is in register 11.)

Step 1: If binary X equals zero, go to step 16.

Step 2: Load bias value (64_{10}) into the exponent counter register [C(Reg 10) = 00000040].

Step 3: Load binary X into register 3.

Step 4: Isolate sign of binary X (*and* register 3 with X'80000000').

Step 5: Set register 5 to zero.

Step 6: Load absolute value of binary X into register 4.

Step 7: Add 1 to the exponent counter register.

Step 8: Shift registers 4 and 5 right double logical one hex digit.

Step 9: If value in register 4 equals zero, go to step 11.

Step 10: Go to step 7.

Step 11: Add value in exponent counter register to register 4.

Step 12: Shift registers 4 and 5 left double logical six hex digits.

Step 13: ØR sign of X into bit position zero of register 4 (ØR 4,3).

Step 14: Store registers 4 and 5 into FLØAT and FLØAT+4, respectively.

Step 15: Go to step 17.

Step 16: Move a true zero to FLOAT.

Step 17: Stop.

The right shift (Step 8) determines the true exponent. Each right shift of 4 binary digits (1 hex digit) is equivalent to a division by 16. If it takes six hex digit shifts to "zero out" the contents of register 4, then the true exponent of X with respect to a base 16 floating-point number is 6.

Example 12.10

Convert -123 to floating-point.

The solution is:

Step 0: C(Reg 11) = FFFFFF85.
Step 1: Binary X is not zero.
Step 2: C(Reg 10) = 00000040.
Step 3: C(Reg 3) = FFFFFF85.
Step 4: C(Reg 3) = 80000000. (The sign has been isolated.)
Step 5: C(Reg 5) = 00000000.
Step 6: C(Reg 4) = 0000007B.
Step 7: C(Reg 10) = 00000041.
Step 8: C(Reg 4) = 00000007, C(Reg 5) = B0000000.
Step 9: The value of register 4 is not zero.
Step 7: C(Reg 10) = 00000042.
Step 8: C(Reg 4) = 00000000, C(Reg 5) = 7B000000.
Step 9: C(Reg 4) = 00000000.
Step 11: C(Reg 4) = 00000042.
Step 12: C(Reg 4) = 427B0000, C(Reg 5) = 00000000.
Step 13: C(Reg 4) = C27B0000.
Step 14: C(FLOAT) = C27B000000000000.

Figure 12.3 is a program segment which implements the ideas expressed in the integer-to-floating-point algorithm.

The Conversion Algorithm: Decimal Fraction to Floating-point is quite similar to our first algorithm in this section.

The program segment in Figure 12.4 which converts a decimal fraction to a floating-point number is quite similar to our first program. The important difference is the final division by 10^6. The rationale behind this step is the fact that we do not convert a decimal fraction to floating-point. Instead, we convert a six digit decimal integer.

FIGURE 12.3 The Integer to Floating-point Conversion

```
        CVB   11,X              CONVERT X TO BINARY
        C     11,=F'0'          IF X = 0, MOVE TRUE ZERO TO FLOAT
        BE    ZERO              IF X IS NOT 0, RNI FROM P + 1
        L     10,=F'64'         LOAD BIAS VALUE INTO REGISTER 10
        LR    3,11              GET READY TO ISOLATE SIGN OF X
        N     3,ISOLATE         C(ISOLATE) = 80000000
        SR    5,5               REGISTER 5 WILL HOLD MANTISSA
        LPR   4,11              ABSOLUTE VALUE OF X GOES TO REGISTER 4
LOOP1   A     10,=F'1'          X IS NOT ZERO, SO ADD 1 TO CHARACTERISTIC
        SRDL  4,4
        C     4,=F'0'           HAVE ALL HEX DIGITS BEEN SHIFTED
        BE    DONE              IF C(REG 4) = 0, WE ARE DONE
        B     LOOP1             IF C(REG 4) NOT 0, RNI FROM LOOP1
DONE    LR    4,10              LOAD CHARACTERISTIC INTO REGISTER 4
        SLDL  4,24              SHIFT FLOATING-POINT X INTO POSITION
        OR    4,3               OR SIGN OF X INTO SIGN BIT
        STM   4,5,FLOAT         STORE FLOATING-POINT X INTO FLOAT
        B     MOVE              SKIP NEXT INSTRUCTION
ZERO    MVC   FLOAT(8),=8X'00'  MOVE TRUE ZERO TO FLOAT
MOVE    LD    0,FLOAT           LOAD FLOATING-POINT X INTO FL-REGISTER 0
```

For example, assume that location DECFRAC contains .9 where the decimal point is, of course, assumed. We take the value to be the integer 9. Then we multiply it by a sufficiently large enough power of 10 so that we have a six-digit decimal integer. In this particular case, we would multiply 9 by 100,000. Hence, our routine would convert 900,000 to floating-point. The converted number is too large by a factor of 10^6, so we divide by that amount. This division, incidentally, not only scales the number to its proper value but also changes it to a hex fraction. (Note how different the hex digits are that represent 900,000 and .900000: $900000_{10} = DBBA0_x$, $.900000_{10} = .E66666_x$.) We choose to work with a six-digit decimal integer since a six-digit decimal integer always converts to a five-digit hex integer. ($100,000_{10} = 186A0_x$ and $999,999_{10} = F423F_x$.) Hence the true exponent of our augmented DECFRAC is five and the number of left shifts needed to normalize is three. Hence our routine does not need to determine these values.

Our algorithm and program segment make the following assumptions:

1. The value of DECFRAC is nonzero.
2. The first digit after the assumed decimal point is also nonzero.
3. The absolute value of DECFRAC is less than 10^6.

Conversion Algorithm: Decimal Fraction to Floating-point

Step 0: Convert DECFRAC to binary.

Step 1: If the absolute value of DECFRAC is greater than or equal to 10^5, go to step 4.

Step 2: Multiply DECFRAC by ten.

Step 3: Go to step 1.

Step 4: Load DECFRAC into register 4.

Step 5: Isolate sign of DECFRAC.

Step 6: Shift sign of DECFRAC to bit position 24 of register 4.

Step 7: Add the bias value plus the true exponent, five, to register 4.

Step 8: Load the absolute value of DECFRAC into register 5.

Step 9: Shift DECFRAC three hex digits to the left.

Step 10: Shift floating-point DECFRAC 24 bits to the left. (Shift the concatenation of registers 4 and 5 to the left.)

Step 11: Store floating-point DECFRAC into FLOAT. (Store Multiple registers 4 and 5.)

Step 12: Load (double-precision) FLOAT into floating-point register 2.

Step 13: Divide floating-point register 2 by 10^6.

Step 14: Add Flreg 2 to Flreg 0.

Step 15: Stop.

The program segment in Figure 12.4 implements the decimal-fraction-to floating-point algorithm.

FIGURE 12.4

```
NEXT    CVB   11,DECFRAC
        LR    4,11
        LPR   11,11
LOOP    C     11, = F'100000'    SIX DIGITS LONG?
        BNL   START              IF SO, BRANCH
        M     10, = F'10'        MULTIPLY BY 10
        B     LOOP               TEST AGAIN
START   N     4,ISOLATE          C(ISOLATE) = X'80000000'
        SRL   4,24               PUT SIGN IN PROPER SPOT
        A     4, = F'69'         ADD BIAS VALUE + EXPONENT
        LPR   5,11               |DECFRAC| → REG 5
        SLL   5,12               NORMALIZE
        SLDL  4,24               READY TO STORE
        STM   4,5,FLOAT          STORE
        LD    2,FLOAT            LOAD
        DD    2, = D'1.0E+6'     DIVIDE TO SCALE
        ADR   0,2                ADD TO INTEGER PART
```

12.4 Some Miscellaneous Instructions

In this section we discuss three rather unrelated sets of floating-point instructions: Compare, Halve, and the unnormalized arithmetic operations. Our first topic is Compare.

Compare. Table 12.4 lists the four floating-point Compare instructions. Schedule E in Figure 12.5 gives the status of the condition code for each of the three possible relationships which may exist between the compared operands. The comparison is algebraic, which takes into account the sign, the characteristic, and the magnitude of the fraction of each number.

TABLE 12.4 The Floating-point Compare Instructions

Mnemonic		Mode	Condition code
COMPARE			See
CE	FLP1,S2	SINGLE	Schedule
CD	FLP1,S2	DOUBLE	E
COMPARE REGISTER			
CER	FLP1,FLP2	SINGLE	
CDR	FLP1,FLP2	DOUBLE	

CONTROL might follow the Compare Algorithm to determine the relationship between two floating-point operands. The work of the algorithm is done in special registers so that the actual operands are not changed by the comparison techniques. The algorithm follows, to a large extent, the rules for normalized floating-point subtraction.

Since the operands are not prenormalized, it is possible to set the condition code to zero, even though the compared operands are unequal. Because of this incongruity, we suggest that the programmer take considerable care when using floating-point comparisons. We note two additional facts: (1) Compare cannot set the condition code to three, and (2) the guard digits of both operands participate in the comparison.

FIGURE 12.5 Schedule E

Comparison result	Condition code
op1 = op2	0
op1 < op2	1
op1 > op2	2

The Compare Algorithm

Step 0: Invert the sign of the second operand.
Step 1: If the characteristics of the operands are equal, go to step 5.
Step 2: Shift the fraction of the operand with the smaller characteristic one hex digit to the right.
Step 3: Add one to the characteristic of the operand whose fraction was shifted.
Step 4: Go to step 1.
Step 5: Add the fractions algebraically.
Step 6: If the fraction of the sum is zero, go to step 12.
Step 7: If the sign of the sum is positive, go to step 10.
Step 8: Set the condition code to one.
Step 9: Go to step 13.
Step 10: Set the condition code to two.
Step 11: Go to step 13.
Step 12: Set the condition code to zero.
Step 13: Stop.

The student should verify that the algorithm does indeed set the condition code to 0,1,2 whenever op1 = op2, op1 < op2, and op1 > op2, respectively.

Example 12.11

a. Compare 42164322 and C3046743.
The solution is:

Step 0: Invert the sign of the second operand.

43046743

Step 1: The characteristics are unequal.
Step 2: Shift the fraction of the operand with the smaller characteristic one hex digit to the right.

42016432 [2]
          0
           ↘

Step 3: Add one to the characteristic of the operand whose fraction was shifted.

43016432 [2]

Step 1: The characteristics are equal.
Step 5: Add the fractions algebraically.

43   016432   [2]
43   046743   [0]
───────────────
43   05CB75   [?]

Step 6: The fraction is not zero.

Step 7: The sign is plus.

Step 10: Set the condition code to two.

b. Compare C3001000 and C1100002.

The solution is:

Step 0: Invert the sign of the second operand.

41100002 [0]

Step 1: The characteristics do not agree.

Step 2: Shift the fraction of the operand with the smaller characteristic one hex digit to the right.

41010000 [2]

$$0 \searrow$$

Step 3: Add one to the smaller characteristic.

42010000 [2]

Step 1: The characteristics do not agree.

Step 2: Shift the fraction of the operand with the smaller characteristic one hex digit to the right.

42001000 [0]

$$2 \searrow$$

Step 3: Add one to the smaller characteristic.

43001000 [0]   .

Step 1: The characteristics agree.

Step 5: Add the fractions algebraically.

C3001000 [0]
43001000 [0]
00000000 [0]   true zero

Step 6: The fraction is zero.

Step 12: Set the condition code to zero.

Note: The condition code is set to zero even though the operands are unequal. See comments in the second paragraph which follows Table 12.4.

Example 12.12

Assume that the contents of the floating-point registers and location SAM are as follows:

C(Flreg 0) = 41001000 FA0FA000
C(Flreg 2) = C1121212 12121212
C(Flreg 4) = 43124641 F1F1F1F1
C(Flreg 6) = 43124641 00000000
C(SAM)   = 391000FA 46723400

What is the setting of the condition code after execution of each of the following instructions?

   ① CER   4,6
   ② CE   0,SAM
   ③ CDR   4,6
   ④ CD   2,SAM

The solutions are:

   ① Sets the code to zero.
   ② Sets the code to one.
   ③ Sets the code to two.
   ④ Sets the code to one.

We suggest that the student use the Compare Algorithm to verify our results. Recall that the guard digit plays a role in the comparison.

Halve. The Halve operation, which is nothing more than a division by two, is in both the single- and double-precision instruction sets. Halve uses two register operands. The second operand is divided by two and the normalized quotient is copied into the first operand location. The second operand remains unchanged.

The division is accomplished by shifting the fraction of the second operand one bit to the right. (This is done in a special register.) The low order bit enters the high order bit position of the guard digit. This intermediate quotient is normalized, if necessary, before being copied into the first operand location. The guard digit participates in this postnormalization step.

The general form of the single-precision instruction is:

   HER   FLP1,FLP2

The action of this instruction is:

   $FLP1 \leftarrow C(FLP2) / 2$

Note that only the first 32 bits of FLP2 and FLP1 participate in the action of the instruction.

Example 12.13

a. HER 0,2

    Before execution   *After execution*
    C(Flreg 0) = 40001212 FFFFFFFF   C(Flreg 0) = 41432A19 FFFFFFFF
    C(Flreg 2) = 41865432 AAAAAAAA   C(Flreg 2) is unchanged

b. HER 0,4

    Before execution   *After execution*
    C(Flreg 0) = 40432A19 FFFFFFFF   C(Flreg 0) = 389230B8 FFFFFFFF
    C(Flreg 4) = 39124017 00000000   C(Flreg 4) is unchanged

Do the results seem strange? We suggest that the reader follow the procedure outlined in the discussion which preceded the example. Remember our arithmetic is in base 16.

The general form of the double-precision Halve instruction is:

HDR   FLP1,FLP2

The action is:

FLP1 ← C(FLP2) / 2

Note that all 64 bits of both FLP1 and FLP2 participate in the action of the instruction.

Example 12.14

HDR   4,6

Before execution
C(Flreg 4) is immaterial
C(Flreg 6) = 40234567 89ABCDEF

After execution
C(Flreg 4) = 4011A2B3 C4D5E6F7
C(Flreg 6) is unchanged

Unnormalized Arithmetic Instructions. The eight unnormalized arithmetic operations in the System/360 floating-point instruction set perform addition and subtraction as depicted in the algorithms of the previous sections. The results of the operations are, however, not normalized. When the sum or difference has been determined, it is copied into the recipient without a check for normalization. If a carry occurs in the high order digit position, the fraction will be shifted to accommodate the overflow. A test is also made to determine if the fraction of the intermediate result equals zero. If it does, a true zero will be forced into the recipient.

The importance of these unnormalized instructions is that they allow us to extend the range of floating-point numbers as their values approach zero. The smallest value which can be expressed by a normalized floating-point number in the interval between 0 and 1 is 16^{-65}, or approximately 5.4×10^{-79}. The smallest value which can be expressed in unnormalized single-precision is 16^{-70}, whereas the minimum value which can be expressed in double-precision is 16^{-78}. The fraction of the short form's minimum value consists of 23 leading zeros followed by a 1. That of its long form counterpart has 55 leading binary zeros followed by a 1.

Table 12.5 lists the unnormalized arithmetic instructions. We present these instructions for completeness, since a detailed discussion of them is not within the scope of this text. (Note that there are no multiplication or division instructions.) We suggest that interested readers refer to the manual *IBM System/360 Principles of Operation, Form A22-6821.*

TABLE 12.5   Unnormalized Arithmetic Instructions

Mnemonic		Action	Mode	Condition code set
ADDITION				
AUR	FLP1,FLP2	FLP1 ← C(FLP1) + C(FLP2)	SINGLE	YES
AU	FLP1,S2	FLP1 ← C(FLP1) + C(S2)	SINGLE	YES
AWR	FLP1,FLP2	FLP1 ← C(FLP1) + C(FLP2)	DOUBLE	YES
AW	FLP1,S2	FLP1 ← C(FLP1) + C(S2)	DOUBLE	YES
SUBTRACTION				
SUR	FLP1,FLP2	FLP1 ← C(FLP1) − C(FLP2)	SINGLE	YES
SU	FLP1,S2	FLP1 ← C(FLP1) − C(S2)	SINGLE	YES
SWR	FLP1,FLP2	FLP1 ← C(FLP1) − C(FLP2)	DOUBLE	YES
SW	FLP1,S2	FLP1 ← C(FLP1) − C(S2)	DOUBLE	YES

Answers to the Floating-point Quiz

1. The first hex digit of the fractional part of a normalized floating-point number is nonzero.
2. Every floating-point number has a sign, a characteristic, and a fractional part.
3. The sign occupies bit position zero; the characteristic occupies bit positions 1–7. The fractional part of a single-precision number is 24 bits, and the fraction of the long form is 56 bits long. They occupy bit positions 8–31 and 8–63, respectively.
4. The bias value of a BAL floating-point exponent is $64_{10} = 40_x$.
5. SAM DC E'3.14' is one way it could be defined.
6. BLUE DC D'14.76' is perhaps the simplest definition.
7. The radix of a BAL floating-point constant (or the base of the exponent) is 16_{10}.
8. Statement (a) is correct.
9. 41110000 is equivalent to 17/16.
10. There are four floating-point registers. Their addresses are 0, 2, 4, 6.

Computer Notebook

TOPIC 1   Floating-point Exceptions

There are four exceptions which are peculiar to floating-point arithmetic. All of them—significance, exponent underflow, exponent overflow, and floating-point divide—can lead to a program interrupt. An interrupt is always taken for the overflow and divide exceptions. The status of the significance bit and the exponent underflow bit in the program mask determines if their associated exceptions will lead to an interrupt. (See Topic 2 of the Computer Notebook in Chapter 8 for a discussion of interrupts.)

The set of bits 36, 37, 38, and 39 of the program status word is called the program mask. Bit 36 is associated with fixed-point arithmetic overflow, bit 37 with packed decimal overflow, and bits 38 and 39 with the exponent underflow and significance exceptions, respectively. If any one of these four exceptions occurs and its associated bit in the program mask is *on,* then a program interrupt will be taken. If the bit is *off,* the exception will be ignored by the interrupt hardware. For instance, if bit position 38 equals 1 and bit position 39 equals 0, then an exponent underflow will cause an interrupt whereas the significance exception will not.

Although a full discussion of the program mask appears in Chapter 17, we note here that the program mask and the condition code are the only bits in the PSW that can be changed by the user. One of the exercises at the end of this chapter involves the setting of the program mask. We suggest that interested readers "do" this problem. We now discuss each of the floating-point exceptions individually.

Exponent Overflow—Completion Code: OCC. An exponent overflow exception occurs when the characteristic of the result of any addition, subtraction, multiplication, or division operation is greater than 127. The operation will be completed before the program interrupt takes place. The result, which will be normalized, will be correct with respect to the sign and the fraction. The characteristic, however, will be 128 smaller than the correct characteristic.

Exponent Underflow—Completion Code: OCD. An exponent underflow exception exists when the characteristic of the result of any arithmetic instruction (including halving) is less than zero. A program interrupt will occur if bit 38 of the PSW is 1. Before this interrupt occurs, however, the operation will be completed. The sign and the fraction of the normalized result will be correct. The characteristic, however, will be 128 too large.

If the exponent underflow bit of the program mask (that is bit 38 of the PSW register) is not on, that is, it is equal to zero, then no interrupt will take place. A true zero, however, will be forced into the recipient. The condition code will be set to zero to reflect this fact when the operation was subtraction or addition. Recall that multiplication and division do not set the code.

Significance—Completion Code: OCE. A program interrupt will not be taken if a significance exception exists because of a division or multiplication operation. In other words, if the fraction of a quotient or of a product is zero, no program interrupt will occur. The significance exception will result in a true zero being forced into the recipient. An interrupt will most likely occur, however, if the true zero in the recipient is used as an operand in a subsequent floating-point instruction.

A program interrupt will occur if the significance exception exists because of an addition or subtraction operation and if the significance bit of the program mask (bit 39 of the PSW register) is turned on. The operation is completed, but the characteristic is not set to zero.

If the significance bit of the program mask is turned off, and if the fraction of a sum or of a difference is zero, then no program interrupt will occur. A true zero will be forced into the recipient.

Floating-point Divide—Completion Code: OCF.   A floating-point divide exception occurs when an attempt is made to divide by a number with a zero fraction. The operation is suppressed. All data remains unchanged. A program interrupt will be taken.

Many of the exceptions that lead to program interrupts which were discussed in Topic 2 of the Computer Notebook in Chapter 8 can occur when an attempt is made to execute floating-point instructions. These exceptions and interrupts are, however, common to many types of instructions. Many of the comments made in Topic 2 are pertinent here. We suggest that the reader review that section to determine which of the exceptions listed there apply to floating-point instructions.

The Multiplication Algorithm presented below takes into consideration the exceptions which are peculiar to floating-point instructions. All other exceptions are ignored. Note that the algorithm ignores the exponent underflow which might occur when the factors of a multiplication operation are normalized.

Multiplication Algorithm #2

Step 0: Prenormalize both operands, if necessary.

Step 1: Multiply the fraction of the multiplicand by the fraction of the multiplier.

Step 2: If the fraction of the intermediate product equals zero, go to step 14.

Step 3: Find the algebraic sign of the product.

Step 4: Add the characteristics of the multiplicand and the multiplier.

Step 5: Subtract 64_{10} from the sum of the characteristics.

Step 6: If the characteristic of the product is now less than zero, go to step 16.

Step 7: If the fraction is normalized, go to step 11.

Step 8: Shift the fraction of the intermediate product one hex digit to the left.

Step 9: Subtract one from the characteristic of the intermediate product.

Step 10: Go to step 6.

Step 11: If the characteristic of the product is now greater than 127, go to step 21.

Step 12: Copy product into recipient.

Step 13: Go to step 25.

Step 14: Set recipient to a true zero.

Step 15: Go to step 25.

Step 16: If the exponent underflow bit in the program mask equals zero, go to step 14.

Step 17: If the fraction is normalized, go to step 21.

Step 18: Shift the fraction of the product one hex digit to the left.

Step 19: Subtract one from the characteristic of the intermediate product.

Step 20: Go to step 17.

Step 21: Copy the product into the recipient.

Step 22: Cause an interrupt.

Step 23: Go to step 25.

Step 24: Cause an interrupt.

Step 25: Stop.

TOPIC 2 An Example from Numerical Analysis

In order to illustrate the use of the floating-point instructions, we offer in this topic a program taken from the literature of numerical analysis. Our example uses the secant method to find one root of the third degree polynomial $AX^3 + BX^2 + CX + D$.

The first step in the procedure to find the root is to choose two initial values which we label X0 and X1. (The better our guesses, the sooner our computation will be done.) Our second step is to determine a new value, X2, using the formula

$$X2 = X1 - \frac{(X1 - X0)F(X1)}{(F(X1) - F(X0))}$$

where the function F is the third degree polynomial. That is, F(X1) and F(X0) are the values of the polynomial at X1 and X0, respectively.

This new value, X2, should be closer to a root than either X1 or X0. And if X2 differs from X1 by less than .005, then we will accept X2 as a root. But if $|X2 - X1| \geq .005$, then we set X0 = X1 and X1 = X2, and we use the formula to find a new X2. We continue this process until we find an X1 and X2 which satisfy our requirement. (It should be noted that the procedure will fail if F(X1) = F(X0).) The Secant Method Algorithm should be helpful in providing additional information about our example.

In the program we use Horner's method of polynomial evaluation to obtain the value of the cubic at X1. The third degree polynomial in Horner's form is $((AX + B)X + C)X + D$. When written in this form, the number of multiplications necessary to evaluate the polynomial at X1 is reduced to three.

We have listed the code for the evaluation of a third degree polynomial by Horner's method in Figure 12.6. We assume that the coefficients A, B, C, and D are in consecutive double-word locations. General purpose register 2

```
          LA    3,3        BCT REGISTER
          LA    2,0        INDEX REGISTER
          SDR   2,2        SET FLOAT 2 TO 0
LOOP1     AD    2,A(2)     C(A) INDEX BY 2 → FLOAT 2
          MD    2,X1       MULTIPLY BY X1
          LA    2,8(2)     MOVE POINTER
          BCT   3,LOOP1    BRANCH IF NECESSARY
          AD    2,A(2)     ADD D, F(X) IS IN FLOAT 2
```

FIGURE 12.6

is used as an index to modify the effective address of the coefficients referenced by the double-precision floating-point Add. Since our polynomial is a
cubic, we must traverse the loop three times.

The program segment which finds the value X2 is given in Figure 12.7.
Our code assumes that floating-point registers 0 and 2 contain F(X0) and
F(X1), respectively.

If $|X2 - X1| \geq .005$, then we must set X0 = X1 and X1 = X2. Notice that
since we have saved F(X1) in floating-point register 6, we do not need to
evaluate the polynomial at the "new" X0. F(X0) for the "new" X0 is equal
to F(X1) for the "old" X1. Our code in Figure 12.8 takes advantage of this
fact.

The value F(X0) is available for use in the formula, without evaluating

FIGURE 12.7

```
LDR    6,2          SAVE F(X1)
SDR    2,0          F(X1) − F(X0)
LD     4,X1         X1 → FLOAT 4
SD     4,X0         X1 − X0
MDR    4,6          (X1 − X0) * F(X1) = Z
DDR    4,2          Z / (F(X1) − F(X0))
LD     2,X1         X1 → FLOAT 2
SDR    2,4          X2 IS IN FLOAT 2
LDR    4,2          SAVE X2
SD     2,X1         X2 − X1
LPDR   2,2          |X2 − X1|
CD     2,=D'.005'   |X2 − X1| < .005?
BL     BLUE
```

FIGURE 12.8

```
LD     2,X1     X1 → FLOAT 2
STD    2,X0     SET X0 = X1
STD    4,X1     SET X1 = X2
LDR    0,6      SET F(X0) = F(X1)
```

the polynomial, in each pass through the program except the first. The evaluation of the cubic in the first pass at the point X0 will require about eight instructions. We can save these instructions if we approximate the first value of F(X0) when we choose the initial value of X0. Since this will not affect the final result, and since the prospect of saving eight instructions is so appealing, we have assumed that the initial value of X0 is zero and that F(X0) = D. We note that if D equals zero, then X0 equals zero is a root. In this case there is no need to run the program. We present the Secant Method Algorithm below and the code for the complete program in Figure 12.9. The secant method works best if the initial values of X1 and X0 are close to a root. We suggest, therefore, that X1 be picked so that F(X1) is close to zero.

The Secant Method Algorithm

Step 1: Pick the initial value of X0.
Step 2: Approximate F(X0).
Step 3: Pick the initial value of X1.
Step 4: Calculate F(X1) by evaluating the polynomial.
Step 5: Calculate X2 by the formula.
Step 6: If $|X2 - X1| < .005$, go to step 11.
Step 7: Set X0 = X1.
Step 8: Set F(X0) = F(X1).
Step 9: Set X1 = X2.
Step 10: Go to step 4.
Step 11: Set ROOT = X2.
Step 12: Stop.

EXERCISES

1. Many computers use two as the base of the exponent in a floating-point number. In that case, a normalized floating-point number is defined as one whose first digit after the binary point is nonzero.
   Contrast a base 2 floating-point number to the System/360 base 16 floating-point number. What are the advantages and disadvantages of each? For instance, which type would have the larger range given that the number of bits in a word is the same?

2. Give the System/360 single-precision floating-point representation of:
   a. 14.0   b. 23.0   c. 1225.0
   d. 14.5   e. 505.5   f. Pi = 3.1416

3. Give the normalized version of the following floating-point numbers:
   a. 41002316   b. 39012471
   c. C1000432   d. 33001234

4. What decimal value is represented by the following floating-point numbers:
   a. 42110000   b. 43010000
   c. C2110000   d. 40100000

```
          LD     0,D
LOOP2     LA     2,0           INDEX REGISTER
          LA     3,3           BCT REGISTER
          SDR    2,2           SET FLOAT 2 TO 0
LOOP1     AD     2,A(2)        C(A) INDEX BY 2 → FLOAT 2
          MD     2,X1          MULTIPLY BY X1
          LA     2,8(2)        MOVE POINTER
          BCT    3,LOOP1       BRANCH IF NECESSARY
          AD     2,A(2)        ADD D, F(X) IS IN FLOAT 2
          LDR    6,2           SAVE F(X1)
          SDR    2,0           F(X1) − F(X0)
          LD     4,X1          X1 → FLOAT 4
          SD     4,X0          X1 − X0
          MDR    4,6           (X1 − X0) * F(X1) = Z
          DDR    4,2           Z / (F(X1) − F(X0))
          LD     2,X1          X1 → FLOAT 2
          SDR    2,4           X2 IS IN FLOAT 2
          LDR    4,2           SAVE X2
          SD     2,X1          X2 − X1
          LPDR   2,2           |X2 − X1|
          CD     2,=D'.005'    |X2 − X1| < .005?
          BL     BLUE
          LD     2,X1          X1 → FLOAT 2
          STD    2,X0          SET X0 = X1
          STD    4,X1          SET X1 = X2
          LDR    0,6           SET F(X0) = F(X1)
          B      LOOP2
BLUE      STD    4,ROOT
```

FIGURE 12.9

5. Consider the Newton iterative method to find the root of a polynomial. The formula used to derive X_{i+1} for any X_i is $X_{i+1} = X_i − (F(X_i)/F'(X_i))$ where F' is the derivative of F.

   Write a program segment to find a root of the quartic $X^4 + 2X^3 − 13X^2 − 4X − 6$.

   Stop the iteration when $|X_{i+1} − X_i| < .005$. Submit an algorithm and flowchart with your solution.

6. Write a program segment which uses Newton's method to find a square root of a real number. Newton's iterative formula can be written in this case as $X_{i+1} = X_i + ((R − X_i^2)/2X_i)$ where R is the square of the value we want. Choose X_0, the first X_i, greater than the square root of R. Stop when $X_{i+1} > X_i$. Submit an algorithm and flowchart with your solution.

7. Submit a program which reads a base 10 real number into MEMORY. (Include the decimal point.) Convert this value to single-precision floating-point by combining the programs in Figures 12.3 and 12.4.

8. Submit a program which converts a floating-point number to EBCDIC form. Do this in two program segments. Convert the integer portion, then the fractional part. Move a decimal point to the appropriate byte. Print the result. Submit an algorithm and a flowchart with your solution.

9. Write a program which causes an interrupt. Issue the following pair of instructions so that the CPU will accept an exponent underflow interrupt.

```
L     3, = F'2'
SLL   3,24
SPM   3
```

Now write a program segment that causes an exponent underflow exception.

10. Assume (for this problem) that the System/360 floating-point instruction set does not contain the floating-point Compare instructions. Let FRED and EMILY contain floating-point numbers. Use the condition code to branch to ALEX if C(EMILY) > C(FRED). (Hint: See the Compare Algorithm.)

11. Write a program segment which finds the roots of a quadratic equation. Test for imaginary roots.

12. Write a program segment which finds the area of a circle. Do all work in double-precision. Define Pi in double-precision. Compare this program to that in Section 6.4 of Chapter 6.

13. Consider the computer you chose for exercise 14 of Chapter 6. Contrast the floating-point repertoire of that computer with the System/360 floating-point instruction set.

14. Submit a program segment which checks for possible exponent overflow before a floating-point multiplication instruction is issued.

15. Submit a program which gives the probability of getting three aces in a poker hand.

$$P(3 \text{ aces in 5 cards}) = \frac{\binom{4}{3}\binom{48}{2}}{\binom{52}{5}}$$

13 | Packed Decimal Instructions

We first mentioned packed decimal numbers in Chapter 4 (Topic 3 of the Computer Notebook). The discussion of the P-type Define Constant statement appears in Section 5.3 of Chapter 5. Take the following ten-question quiz to check your understanding of packed decimal operands. The answers to the questions appear on page 333. If a review is indicated, reread Topic 3 of the Computer Notebook in Chapter 4 and Section 5.3.

The Packed Decimal Quiz

1. Where is the sign field of a packed decimal number?
2. Which hex digits are recognized as a plus sign by CONTROL?
3. When the computer generates a positive packed decimal number, what is the code for a plus sign?
4. When the computer generates a negative packed decimal number, what is the code for a minus sign?
5. Why does a decimal integer which has an even number of digits have a leading zero in packed decimal representation?
6. Express +743 as a packed decimal number.
7. Express −4134 as a packed decimal number.
8. What is the largest value that can be contained in location BLUE if BLUE is defined by BLUE DC P'49'?
9. Give the Assembler reply to the Define Constant declarative SAM DC PL3'12'.
10. Give the Assembler reply to the Define Constant declarative GREEN DC PL3' − 14.64'.

We have a few general observations to make before we discuss the decimal instructions in detail.

1. All decimal instructions are of SS type. Since no index register is available, all address modification of packed decimal operands must be made by changing the contents of a base register. (See discussion in Section 9.8, Chapter 9.)
2. The programmer should be very much aware of the implied length concept when he uses the packed decimal instruction set. He should, in his definitions, specify a large enough implied length for his operands so that these operands will be able to accommodate all expected values. The use of leading zeros in packed decimal operands has considerable importance.

	Condition code settings			
	0	*1*	*2*	*3*
ADD PACKED	= 0	< 0	> 0	overflow
SUB PACKED	= 0	< 0	> 0	overflow
COMPARE	op1 = op2	op1 < op2	op1 > op2	—
ZAP	= 0	< 0	> 0	overflow

Note: =0, <0, and >0 refer to the value in the recipient location after execution of the instruction.

FIGURE 13.1   Schedule G

3. A data exception will exist if the right nibble of the low order byte of either operand cannot be interpreted as a sign when a packed decimal instruction is issued. The data exception will also exist if any of the other nibbles in the operands contain anything except a decimal digit. A program interrupt is always taken for a data exception. (See the discussion in Topic 2 of the Computer Notebook in Chapter 8.)

4. Only four decimal instructions—Add Packed, Subtract Packed, Compare Packed, and Zero and Add Packed (ZAP)—set the condition code. The code is set according to Schedule G in Figure 13.1.

5. We note that two instructions, Pack and Unpack, of the decimal instruction set were discussed in Chapter 8. We have included them in the list of the decimal instructions which appears in Figure 13.2.

13.1   Add, Subtract, and Compare

The three instructions presented in this section are fairly straightforward. The examples should provide the student with sufficient information to use all instructions effectively. However, before presenting these examples we will discuss the decimal overflow exception. This exception is peculiar to Add Packed, Subtract Packed, and to Zero and Add Packed (ZAP). Therefore, the comments we make here apply to ZAP also.

FIGURE 13.2   The Packed Decimal Instruction Set

Instruction	*Mnemonic*		*Action*
Add Packed	AP	S1,S2	$S1 \leftarrow C(S1) + C(S2)$
Subtract Packed	SP	S1,S2	$S1 \leftarrow C(S1) - C(S2)$
Multiply Packed	MP	S1,S2	$S1 \leftarrow C(S1) * C(S2)$
Divide Packed	DP	S1,S2	SEE DISCUSSION
Zero and Add Packed	ZAP	S1,S2	SEE DISCUSSION
Compare Packed	CP	S1,S2	SEE DISCUSSION
Pack	PACK	S1,S2	SEE CHAPTER 8
Unpack	UNPK	S1,S2	SEE CHAPTER 8
Move with Offset	MVO	S1,S2	SEE DISCUSSION

First, let us see why the sum or difference of a decimal operation can overflow the recipient location. Recall that the number of digits in a packed decimal operand is determined by its implied length. A decimal operand with an implied length of one will possess one digit. The maximum value that this operand can express is nine. A packed decimal operand whose implied length is 2 bytes has 3 digits, and the maximum value it can attain is 999. In general, a packed decimal operand with an implied length of n bytes has $2n - 1$ digits. (What is the maximum value that can be "held" by the operand?) The implied length attribute, which determines the size of the operand, is established when the symbolic name is defined. If the recipient of an add or subtract operation cannot hold the sum or the difference, that is, the sum or difference has too many digits for the implied length of the recipient, then the recipient is said to overflow. The high order or most significant digits are lost. A decimal overflow exception exists.

A program interrupt will be taken if the decimal overflow bit in the program mask is turned on. (See Chapter 12, Topic 1 of the Computer Notebook.) If the decimal overflow bit is zero, then no interrupt will occur. In this case, however, the result has been truncated. Serious programming errors may result if the truncated value in the recipient is used in further calculations.

We also note that while a zero sum or difference will have a plus sign, a truncated zero result will have the sign of the correct sum or correct difference. This means that it is possible to have a negative packed decimal zero.

Add Packed. The general form of *Add Packed* is:

    AP   S1,S2

The action of AP is:

$$S1 \leftarrow C(S1) + C(S2)$$

Example 13.1

a. AP   SAM,BLUE

    Before execution   *After execution*
    C(SAM)   = 00004C   C(SAM) = 00018C
    C(BLUE) = 014C   C(BLUE) is unchanged

b. AP   DATA1,DATA2

    Before execution   *After execution*
    C(DATA1) = 00014C   C(DATA1) = 00130D
    C(DATA2) = 00144D   C(DATA2) is unchanged

c. AP   PAYROLL,BKPAY

    Before execution   *After execution*
    C(PAYROLL) = 100C   C(PAYROLL) = 562C
    C(BKPAY)   = 10462C   C(BKPAY) is unchanged

Location PAYROLL overflowed since the result is a five-digit decimal number. The recipient, PAYROLL, can hold only three digits. Two significant digits have been lost.

d. AP   ACCT1,ACCT1

    Before execution   *After execution*
    C(ACCT1) = 0000146C   C(ACCT1) = 0000292C

A decimal number may be added to itself.

e. AP   ACCT,PASTDUE

    Before execution   *After execution*
    C(ACCT) = 99494C   C(ACCT) = 00358C
    C(PASTDUE) = 864C   C(PASTDUE) is unchanged

ACCT had a carry overflow. The high order digit 1 has been lost. What is the setting of the condition code?

Subtract Packed.   The general form of *Subtract Packed* is:

    SP   S1,S2

The action of SP is:

    $S1 \leftarrow C(S1) - C(S2)$

Example 13.2

a. SP   BLUE,BLACK

    Before execution   *After execution*
    C(BLUE)   = 143C   C(BLUE) = 101C
    C(BLACK) = 42C   C(BLACK) is unchanged

b. SP   ACCT,PAY

    Before execution   *After execution*
    C(ACCT) = 849C   C(ACCT) = 095C
    C(PAY)   = 0000246D   C(PAY) is unchanged

Subtraction is algebraic. The algebraic difference overflowed. The high order digit has been lost.

c. SP   DATA1,DATA2

    Before execution   *After execution*
    C(DATA1) = 014C   C(DATA1) = 000D
    C(DATA2) = 01014C   C(DATA2) is unchanged

The algebraic difference overflowed. The correct difference is 01000D, hence the sign of the correct difference is in the sign byte of the recipient.

Compare Packed.   The general form of *Compare Packed* is:

CP   S1,S2

When this instruction is executed, the contents of S2 are compared with the contents of S1. The condition code is set according to Schedule G in Figure 13.1.

The comparison is from right to left. A negative zero is considered equal to a positive zero. The contents of the operands are not affected by the comparison. A data exception will occur if the signs and digits are not valid.

Example 13.3

We assume the following:

```
C(ACCT)   = 00000C
C(DATA)   = 01000D
C(PAY)    = 3C
C(RATE)   = 01235C
C(HOUR)   = 456D
C(OLDPAY) = 617C
C(AB)     = 000D
```

Give the status of the condition code after the execution of each of the following instructions:

① CP   HOUR,ACCT
② CP   RATE,OLDPAY
③ CP   AB,ACCT
④ CP   DATA,ACCT
⑤ CP   PAY,HOUR

The solution is:

① CC = 1   op1 < op2
② CC = 2   op1 > op2
③ CC = 0   op1 = op2
④ CC = 1   op1 < op2
⑤ CC = 2   op1 > op2

13.2   ZAP and MVO

Zero and Add Packed (ZAP) and Move with Offset (MVO) are the two most ingenious instructions in the packed decimal set. Both can be used to truncate digits from decimal operands. ZAP will truncate high order digits of pack decimal operands while MVO can be used to truncate the low order digits.

ZAP, the first instruction we discuss in this section, sets the condition code according to Schedule G of Figure 13.1. MVO does not affect the code.

Zap. The general form of *Zero and Add Packed* is:

    ZAP   S1,S2

The action of ZAP is:

    S1 ← C(S2)

This action is equivalent to the following two steps:[1]

   1. S1 is set equal to a packed decimal zero.
   2. S1 ← C(S1) + C(S2)

The effective address of the first operand, S1, need not contain a packed decimal number.

Example 13.4

a. ZAP   BLUE,DATA

We assume that the implied lengths of BLUE and DATA are equal, that is, L'BLUE = L'DATA

Before execution	After execution
C(BLUE) = 46231D	C(BLUE) = 12122C
C(DATA) = 12122C	C(DATA) is unchanged

b. ZAP   ACCTPAY,ACCT

We assume that L'ACCTPAY < L'ACCT

Before execution	After execution
C(ACCTPAY) = 00164C	C(ACCTPAY) = 32174D
C(ACCT) = 1432174D	C(ACCT) is unchanged

The operand value in ACCT is truncated when placed into ACCTPAY since ACCTPAY can accommodate only five digits.

An exception exists. If the decimal overflow bit of the program mask, bit 37 of the program status word, is on, then an interrupt will be taken for this exception. Otherwise, the condition code is set to three to signal the overflow. The program will continue to execute. (See the discussion of the program mask in Section 17.1.)

c. ZAP   QUOREM,DIVI

We assume that L'QUOREM > L'DIVI

Before execution	After execution
C(QUOREM) = 164327149C	C(QUOREM) = 000000431C
C(DIVI) = 431C	C(DIVI) is unchanged

---

[1] If S1 = S2, that is, if S1 is "zapped" into itself, then statements 1 and 2 must be modified.

We have moved the contents of DIVI to a larger field. We have also increased the number of digits in the operand without changing its value.

Move with Offset. The general form of *Move with Offset* is:

MVØ S1,S2

The action of MVO is S1 ← C(S2), so that the right nibble of the low order byte of S2 is copied in the left nibble of the low order byte of S1. The contents of the right nibble of the low order byte of S1 are unchanged.

The fields are processed from right to left. Since MVO is a class II SS type instruction, the implied lengths of both S1 and S2 monitor the action. If S1 cannot hold all of the information passed from S2, the leftmost bytes are truncated. If S2 cannot fill all the bytes of S1, CONTROL supplies leading zeros.

Example 13.5

a. MVØ DATA,ACCT(3)

Before execution	*After execution*
C(DATA) = 0042137C	C(DATA) = 0120643C
C(ACCT) = 120643171C	C(ACCT) is unchanged

The three low order digits of the packed decimal operand in ACCT have been truncated in the move. The new operand is available in DATA.

b. Truncate the three low order digits of the operand in location PAY. L'PAY = 4.

The solution is:

MVØ PAY,PAY(2)

Before execution	*After execution*
C(PAY) = 1643721C	C(PAY) = 0001643C

The result is equivalent to a division of PAY by 1000.

c. The positive decimal value in ACCT has an assumed decimal point before the two low order digits. Round the value to the nearest integer. Truncate the fractional part of the operand. L'ACCT = 3. Assume C(ACCT) = 17367C.

The solution is:

① AP   ACCT,=P'50'
② MVØ ACCT,ACCT(2)
③ MVØ ACCT,ACCT(2)

Note that:

before execution of ① ;	C(ACCT) = 17367C
after execution of ① ;	C(ACCT) = 17417C
after execution of ② ;	C(ACCT) = 01741C
after execution of ③ ;	C(ACCT) = 00174C

13.3 Multiplication and Division

Both multiplication and division have restrictions placed on the packed decimal numbers which they can use as operands. These restrictions, if not complied with, result in data or specification exceptions. The demands imposed by these restrictions are best met when the programmer is preparing his declarative section, that is, when he defines the packed decimal constants and the packed decimal storage locations for his program.

We now discuss each operation in detail. First, multiplication.

Multiply Packed. The general form of *Multiply Packed* is:

MP   S1,S2

The action of this instruction is:

S1 ← C(S1) * C(S2)

There are several restrictions.

The multiplier, the second operand, cannot be larger than 15 decimal digits. Another length restriction is also placed on the multiplier: its length must be less than the implied length of the first operand, the multiplicand. A significance exception will exist if either of these restrictions are not complied with. The operation is suppressed and a program interrupt occurs.

A restriction is also placed on the multiplicand. The number of leading zeros in this operand must be greater than or equal to the implied length of the multiplier. Suppose, for instance, that the implied length of the multiplier is three, then the number of leading zeros in the multiplicand must be at least six. A data exception will result if the multiplicand does not have a sufficient number of leading zeros. A program interrupt will follow.

Table 13.1 lists the restrictions and their associated exceptions. Note that the table gives the exception which will result if the operands do not satisfy the requirements imposed by the restrictions.

TABLE 13.1   Schedule H

Restriction	*Exception*
L'S2 < L'S1	Specification
L'S2 ≤ 8	Specification
Leading Zeros	Data

These restrictions on the operands insure that no decimal product will overflow. In fact, it insures that every product has at least one leading zero. Note that in spite of these restrictions, we have succeeded in multiplying a decimal number by itself in the examples.

We now discuss a programming technique which enables the user to avoid being concerned about the number of leading zeros in the multiplicand. Example 13.6 is a short program segment which uses this technique.

Example 13.6

```
                    ⋮
①          ZAP      TEMPRO,DATA
②          MP       TEMPRO,HOUR
③          ZAP      DATA,TEMPRO
④          BØ       TOOBIG
                    ⋮
           GOBACK
DATA       DS       PL4
HOUR       DS       PL2
⑤ TEMPRO   DS       PL6
           END
```

We want to multiply DATA by HOUR. We do not, however, want to concern ourselves with the number of leading zeros in DATA. We have, therefore, defined in ⑤ a decimal storage location named TEMPRO with an implied length equal to the sum of the implied lengths of HOUR and DATA.

At execution time, the execution of ① ZAPs our multiplicand into TEMPRO. ② will execute since we have a sufficient number of leading zeros in TEMPRO. The product is in TEMPRO after the execution of ②. Then we ZAP DATA with the product (see ③).

Did our product overflow? In ④ we check the status of the condition code. If any significant digits of the product have been lost, we branch to TOOBIG. Otherwise, we proceed in the normal maner. (Be sure the decimal overflow bit in the program status word is turned off when using this technique.) (See discussion of Set Program Mask in Section 17.1.)

Example 13.7

We wish to multiply DATA1 by PAYREC. We know that the absolute values of DATA1 and PAYREC never exceed 100_{10} and 50_{10}, respectively.

In this case, we do not need to define a temporary storage location into which we ZAP DATA1. Instead, we define DATA1 with an implied length of four. This insures that the multiplicand, DATA1, will have at least four leading zeros when it attains its maximum value of 0000100C.

Since the maximum value that PAYREC can attain is 050C, we are sure that the CPU will do the multiplication. We save a few instructions and some storage locations. We note, however, that this case is not the usual one.

```
          ⋮
          MP        DATA1,PAYREC
          ⋮
          GOBACK
DATA1     DS        PL4
PAYREC    DS        PL2
          ⋮
```

Example 13.8

a. MP   RATE,TIME

Before execution   *After execution*
C(RATE) = 0000175C   C(RATE) = 0002450C
C(TIME) = 014C   C(TIME) is unchanged

b. MP   SSOC,INCOME

Before execution   *Result*
C(SSOC) = 01743C   DATA exception leads to
C(INCOME) = 175C   program interrupt

SSOC has an insufficient number of leading zeros.

c. MP   INC,TIME

Before execution   *Result*
C(INC)   = 00005C   Specification exception leads
C(TIME) = 0000001C   to program interrupt

Note that $L'TIME > L'INC$

d. Multiply the contents of location BLUE by itself.

We assumed that the implied length of DBLUE is equal to twice the implied length of BLUE.

The solution is:

```
ZAP   DBLUE,BLUE
MP    DBLUE,BLUE
ZAP   BLUE,DBLUE
BØ    TØØBIG
```

Divide Packed.   The general form of *Divide Packed* is:

DP   S1,S2

When DP is executed the quotient and the remainder are both placed into the dividend's former location (S1). The quotient occupies the first (high order) $L1 - L2$ bytes, and the remainder occupies the low order L2 bytes.

(Recall that L1 and L2 stand for the implied lengths of the first and second operands, respectively.) The sign of the quotient is determined by the rules of algebra. The remainder carries the original sign of the dividend. Example 13.9 will clarify these assertions.

The restrictions placed on the operands of the division instruction are quite similar in nature to those on the multiplicative operands. The implied length of the divisor, the second operand, must be less than or equal to eight. It must also always have a smaller implied length than the first operand, the dividend. A specification exception will be recognized if these restrictions are not complied with. A program interrupt will occur after the operation is suppressed.

Overflow is not permitted. If the quotient cannot fit into the $L1 - L2$ bytes allotted to it, a decimal divide exception will occur. A program interrupt will be taken after the operation is suppressed. The dividend and divisor will be unchanged.

A decimal divide exception will always occur if the dividend does not have at least one leading zero. But one leading zero in the dividend does not insure that the quotient will fit into its allotted space. Overflow will *not* occur if the dividend has two more leading zeros than the divisor *or* if the dividend has one more leading zero than the divisor *and* the first nonzero digit in the dividend is less than the first nonzero digit in the divisor.

The rule for determining if the condition for a decimal divide exception exists is cumbersome to use. We, therefore, suggest that a quotient-remainder field with an implied length equal to $L1 + L2$ be defined for each dividend-divisor pair. We will call this field QUOREM.

To accomplish our division, we use a technique quite similar to the one that was used in multiplication. We ZAP the dividend into QUOREM. Then we divide QUOREM by the divisor. We do not need to be concerned about a decimal divide exception since QUOREM has at least two more leading zeros than the divisor. We can retrieve the quotient and the remainder from their respective fields in QUOREM at our leisure. Example 13.9 is a short program segment in which we employ the techniques we have discussed. Further discussion appears after the example.

Example 13.9

```
                    ⋮
①          ZAP    QUOREM,DIVI
②          DP     QUOREM,DIVISOR
③          ZAP    DIVI,QUOREM(4)
④          ZAP    REM,QUOREM+4(3)
                    ⋮
           GOBACK
⑤ DIVISOR  DC     P'1423'
⑥ DIVI     DC     P'465327'
```

⑦ REM   DS   PL3
⑧ QUOREM   DS   PL7
        ⋮
        END

1. QUOREM is defined so that its implied length is equal to the sum of the implied lengths of DIVI and DIVISOR.
2. C(QUOREM) = 0000000465327C after execution of ①.
3. C(QUOREM) = 0000327C00006C after execution of ②.
4. C(DIVI) = 0000327C after execution of ③. The condition code is set to two. Note that only the first four bytes from QUOREM are "zapped" into DIVI.
5. C(REM) = 00006C after execution of ②.

The definition of a quotient-remainder field for each dividend-divisor pair is a good programming practice since it helps prevent most decimal divide exceptions. It is possible, however, to divide without establishing such fields. We offer, therefore, in Example 13.10 (although we do not recommend the technique) a discussion of decimal division when no quotient-remainder field has been established. The student should look at these examples, because they do illustrate a few points made in the text about the decimal-divide and specification exceptions.

Example 13.10

a. DP   PAY,RATE

Before execution	*After execution*
C(PAY) = 00464C	C(PAY) = 1C220C
C(RATE) = 244C	C(RATE) is unchanged

b. DP   ABLE,SAM

Before execution	*After execution*
C(ABLE) = 04632D	C(ABLE) = 9C141D
C(SAM) = 499D	C(SAM) is unchanged

The quotient has the algebraic sign of the division. The remainder has the sign of the dividend.

c. DP   FICA,TAX

Before execution	*Result*
C(FICA) = 00460C	A specification exception
C(TAX) = 0000012C	exists. L'TAX > L'FICA

d. DP   RATE1,RATE2

Before execution	*Result*
C(RATE1) = 123C	A decimal divide exception exists.
C(RATE2) = 4C	No leading zero in RATE1.

e. DP   TAX,PERCENT

> *Before execution*   *After execution*
> C(TAX) = 04643C   C(TAX) = 7C142C
> C(PERCENT) = 643C   C(PERCENT) is unchanged

Does a decimal divide exception exist? No. TAX has a leading zero, and the first nonzero digit in TAX is less than the first nonzero digit in PERCENT.

13.4   Edit and Edit and Mark

The purpose of the edit instructions is to prepare packed decimal results for output. These flexible instructions can replace an operand's leading zeros by blanks and convert significant decimal integers into EBCDIC form. They may insert commas to block large values so that the printed results can be read easily. Decimal points can be placed where they are needed. A dollar sign ($) can be placed into a particular spot in the numeric string that is to be printed, or the dollar sign may be "floated" to a more appropriate location in the text.

Both edit instructions, Edit (ED) and Edit and Mark (EDMK), convert packed decimal operands into printable code in exactly the same way. The only difference between the two instructions is that EDMK usually creates a pointer to the first nonzero digit in the edited result, whereas ED does not. Hence, all of the discussion which follows applies to both instructions.

The edit instructions are SS type, class I. The first operand, the recipient, is an editing pattern. This pattern, which is usually moved into the recipient prior to the issuance of the Edit instruction, is destroyed by the action. The edited results become the new contents of the recipient.

The pattern is composed of characters, each of which requires one byte of storage. Table 13.2 lists the pattern characters and their names. Since the pattern character 21 has two functions to perform, we have given it two names. We note that the EBCDIC characters are equivalent to the message characters.

TABLE 13.2   Editing Characters

Character	Name
20	Digit selector
21	Digit selector
21	Significance starter
22	Field separator
Any other	Message characters

The character in the first byte (the high order byte) of the pattern is called the *fill* character. It must be a message character. For example, if C(BLUE)

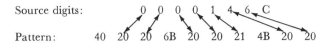

FIGURE 13.3

is a pattern equal to 402020202120, then the message character 40_x is the fill character. (Recall that 40_x is the EBCDIC form for a blank.)

There must be exactly one digit selector in the pattern for each digit in the second operand. These decimal digits, called the *source digits,* are in a one-to-one correspondence with the digit selectors. Suppose C(DATA) = 0000146C. The pattern, 4020206B2020214B2020, could be used to edit DATA. The one-to-one correspondence between the source digits and the digit selectors is given in Figure 13.3.

A signal, called the *significance indicator,* is used to monitor the action of the instruction. This signal, which we will also call *the trigger,* can be *on* or *off.* Initially it is off. How it is turned on and off will be covered in the discussion of the editing process. We now turn to that topic.

The editing proceeds in the pattern, byte by byte, from left to right. The content of each byte is converted to a printable EBCDIC character. (Recall that message characters are EBCDIC characters.) Any message character encountered when the trigger is off is replaced by the fill character. All message characters encountered when the trigger is on are left undisturbed.

Each digit selector examines its associated source digit in turn. If the source digit is zero and the trigger is off, the digit selector is replaced by the fill character. If the source digit is zero and the trigger is on, the digit selector is replaced by F0. If the source digit is nonzero and the trigger is off, the trigger is turned on and the digit selector is replaced by the EBCDIC equivalent of the source digit. If the source digit is nonzero and the trigger is on, the digit selector is replaced by the EBCDIC equivalent of the source digit.

The pattern character 21 plays a dual role; it is both a digit selector and a significance starter. That is, if the source digit associated with 21 is zero and the trigger is off, then 21 assumes its role as a significance starter. In this role, 21 turns the trigger on. The trigger is turned on for the next pattern character; 21, itself, is replaced by the fill character. Significance is said to be *forced* when this occurs.

Table 13.3 lists the various situations and the actions taken for the digit selectors.

Table 13.4 lists the options for the message characters.

What is the edited result of the packed decimal number in Figure 13.3? The answer appears in Figure 13.4.

The sign of the positive source operand will turn the significance indicator off, but the sign of a negative operand will leave it on. We can use this fact to append a note to the edited result. Suppose, for instance, that we have a

Solution:

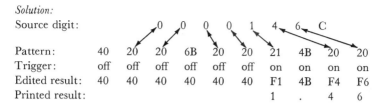

Source digit:		0	0	0	0	1	4	6	C	
Pattern:	40	20	20	6B	20	20	21	4B	20	20
Trigger:	off	off	off	off	off	off	on	on	on	on
Edited result:	40	40	40	40	40	40	F1	4B	F4	F6
Printed result:							1	.	4	6

FIGURE 13.4

TABLE 13.3   Digit Selectors

Trigger	Source	Digit selector
ON	= 0	⌈ REPLACED BY
ON	≠ 0	⎰ EBCDIC EQUIVALENT ⎱
OFF	≠ 0	⌊ OF SOURCE
OFF	= 0	REPLACED BY FILL

TABLE 13.4   Message Characters

Trigger	Message character
ON	UNDISTURBED
OFF	REPLACED BY FILL CHARACTER

packed decimal number which may be positive or negative. If positive, the value represents an amount due. If negative, the value is a credit balance.

We can pass this information in the printed result by including the message characters C3D9 after the last digit selector. (These message characters are equivalent to the EBCDIC form for "CR.") If our source operand is positive, these message characters will be replaced by the fill character. (In this case the fill character should be a blank.) If the source operand is negative, "CR" will be appended to the printed result. Example 13.11 illustrates our discussion.

Example 13.11

a. Source operand:

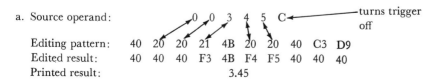

turns trigger off

	0	0	3	4	5	C			
Editing pattern:	40	20	20	21	4B	20	20	40	C3	D9
Edited result:	40	40	40	F3	4B	F4	F5	40	40	40
Printed result:				3.45					

b. Source operand: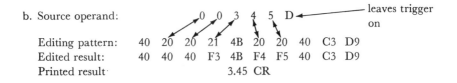

Editing pattern:	40	20	20	21	4B	20	20	40	C3	D9
Edited result:	40	40	40	F3	4B	F4	F5	40	C3	D9
Printed result·					3.45 CR					

The field separator, pattern character 22, is always replaced by the fill character. The field separator turns the significance indicator off before it is replaced. The field separator is used only when two or more packed decimal fields are edited by a single pattern. An illustration of its use appears in the examples which follow the general form of Edit.

The material we have presented in this section is extremely complex and interrelated. We suggest that the student reread the entire section after using the Edit Algorithm to obtain the results we have given in Figure 13.4 and Example 13.11.

The Edit Algorithm, which follows, was simplified by omitting all references to the field separator. The pattern character that the pointer points to has been labeled CHAR. If CHAR is a digit selector, then its associated source digit has been labeled SOURCE-DIGIT. These innovations should make the algorithm easier to follow.

Edit Algorithm

Step 1: Set the pointer so it points to the fill character in the pattern.
Step 2: Move the pointer to the next pattern character in sequence.
Step 3: If CHAR is a message character, go to step 14.
Step 4: If the trigger is off, go to step 8.
Step 5: Replace CHAR with the EBCDIC equivalent of the SOURCE-DIGIT.
Step 6: If CHAR was the last digit selector, go to step 17.
Step 7: Go to step 2.
Step 8: If SOURCE-DIGIT is nonzero, go to step 12.
Step 9: Replace CHAR with the fill character.
Step 10: If CHAR is the significance starter, turn the trigger on.
Step 11: Go to step 6.
Step 12: Turn the trigger on.
Step 13: Go to step 5.
Step 14: If the trigger is on, go to step 2.
Step 15: Replace CHAR with the fill character.
Step 16: Go to step 2.
Step 17: If the source operand is positive, turn the trigger off.
Step 18: If CHAR was the last pattern character, go to step 23.
Step 19: Move the pointer to the next pattern character in sequence.
Step 20: If the trigger is on, go to step 18.
Step 21: Replace CHAR by the fill character.

Step 22: Go to step 18.
Step 23: Stop.

The general form of *Edit* is:

ED   S1,S2

See the Edit Algorithm for the action of this instruction.

The condition code is set according to Schedule I of Table 13.5. If more than one field is edited by the instruction, the setting of the code refers to the contents of the last field.

TABLE 13.5   Schedule I

Source field	Code
= 0	0
< 0	1
> 0	2

Example 13.12

a. ED   PATTERN,DATA

Before execution   *After execution*
C(PATTERN) = 4020206B2020214B2020   C(DATA) is unchanged
C(DATA) = 0000012C   C(PATTERN) = 404040404040404BF1F2

The printed result is .12.

The trigger was set by pattern character 21 in its role as the significance starter. Note that 21 set the trigger for the next pattern character.

b. ED   PATTERN,ACCT

Before execution   *After execution*
C(PATTERN) = 4020206B2020214B2020   C(ACCT) is unchanged
C(ACCT) = 0123456C   C(DATA) = 4040F16BF2F3F44BF5F6

The printed result is 1,234.56.

c. ED   PATTERN,OUTPUT

Before execution   *After execution*
C(PATTERN) = 4020212022202120   C(OUTPUT) is unchanged
C(OUTPUT) = 000C012C   C(PATTERN) = 404040F04040F1F2

The printed result is bbb0bb12 where b is a blank.

Two fields have been edited by the single pattern. The field separator, 22, is replaced by the fill character. The condition code is set to two, since the value of the last field edited is greater than zero.

Edit and Mark. The general form of *Edit and Mark* is:

EDMK   S1,S2

See the Edit Algorithm for the action of this instruction. The address of the digit selector which turns the significance indicator on is placed into register 1.

If significance is forced, that is, if the pattern character 21 in its role as the significance starter turns the trigger on, no address is placed into register 1. If any digit selector, 20 or 21, turns the trigger on, then its address is placed into register 1. (Recall that pattern character 21 has two roles.) The condition code is set according to Schedule I of Table 13.5.

Example 13.13

a. ACCT is a seven-digit packed decimal number. Print the value of ACCT in the form X1X2,X3X4X5.X6X7. Remove all leading zeros except X5. Put a dollar sign in front of the first nonzero digit which precedes the decimal point. If all digits preceding the decimal point are zero, print $0.X6X7.

We find that the pattern will be 4020206B2021204B2020. If significance is forced, no address will be replaced into register 1. Hence we load register 1 with the address of the first digit that will precede the decimal point.

FIGURE 13.5

① LA   1,PATTERN+6   IN CASE ALL DIGITS ARE ZERO
② EDMK   PATTERN,ACCT
③ BCTR   1,0
④ MVI   0(1),C'$'   MOVE $ INTO POSITION

① Register 1 points to the first digit which precedes the decimal point.
② The source operand is edited.
③ C(Reg 1) − 1 → Reg 1. No branch is made since register 0 cannot be used as a pointer. If 21 turns the trigger on in its role as the significance starter, then register 1 now points to the second byte that precedes the decimal point. Otherwise, register 1 points to the first byte which precedes the first significant digit.
④ The dollar sign is moved into position just preceding the first EBCDIC digit.
   Give the edited results and the printed results if C(ACCT) = 0146723C. The edited result is 4040F16BF4F6F74BF2F3. The printed result is b$1,467.23 where b stands for a blank. Give the edited results and the printed results if C(ACCT) = 0000042C. The edited result is 404040404040F04BF4F2. The printed result is bbbbb$0.42 where b stands for a blank.

b. DATA is a five-digit packed decimal number. Print its value in the form X1X2, X3X4X5. If the value is negative, put a minus sign in front of the first nonzero digit. If positive, put a plus sign in front of the first nonzero digit. If the value is zero, print 0.

We find that our pattern is 4020206B202120.

```
             EDMK   PATTERN,DATA
             BCTR   1,0
             BC     B'1000',PRINT
             BC     B'0100',MINUS
             MVI    0(1),C'+'
             B      PRINT
   MINUS     MVI    0(1),C'-'
             B      PRINT
```

FIGURE 13.6

We use the condition code to force a branch to the proper instruction. If the value of the source operand is zero, then we branch directly to the print routine. If the value of the source operand is negative, then we branch to location MINUS. At MINUS we use the address in register 1 to move a minus sign, then we branch to print. Otherwise a plus sign is moved into place before the branch to PRINT is made.

Answers to the Packed Decimal Quiz

1. The sign field of a packed decimal number is the right nibble of the operand's low order byte.
2. CONTROL recognizes hex "A," "C," "E," and "F" as positive signs.
3. CONTROL generates a hex "C" for a positive sign.
4. CONTROL generates a hex "D" for a negative sign.
5. See the discussion in Topic 3 in the Computer Notebook of Chapter 4.
6. 743_{10} has | 7 | 4 | 3 | C | as its packed decimal representation.
7. -4134_{10} has | 0 | 4 | 1 | 3 | 4 | D | as its packed decimal representation.
8. The largest value that BLUE can hold is 999.
9. The Assembler reply to the DC is 00012C.
10. The Assembler reply to the DC is 01464D.

EXERCISES

1. A student's grades in a series of tests are 90, 60, 95, 82, 73, 84. Find the average grade. Use packed decimal arithmetic. Use the Edit instruction to prepare his average for the output. Print the result in good form.

2. Write a program segment which causes an interrupt. Issue the following pair of instructions to ensure that the CPU will accept a decimal overflow interrupt. Then write the program segment which causes a decimal overflow exception.

```
   L     4,=F'4'
   SLL   4,24
   SPM   4
```

3. L'X = 3,DOUBLE is a double word. Location X is associated with columns 7, 8, and 9 of the punch card. These columns were punched *43b*. The card was read in. C(X) = F4F340. A program interrupt occurred when ② was executed. Why?

    PACK   DOUBLE,X
  ② CVB   3,DOUBLE

4. a. What anomaly causes the divide exception?
   b. Does the CPU complete the instruction when a divide exception occurs, or is the execution of it suppressed? Use *Principles of Operation* as your reference.

5. L'CONVERSE = 4. It is assumed that three digits follow the decimal point. That is, the decimal number contained in CØNVERSE has the form X1X2X3X4.X5X6X7. Round C(CØNVERSE) to two decimal places and then truncate the last digit. The decimal point is an assumed one.

6. Do this problem without using any reference. Divide C(MAN) by C(BUSCH). L'BUSCH = 4, L'MAN = 5. Store the quotient in QUOT. Convert the remainder to binary.

7. Write a program segment in which you use the condition code to determine if there is a nonzero remainder after a packed decimal division operation. Recall that division does not set the condition code.

8. What happens if a programmer ZAPs a nonpacked decimal operand into a packed decimal location? What happens if a packed decimal operand is "zapped" into a character location? Use *Principles of Operation* as your reference.

9. L'DATA = 4. Print the value in DATA in the form X1X2,X3X4X5. X6X7. Remove all leading zeros. Print .X6X7 if there are no nonzero digits before the decimal point. Otherwise, put a dollar sign in front of the first nonzero digit. Submit an algorithm and a flowchart with your solution.

10. ACCT is a data item which may be negative, zero, or positive. The customer has a credit balance when the value in ACCT is negative. L'ACCT = 4. Write the program segment which will print the contents of ACCT as X1X2,X3X4X5.X6X7 when positive and as X1X2,X3X4X5.X6X7 CR when negative. Put a dollar sign in an appropriate place.

11. A baseball file has the following format. (The values are given as they appear in MEMORY.)

NAME	AB	HITS	RUNS	HR	BA
KELLER	006C	004C	000C	000C	667C
LOWRY	006C	003C	003C	003C	500C
ANDREINI	007C	003C	001C	001C	429C
STUBBS	008C	002C	001C	001C	225C
MAKSOUDIAN	005C	001C	001C	001C	200C

a. Define the storage for this file.
b. Initialize the file.
c. Update this file by reading in the daily result. (Don't forget to find a new batting average for each player.)
d. Print the updated results. Use the Edit instruction to remove the leading zeros. (Use the field separator character so that the editing can be accomplished by a single pattern.)

Note: All arithmetic must be in packed decimal.

14 | Introduction to Input and Output

In Chapter 8 we introduced a macro named **PROLOG** which handled our input and output needs. Now we have arrived at a point in our study where we consider the programming that is necessary to write input/output (I/O) routines such as PROLOG. We intend to provide, in this chapter, the answers to the questions: How do we read in a card? How do we get the printer to print a line? How do we set up a data set (file) on a tape or a disk? How do we set up an indexed sequential file?

We cannot, of course, cover the entire story of the System/360 access methods. That perhaps would take another text equivalent in size to this one. All we hope to do is provide an elementary unedrstanding of the I/O routines and how to program them. The student should be able, after he completes this chapter, to read in data via the CARDREADER, print his results, and store information into data sets which exist on a tape or a disk. In addition, he should gain sufficient background so that his research in the IBM manuals will be more meaningful.

All the material in this chapter is interrelated and very difficult. We suggest, therefore, that the student read the entire chapter once before making a detailed study of any one item. It will soon be apparent that the information provided in this chapter will not be gained by a casual reading of it. But if you program the concepts, learn the terminology (say "logical record length," for example, when reading the keyword LRECL), and research the appropriate manuals, the subject matter will soon become very meaningful.

14.1 An Input/Output Routine

First, let us examine a program which reads data into MEMORY via the CARDREADER (see Figure 14.1). The data is read in and moved to location BLUE. The next instruction causes the same data to be printed. We have also listed (in the figure) the job control cards that must be submitted with the program, since two of these cards are part of our input-output package. The circled numbers in the remarks field are reference numbers. We will use these reference numbers as pointers in our discussion.

We assume in the comments which follow the program that the information about job control language in Topic 1 of the Computer Notebook in

336

```
      //CSC222     JOB      '2028    88    010    02',1    HANNULA
      //           EXEC     ASMFCLG
      //SYSIN      DD       *
                   TITLE    'AN INPUT-OUTPUT ROUTINE'
                   PRINT    NOGEN
                   INIT
①                  OPEN     (READER,INPUT)
②                  OPEN     (PRINTER,OUTPUT)
③                  GET      READER,BLUE
④                  PUT      PRINTER,BLUE
⑤                  CLOSE    READER
⑥                  CLOSE    PRINTER
                   GOBACK
      BLUE         DS       CL20
⑦     READER       DCB      DSORG=PS,MACRF=GM,DDNAME=BROWN,              X
                            RECFM=F,LRECL=20,BLKSIZE=20
⑧     PRINTER      DCB      DSORG=PS,MACRF=PM,DDNAME=BLACK               X
                   END
      /*
⑨     //GO.BLACK   DD    SYSOUT=A,DCB=(LRECL=20,BLKSIZE=20,RECFM=FA)
⑩     //GO.BROWN   DD    *
         THIS IS A TEST CARD
      /*
```

FIGURE 14.1

Chapter 11 has been understood. Note that statement ⑦ has been "punched" on two cards. A DCB (Data Control Block) statement such as ⑦ can be continued on a second card if three simple rules are followed:

1. The last character in the operand field of the first card must be a comma.
2. A nonblank character must appear in column 72.
3. The continuation card must begin in column 16.

A DD job control card (see ⑨) is continued in a somewhat similar fashion. Here are three simple rules:

1. Interrupt the operand field after a complete parameter on or before column 71 (include the comma).
2. Put a double slash (//) in columns 1 and 2 of the continuation card.
3. Start the continuation in any column from columns 4 to 16 inclusive.

Consider ③ and ④. GET and PUT are two data management macros. This means that they are two subroutines which have been written by IBM (IBM programmers) and supplied to the computer installations. The application programmer uses these macros when he wants the data management routines of the Operating System to read or write a record from a data set which is associated with the first operand of the macro instruction. Let us see how this association is made.

The Operating System maintains a *data control block* for every data set defined by every job. This data control block, or DCB, provides a good deal of information to the access method subroutine which monitors the way in which the data set is referenced. Among the many items which the DCB may describe to the access method subroutine are the length of each logical record, the length of a block of records, how the records are organized, how the data set is organized, what system macros will be used with respect to the data set, and where the data set is located. The data control block for a data set which belongs to the user's program will be maintained by OS in the declarative section of the user's program.

Now consider ⑦ and ⑧. The DCB statement in each declarative is again a system macro which has been devised so that an application program can describe the data control block for a data set by using keyword parameters in the operand field. The keyword parameters of the DCB named PRINTER are DSORG, MACRF, and DDNAME. These keywords are mnemonics for data set organization, macro forms, and data definition name, respectively. We will return to a discussion of these DCB keywords at a later point in this chapter.

Every DCB statement and hence every data control block must be associated with a job control language DD card. The keyword DDNAME in the operand field of the DCB statement is used to create this association. For instance, DDNAME=BLACK, which appears in the operand field of the PRINTER DCB statement (see ⑧), tells the Operating System that the DD card named BLACK (see ⑨) contains more information about the data control block named PRINTER.

Now let us look at the DD card. The operand field of most DD cards is composed of keyword parameters. In our case we have the keyword parameters RECFM, LRECL, BLKSIZE, and SYSOUT. The first three keywords are mnemonics for record form, logical record length, and block size, respectively. SYSOUT=A is the traditional way of specifying that the data set will be assigned to the PRINTER.

There is one DD card keyword parameter, DSNAME (data set name), which associates the DD card to the data set that we want to manipulate in our program. The DSNAME parameter (this can be abbreviated to DSN) is not used with PRINTER or CARDREADER data sets. It should always be used, however, with data sets that are on a disk pack or tape reel. Example 14.15 shows how to use the keyword DSNAME for a disk pack data set. Its use for a data set that exists on a tape reel is similar.

If DSNAME is omitted by the programmer, the Operating System will assign a unique temporary name to the data set. The programmer, if he chooses to name his data set, must limit the label to eight characters such that the first character is alphabetic or one of the three characters @, #, or $.

Figure 14.2 depicts the logic of the steps which associates the PUT macro in ④ to our print data set. Remember the logic in Figure 14.2 holds no matter who, the Operating System or the programmer, named the data set.

Now let us consider the data set we manipulate by our GET instruction in ③. All of the keyword parameters which are necessary to define a data control block appear in the DCB statement in ⑦. The DDNAME keyword refers to the DD card whose name is BROWN. Since all of the required

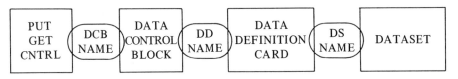

FIGURE 14.2

keyword parameters were given in the DCB statement, all we need on the DD card is the device specification. The asterisk (*) in the operand field of the BROWN DD card (see ⑩) is a special code which informs the Operating System that data cards for the data set follow immediately in the input stream of the CARDREADER.

We now turn to a discussion of the various access methods. Before we do, however, we note that each GET brings one record into MEMORY and each PUT writes one record from MEMORY onto an auxiliary storage device. We suggest that the student run the program in Figure 14.1.

14.2 The Access Methods

Every input and output operation must use one of the several available access methods. We list five of these in Table 14.1. We cover QSAM in considerable depth in this chapter. We also provide sufficient information about QISAM so that the student should be able to create, update, and retrieve an indexed sequential data set. We shall discuss various aspects of the basic access methods but we will *not* give any examples of data sets which require processing by the basic access methods.

TABLE 14.1 Five Access Methods

QSAM	Queued Sequential Access Method
QISAM	Queued Indexed Sequential Access Method
BSAM	Basic Sequential Access Method
BISAM	Basic Indexed Sequential Access Method
BDAM	Basic Direct Access Method

The user does not call an access method routine by name. Rather, he states his requirements in the DCB statement and in the associated DD card. The appropriate access method will be made available to his program by the data management routines of the Operating System.

Consider, for instance, the requirements we specified in the data control block named PRINTER. We specified DSØRG=PS, which stated that our data set was in a sequential mode. That is, our data set is organized so that all records must be processed in order. There is no "skipping around." The fourth record must be processed before the fifth.

All data sets read by the CARDREADER are sequential. So are the data sets that reside on magnetic tapes. All print data sets are also sequential. One can easily ascertain which access methods process sequential data sets by glancing at the names in Table 14.1.

Our second keyword parameter in the PRINTER DCB statement, MACRF=PM, tells the Operating System that we intend to use the data management macro instruction PUT in the move mode. PUT (in any mode) can only be used by a queued access method. We then spell out the additional requirements on the DD card. We tell OS via the data management routine (by LRECL=20) that the length of a logical record is 20 bytes. The BLKSIZE=20 specifies that there is one record per block. If we code BLKSIZE=40, then each block should contain two records. RECFM=FA passes two pieces of information. The first letter after the equal sign, F, signifies that all records in the data set are of the same (fixed) length. (That certainly is true, since it contains exactly one record.) The second letter, A, designates the character in the first byte of the record as the carriage control character. (Glance at the first character in the record. It is a blank. A blank carriage control character signifies that one space should be skipped before printing.)

Finally, SYSOUT=A specifies the PRINTER as the output device for our data set. We have listed our requirements. What access method will the data management routine provide to process our data set? QSAM. Let us see why.

Although both the basic sequential access methods and queued sequential access methods process sequential data sets, a queued sequential access method will be assigned to the file since the PUT macro was specified. The use of the PUT macro instruction, as we have pointed out, is restricted to the queued sequential access methods. WRITE is the analogous basic sequential access method's macro instruction which outputs a record. We note that GET is restricted to the queued techniques and READ to the basic methods. (We carry this topic a little further in Section 14.4, where we discuss buffering and blocking.)

We have two queued access methods. Why is QSAM, instead of QISAM, assigned to our data set? QISAM processes indexed sequential data sets and ours is not indexed. An indexed data set is specified by choosing the option IS (indexed sequential) when specifying the value for DSORG. (See Section 14.5.) We note that there are two modes for QISAM, the load mode and the scan mode. Both, however, use the same DSORG keyword option. (In conclusion, let us point out here that only QSAM data sets may be assigned to the CARDREADER or to the PRINTER.)

Now let us take a quick look at the difference between a sequential and an indexed sequential data set. Although an indexed sequential file may be processed sequentially, its great utility lies in the fact that the application programmer may skip to any record in the data set. Each record has a key. The indexed sequential access routines maintain an index of the keys for each data set they process. This index has a pointer to the track on a disk in which a record with that particular key resides.

When, for example, a programmer wishes to retrieve a record from an indexed file, he gives the key to the access method. The index is searched first to find the pointer to the track. The track is searched for the block which contains the record. The block is brought into a buffer in MEMORY (see Section 14.4 on blocking and buffering).

The QISAM routine retrieves the record from the block and places it at the disposal of the programmer. (Again we note, however, that an indexed sequential file may be processed as if it were a regular sequential data set.)

Each record of a data set that is processed by the basic direct access method has a key, as do the records processed by the indexed access methods. BDAM (Basic Direct Access Method), however, does not maintin an index. The record key itself points to the location of the record on the direct access device. In other words, the record key serves as a pointer to the record.

The technique is fast. Suppose we want to retrieve a record. We supply BDAM with the key. Immediately, that is, without a search, the record is supplied to us by the access method.

We now turn to a discussion of the data management macros.

14.3 Data Management Macros

Table 14.2 lists some of the more common data management macro instructions. If an X appears in an access method column, then that access method uses the macro which is in the same row as X. For instance, the SETL macro is used only by QISAM, since the only X in the SETL row is in the QISAM column.

The list of macros is alphabetized. We will, however, discuss them in the order specified by the circled numbers. (A complete list of the data management macro instructions appears in the IBM manual, *System/360 Operating*

TABLE 14.2 Data Management Macros

Macro	QSAM	QISAM
③ CLOSE	X	X
⑦ CNTRL	X	
① DCB	X	X
⑨ ESETL		X
④ GET	X	X
② OPEN	X	X
⑤ PUT	X	X
⑥ PUTX	X	X
⑧ SETL		X

System: Supervisor and Data Management Macro Instructions (Form C28-6647).)

We also note that our discussion from now on will be limited to the two queued access methods. The student should, however, gain sufficient background so that his research in the IBM manual listed above will be profitable.

DCB Construct a Data Control Block. The general form of DCB is:

> name DCB keyword operands

1. The name may be any valid Assembler Language symbol.

2. The operands are the DCB keyword parameters. Three of these keyword parameters must appear in the DCB operand field. They are DDNAME, MACRF, and DSORG. A partial list of the DCB operands appears in Section 14.5. A complete list is in the data management macro manual listed above.

3. The data management routines will start to construct the data control block with the information supplied by the keyword parameter values. Additional information about the data control block is given by the values of the keyword parameters on the DD card. The final source of information is the data set label, if it exists.

If more than one source supplies information about a particular field in the data control block, then the DD card has precedence over the data set label. The DCB macro statement has precedence over both.

4. See Figure 14.1 for an example.

OPEN Activate a Data Control Block. The general form of *OPEN* is:

> OPEN (dcbname,([option 1,option 2]))

1. The dcbname is the symbolic address of any previously defined data control block.

2. The choices for option 1 are:

QSAM	QISAM
INPUT	INPUT
OUTPUT	OUTPUT
UPDAT (direct access device only)	

3. QISAM does not use option 2. QSAM may. If both options are chosen for QSAM, then the two options must be enclosed in an inner set of parentheses. For example,

> OPEN (BLUE,(OUTPUT,REREAD))

4. The second option in QSAM controls the positioning of the data set. If omitted, the data set will be positioned at the beginning.

5. UPDAT enables the application programmer to retrieve a record from a file on a direct access device, update the information on the record, and then write the updated record back into the data set. This is called updating in place.

Example 14.1

a. OPEN   (BLUE,OUTPUT)

b. OPEN   (DISC,UPDAT)

c. OPEN   READER

If option 1 is omitted, the default is INPUT.

d. OPEN   (READER,INPUT,DISC,UPDAT)

Two or more DCB's may be activated by one OPEN statement.

e. OPEN   (READER,,DISC,UPDAT)

The missing positional parameter, option 1, must be noted by the extra comma. The default INPUT will be assumed.

CLOSE   Deactivate a Data Control Block.   The general form of *CLOSE* is:

CLOSE   (dcbname,option)

1. CLOSE disconnects the data set from the program. That is, the data set is no longer available.
2. The options for a data set which resides on a magnetic tape or a direct access device are REREAD, LEAVE, or DISP. If REREAD is chosen, the data set is positioned at the beginning. LEAVE positions it at the logical end of the records. If DISP is coded, the value that is assigned to the DISP keyword on the DD card will be assumed. If the option is omitted, then DISP will be assumed. (See Section 14.6 where DISP is discussed in greater detail.)

Example 14.2

a. CLOSE   (BLUE,REREAD)

b. CLOSE   READER

c. CLOSE   (READER,,BLUE,REREAD)

1. Both READER and BLUE are closed by the CLOSE statement.
2. The missing option for READER is designated by a comma. DISP is assumed.

GET   Retrieve a Record.   The general form of GET in the move mode is:

GET   dcbname,address

One record is made available by the access method to the application program. In the move mode, this record is moved from the buffer area into the address which is specified in the second operand.

The general form of *GET* in the locate mode is:

GET   dcbname

One record is retrieved. The address of the buffer where the record has been placed by the access method is in register 1. The application program must move the record from this buffer to its own work area. The following examples should clarify the use of this mode.

Example 14.3

a. GET   BLUE,AREA

1. QSAM—The next logical record is retrieved by QSAM and moved to location AREA. The implied length of AREA should equal the length of the record.
2. QISAM—Usually GET is preceded by the SETL macro. The SETL macro positions the data set at a specified record or device address. GET then causes QISAM to retrieve that record. Since this is the move mode, QISAM will move the record to location AREA. Sequential retrieval of records using the GET macro will continue from this point. The data set can be repositioned by issuing an ESETL macro, then a new SETL.

   If no SETL macro instruction has been issued prior to the first GET, QISAM will start processing the data set at the first record.
3. The mode must be specified in the MACRF keyword parameter. The GET macro instruction in the move mode was specified for the READER DCB in Figure 14.1 by MACRF=GM.

b. GET   DATA

1. QSAM—This is the locate mode. The next logical record in the data set is retrieved by QSAM. The address of the buffer which contains the retrieved record is placed into register 1. Or to say it another way, register 1 points to the retrieved record.
2. QISAM—The information about the SETL macro instruction which was given in the previous example is pertinent here also. Since this is the locate mode of the GET macro, QISAM places the address of the retrieved record into register 1.
3. The code in (i) and (ii) are equivalent. We assume that the implied length of AREA is equal to the length of the retrieved record. The mode must be specified in the DCB statement as an option for the MACRF keyword.

Locate mode		*Move mode*
i. GET	DATA	ii. GET DATA,AREA
MVC	AREA,0(1)	

PUT   Write a Record.   The general form of *PUT* in the move mode is:

PUT   dcbname,address

PUT causes the access method to write one record in the sequential data set associated with the dcbname. The record is moved by the access method to the OUTPUT buffer.

The general form of PUT in the locate mode is:

    PUT   dcbname

1. Register 1 points to the location in an output buffer which will be used by the access method. The application programmer must move the record to this buffer before issuing the PUT. After the PUT instruction is executed, the address of a new location in an output buffer is returned in register 1.
2. The first PUT issued in a program does not cause a record to be written. The first PUT merely causes the address of the first location (record) to be placed into register 1. However, the access method, QSAM or QISAM, will remember that it owes the user a "PUT." This PUT will be made when the data set is closed.

Example 14.4

a. PUT   DATABLK,BLUE

1. QSAM—The record at location BLUE is moved to the output buffer by QSAM. QSAM then writes it into the sequential data set.
2. QISAM—The PUT macro causes the access method to write a record into the indexed sequential data set. The PUT macro can also be used to create an indexed sequential data set or to extend an existing data set. If the data set is being extended, then the key of the record which is being added must be higher than the key of any existing record in the data set.

b. Consider the following problem. A data set consists of five punched cards. Read in these cards using the GET macro in the move mode. Print the five records using the PUT macro in the locate mode.

We assume that:

1. the input file is READER. MACRF=GM has been coded in the operand field of its DCB statement.
2. the output file is PRINTER. MACRF=PL and RECFM=FA have been coded in the PRINTER DCB statement.
3. the first byte of each record is blank.

FIGURE 14.3

```
          :
          :
          LA    5,5                BCT REGISTER
LOOP1  ①  PUT   PRINTER            BUFFER ADDR IN REG 1
       ②  LR    2,1                SAVE BUFFER ADDRESS
       ③  GET   READER,DATA        READ A CARD
       ④  MVC   0(80,2),DATA       MOVE RECORD TO BUFFER
          BCT   5,LOOP1
```

The first PUT PRINTER (see ①) did not print any record. The command merely caused the access method to return the address of an output buffer location in register 1. The address of this location was saved (see ②) because the GET macro (see ③) destroys the contents of register 1.

Since register 2 points to the output buffer location, the instruction MVC (see ④) moves the record to the buffer. The second PUT (see ①) causes a record to be printed. When the data set is closed, the access method will cause the "PUT" of the last record.

PUTX   Update a Record.   The general form of PUTX is:

PUTX   dcbname

The PUTX macro rewrites an updated record into a QSAM or QISAM data set. There is one restriction. A locate-mode GET macro must have brought the original record into MEMORY.

Example 14.5

Replace the fifth record of DISKFILE, a QSAM data set, by the record located at DATA. The locate mode has been chosen for the GET macro. The length of a record is 80 bytes. Assume that DISKFILE is positioned at the first record.

The solution appears in Figure 14.4.

CNTRL   Control Online Printer.   The general form of CNTRL is:

CNTRL   dcbname,options

The options are:

Line spacing		Carriage control	
Option	Result	Option	Result
SP,1	single line skipped	SK,1	skip to a new page
SP,2	two lines skipped	SK,n	see below
SP,3	three lines skipped		

Note that the punched carriage tapes vary from installation to installation. SK,n causes a carriage skip to a position which corresponds to the nth channel of the carriage tape. n must be an integer from 1 to 12 inclusive.

FIGURE 14.4

```
        LA    5,5
LOOP    GET   DISKFILE
        BCT   5,LOOP
        MVC   0(80,1),DATA
        PUTX  DISKFILE
```

The use of the CNTRL macro must be specified as an option to the MACRF keyword parameter in the DCB statement. MACRF=PMC specifies PUT in the move mode and the use of the CNTRL macro. See the discussion of MACRF in Section 14.5.

Example 14.6

a. CNTRL   DATA,SP,3

Three lines will be skipped.

b. CNTRL   DATA,SK,1

The next line will be printed on a new page (fourth line from the top).

SETL   Position QISAM Data Set.   We limit our discussion to two options, K and B. The general form of SETL with option K is:

SETL   dcbname,K,address

1. The third operand is the address of a MEMORY location in the user's program. The user must place the key of the record he wishes to retrieve into this location. The QISAM data set is positioned by this macro to the record whose key matches the key in the location specified by *address*.
2. The QISAM data set will be processed sequentially from this record until the end of the data set or until an ESETL instruction is issued.
3. An ESETL instruction must be issued between two SETL macros.
   The general form of SETL with option B is:

SETL   dcbname,B

1. The QISAM data set is positioned to the first record. Items 2 and 3 in the above list are pertinent here.

Example 14.7

Retrieve the record whose key is equal to TULIP from the QISAM file named DATAIN.
   The solution to this problem appears in Figure 14.5.

FIGURE 14.5

```
MVC    BLUE, = C'TULIP'
SETL   DATAIN,K,BLUE
GET    DATAIN,WORKAREA
```

ESETL   End Sequential Retrieval.   The general form of ESETL is:

    ESETL   dcbname

The ESETL macro ends the sequential retrieval of a data set. In a sense it is the inverse of SETL. Remember, an ESETL must be issued between two SETL macros.

Example 14.8

Retrieve the records in DATAIN whose keys are equal to SMITH and BULTY. Retrieve the record which follows SMITH in the data set also.

The solution to this problem appears in Figure 14.6.

LA	3,0	INDEX REGISTER
MVC	BLUE, = C'SMITH'	KEY → BLUE
SETL	DATAIN,K,BLUE	POSITION DATASET
GET	DATAIN,AREAIN(3)	RETRIEVE RECORD
LA	3,80(3)	INCREMENT INDEX
GET	DATAIN,AREAIN(3)	RETRIEVE RECORD
ESETL	DATAIN	END SEQUENTIAL
MVC	BLUE, = C'BULTY'	NEW KEY
SETL	DATAIN,K,BLUE	POSITION DATASET
LA	3,80(3)	INCREMENT INDEX
GET	DATAIN,AREAIN(3)	RETRIEVE RECORD

FIGURE 14.6

14.4   Buffering and Blocking

The Operating System subroutine which is responsible for all input and output operations is called the Input/Output Supervisor. The application program does not communicate directly with this I/O Supervisor. Rather, the application program notifies the access method (by GET or PUT) when it wants an input record or when it wishes to write a record on an output device.

Buffering.   The access method maintains a supply of input records (which belong to the data set it is servicing) in a block in MEMORY. The request for an input record is met by making one available from this block. This block of MEMORY which is reserved by the access method when the application program issues an OPEN macro instruction is called a *buffer*. The queued access methods reserve (or provide) two buffers for each data set they service. The length (number of bytes) of each buffer is equal to the length of the longest block of records in the data set.

Let us suppose we have a QSAM data set named MAUD which resides on a disk. LRECL (the logical record length) is 60. BLKSIZE is 300. In other words, there are five records per block. When we issue the OPEN macro for

MAUD, QSAM will provide two buffers equal in length to the BLKSIZE, each 300 bytes long. We do not know the addresses of these buffers but that does not matter if we are in the move mode. If we had specified the locate mode in the DCB statement, QSAM would place the address (when needed) of the pertinent location of the buffer into register 1.

Suppose MAUD has been opened as an output data set and we have specified MACRF=PM, which means we will PUT records in the move mode. When we issue PUT MAUD,AREAOUT, QSAM will move our record from AREAOUT to the buffer. After we issue five PUTs, one buffer will be full. QSAM will notify the I/O Supervisor that an output operation is needed. The Supervisor will command the channel to write the block of records from the buffer into the output data set.

Once the channel has started writing the records into the data set, control will be returned to our program. Both the channel and our program will perform simultaneously. This *overlapping* of functions increases efficiency, made possible by the use of buffers.

The action in the locate mode is the same. The only difference is that QSAM, instead of moving the logical record to our program, will provide us with the address of this record in register 1. Remember, this will be an address of some location in one of the buffers. We must move the records from our work area to that location.

If MAUD has been opened as an input data set, then the OPEN instruction causes QSAM to inform the I/O Supervisor to start an input operation. (This is done even before we request a record!) The I/O Supervisor will command the appropriate channel to fill both buffers with the records of two sequential blocks from MAUD. These records are "queued"—waiting for the user program to request them. (This input operation is done while our program is executing its instructions.)

When we issue our first GET, the first record in buffer 1 is made available to our program by QSAM. After the fifth GET, buffer 1 is "empty," that is, we have exhausted the records in the buffer. QSAM notifies the I/O Supervisor that another input operation is needed. The Supervisor again commands the appropriate channel to read a block of records into buffer 1.

The important point is that the input or output operations and the processing by the application program can occur simultaneously. This phenomenon is made possible by the use of buffer areas. Think of the havoc that would result if the input records were read directly into the work area which was being processed by the application program at the same time.

Blocking. The queued access methods, once the block of records is in the buffer, make individual records available to the application program as requested. We have seen that when the request for records by the application program exhausts the supply in one buffer, the access method causes another block to be retrieved. The time saved by the simultaneous input operations by the channel and the data processing by the CPU is very appealing. But there is also another reason for blocking records. We now consider that rea

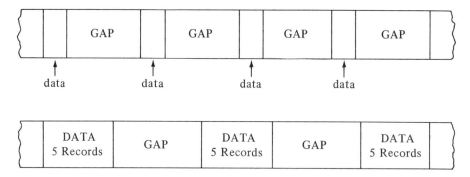

FIGURE 14.7

son by looking at the records on a magnetic tape. (A discussion of records on a disk pack is in Topic 1 of the Computer Notebook.)

When a record is placed on a tape there must be some way to differentiate it from another record. The best way to separate them is by space. The space is known as an *interrecord gap* (IRG). Now suppose that our record is 80 bytes long and that the tape holds 800 bytes (or characters) per inch. (This is called 800 bpi density.) Hence the amount of space occupied by each record will be one-tenth of an inch.

The interrecord gap (IRG) must be close to six-tenths of an inch; that is, we must keep about six-tenths of an inch of space between each record. Now suppose we have 1000 records. The amount of space required by our data set for the records is 100 inches. The amount of space required by IRG is 600 inches. This situation is depicted in the first diagram of Figure 14.7.

This six-to-one ratio of IRG to record space is cut drastically when we block the records. Suppose we put just five records in a block. That means we can hold all of our records in 200 blocks. Our data still requires the 100 inches of space on the tape, but the space needed for the interrecord gaps has been cut to 120 inches. The length of magnetic tape needed for our data set has been reduced from 700 inches to 220 inches! The second diagram in Figure 14.7 depicts the tape when the records are blocked.

What is the optimum block size? The answer to that question depends on a number of factors. We mention two here: one is the length of the logical record, the other is the amount of space available in MEMORY for buffers. Recall that the blocks will be read into the buffers by the channels. Hence, the blocks must be small enough to leave sufficient space in MEMORY for the problem programs.

14.5 The DCB Keyword Parameters

Space for the data control block is reserved in the application program by the DCB macro instruction. The data control block is constructed in that space by information provided by the DCB keyword operands. There are over 25 of these parameters, but we shall limit our discussion to 14 of them. Table 14.3 lists these parameters. An X in an access method column means that the keyword in that row is applicable to that access method. The circled numbers give the order in which we discuss the items.

TABLE 14.3 DCB Keyword Parameters

		QSAM	QISAM
⑨	BFTEK	X	
⑤	BLKSIZE	X	X
⑩	BUFNO	X	X
⑬	CYLOFL		X
③	DDNAME	X	X
⑦	DEVD	X	
①	DSØRG	X	X
⑧	EODAD	X	X
⑪	KEYLEN		X
④	LRECL	X	X
②	MACRF	X	X
⑭	OPTCD		X
⑥	RECFM	X	X
⑫	RKP		X

We called attention to the fact, when we studied the example in Section 14.1, that many of these keyword parameters may appear in either the operand field of the DCB statement or in the operand field of the job control language DD card. Three of the keywords—DSORG, DDNAME, and MACRF—must, however, appear in the DCB statement. The others may appear on either card.

The minimum number of DCB keywords necessary to complete a QSAM data control block is six. We list these in Table 14.4. Both data sets described in Figure 14.1 adhered to this minimum list.

TABLE 14.4 QSAM Minimum Set

	Required in DCB	Required in DCB or DD
BLKSIZE		X
DDNAME	X	
DSØRG	X	
LRECL		X
MACRF	X	
RECFM		X

We now consider each of the keyword parameters in Table 14.3.

DSORG   Data Set Organization.   DSORG specifies the way the data is organized. The information must be given in the DCB statement. The option for QSAM is PS and that for QISAM is IS. PS stands for physical sequential and IS stands for indexed sequential.

MACRF   Macro Forms.   MACRF specifies which data management macros will be used to process the data set. The keyword also designates the mode for GET and PUT—locate or move. (There is also a substitute mode which we do not cover.) The order in which the options are specified must be followed.

QSAM

Option	*Meaning*
PM	PUT (move mode)
PL	PUT (locate mode)
PMC	PUT (move mode),CNTRL
PLC	PUT (locate mode),CNTRL
GM	GET (move mode)
GL	GET (locate mode)
GLC	GET (locate mode),CNTRL
GMC	GET (move mode),CNTRL

QISAM

Option	*Meaning*
PM	PUT (move mode)
PL	PUT (locate mode)
GM	GET (move mode)
GM,S	GET (move mode),SETL
GL	GET (locate mode)
GL,S	GET (locate mode),SETL
GL,S,PU	GET (locate mode),SETL,PUTX

GL,SK has been omitted from the QISAM options. GL and S have the meaning described above. Example 14.7 is an illustration of the use of K and should clarify the meaning of K.

DDNAME   Data Definition Name.   The DDNAME keyword specifies the name of the DD card which may have more information about the data control block. This keyword must appear in the operand field of the DCB statement. Examples of its use appear in Figure 14.1.

LRECL   Logical Record Length.   LRECL specifies the length of a record. Consider LRECL=20 in the READER DCB of Figure 14.1. We might say that the keyword with the option of 20 passed a message to the CARD-

READER: "Read the first 20 columns of the card." Similarly, LRECL=20 in the PRINTER DCB told the PRINTER: "Print a line with 20 characters." See Figure 14.1 for an example of the use of LRECL.

BLKSIZE Length of a Block of Records. BLKSIZE specifies the number of bytes that must be reserved for a block. The value given must be a multiple of the record length. That is, the division of the value of the BLKSIZE by LRECL gives the number of records in a block.

RECFM Record Form. RECFM specifies information about the format and characteristics of the records. (The letter A in the option designates the first byte of the record to be the carriage control character. The option A must not be chosen if the macro CNTRL is specified in MACRF.)

QSAM

Option	*Meaning*
RECFM = FA	fixed length; carriage control
RECFM = FB	fixed; blocked
RECFM = FBA	fixed; blocked, carriage control
RECFM = VA	variable length records; carriage control

Fixed means all records are of the same length.

QISAM

Option	*Meaning*
RECFM = V	variable length records
RECFM = VB	variable length, blocked
RECFM = F	fixed length records
RECFM = FB	fixed, blocked

DEVD Device Type. DEVD specifies the type of device that is to be associated with the data set. If DEVD=DA, the data set may be on a direct access device, magnetic tape, or cards. If DEVD is omitted, then DA is assumed by the data management services.

The DEVD option DA gives the data set the greatest amount of device independence by assuring that the DCB block is as large as possible. We suggest, therefore, that DEVD be omitted since the default is DA.

Consider the PRINTER DCB statement in Figure 14.1. The DEVD operand was omitted; hence DA was assumed. The SYSOUT=A in the associated keyword directed the data set to the printer.

DEVD must not appear on the DD card.

EODAD End of Data Set Address. EODAD specifies the address to which control is transferred when the end of a data set is reached. EODAD is optional. An application program will be abnormally terminated if the end of a data set is reached and EODAD has been omitted.

Example 14.9

Let us assume that a data set assigned to the READER has five data cards, and the characteristics of the data set were given by the following DCB statement and DD card:

```
BLUE    DCB    DSORG = PS,DDNAME = RED,LRECL = 80,
               BLKSIZE = 80,RECFM = F,MACRF = GM,
               EODAD = VERYL
          ⋮
RED     DD     *
```

The program segment is:

```
LOOP    GET    BLUE,AREAIN(5)
        LA     5,80(5)
        B      LOOP
```

In the sixth execution of the GET instruction, an attempt will be made to read the delimiter (/*) card. Since the end of the data set has been reached, a branch will be made to VERYL, the address specified by EODAD. If EODAD and its option are removed from the DCB statement, the program will terminate abnormally.

BFTEK   Buffering Technique.   BFTEK specifies the type of buffering the control program (the access method) should use. QSAM has two options: simple and exchange. If the keyword is omitted, simple buffering is assumed. We restrict ourselves to simple buffering in this chapter.

BUFNO   Number of Buffers.   BUFNO specifies the number of buffers the application program needs for its data set. If the operand is omitted, two buffers will be assigned. Two buffers are usually enough to obtain the maximum I/O efficiency. Programs which do a lot of input and output (that is, programs that are I/O bound) should request additional buffers to increase the processing efficiency.

BUFNO=3 will result in the assignment of three buffers for the data set.

KEYLEN   Length of Key (QISAM).   KEYLEN specifies the length (in bytes) of the key associated with each record in the data set. KEYLEN is specified only when the QISAM data set is created. The key length appears in the data set label of existing QISAM data sets. See the following example.

Example 14.10   Creation of a QISAM Data Set

```
TARMO    DCB    DSORG = IS,KEYLEN = 5,BLKSIZE = 47,RKP = 10,
                LRECL = 47,MACRF = PM,DDNAME = BB
```

1. The key is part of the logical record length. Hence the LRECL=47 includes the key length.

2. A QISAM file has two modes: load and scan. The key length is specified in the load (creation) mode. The keyword KEYLEN must be omitted in the scan mode.

RKP   Relative Key Position (QISAM).   RKP specifies the position of the key relative to the first byte of the record. RKP=5,KEYLEN=6 specifies that the key occupies bytes 5 through 10 inclusive. Recall that the first byte is byte 0. RKP must not be specified in the scan mode.

RKP=0 when the key field starts in the first byte of the record. In this case QISAM doesn't consider the key field to be part of the record field. This means that block size will be the sum of the logical record length and the key length. In Example 14.16 we create a QISAM data set with one record in each block. We specify: RKP=0,KEYLEN=20,LRECL=60,BLKSIZE= 80.

We might have specified RKP=10,KEYLEN=20,LRECL=80,BLKSIZE =80. Our key in this case would occupy bytes 10–29 inclusive. Notice the difference in the specification of block size.

If the key is imbedded in the record, that is, RKP≠0; then QISAM will copy the key in front of the logical record when that record is stored on a disk. (The key is in two places.) When RKP=0, QISAM doesn't have to do this.

Is this important? Yes. The storage space in MEMORY for retrieved records should be equal to the block size when RKP=0. The storage should be equal to the sum of the block size and the key length when RKP≠0. QISAM retrieves the key in front of the record along with the record.

CYLOFL   Cylinder Overflow.   CYLOFL specifies the number of tracks the application programmer wishes to reserve on each cylinder for records that overflow from the other tracks in that cylinder.

CYLOFL=1 will set aside one track for overflow records.

OPTCD   Optional Services.   Our discussion refers to QISAM only. OPTCD specifies the optional services that the application program wants from the operating system with respect to the QISAM data set. We discuss the optional services represented by the letter codes L,M, and Y.

Code	Meaning
L	delete marked records when space is needed for new records (see discussion below)
M	create master index when required
Y	use cylinder overflow areas

A programmer may insert all ones into the bits of the first byte of any record. A record marked in this manner will be deleted by the access method when space is needed for a new record, if the L option is chosen. OPTCD = L must not be chosen when the relative key position is zero.

OPTCD concludes our discussion of the DCB keyword parameters. Again we point out that we have not exhausted the list of DCB parameters nor have we exhausted the options available with the parameters that we have presented.

Section 6 presents a second set of keyword parameters. Since these parameters must be coded on the DD cards, we will refer to them as the DD keyword parameters.

14.6   The DD Card Keyword Parameters

We have divided the set of DD card keywords into three groups in order to simplify our discussion of them. We list these groups in Table 14.5. We discuss each group in turn. The student may find additional information about these parameters and job control language in particular in the IBM manual, *JOB Control Language User's Guide,* Form GC 28-6704.

TABLE 14.5   The DD Card Groups

Group	Name
I	Data set information
II	Data set location
III	Data set size

Group I   Data Set Information.   Group I has two parameters: DSNAME and DISP. DSNAME (data set name) may be omitted. If omitted, the Operating System assigns a unique name to the data set. If the user chooses to name his data set, he is limited to an eight character name such that the first character is alphanumeric (A through Z, 0 through 9) or national (@, #, $). The remaining characters may include a hyphen.

If the name is omitted, the data set will be temporary; that is, all nontemporary data sets must be named by the programmer.

The DISP (disposition) keyword parameter is composed of three positional subparameters which specify the current status of the data set, its disposition at end of the job step, and its disposition should the job step terminate abnormally.

The general form is:

DISP = (current status,normal disp,abnormal disp)

Table 14.6 lists some of the options available for each of the three positional subparameters.

1. *OLD* means that the data set already exists.
2. *NEW* means that the data set is being created in this job step.
3. *KEEP* tells that the access method to "save" the data set when the job step is completed.

TABLE 14.6   DISP Subparameter Options

Current	Normal	Abnormal
OLD	KEEP	KEEP
NEW	DELETE	DELETE

4. *DELETE* tells the access method to "erase" the data set when the job step has terminated.

Example 14.11

a. DISP=(NEW,KEEP,DELETE)

The data set is being created in this job step. It will be saved if the job step terminates normally. If the job step terminates abnormally, the data set will be scratched.

b. DISP=(OLD,DELETE,DELETE)

The DISP parameter specifies an existing data set. It will be deleted at the end of the job step.

Note: DISP=(NEW,DELETE,DELETE) will be assumed if the disposition parameter is omitted.

Group II   Data Set Location.   We discuss three of the available keyword parameters: UNIT, VOLUME, and SYSOUT.

The SYSOUT parameter is a convenient method of specifying the output device such as a printer, card punch, disk, or tape drive. Traditionally, SYSOUT=A directs a data set to the printer, and SYSOUT=B directs it to the card punch.

The UNIT keyword requests an I/O unit by address, by type, or by group. If SYSOUT is coded, UNIT may be omitted. It also may be omitted if the data set already exists and the data set is catalogued or has been passed from another job step.

Example 14.12 illustrates the coding for each kind of request.

Example 14.12

a. by address

UNIT=191

The direct access device whose hardware address is 191 is requested. *Do not* request an I/O UNIT by hardware address unless there is a need for the particular device. If the particular UNIT is not available, the execution of the user program may be delayed.

b. by device type

> UNIT = 2311

The data set will be placed on any available 2311 disk storage drive. The device type option provides the programmer with a greater degree of device independence than the hardware address option.

c. by group name

> UNIT = SYSDA

Requesting an I/O unit by group name provides the programmer with the greatest degree of device independence. The group name for devices of the same kind is selected by the installation during system generation. SYSDA is the traditional way of specifying a direct access storage device. Ask the installation manager for the group names.

The VOLUME or VOL keyword parameter requests a specific volume of the kind specified by the UNIT keyword. A volume can be a tape reel, a disk, pack, a drum, a bin in a 2321 data cell, etc. VOLUME must always give the volume serial number for an existing but not catalogued data set. The VOL keyword may be omitted if the data set is being created in the program. The Operating System will pick an appropriate volume of the kind specified by the UNIT parameter. If the data set already exists, it may be necessary to tell the operating system where it is.

Example 14.13

> UNIT = SYSDA,VOL = SER = PCPRES

The data set is assigned to a direct access device which has been labeled PCPRES.

Group III   Data Set Size.   The keyword parameter options in Group I name the data set and give its disposition at the end of the job step. The options in Group II specify its location. The final group that we discuss consists of one keyword parameter, SPACE. There are others, but we omit discussion of them in this text. (See the JCL User's Guide.)

SPACE specifies the amount of space to be allocated to the data set. On a direct access volume this allocation may be by block, track, or cylinder. The general form of SPACE is:

> SPACE = (method,(amount,increment))

We have omitted several optional positional subparameters from the general form to simplify our discussion.

Example 14.14

a. SPACE=(80,(300,100))

The application program requests 300 80-byte blocks. This allocation will be incremented by 100 80-byte blocks if the first amount proves insufficient.

b. SPACE=(80,300)

An allocation of 300 80-byte blocks is requested. Since no secondary allotment is requested, the inner parentheses may be dropped.

c. SPACE=(TRK,(200,10))

The space is requested by tracks. The initial request is for 200 tracks with an increment of 10 tracks if needed. (A track contains 3625 bytes on a 2311 disk pack.)

d. SPACE=(CYL,(15,5))

The initial allocation to the data set will be fifteen cylinders. The secondary allotment is five cylinders. A cylinder consists of ten tracks.

14.7 Examples of Data Set Definitions

In this section we present several examples of the definitions of various types of data sets. We include only the DCB statement and the DD card.

Example 14.15

```
a. DATA       DCB   DSØRG = PS,MACRF = (GL,PM),DDNAME = BLUE,
                    LRECL = 80,BLKSIZE = 400,RECFM = F
              ⋮
   //GØ.BLUE   DD   DSNAME = ALICE,SPACE = (TRK,(10,5)),
                    UNIT = SYSDA
```

A QSAM direct access file has been defined. There are five records in each block. The GET macro will be used in the locate mode when the data set is opened as an input file. The PUT macro will be used in the move mode when the data set is opened for output. The initial allotment will be 10 tracks or 36,250 bytes. The data set, ALICE, will be deleted at the end of the job step.

b. Creation of a QISAM data set.

```
DISK            DCB   DSØRG = IS,MACRF = PL,DDNAME = ONDISK,
                      KEYLEN = 4,BUFNØ = 3,RECFM = F,LRECL = 80,
                      BLKSIZE = 80,RKP = 10
                ⋮
//GØ.ØNDISK   DD    SPACE = (CYL,10),UNIT = 2311,DSNAME = CARØL,
                    DCB = DSØRG = IS,DISP = (NEW,KEEP,DELETE),
                    VØL = SER = PCPRES,CYLØFL = 1,ØPTCD = YM
```

A QISAM data set has been defined. It is in the load mode. The data set will be organized on a 2311 disk pack. Ten cylinders, 362,500 bytes, will be allocated to CAROL. One track per cylinder will be allotted to record overflow. A master index will be created.

Note that all DCB keywords which appear on the DD card must be in the form DCB=(keyword=,keyword=). If there is only one keyword on the DD card, then the parentheses can be omitted. For example, DCB=DSORG=IS.

The general form of SPACE for QISAM is SPACE=(CYL,(quantity,,index)). SPACE is allocated by cylinders. The index specifies the number of cylinders to be reserved for indexes. In this text we choose the simplest form. We let the system worry about the indexes. We note that there are other ways to request allocation of space for an indexed sequential data set.

c. Code the DCB statement and the DD card so that the data set named CAROL can be retrieved. In other words, define the scan mode of the QISAM data set created in the last example.

The solution to this problem is:

```
BLUE        DCB     DSØRG = IS,MACRF = (GL,SK),DDNAME = SAM
            ⋮
//GØ.SAM   DD      DSNAME = INDEX,UNIT = 2311,DCB = DSØRG = IS,
                    VØL = SER = PCPRES,DISP = (ØLD,KEEP,KEEP)
```

The SETL macro instruction will be used. The search for a record will be by key. The application programmer will put the key in some four-byte location in MEMORY. He will pass the address of this location to QISAM via the SETL instruction.

```
d. TAPE     DCB   DSØRG = PS,MACRF = GM,DDNAME = TPI,
                  LRECL = 80,BLKSIZE = 800,RECFM = F
            ⋮
//GØ.TPI   DD    DISP = (ØLD,KEEP),DSNAME = AL121,
                  VØL = SER = ABC,UNIT = 2400 − 2
```

A QSAM data set which resides on a magnetic tape will be retrieved.

Example 14.16

a. A card file consists of 200 80-byte records. Read in the card file. Create an indexed sequential data set for the 200 records. Let the key be the name field, bytes 0–19 of each record. Put the records from the card file into this QISAM data set.
The solution appears in Figures 14.8 and 14.9.

b. The following problem refers to the QISAM data set created in part (a).

1. A card file contains the keys to several of the records in the QISAM data set named ARVO. Read in this card file. Retrieve each record in ARVO which is associated with a key in the card file.

```
          PRINT  NOGEN
          INIT
          OPEN   (CARDIN,INPUT)
          OPEN   (DISKFILE,OUTPUT)
LOOP      GET    CARDIN,AREAIN
          PUT    DISKFILE,AREAIN
          B      LOOP
EOJ       CLOSE  CARDIN
          CLOSE  DISKFILE
RED       GOBACK
AREAIN    DS     CL80
CARDIN    DCB    DSORG=PS,MACRF=GM,DDNAME=BLUE,                    X
                 LRECL=80,BLKSIZE=80,RECFM=F,EODAD=EOJ
DISKFILE  DCB    DSORG=IS,MACRF=PM,DDNAME=ONDISK,LRECL=60,         X
                 BLKSIZE=80,RECFM=F,KEYLEN=20,RKP=0
          END
```

FIGURE 14.8 The Program (Load Mode)

```
//GO.ONDISK   DD    DSN=ARVO,SPACE=(CYL,2),UNIT=SYSDA,
//                  DCB=DSORG=IS,VOL=SER=PCPRES,DISP=(NEW,KEEP)
//GO.BLUE     DD    *
```

FIGURE 14.9 The DD Cards

FIGURE 14.10 The Program (Scan Mode)

```
          PRINT  NOGEN
          INIT
          OPEN   (CARDIN,INPUT)
          OPEN   (DISKFILE,INPUT)
          OPEN   (RECDISC,OUTPUT)
LOOP1     GET    CARDIN,KEY
          SETL   DISKFILE,K,KEY
          GET    DISKFILE,AREAIN
          ESETL  DISKFILE
          PUT    RECDISC,AREAIN
          B      LOOP1
EOJ1      CLOSE  (CARDIN,,DISKFILE)
          CLOSE  (RECDISC,REREAD)
          OPEN   (PRINTER,OUTPUT)
          OPEN   (RECDISC,INPUT)
LOOP2     GET    RECDISC,AREAIN
          PUT    PRINTER,AREAIN-1
          B      LOOP2
EOJ2      CLOSE  PRINTER
          CLOSE  RECDISC
          GOBACK
CARDIN    DCB    DSORG=PS,MACRF=GM,DDNAME=BLUE,LRECL=20,           X
                 BLKSIZE=20,RECFM=F,EODAD=EOJ1
DISKFILE  DCB    DSORG=IS,DDNAME=INDEX,MACRF=(GM,SK),EODAD=EOJ1,   X
                 BLKSIZE=80,LRECL=60,RECFM=F
PRINTER   DCB    DSORG=PS,MACRF=PM,DDNAME=SAM,RECFM=FA,            X
                 LRECL=80,BLKSIZE=80
RECDISC   DCB    DSORG=PS,DDNAME=GREEN,MACRF=(GM,PM),RECFM=F,      X
                 LRECL=81,BLKSIZE=81,EODAD=EOJ2
KEY       DS     CL20
          DC     C' '         USED FOR CARRIAGE CONTROL
AREAIN    DS     CL80
          END
```

2. Create a QSAM file on the disk. Store all records retrieved from ARVO in this file.

3. When all records have been retrieved and stored on the QSAM data set, open a print file and print all the records in the QSAM file.

The number of keys in the card file is immaterial since the EODAD option will specify the branch address when the end of the card file is reached.

We need four data sets:

        a. the scan mode of the QISAM data set named ARVO (See Figure 14.8.)

        b. a print data set

        c. a card file

        d. a QSAM disk file

The solution appears in Figures 14.10 and 14.11.

```
//GO.GREEN    DD    UNIT=SYSDA,SPACE=(80,(50,10)),DSN=NAMES,
//                  VOL=SER=PCPRES,DISP=(NEW,KEEP)
//GO.INDEX    DD    DSN=ARVO,UNIT=SYSDA,VOL=SER=PCPRES,DISP=(OLD,KEEP),
//                  DCB=DSORG=IS
//GO.SAM      DD    SYSOUT=A
//GO.BLUE     DD    *
```

FIGURE 14.11 The DD Cards

Computer Notebook

TOPIC 1 Disk Storage

If the programmer desires to make efficient and effective use of the input/output access methods, he should be conversant with the characteristics of the auxiliary storage mediums where he stores his data sets. We have, therefore, devoted the Computer Notebook of this chapter to a discussion of the direct access storage medium, the disk pack. Most of the figures that we cite in this topic refer to the IBM 2311 disk pack.

The common phonograph record is an example of a disk with which every reader should be familiar. The phonograph record has one track which spirals inward. The "data" that is recorded on the track produces a "noise" (music?) as it is read by the needle on the phonograph arm. The needle is able to "read" the entire distance from the beginning of the track to the end near the center of the record.

A direct access storage medium disk differs from a phonograph record in that each face (each side) of the disk contains 203 tracks. That is, the disk has 203 concentric circular tracks. The mechanism, the *head* (which corresponds to the needle on the phonograph arm), which is attached to the *access arm,* cannot by itself move from one track to another. The access arm must be physically moved if, for some reason, one wanted to read or write another track on the same side of the disk. (Compare this to the phonograph access arm which can traverse the phonograph record track from the beginning to the end.)

One track can store 3625 bytes of information. Since we have 203 tracks on each side, we can store approximately 1,471,750 bytes of data on one disk. Since this is an insufficient amount of space for many needs, the disks are grouped together into a pack by inserting a shaft through the center of six disks. (The disks in this pack are about an inch apart.) The upper face of the top disk and the lower face of the bottom disk in the pack are not used for storage purposes since these surfaces are so vulnerable to damage.

That leaves ten surfaces for our data. Now let us order these surfaces as follows: the lower face of the top disk is surface 0; the upper and the lower faces of the next disk are surfaces 1 and 2, respectively. We proceed in this fashion to the upper face of the bottom disk which we label surface 9.

Now let us make a temporary ordering of the tracks so that we can explain the *cylinder concept* more readily. We number the tracks for this purpose from 0 (the first track on the outer edge) to 202 (the track closest to the center of the disk). Remember that this is only a temporary ordering. The final track numbers will depend on their relative position in a *cylinder.*

The set of all tracks which have been numbered 0 (there are 10 of them) make up cylinder 0. Cylinder 1 of the disk pack is the set of tracks we have temporarily numbered as 1. Hence, it follows that our disk pack contains 203 cylinders such that each cylinder consists of ten tracks.

Now let us drop our temporary ordering and reorder our tracks. Track 0 of cylinder 0 will be the first track in the lower face of the first disk. (Recall that the upper face of the first disk is not used.) Track 1 of cylinder 0 is the first track in surface 1. Track 9 of cylinder 0 is the first track of surface 9. This is the former track 0 of surface 9.

Example 14.17

We wish to locate track 8 of cylinder 9 in the disk pack.

We find that track 8 of cylinder 9 is on the lower face of the fifth disk from the top of the pack. It is the tenth track from the outer edge. (In the old ordering it was track 9 on surface 8.)

Instead of having 203 tracks on each of 10 surfaces, we now have 10 tracks on each of 203 cylinders. The cylinders are on the 10 surfaces.

Each track has 3625 bytes available for storing information. Each cylinder, therefore, has 36,250 bytes of storage space. Hence the disk pack has a capacity of about $7\frac{1}{4}$ million bytes.

We ordered the tracks to explain the very important cylinder concept. Our ordering may not be related to any IBM ordering.

Now let us suppose that a disk pack is placed on the drive spindle. The protective covering is removed. The START button is depressed. When the disk pack attains a speed of about 2400 revolutions per minute (rpm), it is automatically cleaned. A set of brushes scan each disk to remove the dust which might affect the reading and writing on the disk. (Compare this speed with the 78 rpm of the turn-table of an ordinary phonograph.) A green light will signify when the disk pack is cleaned and ready for use.

Each surface has its own read-write head. Two read-write heads are attached to one access arm. All five of the access arms are positioned in such a way that the heads can read or write one complete cylinder without any physical movement with respect to the access arms. That is, suppose the arms are at cylinder 27; then we can write on every track of cylinder 27 without further physical movement of either the arms or the heads.

The time required to move the access arms from, say, cylinder 40 to another cylinder is called *access time* or *seek time*. It, of course, takes more time to move the arms a distance of 40 cylinders than it does to move them 10 cylinders. The average access time is about 75 milliseconds. (A millisecond is 1/1000 of a second.) The time required to find the record in the track is called the *rotational delay*. In the 2311 disk pack, the average rotational delay is about 12 milliseconds.

Figure 14.12 is a straight line projection of a disk track. The index point is an actual physical hole in the disk which is sensed by the read-write head as the starting point of the track. Both the cylinder number and the head number (this is equal to the surface number) are recorded in the HOME ADDRESS field along with other pertinent information about the track.

The next field, the TRACK-ID, contains a considerable amount of information about the track and about the records which have been recorded on the track. The TRACK-ID field contains both the track number and the cylinder to which the track belongs. It also gives the record number (within the track) along with the length of a physical record. (See Section 14.4 of this chapter for a discussion of the difference between a physical and logical record.) If the record has been written with a key, the length of the key is recorded in the TRACK-ID field. Figure 14.13 projects a straight line image of a track which contains records written with keys.

An ADDRESS MARKER field, consisting of a one-byte character and a

FIGURE 14.12

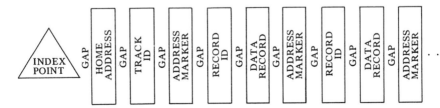

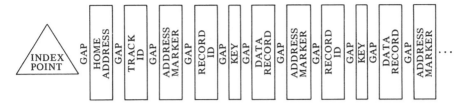

FIGURE 14.13

two-byte data cyclic check field, precedes each physical record that has been placed on the track.

The Operating System stores information pertinent to the physical record that follows in the RECORD-ID field. This information includes:

1. the cylinder number
2. the track number
3. the record number (within the track)
4. the length of the physical record
5. the key length (if a key is used)

If the length of the key field is zero, then no key has been designated. If the length of the data field is zero, then no data has actually been written. This fact usually signifies the end of the data set.

A gap, a space with no recorded information—somewhat analogous to the interrecord gap discussed in Section 14.4—exists between each field. This gap is depicted in both Figure 14.12 and Figure 14.13. The length of the gap varies depending on the length of the field which precedes it. The gap between the key field and the data field is always at least 18 bytes long.

The number of blocks that can be placed on a track can be determined by two formulas. If no key is written, then formula I applies; otherwise use formula II. B is the number of bytes required for any block except the last. BL is the number of bytes required for the last block on the track.

Formula I
$B = 61 + 1.049 \times DL$
$BL = DL$
Where DL is data length.

Formula II
$B = 81 + 1.049 \times (KL + DL)$
$BL = 20 + KL + DL$
Where DL is data length and KL is key length.

EXERCISES

1. Write an input routine which reads in the first 39 bytes of an IBM card. Let the program segment include an output routine which prints the last 26 bytes of the 39 bytes that were read in.

2. Consider the baseball file problem in exercise 11 of Chapter 13. Define a disk QSAM data set for these records. Read the records into MEMORY, put them on the disk data set, update them, and print the updated data set. (Hint: consider the PUTX macro.) Use the IBM manual *Supervisor and Data Management Macros* as a reference.

3. Consider the baseball file once again. Add a key field to each field (or use the name field as a key). Define a QISAM file for the baseball records, then follow the procedure in exercise 2. Show how to retrieve the record of any player. (Hint: consider the SETL macro.) ·

4. BFTEK (buffer technique) is one of the keyword options that may be specified in a DCB macro instruction. Discuss this keyword and the options that may be chosen when it is coded. Show how to use these options. Use *Supervisor and Data Management Macros* as a reference.

5. Give the sources the data management services use to obtain the necessary information to fill the data control block. Which source takes precedence?

6. A data set consists of about 300 records punched in the first 50 columns of each card. The records should be organized into a disk file. Write the necessary DCB statements and DD cards to process this request.

7. One of the positional subparameters of the SPACE keyword on a DD card is RLSE. Explain the significance of the RLSE in SPACE = (CYL, (8,2),RLSE). Use the IBM manual *Job Control Language User's Guide* as your reference.

8. Obtain the macro expansion of any data management macro by coding GEN as an operand of the PRINT pseudo. Notice how register 15 is used as a branch register.

   What would happen if register 15 were the implied base register in the program?

9. Consider exercise 11 of Chapter 9. Define a QISAM data set which will hold all records of the data set mentioned in the exercise. Retrieve, in the scan mode, the records of all class members whose name begins with the letter *R*. (Can you figure out a way to do this exercise in one job step?)

10. Consider the ASMFCLG catalog procedure mentioned in Topic 1 of the Computer Notebook in Chapter 11. Trace the creation of the load module; that is, follow the job control language used in the processing of the source deck to object deck to load module. Use the ASMFCLG procedure given in Part V of *Job Control Language User's Guide* or code MSGLEVEL = 1 on your next assembly job.

    a. What is the data set name of the object module?

    b. What DD card is associated with the object module passed to the Linkage Editor?

    c. What is the data set name of the load module?

11. Choose any data set whose records consist of punch cards. Define the data control block. Specify the GET macro in the locate mode. Print this data set after defining a printer data control block. Use the PUT macro in the locate mode. (Hint: recall that both GET and PUT use register 1 for their own purposes.)

12. Consider the DCB keyword DISP (disposition). PASS is one of the options that may be specified for the *normal* positional subparameter. Discuss the meaning of the PASS option. Refer to the JCL guide.

13. Suppose we have two data sets. Let the first specify RECFM = FA in the Data Control Block statement. (Recall that A in FA designates the first byte of the printer file to be a carriage control character.) Let the DCB statement of the second data set specify MACRF = PMC where the C designates that the CNTRL macro will be used. (This means the first character of the record will be printed. It will not be used for carriage control.)

    Discuss the advantages or disadvantages of both methods of controlling the PRINTER.

14. *The move mode.* The specification MACRF = PM tells the data management services that the PUT macro will be used in the move mode. Explain in detail what this statement means.

15. *The locate mode.* The specification MACRF = GL tells the data management service that the GET macro will be used in the locate mode. Explain in detail what this statement means.

16. *The substitute mode.* The specification MACRF = PT tells the data management service that the PUT macro will be used in the substitute mode. Explain in detail what this statement means. Use the IBM manual *Supervisor and Data Management Macro* as a reference.

17. Give the meaning of each of the following acronyms:

    MACRF   DSØRG   DCB
    LRECL   BLKSIZE RECFM
    DISP   DSN   DDNAME

18. Give the acronym for each of the following concepts:

    buffering technique   end-of-data address
    number of buffers   key length
    device address   relative key position

19. Try to do this problem without using any references. If you cannot, review the chapter.
    a. Define a CARDREADER data set. Use GET in the move mode.
    b. Define a QSAM disk file to hold the card image.
       Use MACRF = (PM,GM).
    c. Define a print file. Use PUT in the locate mode. Use CNTRL.

    d. Read in a record.

    e. Put the record on the disk.

    f. Retrieve the record from the disk.

    g. Print the record.

20. Perform the nine steps listed below, then answer the question at the end of the list.

    a. Prepare and run a program in which you define a CARDREADER and a printer data set. Specify LRECL = 6. Specify an end-of-file address for the CARDREADER DCB.

    b. Prepare five punch cards for the CARDREADER data set. Punch CARD1 in the first six columns of the first card, CARD2 in the first six columns of the second card, etc.

    c. OPEN the CARDREADER and PRINTER DCBs.

    d. GET the first two cards and PUT their card image.

    e. CLOSE the CARDREADER DCB.

    f. OPEN the CARDREADER DCB.

    g. GET the remainder of the cards in the data set and PUT their card image.

    h. CLOSE all data sets.

    i. Read the results on your computer printout. It should read:

        CARD1
        CARD2
        CARD5

QUESTION: What happened to CARD3 and CARD4? (Hint: Read Section 14.4.)

15 | The Execute, Translate and Test, and Translate Instructions

The main purpose of this chapter is to introduce three powerful and sophisticated instructions from the System/360 repertoire. These instructions are Execute, Translate and Test, and Translate.

Before introducing these instructions, however, we present a *search by scanning* problem called "The Case of the Lazy Keypuncher." We pose and solve this problem using the instructions that have been presented up to this point. Then in Section 15.2 we introduce EXECUTE, and we solve the problem again employing this new instruction in the solution.

Note that in our first solution to the Lazy Keypuncher problem we modify the operand of an instruction. Although this procedure was once considered a sophisticated programming technique, it is now frowned upon. There are, however, two good points to our example. It emphasizes the fact that instructions are data to the CPU. It also illustrates that knowledge of the machine language format can be useful to an assembly language programmer.

Let us consider briefly why the instruction modification in Section 15.1 is not accepted as a good programming technique today. First, suppose the program in which instruction modification takes place is maintained over a period of years. It will be difficult, even for the individual who wrote the original code, to recall why the modification technique was used. It may happen that the modification will be forgotten even if the program seems to be well documented. Any results obtained by such a program may not be very meaningful.

The second reason we offer is more important. The program violates the concept of a *pure procedure*. A program that is a pure procedure can be interrupted at any instruction and started again at the beginning. This fact assumes its greatest importance in a multiprogramming environment where it may be necessary or desirable to switch from one user program to another.

Suppose, for instance, that a program has modified one of its instructions and then it is interrupted. If the processing restarts at the beginning of the code, then the CPU will not be executing the same program as the original. We say, in this case, that the program is not *reentrant*.

Our first solution to the Lazy Keypuncher problem modifies the length code of a Pack instruction in each pass through the program. The second solution illustrates how the Execute instruction obviates the need for this length modification. That is, our program will remain a pure procedure and still solve our problem.

Let us now consider "The Case of the Lazy Keypuncher."

15.1 The Lazy Keypuncher

Let us suppose that we have hired a keypuncher who finds that punching data items into a designated field on a punch card is much too restrictive for his life style. Let us suppose further that there are circumstances beyond our control (he might be related to our boss) which force us to retain him on our staff.

After a lengthy conference he agrees to punch data, which consists of decimal integers, on the cards according to the following restrictions:

1. There will be one data item per card.
2. The data item may be punched anywhere on the card. Column 80, however, must be blank.
3. The maximum length of an item will be nine digits.
4. An item may be preceded by a plus or minus sign, or the item may be an unsigned positive integer.
5. An occasional blank card may be inserted into the data set by the keypuncher.

Figure 15.1 depicts a typical record from the data set punched by our lazy keypuncher.

FIGURE 15.1

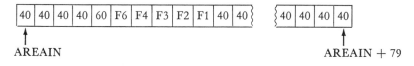

FIGURE 15.2

Our problem is to write a program segment that:

1. reads each data card into an 80-byte MEMORY location called AREAIN;
2. finds a data item in AREAIN and converts that item to a full-word binary integer;
3. prints an appropriate message whenever a blank card has been discovered.

Our program must scan AREAIN to find the data item, determine if it is a signed integer, determine its length (that is, the number of digits it possesses), pack it, and finally convert it from its packed decimal form to a full-word binary integer.

Figure 15.2 depicts the pertinent portion of AREAIN after the typical data item of Figure 15.1 has been read in. Note that AREAIN is blank except for this data item.

The Lazy Keypuncher Program Algorithm gives the procedure we follow in the program. We have made the following register and storage assignments:

1. Register 4 is the BCT register which monitors both loops. It is set to 80 for the first loop and to 9 for the second. If it reaches zero in the first loop, the card read in was blank. If it reaches zero in the second loop, there were more than nine digits in the data item.
2. Register 3 is the sign indicator. It is initialized to positive. (We let zero signify positive and one signify negative.)
3. Register 2 is the base register for the effective address pointer, EFP, which is 0(2), points initially to the first byte in AREAIN.
4. SAVADD is a full-word storage location where the address of the first digit in the data item is saved.
5. LENGTH is a one-byte storage location used to store the length of the data item.

Note that when we modify the length operand of an SS type instruction we must store the machine length into the length field. Recall that the machine length is one less than the actual length.

The Lazy Keypuncher Program Algorithm

Step 1: Set sign indicator to zero (register 3).
Step 2: Set BCT register to 80 (register 4).
Step 3: Set EFP so that it points to the first byte of AREAIN. (Note: the byte that EFP points to will be called *BYTE*.)

Step 4: Read in data item.

Step 5: If BYTE is nonblank, go to step 9.

Step 6: Move EFP so that it points to the next byte in sequence.

Step 7: Subtract one from the BCT register.

Step 8: If C(BCT) = 0, go to step 29; otherwise go to step 5.

Step 9: If BYTE contains minus sign, go to step 12.

Step 10: If BYTE contains plus sign, go to step 13.

Step 11: Go to step 14.

Step 12: Set sign indicator to negative.

Step 13: Move EFP so that it points to the next byte in sequence.

Step 14: Put address of first digit in SAVADD.

Step 15: Set BCT register to nine (no more than nine digits).

Step 16: Move EFP so that it points to the next byte in sequence.

Step 17: If BYTE is blank, go to step 20.

Step 18: Subtract one from the BCT register.

Step 19: If C(BCT) = 0, go to step 31; otherwise go to step 16.

Step 20: Subtract address of first digit in SAVADD from base register associated with EFP. (Note: C(Reg 2) = number of digits in data item.)

Step 21: Subtract one from base register associated with EFP. (Note: C(Reg 2) = machine language length of data item.)

Step 22: Modify length of second operand in Pack instruction.

Step 23: Issue Pack instruction.

Step 24: Convert packed decimal operand to binary.

Step 25: If sign indicator is negative, go to step 27.

Step 26: Go to step 32.

Step 27: Complement binary operand (two's complement).

Step 28: Go to step 32.

Step 29: Print: YOU CAN'T FOOL ME, THE CARD IS BLANK.

Step 30: Go to step 32.

Step 31: Print: YOU GOOFED! THE ITEM HAS MORE THAN NINE DIGITS.

Step 32: Stop.

The program in Figure 15.3 is an implementation of the algorithm.

①, ②, and ③ are used to modify the length of the second operand in the Pack instruction. The modification is accomplished by the following sequence:

1. after ① —C(Reg 2) = 00000004
2. after ② —C(LENGTH) = 0 ④ ⟶ numeric part
3. after ③ —see Figure 15.4

The address of the first digit in the data item was loaded into register 6 by ④. Hence register 6 points to F6 of our typical data item. Five digits are packed by the instruction at BLUE.

```
        PRINT   NOGEN
        INIT
        PROLOG  END=BROWN,CSIZE=80,LSIZE=80
*       THE PROGRAM
GREEN   LA      3,0                     SIGN INDICATOR IS PLUS
        LA      4,80                    BCT SET TO 80
        LA      2,AREAIN                EFP = 0(2) POINTS TO AREAIN
        GET     CARDIN,AREAIN
        PUT     LINEOUT,AREAIN
LOOP1   CLI     0(2),X'40'              NON-BLANK?
        BNE     MINUS                   CHECK FOR MINUS SIGN
        LA      2,1(2)                  MOVE EFP
        BCT     4,LOOP1                 NEXT BYTE
        B       MESSAGE1                CARD IS BLANK
MINUS   CLI     0(2),C'−'               MINUS SIGN?
        BE      NEGATIVE                IF SO, BRANCH
        CLI     0(2),C'+'               PLUS SIGN?
        BE      PLUS                    IF SO, BRANCH
        B       UNSIGNED
NEGATIVE LA     3,1                     SET NEGATIVE SIGN
PLUS    LA      2,1(2)                  MOVE EFP TO FIRST DIGIT
UNSIGNED ST     2,SAVADD                SAVE ADDRESS OF FIRST DIGIT
        LA      4,9                     RESET BCT
LOOP2   LA      2,1(2)                  MOVE EFP
        CLI     0(2),X'40'              BLANK?
        BE      BLANK
        BCT     4,LOOP2
        B       MESSAGE2
BLANK   S       2,SAVADD                AL LENGTH IN REG 2
     ① S        2,=F'1'                 ML LENGTH IN REG 2
     ② STC      2,LENGTH                C(LENGTH) = ML LENGTH
     ③ MVN      BLUE+1(1),LENGTH        LENGTH MODIFIED
     ④ L        6,SAVADD                0(0,6) POINTS TO DIGIT
BLUE    PACK    DOUBLE,0(0,6)           MODIFIED L2 FIELD
        CVB     4,DOUBLE
        C       3,=F'1'
        BNE     BROWN
        LCR     4,4                     MAKE IT NEGATIVE
BROWN   GOBACK
AREAIN  DS      CL80
SAVADD  DS      F
DOUBLE  DS      D
LENGTH  DS      C
MESSAGE1 PUT    LINEOUT,=CL80' HA. YOU CAN''T FOOL ME. THE CARD IS BLANK.'
        B       BROWN
MESSAGE2 PUT    LINEOUT,=CL80' YOU ERRED.THE ITEM HAS MORE THAN 9 DIGITS.'
        B       BROWN
        LTORG
                =CL80' HA. YOU CAN''T FOOL ME. THE CARD IS BLANK.'
                =CL80' YOU ERRED.THE ITEM HAS MORE THAN 10 DIGITS.'
                =F'1'
        END
```

handwritten notes at right:

```
L   6,SAVADD
S   2,=F'1'
IC  2,LENGTH
 MVN
 PACK
 CVB
 LTR  3,3
 BZ   POSITIVE
 LCR  4,4
```

FIGURE 15.3

FIGURE 15.4

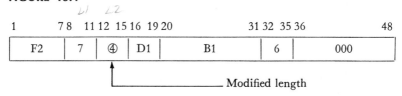

1	7 8	11 12	15 16	19 20		31 32	35 36		48
F2	7	④	D1	B1		6	000		

Modified length

We now present the Execute instruction. We will repeat part of The Lazy Keypuncher problem using Execute to specify the length of the data item.

15.2   The Execute Instruction

The general form of *Execute* is:

EX   R1,S2

When this statement is executed, the instruction at S2, after being fetched, is "modified" by OR'ing it with bits 24–31 of R1. After this modification the instruction is executed. Control is returned to P + 1, the instruction which follows Execute in the normal sequence (see Mini-algorithm).

Bits 8–15 of the instruction at S2 are OR'ed with bits 24–31 of R1. Note that this OR'ing *does not* affect the contents of S2.

S2 may be any location accessible by the user's program. It must, of course, be an Assembler Language instruction whose length is two, four, or six bytes. S2 is not, in general, placed in the normal instruction sequence.

We present a mini-algorithm that CONTROL might follow after it has *fetched* the Execute instruction. We assume the Execute instruction was in location 007000.

Mini-algorithm

Step 1: Update Instruction Address Register by four. (New content of IAR is 007004 = address of the Execute instruction + 4.)

Step 2: Fetch instruction at S2.

Step 3: *OR* bits 8–15 of fetched instruction with bits 24–31 of R1.

Step 4: Execute "modified" instruction.

Step 5: Fetch instruction from 007004.

Example 15.1

Consider the Lazy Keypuncher Program (see Figure 15.3). Rewrite the part necessary so that the Execute instruction is used instead of the instruction modification caused by ② and ③.

We must redefine location BLUE, which contains the PACK instruction. It must not be placed among the instructions which are executed in the normal sequence. Let us, therefore, put BLUE among the declaratives. The declarative section might then appear as:

```
DOUBLE   DS     D
BLUE     PACK   DOUBLE,0(0,6)
SAVADD   DS     F
AREAIN   DS     CL80
```

The solution to our problem appears in Figure 15.5. The first part of the program up to and including ① is the same. We do not repeat that part (see Figure 15.3).

```
                  ⋮
       BLANK    S      2,SAVADD
 ①              S      2, = F'1'
                L      6,SAVADD
 ⑤              EX     2,BLUE
                CVB    4,DOUBLE
                  ⋮
       DOUBLE   DS     D
 ⑥     BLUE     PACK   DOUBLE,0(0,6)
       SAVADD   DS     F
       AREAIN   DS     CL80
                  ⋮
                END
```

FIGURE 15.5 The Execute Instruction

Location LENGTH has been dropped since it is no longer needed. The Execute instruction ⑤ of Figure 15.5 replaces ② and ③ of Figure 15.3. The PACK instruction ⑥, the *subject* instruction of Execute, has been moved out of the normal sequence.

15.3   Translate and Test

The general form of *Translate and Test* is:

TRT   S1,S2

TRT scans the first operand, a character string, using the second operand as a reference table. The Translate and Test Algorithm gives some of the action caused by TRT. We have chosen this rather novel way of presenting the action because Translate and Test is such an unusual instruction. We believe the reader will find this algorithm easier to follow than the conventional explanation of the action.

The following discussion defines the terminology used in the algorithm.

We shall refer to the first operand as the *string*. Each byte in this string will be called an *argument byte*.

We shall refer to the second operand (which is usually 256 bytes long) as the *TABLE*. Each byte in the TABLE will be called a *function byte*. The address of the first byte in the TABLE will be called the *table-address*.

We note here that the programmer must define the TABLE before issuing the TRT instruction. The value of each function byte must be set by the programmer so that TRT will do the job he wants done. This point will become clear as the discussion proceeds.

EFP in the algorithm is just a convenient pointer. Its name and role are not pertinent to the action of the instruction.

Translate and Test Algorithm

Step 1: Set EFP so that it points to the first byte in the string (first operand of TRT).

Step 2: Go to step 4.

Step 3: Move EFP so that it points to the next byte (in sequence) in the string.

Step 4: Find the sum of the table-address and the value of the argument byte EFP points to.
(Note: we will call this sum the *table-reference-address*.)

Step 5: If the value of the function byte in the table-reference-address is nonzero, go to step 7.

Step 6: If EFP is pointing to the last argument byte, go to step 9; otherwise go to step 3.

Step 7: Put the address of the argument byte EFP points to into bits 8–31 of register 1.

Step 8: Put the value of the table-reference-address function byte into bits 24–31 of register 2.

Step 9: Stop.

If, for example, we are searching for a blank in the string, its address, if found, will be placed into register 1 provided the TABLE has been properly initialized.

The condition code is set as follows:

CC = 0   All function bytes referenced in the scan were zero. The search failed.

CC = 1   A nonzero function byte was referenced. The search was successful, but the string has not been completely scanned. There may be other argument bytes associated with a nonzero function byte.

CC = 2   The search was successful. The entire string has been scanned. The last argument byte was associated with a nonzero function byte.

Example 15.2

a. TARMO is a ten-byte character string. Find the address of the first blank in the string if there is one.

We assume that:

1. C(TARMO) = C740D9E2E340F1F2F3Cl, or (in English) TARMO contains GbRSTb123A where b stands for a blank.
2. TARMO's address is 007200.

We need to define a 256-byte function table for our second operand. Since we are searching for a blank in the character string, all bytes in the table should contain 00_x except the function byte associated with the character *blank*. If we name our table by TABLE, then the address of this byte will be $TABLE+40_x$ since the EBCDIC code for a blank is 40_x.

The solution to this problem is:

```
         ⋮
         SR    1,1
         SR    2,2
①        MVI   TABLE+X'40',X'01'
②        TRT   TARMO,TABLE
         ⋮
TABLE DC       256X'00'
```

The instruction at ① inserted a nonzero value into $TABLE+40_x$. If the CPU encounters a blank in TARMO, the nonzero value in TABLE+40 will indicate that this character has a special meaning with respect to the instruction.

We follow the action caused by the execution of ② using the Translate and Test Algorithm:

Step 1: EFP points to G ($C7_x$ in EBCDIC).
Step 4: Table-reference-address = $TABLE+C7_x$ = $TABLE+199_{10}$.
Step 5: The value of the function byte $TABLE+199_{10}$ is 00_x.
Step 6: EFP is not pointing to the last byte in the string.
Step 3: EFP now points to b (blank).
Step 4: Table-reference-address = $TABLE+40_x$ = $TABLE+64_{10}$.
Step 5: $C(TABLE+64_{10})$ is nonzero.
Step 7: $C(Reg\ 1)$ = 00007201.
Step 8: $C(Reg\ 2)$ = 00000001.

Example 15.3

Find the address of the first letter A in the string named TARMO (see Example 15.2). If none, branch to BLUE. Recall that TABLE has 01_x in $TABLE+40_x$.

The solution to this problem is:

```
         ⋮
         SR    1,1
         SR    2,2
         MVI   TABLE+X'40',X'00'
         MVI   TABLE+C'A',X'01'
         TRT   TARMO,TABLE
         BC    B'1000',BLUE
         ⋮
TABLE DC       256X'00'
         ⋮
```

Use the assumptions given in Example 15.2 to answer the following questions:

1. What is the value in register 1?
2. Will the program branch to BLUE?
3. What is the value of the condition code?
4. What is the value in register 2?

```
*  THE IMPERATIVES
          MVI    TABLE+C'B',X'01'     SET TABLE
          SR     1,1                  CLEAR REG 1
      ①  LA     4,255
      ②  LA     3,HELEN              POINTER TO HELEN
BLUE      LR     11,3                 SAVE POINTER
      ③  EX     4,ELMO              SEE 10 AMONG CONSTANTS
      ④  BC     B'0100',RESET        FOUND A 'B' BUT WE ARE NOT DONE
      ⑤  BC     B'0010',LEONY        THE LAST CHAR IS A 'B'
          B      ALLDONE
RESET     AP     COUNT,=P'1'          ADD 1 TO THE COUNT OF B'S
      ⑥  LA     3,1(1)
      ⑦  SR     1,11                 HOW MANY DIGITS SCANNED?
      ⑧  A      1,=F'1'              THE COUNT IS NOW CORRECT
      ⑨  SR     4,1                  REG 4 TELLS HOW MANY TO GO?
          B      BLUE                 SCAN AGAIN
LEONY     AP     COUNT,=P'1'          ADD THE 'B' IN THE LAST BYTE
ALLDONE   AR     4,4                  THIS HAS NOTHING TO DO WITH ALGORITHM
              ⋮
*  THE DECLARATIVES
COUNT     DC     PL2'0'
ELMO  ⑩  TRT    0(0,3),TABLE
TABLE     DC     256X'00'
```

FIGURE 15.6

Example 15.4

Count the number of character B's in the 256-byte character string named HELEN. Use Translate and Test as the subject instruction of Execute.

We present the solution in the program segment given in Figure 15.6.

To check your understanding of the Translate and Test instruction, answer the following seven questions. (The answers to these questions appear on page 380.)

1. Why has register 1 (but not register 2) been cleared?
2. The length of the character string, HELEN, is 256 bytes. Why has 255 been loaded into register 4? (See ①.)
3. Explain the action when ③ is executed.
4. If the program branches to RESET, what is register 1 pointing to?
5. What is register 3 pointing to after each execution of ⑥?
6. Explain the significance of ⑦ and ⑧.
7. What is the significance of the value in register 4? How is it used?

15.4   Translate

The general form of *Translate* is:

    TR   S1,S2

S2 is a 256-byte table which is referenced in the same manner as the table of the TRT instruction. Therefore, in the discussion that follows, the words *function byte, argument byte, string, TABLE, table-address,* and *table-reference-address* have the same meaning as in the last section.

When the Translate instruction is executed, the character string at S2 is scanned byte by byte. The value of a scanned byte—the argument byte—is added to the table-address. The value of the function byte of the resulting table-reference-address replaces the value of its associated argument byte in the string.

The action continues until the value of every byte in the string has been replaced by the value of its associated function byte in the TABLE.

The Translate Algorithm and Example 15.5 should clear up all questions about this instruction.

Translate Algorithm

Step 1: Set EFP so that it points to the first byte in the string.

Step 2: Go to step 4.

Step 3: Move EFP so that it points to the next argument byte in sequence.

Step 4: Find the sum of the table-address and the value of the argument byte that EFP points to (table-address + $(\overrightarrow{EFP})$ = table-reference-address).

Step 5: Copy the value of the function byte in the table-reference-address into the argument byte that EFP points to.

Step 6: If EFP is pointing to the last argument byte in the string, proceed in the normal sequence; otherwise go to step 3.

Step 7: Stop.

Example 15.5

Suppose we have a data set consisting of punched cards in which the letter O has often been punched instead of the correct character, the number 0. We can read these data cards into MEMORY, use Translate to correct the card image, and punch a new corrected deck of cards for our data set.

Our program segment scans and corrects one card image. The segment also illustrates one way to create the function table for Translate.

```
        Declarative section
                    ⋮
        CARDIM  DS      CL80
        TABLE   DS      CL256
        Imperative section
                    ⋮
        *CREATING THE TRANSLATE TABLE
                LA      2,0   index register
        LOOP    STC     2,TABLE(2)
                LA      2,1(2)
                C       2,=F'255'
                BNH     LOOP
                    ⋮
        *EDITING
                MVI     TABLE+C'O',X'F0'
                TR      CARDIM,TABLE
```

Each letter O scanned by TR is replaced by the number 0, which has been placed into the function byte associated with the letter O.

Answers to Questions in Example 15.4

1. TRT ignores bits 0–7 of both registers 1 and 2. Since we use the value placed in bits 8–31 of register 1 in a subtraction instruction, we want to be sure that all bits in register 0 are zero. We do not use register 2 in the program segment.
2. Register 4 is the Execute register. The value in bits 24–31 will be OR'ed with the subject instruction at ELMO. We must put the machine language length, which is one less than the implied length, into register 4.
3. See discussion of the Execute instruction in Section 15.2.
4. Register 1 is pointing to a character B in the character string HELEN. This character is in the last byte that has been scanned by TRT.
5. Register 3 is pointing to the next byte that will be scanned when TRT is activated by EX.
6. ⑦ and ⑧ determine the number of bytes that TRT has scanned. Test the instructions on an example.
7. Register 4 contains, after execution of ⑨, the number of bytes that must still be scanned by TRT. This value will be OR'ed with the 00_x that is in the length field of the TRT instruction.

Computer Notebook

TOPIC 1   Six General Purpose System/370 Instructions

The System/370 instruction set includes all of the instructions in the System/360 repertoire, some seven extended precision floating-point instructions, and the six general purpose instructions which we discuss in this section.

Each of these general purpose instructions will be presented in its own subtopic. We will give the syntax, the action, and examples in a manner similar to our discussion of the System/360 instructions. The instructions we discuss are complicated. We suggest, therefore, that the reader pay careful attention to the discussion. Our first subtopic is Shift and Round Decimal.

Shift and Round Decimal.   The syntax of the instruction is:

    SRP   S1,S2,I3

The first operand, S1, a packed decimal number, is shifted in the direction designated by the binary digit in bit position 26 of the *effective address* of S2. If bit 26 of this effective address is 1, the shift is to the right; otherwise the shift is to the left. (An address is only 24 bits long, but IBM numbers these bits from 8 to 31.)

When bit 26 equals zero, the amount of the designated *left* shift is equal to the value of the binary integer in bit positions 27–31 of the effective ad-

F0	L1	I3	B1	D1	B2	D2

0   7 8   11 12 15 16 19 20   31 32 35 36   47

FIGURE 15.7

dress. These bits are considered a nonnegative binary number. (Recall how CONTROL determines an effective address.)

When bit 26 equals one, a *right* shift is designated. In this case the amount of the right shift is given by the binary number in bits 26–31. These bits are considered a binary number in two's complement form.

The sign of the packed decimal number S1 does not participate in the shift. If the shift is to the left, the CPU supplies trailing zeros. If the shift is to the right, the CPU provides leading zeros.

The I3 field contains a rounding factor. If the shift is to the right, the operand S1 will be rounded by the factor I3 before the shift takes place. No rounding occurs if the shift is to the left.

The first operand, S1, must be in packed decimal form. A data exception will occur if S1 is not composed of decimal digits with a hex sign. Recall that the sign of a packed decimal operand is a hex digit in the rightmost nibble of the rightmost byte.

The second operand, although labeled by IBM in its manuals as S2, is not a data item. It is an "address item" which is 24 bits long. The bit positions are numbered 8–31. Only bit position 26 and bit positions 27–31 pass useful information to CONTROL. The rest of bits are ignored.

I3 is an immediate operand.

Figure 15.7 gives the format of SRP, which is an SS type instruction.

Condition Code

The condition code is set as follows:
0 if C(S1) equals 0 after shift
1 if C(S1) is less than 0 after shift
2 if C(S1) is greater than 0 after shift
3 if C(S1) overflows in shifting

Example 15.5

We assume the L'DATA = 3.

a. SRP   DATA,0(2),5

    Before execution   *After execution*
    C(DATA) = 12346C   C(DATA) = 01235C
    C(Reg 2) = 0000003F   CC is set to 2

b. SRP   DATA,3F,5

    Before execution   *After execution*
    C(DATA) = 06995C   C(DATA) = 00700C
                        CC is set to 2

c. SRP   DATA,1,5

Before execution	*After execution*
C(DATA) = 12648C	C(DATA) = 26480C
	CC is set to 3

Move Long. The syntax of *Move Long* is:

MVCL   R1,R2

Background

1. R1 and R2 are pointers to operand 1 and operand 2, respectively. (Henceforth we shall shorten operand 1 to op1 and operand 2 to op2.) Each register points to the leftmost byte of its operand.
2. Both R1 and R2 must be even numbered registers. Each designates an even-odd pair.
3. Bit positions 8–31 of the odd registers—R1 + 1 and R2 + 1—pass the length of op1 and op2, respectively, to CONTROL.
4. Bit positions 0–7 of the odd register R2 + 1 contain the padding character that will be used if the length of op1 is greater than the length of op2.
5. Bit positions 0–7 of registers R1,R1 + 1 and R2 are ignored by CONTROL.

The contents of the location pointed to by R2 (operand 2) is moved byte by byte into operand 1. Execution ceases when the number of bytes specified by bits 8–31 of R1 + 1 have been moved.

If the length of op1 is greater than the length of op2, the rightmost bytes of op1 are padded with the character designated by bits 0–7 of R2 + 1.

Operand 1 and operand 2 are said to *overlap destructively* if any byte in operand 1 is used as a source after data has been moved into it.

CONTROL checks for destructive overlap before executing the instruction. If such an overlap will occur, the instruction *will not* be executed. In this case, the condition code will be set to 3.

Condition Code

The condition code is set by MVCL as follows:
0 if length of op1 equals length of op2
1 if length of op1 is less than that of op2
2 if length of op1 is greater than length of op2
3 if destructive overlap exists

Example 15.6

MVCL   2,4

C(Reg 2) = 00007000
C(Reg 3) = 00000100

C(Reg 4) = 00006000
C(Reg 5) = 40000090

One hundred forty-four bytes are moved starting at location 6000_x to locations starting at 7000_x. Since the length of op1 is greater than op2, blanks (as designated by bits 0–7 of register 5) are moved into 112 byte locations starting at 7090_x. The condition code is set to 2.

Compare Logical Long.   The syntax of *Compare Logical Long* is:

   CLCL   R1,R2

1. R1 and R2 are pointer to op1 and op2, respectively.
2. R1 and R2 designate two even-odd pairs. Both R1 and R2 must be even or a specification exception will occur.
3. The lengths of op1 and op2 are in bit positions 8–31 of registers R1 + 1 and R2 + 1, respectively.
4. Bit positions 0–7 of R2 + 1 contain a padding character which will be used in the comparison if the lengths are not equal. CONTROL will assume that the shorter operand is extended with the padding character in R2 + 1.
5. Bit positions 0–7 of R1,R2, and R1 + 1 are ignored.

A bit-by-bit comparison is made of op1 and op2. The comparison ceases when two unlike bits are matched. The condition code is set according to the schedule given under the heading *Condition Code*. (See also the discussion of Compare Logical Character in Topic 3 of the Computer Notebook, Chapter 9.)

   Condition Code

   The Condition Code is set as follows:

   0 if op1 = op2
   1 if op1 < op2
   2 if op1 > op2
   3 ——

Example 15.7

CLCL   2,4

C(Reg 2) = 00007000   C(Reg 4) = 00006000
C(Reg 3) = 00000005   C(Reg 5) = 40000004

C1	C2	C3	F9	C1

└— location 7000_x

C1	C2	C3	F9

└— location 6000_x

After execution. The condition code has been set to 2 since op1 is logically greater than op2.

(The comparison was equal until the bits in op2 were exhausted. C1 in location 7004_x was compared to the padding character 40 in bits 0–7 of register 5.)

A Discussion of the Mask. Each of the next three instructions that we discuss uses an immediate operand called a *mask* to monitor the action caused by the execution of the instruction.

The mask field is 4 bits long. The bits are placed in a natural 1:1 correspondence with the bytes of the first operand which, in each case, is a register operand. That is, bit positions 0, 1, 2, and 3 of the mask given in the M3 field are associated with byte 0, byte 1, byte 2, and byte 3, respectively, of the general purpose register given in the R1 field.

Each byte in the general purpose register (designated by the R1 field) which is associated with a mask bit position that contains a binary 1 participates in the action of the instruction. If a mask bit position is binary zero, then its corresponding byte in the general purpose register does not participate in the action.

For example, if M3 = 1010, then bytes 0 and 2 of R1 are involved in the execution of the instruction. If M3 = 0110, then only bytes 1 and 2 participate. The mask, M3 = 0000, sets the condition code to 0 in case of Compare Logical Under Mask and Insert Character Under Mask. This mask, M3 = 0000, is tantamount to a no operation instruction with respect to Store Characters Under Mask.

We now consider each of these "under mask" instructions separately. The examples which follow the discussion should help clarify the function of the mask.

Compare Logical Under Mask. The syntax of this compare instruction is:

CLM   R1,M3,S2

The contents of the register designated by R1 are compared with the contents of the MEMORY locations designated by S2. A 4-bit binary mask controls the comparison. (See the preceding discussion of the mask.)

The condition code indicates the result of the comparison. (See the schedule of the condition code in the discussion of Compare Logical Long.)

The machine language format is given in Figure 15.8. (We note here that the two other instructions which are monitored by a mask have a similar machine language format.)

FIGURE 15.8

0	7 8	11 12	15 16	19 20	31
BD	R1	M3	B2	D2	

Example 15.8

a. CLM   3,B'0101',DATA

Before execution	*After execution*
C(Reg 3) = 00104A40	CC is set to 2. The contents
C(DATA) = 004300	of register 3 and DATA are
	unchanged.

The comparison is made between bytes 1 and 3 of register 3 and the first two consecutive bytes of DATA. That is, 1040_x *is* compared logically to 0043_x. The first three bits match. Bit 4 of op1 is 1 and bit 4 of op2 is 0. Hence the comparison stops. op1 > op2. CC is set to 2.

b. CLM   3,B'0001',BLUE

Before execution	*After execution*
C(Reg 3) = 000000FF	CC is set to 2
C(BLUE) = AB	

c. CLM   3,B'0000',DATA

Before execution	*After execution*
C(Reg 3) is immaterial	CC is set to 0
C(DATA) is immaterial	No comparison is made

Insert Characters Under Mask

ICM   R1,M3,S2

The contents of the mask M3 monitors the action of the instruction. (See the discussion in the subtopic *A Discussion of the Mask* in this topic.)

The contents of consecutive bytes in MEMORY starting at the address specified by S2 are inserted into those bytes of R1 that are associated with nonzero bits in the mask.

The condition code is set as follows:

0 if all bits inserted into R1 are zero (or if the mask has all zero bits)
1 if the first bit of the inserted field is 1
2 if the first bit in the inserted field is 0 *and* not all of the other inserted bits equal zero
3 not possible

Example 15.9

ICM   3,B'1010',DATA

Before execution	*After execution*
C(BLUE) = 1764ABCD	C(BLUE) is unchanged
C(Reg 3) = 76431200	C(Reg 3) = 17436400

17_x is copied into byte 0 of register 3 since bit 0 of the mask is 1.
64_x is copied into byte 2 of register 3 since bit 2 of the mask is 1.
The condition code is set to 2.

Store Characters Under Mask

STCM   R1,M3,S2

1. The contents of the mask M3 monitor the action of the instruction. (See the discussion of the mask on page 384 in this topic.)
2. The contents of those bytes in R1 which are associated with a nonzero mask bit are stored in consecutive MEMORY locations starting at S2.
3. The condition code is not affected by the instruction.

Example 15.10

a. STCM   5,B'1010',DATA

Before execution	*After execution*
C(Reg 5) = A20F1234	C(Reg 5) is unchanged
C(DATA) is immaterial	C(DATA) = A212

b. STCM   3,B'0111',SAM

Before execution	*After execution*
C(Reg 3) = 011F2B3C	C(Reg 3) is unchanged
C(SAM) is immaterial	C(SAM) = 1F2B3C

EXERCISES

1. Consider the character string which is given below. Write a program segment which will count the number of letter O's in the string. Write a second segment which will count the number of letter O's that are followed by a comma. Use Translate and Test and the Execute instructions.

    The String: MY BROTHERS' AND SISTERS' NAMES ARE TOIVO, ARVO, VIENO, TARMO, WAINO, LILJA.

2. An execute exception will occur if the subject of an Execute instruction is another Execute. What other exceptions can occur when Execute is used? What action will the Operating System take when these exceptions occur? Use *Principles of Operation* as your reference.

3. Consider exercise 11 in Chapter 9. Some students forget the instructions when they prepare their own records for the class. At least some records in this class data set always seem to have a blank in column 1. Write a program segment which checks every record in the class data set. Correct the records which have a blank in column 1 by moving the data in the first

record one byte to the left. Be sure to blank out the byte that contained the last nonblank character in the former record. Submit an algorithm and a flowchart with your solution.

4. Assume that there exists a data set punched on cards. Each record is 80 bytes long. The records have three errors. The letter Ø has been punched for the number 0, the letter A has been punched for the number 2, and the letter P has been punched for the number 9.

   Write a program segment which reads in the cards. Correct the card image. Put the corrected card image on a QSAM file which has been created on a disk. Submit an algorithm with your solution.

5. Consider a modification of the Lazy Keypuncher problem. Let up to five data items be punched on a card. Read in the card. Find the data items in the card image. Convert them to packed decimal arithmetic. Print the result after editing it by the Edit instruction. Submit an algorithm with your solution.

6. Consider another modification of the Lazy Keypuncher problem. Let a data item, which might include a decimal point, be punched anywhere on a punch card. Write a program segment which reads in this data item. Find the data item in the card image. Convert both the integral and fractional parts to floating-point representation. Submit an algorithm with your solution.

7. Suppose we have a data set composed of base ten integers punched in columns 1–9 (inclusive) right justified on some punch cards. Assume that there is one integer per card. Read in the data set. Write a program segment which converts the base ten integer to a full-word binary constant directly. That is, do not convert your EBCDIC constant to packed decimal; convert it directly to a full-word binary constant. Submit a flowchart and an algorithm with your solution. (Remember you do not know how many digits there are in the base ten integer.)

8. The Welty Way. Write a program which will print the contents of a register. For instance, suppose C(Reg 5) = 0A104321. Your program must print: *THE CONTENTS OF REGISTER 5 ARE 0A104321*.

   Hint: set up a table similar to the table used by the Translate instructions. Use the value in each nibble in the register as an index to move its associated value in the table to the proper output byte. Your table might be defined by:

   TABLE   DC   X'F0F1F2F3F4F5F6F7F8F9C1C2C3C4C5C6'

9. Primitive Root. (You will not need the Translate instructions or EXECUTE to solve this problem.)

   First we make an observation. The integer 2 is a *primitive root* of a prime number P if the following algorithm produces $P-1$ distinct integers.

Dourson Prime Root Algorithm

Step 1: Pick a prime number P.
Step 2: Pick Y so that $Y < P$.
Step 3: Set $i = 1$.
Step 4: Set $Xi = Y$.
Step 5: Set $i = i + 1$.
Step 6: If $i = P$, go to step 11.
Step 7: Set $Y = 2 * Y$.
Step 8: If $Y < P$, go to step 4.
Step 9: Set $Y = Y - P$.
Step 10: Go to step 4.
Step 11: Stop.

Write a program segment which will generate the first 100 primes that possess 2 as a primitive root.

Pick Y so that $Y = 2$; then if $P = 5$, our algorithm will generate 2, 4, 3, 1—hence 2 is a primitive root of 5. If $P = 7$, we will generate the sequence 2, 4, 1, 2, 4, 1. Since we do not have six ($P = 7$, so $P - 1 = 6$) distinct integers in our sequence, 7 does not have 2 as primitive root. How about 11 and 13?

10. Create a simplified symbol table.
   a. Define an appropriate amount of STORAGE for your entries.
   b. Let each record in the symbol table have two fields—the symbolic address field and its associated numeric value field.
   c. Initialize a counter (LOCATION COUNTER) to zero.
   d. Write a program segment which scans the label field of an assembly instruction for an entry. Enter any legitimate symbolic names found into the symbol table with their associated numeric values. Print appropriate messages for rejected names—DUPLICATE, TOO LONG, etc. Update the counter after each instruction. Assume that all instructions are one word in length.
   e. Print the symbol table after the pass has been completed.

11. Test Under Mask. The general form of *Test Under Mask* is:

   TM   S1,I2

A natural one-to-one correspondence is made between the bit positions of S1 (one byte) and the mask I2. That is, bit position i of S1 is associated with bit position i of I2.

The instruction is used to set the condition code. When TM is executed, the one bits of the mask test their associated bits in S1. The condition code is set as follows:

CC = 0 if all tested bits are 0
CC = 1 if some tested bits are 1 and some tested bits are 0
CC = 3 if all tested bits are 1

Example 15.5

TM   BLUE,B'10100010'

We assume that:

C(BLUE) = 11110000_2

The mask tests bit positions 0, 2 and 6 of BLUE.
The condition code equals one, since some bits tested are one and some are zero. TM does not set the condition code to two.

Assume that CURRY is a packed decimal operand such that L'CURRY = 3. Write a short program using Test Under Mask which will determine if C(CURRY) is negative or positive.

12. Consider the following character string which is a table of names.
HENRY, ROLAND, BARBARA, MARTHA, VICTOR, DAVID, ELLEN, MICHAEL, LINDA, WENDY, STEVEN, PETER, KEVIN, POLLY, DOUGLAS, RICHARD, ROBERT, DANIEL, CYNTHIA, JEANNE, MARK, BRUCE, CAROL, SUSAN, CRAIG, CHRISTINE, BRADLEY, STACEY
   a. Write a program segment which uses Translate and Test as the subject instruction of EXECUTE to count the number of names in the table.
   b. Write a program segment which uses Translate and Test as the subject instruction of EXECUTE to count the number of five-letter names.

13. Example 15.5 gives one way to create a translate table. The table can also be created by using the Define Constant instruction. We illustrate:
   TABLE   DC   256AL1(*−TABLE)
   Compare the two methods. Explain how CONTROL creates the translate table at execution time when the former method is used. Explain how the Assembler creates the table when the Define Constant instruction is issued.

16 | Macros and Conditional Assembly

We have used macro instructions (usually called macros) throughout this text as an extension of Basic Assembler Language. We used macros in early chapters to establish base registers and to do the housekeeping chores that are necessary before a program can be run on a System/360 computer. In Chapter 14 we introduced the student to some data management macro instructions which are supplied by IBM. All of these macros had one thing in common: they saved the programmer the work of writing the same piece of code several times.

This chapter is devoted to a discussion of macro writing. The student is probably aware that the System/360 Assembler has macro capabilities. That is, the student may define his own macros in his program and call them when needed. The student should be able to write simple macros and use them effectively after completing this chapter.

Macros are, in general, easier to understand than the discussion about them. Most of our presentation will, therefore, be in the form of examples. We note, however, that our examples necessarily will be simplified. The source language statements used to expand macros, such as GET, PUT, and the like, are stored in the SYS1.MACLIB. These macros have been written by sophisticated programmers. Therefore, we suggest that the student, after he has gained the background offered by this chapter, access and study some of the macros in this Operating System library (SYS1.MACLIB). Use the IEBPTPCH system utility. Consult the System/360 OS *Utilities* manual.

Let us answer the question "What is a macro?" in a gross fashion. A macro instruction is an extension of Assembler Language. It is a convenient way to generate a sequence of instructions which must be repeated many times in a program. It is also a convenient way to generate a detailed or complex segment of coding that is used in many programs. (INIT is an example of such a segment.)

The application programmer may make a program segment into a macro by a macro-definition. This definition is written only once, and then, as we have seen, a single macro instruction will cause the entire program segment to be generated and inserted in the program at the desired point.

16.1 The Macro-definition

A local macro-definition must appear in an application program before any instruction—imperative or assembly control statement—which belongs to the first control section of the program. To be specific, only EJECT, PRINT, SPACE, TITLE, OPSYN, ICTL, and ISEG—all pseudo instructions—may appear before the macro-definition in the source deck.

The macro-definition consists of four parts which must appear in the order given below:

1. a macro header
2. a prototype statement
3. the model statements
4. a trailer statement

The header consists of a single line with the word MACRO written in the operation field. Since operation MACRO has a blank name field and a blank operand field, the only form of *Macro* is:

blank   MACRO   blank

The trailer statement also consists of a single line. The operation field must consist of the word MEND (macro end). The operand field must be blank, but the label field may have a sequence symbol. (Sequence symbols will be discussed at a more convenient point. They are analogous to symbolic names in an Assembler Language instruction.) The general form of *Mend* is:

seq.symbol or blank   MEND   blank

The prototype statement specifies both the name of the "new" macro instruction and the formal arguments (parameters) that will be used by the macro instruction. The name field may be blank, or it may contain a formal parameter. The general form of the prototype statement is:

parameter or blank   symbol   arguments

The symbol is the name of the "new" macro instruction. This symbol may consist of any alphabetic characters, but it must not be the same as any Assembler Language operation name.

The formal arguments or parameters are often called *symbolic variables*. They may be one to seven alphanumeric characters long. The first character must be alphabetic. The entire string of characters must be preceded by an ampersand. (&ABLE and &BL100 are examples of two acceptable symbolic variables.)

The prototype statement may contain from 0 to 200 of these formal parameters.

Example 16.1

a. &BLUE   CIRCLE   &A,&B1

&BLUE, &A, and &B1 are the three symbolic variables of the macro whose name is CIRCLE. The action caused by CIRCLE will be completely defined by the model statements.

b.   GODATA   &A,&RED,&B1,&ABLE

The GODATA macro prototype statement does not possess a symbolic variable in the name field. It does, however, have four formal arguments.

The Model Statements.   The model statements define the action of the macro instruction. There is no limitation with respect to the number of instructions that may appear in the set of model statements except the one imposed by the size of storage.

The fields of the model statements are the same as those of an Assembler Language instruction, and the rules for forming a model statement are about the same as the rules for forming an Assembler Language instruction. Sample model statements are included in the full macro-definition of Example 16.2. In the second half of the example we show the expansion of the macro (the code that is generated) when it is called.

Example 16.2

```
a.              MACRO
                DIVIDE   &EVEN,&ODD,&A,&B,&C
                ┌L       &EVEN,&A
      model     │SRDA    &EVEN,32
      statements│D       &EVEN,&B
                └ST      &ODD,&C
                MEND
```

The four model statements define the action of DIVIDE.

Part *b* of the example shows how to call the macro in the user program. The plus symbols are generated by the Assembler to signify that the corresponding assembly statement is part of the macro expansion.

b. DIVIDE   2,3,SAM,TOIVO,DATA

The Assembler inserts the machine language equivalent of the following assembly code into the program starting at the point where it encountered the DIVIDE macro call.

```
        +    L       2,SAM
        +    SRDA    2,32
        +    D       2,TOIVO
        +    ST      3,DATA
```

Note the substitution of the actual parameters of the call—2, 3, SAM, TOIVO, and DATA—for the symbolic variables of the prototype statement—&EVEN, &ODD, &A, &B, and &C. Note further that the *i*th symbol in the actual parameter list is substituted for the *i*th symbolic variable in the formal parameter list.

We now discuss the relationship between the symbolic variables of a macro-definition and various other concepts related to these symbolic parameters.

16.2 The Symbolic Variables

Two types of symbolic variables may appear in the operand field of a prototype statement. They are positional and keyword parameters. The positional parameters must appear first. (We limit our discussion in this section to the positional symbolic variables; the keyword variables are discussed in Topic 1 of the Computer Notebook of this chapter.

The positional parameters are placed into a natural one-to-one correspondence with actual parameters that appear in the call.

Consider Example 16.2. The order of the symbolic parameters was &EVEN, &ODD, &A, &B, &C. The order of the actual parameters in the call was 2, 3, SAM, TOIVO, DATA. Hence *2* was associated with &EVEN, *3* with &ODD, *SAM* with &A, *TOIVO* with &B, and *DATA* with &C. (Always bear in mind that the symbolic variables are associated with character strings. For instance, &A is associated with the character string *SAM*.)

Concatenation. The symbolic variables may also be *concatenated*. For example, we might have written the macro-definition of Example 16.2 as

```
      MACRO
①    DIVIDE   &EVEN,&A,&B,&C
      L        &EVEN,&A
      SRDA     &EVEN,32
      D        &EVEN,&B
②    ST       &EVEN.+1,&C
      MEND
```

Note the omission of &ODD in the prototype statement ①. Consider the operand field in ②. *+1* is said to be concatenated to &EVEN. When the macro is called by, say,

```
DIVIDE   4,DATA,ACCT,RESULT
```

the macro expansion will be

```
      L        4,DATA
      SRDA     4,32
      D        4,ACCT
④    ST       4+1,RESULT
```

The Assembler will add four and one and place the value five in the machine language instruction when ④ is encoded. Notice that the period which follows &EVEN does not appear in the macro expansion. The period was used to signify (to the *macro processor*) that the character string *+1* was to be concatenated to the actual parameter associated with &EVEN.

Let us now turn to another example of concatenation of character strings.

Example 16.3

Definition

```
MACRO
SUBTRACT   &TYPE,&A,&B,&C
L&TYPE     4,&A
S&TYPE     4,&B
S&TYPE     4,&C
ST&TYPE    4,&A
```

First call

```
SUBTRACT   E,DATA,ACCT,RITA
```

First expansion

```
LE         4,DATA
SE         4,ACCT
SE         4,RITA
STE        4,DATA
```

Second call

```
SUBTRACT   ,NUMBER,DAYS,JINGER
L          4,NUMBER
S          4,DAYS
S          4,JINGER
ST         4,NUMBER
```

Recall that the formal symbolic parameters are associated with character strings. &TYPE was associated with *E* in the first call. In the second call, a comma signified the absence of an actual parameter, so &TYPE was associated with a *null character*. The difference between null and blank is explained in Example 16.11.

The mnemonics in the first call were concatenated with an *E*. Hence the code involved single-precision floating-point constants. The code in the second call involved full-word binary integers.

Note the two different methods of concatenation. No period is needed when a character string is concatenated to a symbolic variable (L&TYPE, ST&TYPE), but a period is required when a symbolic variable is concatenated to a character string (&EVEN.+1).

Sublists. A symbolic variable of a prototype statement may be associated with a sublist or a set of actual parameters. For instance, &A might be associated with the sublist (RED,DATA,PAY) in the macro call. The Assembler would associate RED with &A(1). &A(2) and &A(3) are associated with DATA and PAY, respectively.

Example 16.4

Definition

```
MACRO
AVERAGE   &DATA,&N
L         4,&DATA(1)
A         4,&DATA(2)
A         4,&DATA(3)
SRDA      4,32
D         4,&N
MEND
```

Call

```
AVERAGE   (WK1,WK2,WK3),=F'3'
```

Expansion

```
L         4,WK1
A         4,WK2
A         4,WK3
SRDA      4,32
D         4,=F'3'
```

To check your understanding of this material, write the macro, the macro call, and the expansion to find the average of four data items.

Set Symbols.   There is another type of symbolic variable called *set symbols* or *set variables* which may be used in a macro-definition. These variables are written in exactly the same way as the symbolic parameters. That is, each must be one to seven characters long and each must be preceded by an ampersand.

How, then, does one distinguish between these two types? By the manner in which they are defined. The symbolic variables are defined in the proto- type statement. Set symbols are defined by one of the following *conditional assembly* instructions: LCLA, LCLB, LCLC, GBLA, GBLB, GBLC. (See Section 16.3.)

The three instructions LCLA (local A), LCLB (local B), and LCLC (local C) define set symbols which are *local* to the macro definition in which they appear. GBLA (global A), GBLB (global B), and GBLC (global C) de- fine set symbols which are *global*. They are global in the sense that they are available not only in the macro definition in which they were defined but also in the main program, its subroutines, and in all other macro-definitions that belong to the main program.

We will discuss the set symbols in greater detail in the next section.

16.3 Conditional Assembly Instructions

There are 13 conditional assembly instructions which enable the programmer to vary the sequence of the statements generated by a macro call. We list these instructions in Table 16.1. We note that these instructions may be used in conditional assembly statements which are interspersed among the model statements of a macro definition. These conditional assembly statements, however, will not be generated when the macro is called. They are used by the macro processor to monitor the "flow" of the generated statements.

TABLE 16.1 Conditional Assembly Instructions

LCLA	GBLA	SETA	AIF	
LCLB	GBLB	SETB	AGO	ACTR
LCLC	GBLC	SETC	ANOP	

The set symbols that were mentioned in the last section are divided into three types: *arithmetic, Boolean,* and *character.* LCLA (local A) and GBLA (global A) define the arithmetic set symbols. LCLB (local B) and GBLB (global B) define the Boolean (logical) set symbols. LCLC and GBLC define the character set variables.

Example 16.5

a.   LCLA &BET

&BET is defined as a local integer arithmetic set variable. It is available only in the macro definition in which it has been defined. &BET has the initial value of zero. The values that &BET may attain range from a low of -2^{31} to a maximum of $+2^{31} - 1$.

b.   GBLA &DAY

&DAY is a global set variable. It is available in any macro definition or in any program segment of the jobstep. The other attributes of &DAY are the same as those which belong to &BET.

c.   LCLB &BOOL

&BOOL is a local Boolean or logical set variable. Its initial value is false. The code for false is a binary zero, and that of true is a binary one.

d.   GBLB &BLUE

&BLUE is a global Boolean set variable. The attributes of &BLUE, except for its global aspects, are the same as those of &BOOL.

e.   LCLC &VIENO

&VIENO is a local character set variable. Its initial value is the null character. (Note: the null character is not a blank. Example 16.11 distinguishes between a null character and a blank.) The maximum length of the character string which can be contained in &VIENO is eight. The length of &VIENO depends on the character string it contains.

f.   GBLC &ALICE

&ALICE is a global character set variable. The attributes &VIENO and &ALICE are the same, except for the global and local attributes.

The initial values which have been assigned to the set variables at definition time can be modified by using the set instructions. These instructions—SETA, SETB, and SETC—are used to assign new values to the arithmetic, logical, and character set variables, respectively. Henceforth, we shall refer to the set variables whose values are modified by the SETA instruction as SETA symbols. The names SETB symbols and SETC symbols will be used for the other two types of set variables.

Table 16.2 depicts the relationship between these set variables and their associated set instruction.

TABLE 16.2 The Set Symbols

Type	SETA symbols	SETB symbols	SETC symbols
Local	LCLA	LCLB	LCLC
Global	GBLA	GBLB	GBLC

The syntax of the set instructions is rather unusual. The set variable is placed in the label field, and its associated set instruction appears in the operation field. The new value (which may be an arithmetic or logical expression) that is to be assigned to the set variable appears in the operand field. Example 16.6 illustrates the assignment of new values to each of the three types of set variables. We note, however, that these are rather elementary examples. More advanced examples will be given after we have presented additional background material.

Example 16.6

We assume that &ALICE, &BEATRICE, and &COLOR have been defined as SETA, SETB, and SETC symbols, respectively.

a. &ALICE   SETA   12

The new value of &ALICE is 12.

b. &BEATRICE   SETB   1

&BEATRICE is equal to true.

c. &COLOR   SETC   'BLUE'

&COLOR has been assigned the value BLUE.

We will discuss the remaining four conditional assembly instructions at greater length after we have introduced some additional background material. Here we merely point out that AIF and AGO are conditional and unconditional branch instructions, respectively. ANOP is a no operation instruction used to accommodate the branching instructions. ACTR is used to specify a maximum count to the number of AIF and AGO branches which can be allowed within a macro definition. The default value of the branch counter is 4096.

16.4   Attributes

The Assembler assigns attributes to the symbolic names (operands) that it encounters in its first pass through the main program. (One such attribute, the implied length, should be familiar to all readers.) Table 16.3 has a complete list of the attributes that may be possessed by any operand. The table also lists the attribute notation and a sample reference of each type.

When a program symbolic name is used as an actual parameter in a macro call, it passes its attributes to its corresponding symbolic variable in the macro definition. Hence, a programmer may refer to the attributes of a main program operand in a conditional assembly instruction by referring to the attributes of the associated symbolic variable.

We do not discuss the *integer* and *scaling* attributes in this text. We have included them in the table for the sake of completeness. Interested readers might refer to the IBM manual *Assembler Language* for a complete discussion. We consider each of the other attributes immediately following the table. We assume that &DATA is a symbolic parameter.

TABLE 16.3   Attribute Table

Attribute	Notation	Reference
COUNT	K'	K'&DATA
INTEGER	I'	I'&DATA
LENGTH	L'	L'&DATA
NUMBER	N'	N'&DATA
SCALING	S'	S'&DATA
TYPE	T'	T'&DATA

Count.   The value of the count attribute is an integer equal to the number of characters in the actual parameter of the macro call. If the actual parameter is a list, then the value includes the left and the right parentheses and the commas which separate the members of the list.

The count attribute is applicable only to operands used in a macro call. The count attribute can be used in the operand field of SETA instructions and in arithmetic and logical expressions.

Example 16.7

Prototype statement

>   SAMPLE   &A,&AB,&ABC,&ABCD

Macro call

>   SAMPLE   (A1,A2,A3),LILJA,SAM,DATA1

then

>   K'&A   = 10
>   K'&AB   = 5
>   K'&ABC   = 3
>   K'&ABCD = 5

Length. The student should, by now, be quite familiar with the length attribute. Therefore, we limit our discussion of this entry to the examples that follow.

Example 16.8

Prototype statement

>   ADD   &A,&B,&D,&E

Macro call

>   ADD   BUSH,BLUE,CALL,DAVID

We assume that if BUSH, BLUE, CALL, and DAVID are a full-word storage location, a double-word storage location, a binary integer, and a half-word binary integer, respectively, *then*:

>   L'&A = 4
>   L'&B = 8
>   L'&C = 4
>   L'&D = 2

Number. The number attribute is an integer equal to the number of operands in a list that is associated with a symbolic variable. If, for instance, &A is associated with the list of variables (WAINO,ABLE,TABLE), then N'&A = 3. If &A is associated with a single operand, then N'&A = 1. If N'&A = 0, then the associated operand in the macro call is missing.

We note here that the value of the number attribute of a list of operands is equal to one plus the number of commas. If, for instance, &A is associated with (ABLE,,TABLE), then N'&A = 3.

Type. The value of the type attribute is a letter. Table 16.4 lists the type attribute of some DC and DS pseudo statements. We note that the list in the table is not complete.

TABLE 16.4 Some Type Attribute Values

Operand	*Value*
address constant	A
binary constant	B
character constant	C
long form floating-point	D
short form floating-point	E
full-word binary integer	F
half-word binary integer	H
packed decimal constant	P
zoned decimal constant	Z

Example 16.9

Prototype statement

   SUB   &A,&B,&C

We assume that:

   T'&A = F,   T'&B = E,   T'&C = Z

What type of operand is each of the symbolic variables &A, &B, and &C associated with?

16.5 Conditional Assembly Expressions

There are three kinds of expressions which may appear in the operand field of a conditional assembly instruction—one for each type of set instruction. SETA evaluates an arithmetic expression. SETB and SETC evaluate a logical expression and a character expression, respectively.

Arithmetic Expressions. The value of the arithmetic expression which appears in the operand field of a SETA instruction will be assigned to the SETA symbol—LCLA or GBLA—which has been placed in the label fields. The expressions are evaluated in the usual algebraic manner. There are, however, two restrictions that must be followed: only five levels of parentheses are allowed and there must not be more than 16 terms.

Example 16.10

a. &BOB   SETA   (L'&HEAT+N'&ABLE)*6

If L'&HEAT = 6 and N'&ABLE = 2, then the value +48 is assigned to the SETA symbol &BOB.

b. &A   SETA   12−&B+L'&BLUE

We assume that &B is a SETA symbol whose value is 10. L'&BLUE = 12.

What value is assigned to &A?

c. &A   SETA   &A*&B+N'&ABLE

We assume that:

$$&A = 46_{10}$$
$$&B = 10_{10}$$
$$N'&ABLE = 42$$

What is the new value assigned to &A?

Character Expressions.   A character expression may appear in the operand field of a SETC instruction. The expression may contain a character string up to 256 bytes long. The maximum number of characters that can be assigned to a SETC symbol is eight. The SETC instruction uses the first eight characters of any resulting string. The rest of the string is truncated.

If the string which results from the character expression has less than eight symbols, then the entire string is assigned to the SETC variable. Strings in the expression must be enclosed in apostrophes.

Example 16.11

a. &HELEN   SETC   'ABCD'

The value ABCD is assigned to the SETC symbol &HELEN.

b. &A   SETC   T'&ABLE

&A is equal to the type of operand associated with &ABLE (see Table 16.4).

c. &RITA   SETC   T'&ABLE.'ABC'

The value of T'&ABLE is concatenated with the string ABC. If T'&ABLE = F, then &RITA = FABC.

d. &RED   SETC   ' ' (blank)
    &BLUE   SETC   '' (null)
    &ALICE   SETC   'AB&RED.CD'
    &TWO   SETC   'AB&BLUE.CD'

The value assigned to &ALICE is AB CD, since &RED is equal to a blank.
The value assigned to &TWO is ABCD since &BLUE is equal to the null character.

e. &MARK   SETC   'L''BLUE'

The value of &MARK is L'BLUE. Two apostrophes are needed to create a single apostrophe in the character string. If the macro writer wants an ampersand in a character string, he must provide two ampersands in the expression.

We now present two examples of macro-definitions in which SETC symbols are used.

Example 16.12

a. *Macro-definition*

```
            MACRO
            SWING      &DATA
            LCLC       &PRE,&A
&PRE        SETC       'A'
&A          SETC       'B'
            L          5,&DATA&PRE
            ST         5,&DATA&A
            MEND
```

Macro call

```
            SWING      FIELD
```

Macro expansion

```
            L          5,FIELDA
            ST         5,FIELDB
```

Conditional assembly instructions are not generated by the macro call.
The symbol FIELD was concatenated to A and B.

b. *Macro-definition*

```
            MACRO
            MULTIPLY   &MITCH
            LCLC       &BLUE
&BLUE       SETC       'A'
            L          5,&MITCH&BLUE
```

```
&BLUE     SETC      'B'
          M         4,&MITCH&BLUE
&BLUE     SETC      'C'
          ST        5,&MITCH&BLUE
          MEND
```

Macro call

```
          MULTIPLY  FIELD
```

Macro expansion

```
          L         5,FIELDA
          M         4,FIELDB
          ST        5,FIELDC
```

Logical Expressions. Logical expressions may appear in the operand field of a SETB instruction or the AIF conditional branch instruction. SETB will assign the value of the expression to the set symbol which appears in the name field of the instruction. This value must, of course, evaluate to *true* or *false* (binary zero or binary one). AIF uses the value of the logical expression as a switch for a branch. When the expression is true, the branch is made. If false, the branch will not occur.

A logical expression may consist of a combination of terms. These terms are combined by the *logical operators* AND, OR, and NOT. The terms in the expression may be arithmetic or character relations. These relations are composed of two arithmetic or character terms connected by one of the allowable relational operators—EQ, NE, LT, GT, LE, and GE.

Table 16.5 lists both the logical and the relational operators. The logical operators are Boolean functions which were defined in Chapter 8. The meanings of the relational operators are given in the table. Examples of logical expressions used to assign values to SETB symbols follow the table. Other uses will be discussed in Section 16.6.

TABLE 16.5 Logical Expression Operators

Boolean	Relational operator	meaning
AND	EQ	equal
OR	GE	greater than or equal
NOT	GT	greater than
	LE	less than or equal
	LT	less than
	NE	not equal

Example 16.13

a. &ABLE SETB (0)

&ABLE is assigned the value *false*.

b. &CRAIG SETB (T'&A EQ 'F')

&CRAIG is assigned the value *true* if &A is associated with an F-type operand; otherwise &CRAIG is false.

c. &MAYOR SETB (L'&A NE 4 AND T'&A EQ 'D')

&MAYOR will be assigned the value *true* only if the arithmetic expression L'&A NE 4 is true *and* the relation T'&A EQ 'D' is true.

d. &WAINO SETB (NOT &DATA AND T'&A EQ 'F')

&BLUE will be assigned the value *true* only if &DATA (a SETB symbol) is false *and* &A is associated with an F-type operand.

e. &ALICE SETB (&KAINO EQ 'ABC')

If &KAINO, a SETC symbol, has the value *ABC*, then &ALICE will be assigned the value *true*.

16.6   Conditional Assembly Branch Instructions

Conditional assembly has two branch instructions: AGO, an unconditional branch, and AIF, the conditional branch. AGO must have a sequence symbol in the operand field. AIF must have a logical expression in the operand field which is immediately followed by a sequence symbol. Before we continue our discussion of the conditional assembly Branch instructions, we will discuss the concept of a sequence symbol.

Sequence Symbols.   A sequence symbol consists of one to seven alphanumeric characters preceded by a period. The first character that follows the period must be alphabetic. .RED, .BLUE001, .ABC, and .DATA are all examples of sequence symbols.

Sequence symbols are used by the programmer to monitor the flow of the conditional assembly instructions and/or the flow of the model statements. The sequence symbols are local to the macro definition. They will not be generated by a macro call.

The programmer may use a sequence symbol in the label field of any macro definition statement. "Control" in the conditional assembly may be transferred to this statement by placing its sequence symbol name in the operand field of an AGO or AIF instruction. The Assembler will always "branch" to process the macro definition statement named by the sequence symbol in the operand field of an AGO. The branch to the sequence symbol named in an AIF instruction will be made only if the logical expression in the operand field is true.

Conditional Branch—AIF. The syntax of *AIF* is:

blank or ss AIF (expression)sequence symbol

Note: ss stands for sequence symbol.

Example 16.14

```
        MACRO
        ADD      &REG,&A,&D
        SR       &REG,&REG
        AIF      (T'&A  NE  'F').ABLE
        A        &REG,&A
.ABLE   AIF      (T'&D  NE  'F').END
        A        &REG,&D
.END    MEND
```

Unconditional Branch—AGO. The syntax of *AGO* is:

blank or ss AGO sequence symbol

Example 16.15

```
        MACRO
        LOAD     &REG,&A
        AIF      (T'&A  EQ  'F').ABLE
        AGO      .END
.ABLE   L        &REG,&A
.END    MEND
```

a. We assume that:

   T'&A = F

Macro call

   LOAD 3,BLUE

Macro expansion

   L 3,BLUE

b. We assume that:

   T'&A $\neq$ F

Macro call

      LOAD   3,SAM

Macro expansion
No code is generated, because SAM is not type F.

ANOP. The conditional assembly instruction ANOP (no-operation) is handy when the name field of the macro-definition instruction to which we desire to branch is already occupied. Suppose, for instance, we have the following code:

    ⋮

    &SAM   A   &REG,&DATA(4)

    ⋮

We want to branch to the Add instruction by AGO .BLUE. Since the name field of the Add instruction is already occupied by &SAM, we use the no-operation instruction, ANOP, with .BLUE in the name field just before the Add instruction. Our code now reads:

    ⋮

.BLUE   ANOP
.&SAM   A   &REG,&DATA(4)

    ⋮

    AGO   .BLUE

    ⋮

The student will find the study of Example 16.16 helpful.

Example 16.16

Macro definition

```
            MACRO
            CONVERT   &X,&D,&REG
            LCLA      &LENGTH
            AIF       (T'&D NE 'D').END
            AIF       (T'&X EQ 'Z').AB
            AIF       (T'&X EQ 'C').AB
            AIF       (T'&X EQ 'P').BA
            AGØ       .END
.AB         ANOP
&LENGTH     SETA      3
            PACK      &D,&X.(&LENGTH)
.CVB        CVB       &REG,&D
            AGØ       .END
.BA         ZAP       &D,&X
            AGØ       .CVB
.END        MEND
```

Macro call

>   CONVERT   XCARD,DOUBLE,3

We assume that:

>   T'XCARD = C,   T'DOUBLE = D

Macro generation

>   PACK   DOUBLE,XCARD(3)
>   CVB   3,DOUBLE

What will be the macro generation if T'XCARD = P?

Computer Notebook

TOPIC 1   Advance Features of Macro Language

In this section we discuss some extended features of macro language. We present each topic in its own subsection. Although these topics are more or less independent, we will assume that the student has studied them in order. Concepts developed in the early topics will be used in later subsections. Our first topic is keyword macros.

Keyword Macro-definitions.   If the symbolic operands listed in the prototype statement are positional parameters, then the actual parameters in the macro call must appear in a specified order. The keyword macro feature enables the programmer to specify his symbolic variables as keywords. If he does so, then the actual parameters in the macro call may appear in any order. Example 16.17 has a keyword prototype statement and a typical macro call. (Note that the ampersands are dropped in the call.)

Example 16.17

a. *Macro prototype*

>   ADD   &SUM=,&ADD1=,&ADD2=

Macro call

>   1. ADD   ADD1=BLUE,SUM=DATA,ADD2=RED
>   2. ADD   ADD2=RED,ADD1=SAM,SUM=ACCT

The programmer may provide default values for the keyword symbolic parameters in the prototype statement. The default values become the actual parameters if not overridden in the macro call. The next example illustrates the assignment of a default value to a keyword parameter.

b. *Prototype statement*

      SUM   &REG = 4,&ADD1 = ,&ADD2,&SAM = SAVE

Macro call

    1. SUM   REG = 6,ADD1 = ACCT,ADD2 = PAY

The default value of SAVE is assigned to &SAM. The call overrides the default value given to &REG.

    2. SUM   ADD1 = BLUE,ADD2 = ACCT,SAM = DATA

In this call, the keyword parameter &SAM is associated with DATA, but the default value four is assigned to &REG.

The prototype statement may be in a mixed mode. That is, the symbolic parameters may be specified as positional or keyword. There is one restriction: All positional parameters in both the prototype statement and in the macro call must appear before any keyword parameters. Example 16.18 should clarify this point.

Example 16.18

Prototype statement

      MØVE   &A,&B,&C,&SAVE = STORE,&KEY =

Macro call

      MØVE   X,Y,Z,KEY = BLUE

X, Y, and Z are associated with &A, &B, and &C, respectively. The default value STORE is assigned to &SAVE. BLUE is associated with the keyword &KEY.

MEXIT (Macro Exit). The MEXIT instruction tells the Assembler to terminate the processing of the macro definition. The syntax of MEXIT is:

    blank or seq. sym.   MEXIT   blank

The use of one or more MEXIT instruction in a macro definition does not negate the need for a MEND trailer statement. All macro definitions must end with MEND. Example 16.19 illustrates a use of MEXIT.

Example 16.19

      MACRØ
      CØNVERT   &EBC,&DOUG,&REG
      AIF   (T'&EBC EQ 'Z').RED

```
①          MEXIT
   .RED    PACK    &DOUG,&EBC
           CVB     &REG,&DOUG
           MEND
```

An AGO branch to MEND would be equivalent to the MEXIT statement in ①.

MNOTE (Macro Note). The MNOTE instruction enables the programmer to pass a message, either a comment or an error message, to the calling program. One form of MNOTE is:

blank or seq. sym.   MNOTE   message

The message must be enclosed in apostrophes, and the MNOTE message may *not* be suppressed by PRINT NOGEN.

Example 16.20

```
           MACRO
           MOVE    &TO,&FROM
           LCLA    &LENGTH
①          MNOTE   *,'MOVING TWO OPERANDS'
           AIF     (T'&TO NE T'&FROM).ERROR1
           AIF     (T'&TO EQ 'F').FULL
           AIF     (T'&TO EQ 'D').FLOAT
           AGO     .ERROR2
   .FULL   ANOP
   &LENGTH SETA    4
           MVC     &TO.(&LENGTH),&FROM
           MEXIT
   .FLOAT  ANOP
   &LENGTH SETA    8
           MVC     &TO.(&LENGTH),&FROM
           MEXIT
② .ERROR1 MNOTE   'TYPES DON''T MATCH'
           MEXIT
③ .ERROR2 MNOTE   'OPERANDS WRONG TYPE'
           MEND
```

The MNOTE message in ① will not be printed if PRINT NOGEN is specified. The error messages in ② and ③ will be printed whenever they are applicable; that is, they will not be suppressed by NOGEN.

SYSNDX (System Index). The system index is a four digit counter which is updated by one after each macro call. This index remains constant during any call. Hence it is possible for a programmer to create a unique symbolic name by concatenating a maximum of four characters to the contents of this index.

For instance, if the contents of the system index are 0016 in a macro call, then the concatenated label BUB&SYSNDX in the macro definition will be generated into BUB0016.

Example 16.21 illustrates our comments. The macro instruction COUNTER counts the number of one bits in a word. It is called twice by the main program.

Example 16.21

Macro definition

```
          MACRØ
          CØUNTER  &SAVE,&DATA,&REG,&R0=0,&R1=1
          STM      &R0,&R1,&SAVE
          SR       &R0,&R0
          L        &R1,&DATA
          SR       &REG,&REG
AB&SYSNDX SLDL     &R0,1
          AR       &REG,&R0
          SRL      &R0,1
          LTR      &R1,&R1
          BNZ      AB&SYSNDX
          LM       &R0,&R1&SAVE
```

Macro call (first call)

```
          COUNTER  SAVEIT,ACCT,8
```

We assume that:

```
          C(SYSNDX) = 0147
```

Macro expansion

```
          STM      0,1,SAVEIT
          SR       0,0
          L        1,ACCT
          SR       8,8
AB0147    SLDL     0,1
          AR       8,0
          SRL      0,1
          LTR      1,1
          BNZ      AB0147
          LM       0,1,SAVEIT
```

Macro call (second call)

```
          COUNTER  SAVEIT,PAY,8
```

Macro expansion

```
          STM    0,1,SAVEIT
          SR     0,0
          L      1,PAY
          SR     8,8
AB0148    SLDL   0,1
          AR     8,0
          SRL    0,1
          LTR    1,1
          BNZ    AB0148
          LM     0,1,SAVEIT
```

EXERCISES

1. Do not use the text or any manual as a reference for this problem. Write a short macro. Give a typical call. Give the macro expansion.

2. Write a macro that will enable the user to move a character string whose implied length may vary from 1 to 3500 bytes.

3. Write a macro in which all three types of set variables are defined. Show how to put the values 127, *false*, and CHAR into the arithmetic, Boolean, and character set variables, respectively.

4. Consider the following operation which is not implemented in the System/360 instruction set:

   RAD   R1,S2

   This operation causes

   $$S2 \leftarrow C(R1) + C(S2)$$

   Write a macro which, when called, will accomplish this action. (Note that the contents of the register operand must not be changed by the action of the macro instruction.) For example:

   RAD   5,BLUE

Before execution	*After execution*
C(BLUE) = 00001200	C(BLUE) = 00001304
C(Reg 5) = 00000104	C(Reg 5) is unchanged

5. Many computers have an *end-around* shift. Consider, for instance, a left *end-around* shift of five bits. The bits which leave bit position 0 "re-enter" the register at bit position 31. (Recall that the registers in System/360 computers drop these bits into a bit bucket.) Write a macro which will enable a user to have a circular shift.

6. Consider exercise 6 in Chapter 15. Write your solution to this modified Lazy Keypuncher problem as a macro. Use the defined macro instruction to read in two data items. Add them using single-precision floating-point arithmetic.

7. Distinguish between:
   a. macro definition and macro call
   b. formal parameters and actual parameters
   c. AGO and AIF
   d. sequence symbol and symbolic variable
   e. MACRO and MEND
   f. prototype statement and model statement
   g. ANOP and ACTR

8. Define a macro which will evaluate a polynomial for a given x. Use Horner's method. Let the symbolic parameters be keywords. The macro call should accept a polynomial of the first, second, third, and fourth degree. (Hint: use Conditional Assembly.)

9. Find out what is meant by *nesting of macros*. Distinguish between inner and outer macros. Use the *Assembler Language Manual* as your reference.

10. When we concatenate FIELD to &A by FIELD&A, we may omit the "concatenation" period. But when we concatenate &SAM to BLUE by &SAM.BLUE, we must include the period. Explain the difference.

11. Write a macro which uses the keyword method of naming parameters. Supply default values for some, but not all, of the symbolic parameters. Submit a macro expansion with your definition.

12. Make an attribute table listing the various kinds of attributes. Give the type of value associated with each kind of attribute. What is the range of the value for each type? Give an example of each kind of attribute with its associated value. For example, assume that BLUE is a full-word location; then L'BLUE = 4. Use the *Assembler Language Manual* as your reference.

13. Let &A, &B, &C, &D, &E, &F, &G be set variables. Declare these set variables using the correct set instruction. (Hint: determine the set instruction to use from the information given below.) Then set these set variables to the values specified. (Assume that the undesignated variables are symbolic parameters of the prototype call.)
   a. &A to the length of &SAM
   b. &B to the length of &BOB
   c. &C to the null character
   d. &D to the number of characters in &SAM
   e. &E to the value equal to the type attribute of &SAM
   f. &F to *false* if &SAM is associated with a full-word binary integer
   g. &G to the first character in the actual parameter associated with &SAM (Note: You may have to do some outside research on this one.)

14. Consider Figure 8.2. Recall that when we Unpack a packed decimal number, the contents of the recipient location are in zoned decimal form. We showed how to *OR* positive zoned decimals into EBCDIC form. We "skirted" the problem (in Chapter 8) of negative packed decimal operands. Now consider both cases. Write a macro—using Conditional Assembly—which will print a full-word binary integer which is stored in a full-word MEMORY location. For instance, suppose C(GERALD) = 0000000A; the macro instruction PRINT GERALD should cause the following message to be printed:

    THE VALUE IN LOCATION GERALD IS 10.

    If, on the other hand, C(GERALD) = FFFFFFF6, the macro instruction PRINT GERALD should result in:

    THE VALUE IN LOCATION GERALD IS −10.

15. Write a Conditional Assembly statement which contains all three types of expressions in the operand field. Recall that the three types are arithmetic, Boolean, and character. Assume that all symbolic parameters and set symbols that are used in the expression have been defined.

16. Pick any computer not in the IBM 360 series. Contrast the macro facilities of the computer of your choice with the System/360 macro facilities.
    a. Does the computer of your choice allow nesting of macros?
    b. Does the computer of your choice provide a conditional assembly facility?
    c. How are the parameters passed?
    d. Does the macro facility provide variables such as SETA, SETB, and SETC variables which are local to the definition?

17. Let a data item which has up to nine digits be punched right justified in the first nine columns of a punch card. Write a macro instruction which will read this data item into MEMORY and convert it to a full-word binary integer.

18. Consider the following four macro concepts: MEXIT, MNOTE, ANOP, and SYSNDX. Write a single macro instruction such that its definition requires the use of all four concepts.

17 | Introduction to the Operating System

In this chapter we discuss some topics that might be considered an introduction to the Operating System. These topics divide this chapter into four subdivisions: (1) the program status word, (2) interrupts, (3) the privileged instructions, and (4) channel programming.

These subjects cover a great deal of material, and some of it is quite complex and difficult. But a knowledge of all of it is necessary if a programmer is to make efficient use of the services offered by the Operating System. Although we shall discuss each topic quite thoroughly, the student must bear in mind that this chapter is merely an introduction to these advanced topics.

Our first topic is the program status word, a double-word, which contains considerable information about the state of both the CPU and the program being executed by the CPU.

17.1 The Program Status Word

The PROGRAM STATUS WORD register does not reside in the addressable portion of main MEMORY. Although this register is not generally addressable by the application programmer, we have seen that he can change the contents of one field, the program mask, in this double-word (see exercise 11, Chapter 8).

Figure 17.1 is a diagram of the PSW. We discuss each of the fields in some depth in the text that follows the diagram.

FIGURE 17.1 The Program Status Word

0	7 8	11 12	15 16	31
SYSTEM MASK	PROTEC-TION KEY	CODE FOR AMWP	INTERRUPT CODES	

32	33 34	35 36	39 40	63
ILC	CC	PROGRAM MASK	INSTRUCTION ADDRESS REGISTER (ADDRESS OF NEXT INSTRUCTION)	

System Mask. The bits in bit positions 0–6 of the system mask are associated by a natural one-to-one correspondence with the I/O channels. Table 17.1 lists the mask bit positions and their associated channels. The bit in position 7 is associated with the *timer*, with the interrupt key on the system control panel, and with certain external signal devices. These three sources have been grouped under *external* in the table. Each bit position in the mask is said to be associated with a source. For example, the source channel 0 is associated with bit position 0. The source channel 3 is associated with bit position 3.

When a mask bit is *on* (equals one), then its associated source may cause an interrupt of the CPU. When a mask bit is *off* (equals zero), then its associated source cannot interrupt the CPU. Any communication that the source wishes to pass to the CPU must wait until its associated bit is turned on. In this case the interrupt is said to be *pending*.

TABLE 17.1 System Mask Bits

PSWR bit	Interrupt source
0	channel 0
1	channel 1
2	channel 2
3	channel 3
4	channel 4
5	channel 5
6	channel 6
7	external

We consider in the next few paragraphs some background material about the channel concept so that the function of the system mask will have more meaning to the student.

First, a definition: A *channel* is a logical entity that controls the transmission of information between the CPU and external I/O devices. The channel is actually a small computer which monitors the flow of data between the input/output device and MEMORY. A maximum of seven channels can be attached to a System/360 computer. Each channel will execute a program of *commands* at the behest of the CPU. (Instructions when executed by a channel are called *commands*.)

There are two types of channels called *multiplexor* and *selector*. Each type of channel can monitor several different I/O devices which are attached to them. The multiplexor channel services the "slower" I/O devices such as the CARDREADER and the PRINTER. Since these devices are slow, they share the channel's I/O interface. That is, each takes a "short" interval of time during which they transmit only a segment of the data they are transferring. This mode of operation, called the *multiplex mode,* gives the channel its name.

The I/O devices attached to a selector channel operate in what is called the *burst* mode. These devices are "fast" and monopolize the channel's I/O interface when transmitting data. That is, when a "burst" (of data) is transmitted, no other device can communicate over the interface. We note that while a multiplexor channel can operate, when necessary, in the burst mode, a selector channel never operates in the multiplex mode.

When a channel has finished an input/output action (or if some unusual condition occurs during an I/O routine), the channel sends a signal to the CPU. This signal can interrupt the CPU if the channel's mask bit in the system mask is turned on. If that mask bit is turned off, then the interrupt will be queued. It is said to be pending until the CPU is able to acknowledge the message. (We will return to this discussion in the section on interrupts.)

When bit 7 is on, the CPU will accept an interrupt from any one of three sources: the timer, any of the external signals attached to the direct control feature (another computer), or the operator who has depressed the interrupt key on the system control panel.

Protection Key. Each 2048-byte block of MEMORY is associated with a protection key. A block's key is not addressable by an application programmer, but the key may be accessed by one of the privileged instructions (see Section 17.3). A protection key is used to establish the programmer's right to access a particular block for storing and/or fetching data.

A key appropriate to the needs of the application program is inserted in the user's program status word just before control of the CPU is transferred. Any attempt made to access blocks outside the "domain" of this key will result in a protection exception and a program interrupt.

AMWP Codes. The AMWP field of the PSWR gives miscellaneous information about the status of the CPU. Table 17.2 lists the bit positions of this field and the meanings associated with their values. A discussion of each bit in this field appears after the table.

TABLE 17.2 AMWP Codes

Label	Bit position	Bit off	Bit on
A	12	EBCDIC code	USACII-8 code
M	13	machine int. off	machine int. on
W	14	CPU running	CPU in wait state
P	15	supervisor mode	problem mode

The A-bit specifies whether the signs of the packed decimal operands in AP, SP, ZAP, MP, DP, CVD, ED, and EDMK are in the EBCDIC code or in the UASCII-8 code. (Consult the IBM manual *Principles of Operation* for the difference between these two codes.) We note that this text has assumed that the A-bit is off.

If the M-bit is off, the machine check interrupt is said to be *disabled*. That is, the CPU will not accept an interrupt caused by a malfunction of the computer. An attempt will be made, without any diagnosis of the trouble, to continue running. If the M-bit is on, then a machine check interrupt will be accepted.

The W-bit specifies the status of the CPU. If the bit is on, then the CPU is in the wait state; otherwise the CPU is running.

Do not confuse the wait state and the stop state. It takes manual action to get the CPU out of the stop state; this is not necessary in the wait state. An interrupt will force the CPU out of the wait state, but the CPU cannot accept an interrupt in the stop state. The stop and wait states are alike, however, in that in both states the processing of instructions has ceased.

If the P-bit is one, then the CPU is in the problem mode. It is executing an application program. If the P-bit is zero, the CPU is in the supervisor (or privileged) mode. Certain instructions (the privileged instructions) can be executed only in the supervisor mode.

Interrupt Code.   The interrupt code field will designate the cause of an interrupt, if one occurs. The table which lists the code for each type of interrupt can be found in the *Principles of Operation* manual. It is too long to reproduce in this text. We have listed the code for some of the program interrupts in Topic 2 of the Computer Notebook in Chapter 8.

Instruction Length Code (ILC).   The ILC field (bits 32 and 33) specifies the length of the current instruction. Table 17.3 lists the values in the field which are associated with the various instruction lengths. We note that the ILC is a useful aid in finding the "present" instruction after an abnormal termination.

TABLE 17.3   ILC Code

Code	Bit position 32	33	Instruction length
0	0	0	not available
1	0	1	2 bytes
2	1	0	4 bytes
3	1	1	6 bytes

Condition Code.   The condition code has been discussed in many chapters of this text. The most extensive discussion of this field appears in Chapter 10. We omit any discussion here.

Program Mask. Each bit position in the program mask is associated with a program exception. If a bit is on and its associated exception occurs, then a program interrupt will be taken. No interrupt will occur if the mask bits are off. Table 17.4 lists the bit positions and their associated program exceptions.

The program mask and the condition code are the only fields in the PSW which can be modified by the application programmer directly. The Set Program Mask instruction, which was presented in the exercises of Chapters 8 and 12, will be reviewed here.

The general form of Set Program Mask is:

SPM   R1

Bits 2–7 of R1 are stored into bit positions 34–39 of the PSWR. In other words, bits 2–7 of R1 replace the former values of the condition code and program mask.

Example 17.1

We assume that:

C(Reg 7) = 02000000
SPM   7

Bits 34–39 of the PSW are now 000010. If an exponent underflow exception occurs, an interrupt will be taken. No interrupt will be taken for fixed-point overflow, decimal overflow, or a significance exception.

TABLE 17.4   The Program Mask

Bit position	Associated exception
36	fixed-point overflow
37	decimal overflow
38	exponent underflow
39	significance

Instruction Address.   The instruction address field, bits 40–63, is a pointer to the next instruction that will be executed by the CPU. This field is equivalent to FINAC's INSTRUCTION COUNTER CELL. This instruction address field is updated at the end of each fetch cycle.

17.2   Interrupts

What do we mean by an interrupt? Let us expand on the definition and the discussion we gave in Chapter 2 so that information about the classes of

System/360 interrupts and the technique for handling them will have added significance.

All modern computers have been designed to run with the help of a control program called the Operating System. The nucleus of this control program resides in MEMORY at all times. One of the jobs of the nucleus is to monitor or supervise the many subprograms which compose the Operating System. We shall refer to this nucleus as the Supervisor or Monitor in the discussion that follows.

The main objective of the control program is to increase the efficiency of the computer. That is, the Operating System's job is to maximize the utilization of the resources of the computer. One of its jobs is to keep the CPU running, as much as possible, in the problem state. Let us consider what the control program needs to be able to do its job.

Facilities must be provided so that control of the computer is returned to the Operating System whenever a user program makes a mistake. The control program (OS) must not lose control of the CPU. Allowing the CPU to enter the wait or stop state when a program error occurs is completely unacceptable. It is much faster to return control to the Supervisor, which will diagnose the error, than to allow human intervention. Human intervention is not, as the reader knows, the way to maximize use of the CPU.

Facilities must be provided so that the user program may communicate with the Operating System when the user needs some exceptional service. There also must be a way for the computer operator to communicate with the Supervisor even though, at the moment, an application program has control of the CPU. The Operating System must also be able to respond to signals from the timer, special devices, and/or other computers that may be linked to it.

The Operating System is also responsible for the efficient use of the input/output devices that are attached to the channels. Therefore, facilities must also be provided so that the Supervisor will respond to a signal from a channel when a particular device has finished transmitting data into or out of a buffer.

All these facilities which enable the Operating System to intercept a signal are called the *program interrupt mechanism*. The signals themselves are the program interrupts.

There are five classes of interruptions recognized by the Interrupt Handling Routine of the System/360 Operating System. We list these in Table 17.5. The priority given in the table reflects the order in which an interruption will be recognized by the Interrupt Handling Routine if two or more simultaneous interruption requests are made. We discuss each type of interrupt in the text following the table. The "old" PSW and the "new" PSW will be explained in that discussion. The addresses in the table are in hex.

Program. A program interrupt will occur if any one of the 15 errors listed in Table 17.6 occurs. When a program interrupt is recognized, the Interrupt

TABLE 17.5 Classes of Interrupts

Class	Old PSW	New PSW	Priority
External	000018	000058	3
Supervisor call	000020	000060	2
Program	000028	000068	2
Machine check	000030	000070	1
Input/Output	000038	000078	4

Handling Routine stores the status word (now called the "old" PSW) into location $28_x = 40_{10}$. A "new" PSW which will cause a branch to an error subroutine is loaded from location $000068_x = 104_{10}$.

We have seen that 4 of the 15 program interrupt errors listed in Table 17.6 can be masked in the PSWR. These, recall, are fixed-point overflow, decimal overflow, exponent underflow, and significance. The other 11 error types cannot be masked. An exception caused by any one of these 11 error types will always cause an interrupt.

It is, however, possible to use a Supervisor macro called SPIE to specify an *interruption exit routine address* where the programmer may handle the interrupt himself. The address should, of course, be in a control section that belongs to the application program. We suggest that the information provided in the *Data Management and Supervisor Macros* manual be consulted before issuing a SPIE macro.

TABLE 17.6 Program Exceptions

Number	Type of error
1	Operation
2	Privileged
3	Execute
4	Protection
5	Addressing
6	Specification
7	Data
8	Fixed-point overflow*
9	Fixed-point divide
10	Decimal overflow*
11	Decimal divide
12	Exponent overflow
13	Exponent underflow*
14	Significance*
15	Floating-point divide

* maskable

The general form of *Specify Program Interruption Exit* is:

SPIE   address,(types)

If an interrupt caused by an error of a type listed in the second operand field occurs, then control will be transferred to the address specified by the first operand.

For example:

1. SPIE   BLUE,(6,9) will cause a branch to BLUE if an interrupt is caused by error types 6 or 9 (see Table 17.6).
2. SPIE   BLUE,((6,9)) will cause a branch to BLUE if an interrupt is caused by error types 6 through 9 inclusive.
3. SPIE   BLUE,(4,(6,9)) will cause a branch to BLUE if an interrupt is caused by error types 4 or 6 through 9 inclusive.

Supervisor Call.   When the Supervisor Call instruction is issued, a program interrupt takes place. The "old" PSW is stored in location $20_x = 32_{10}$, and a "new" PSW is loaded from location $60_x = 96_{10}$.

The general form of the *Supervisor Call* is:

SVC   I1

A program interrupt takes place. The "old" PSW is modified before being stored by placing the 8-bit immediate operand I1 into bit positions 24–31 and zeroing out bit positions 16–23. (The "old" PSW now designates the type of Supervisor Call.)

The SVC instruction is the usual way in which the user program communicates with the Supervisor. SVC can be issued in the user mode or in the privileged mode. If issued in the user mode, the computer will, of course, enter the privileged mode.

External.   When the external interrupt takes place, the "old" PSW is stored in location $18_x = 24_{10}$, and the "new" PSW is loaded from $58_x = 88_{10}$. (See Section 17.1 for the causes of an external interrupt.)

Machine Check.   The machine check interrupt will store the "old" PSW into location 48_{10}. The "new" PSW is loaded from 112_{10}. (See the *Principles of Operation* manual for further details.)

Input/Output.   When the Input/Output interrupt occurs, the "old" PSW is stored in location 56_{10}. The "new" PSW is fetched from location 120_{10}. (See Section 17.1 on the causes of an I/O interrupt.)

17.3 Privileged Instructions

The privileged instructions, listed in Table 17.7, can be executed only when the CPU is running in the Supervisor mode. (Recall that the P-bit in the PSW equals zero when the CPU is in the Supervisor mode.) Any attempt to execute a privileged instruction in the user mode will result in a privileged exception. A program interrupt will be taken which will lead to an abnormal termination.

We cover most of the privileged instructions immediately following the table. Three of the instructions, however, will not be discussed since they will lead us too far afield from our main purpose. We mention them briefly now. DIAGNOSE, which has no mnemonic, is used chiefly by the computer engineer to perform diagnostic tests. One of the uses of both Read Direct (RDD) and Write Direct (WRD) is to communicate with other CPUs.

TABLE 17.7 The Privileged Instruction Set

Instruction	Mnemonic	Type
DIAGNOSE	none	SI
Halt I/O	HIO	SI
Insert Storage Key	ISK	RR
Load PSW	LPSW	SI
Read Direct	RDD	SI
Set Storage Key	SSK	RR
Set System Mask	SSM	SI
Start I/O	SIO	SI
Test Channel	TCH	SI
Test I/O	TIO	SI
Write Direct	WRD	SI

Insert Storage Key. The general form of the *Insert Storage Key* instruction is:

ISK   R1,R2

The key of the storage block designated by R2 is inserted into R1.

The address of the storage block whose key is desired must be in bits 8–20 of R2. Bits 0–7 and 21–27 of R2 are ignored by the CPU. However, bits 28–31 must be zero. If these bits are not zero, a specification exception will occur.

The five-bit key of the specified storage block will be inserted into bits 24–28 of R1. Bits 0–23 of this register (R1) will be unchanged, while bits 29–31 will be set to zero.

Set Storage Key. The general form of the *Set Storage Key* instruction is:

SSK   R1,R2

The key in R1 is placed into the storage block addressed by R2.

A new key, which is in R1, replaces the old key in the storage block addressed by R2. The new key is in bits 24–28 of R1. Bits 0–23 and 29–31 of R1 are ignored. The address of the storage block is in bits 8–20 of R2. Bits

0–7 and 21–27 of this register are ignored. Bits 28–31, however, must be set to zero.

Set System Mask. The general form of the *Set System Mask* instruction is:

SSM D1(B1)

The contents of the byte at the address specified by D1(B1) replace the contents of the system mask in the PSWR.

A system programmer can, in the Supervisor mode, mask out (disable) any of the interrupts associated with the system mask. He does this by using SSM to put a zero-bit into the appropriate bit position of the mask. Interrupts masked out in the system mask will be *pending*.

An interrupt that is pending will take place when the bit position associated with that interrupt is turned on. That is, the pending interrupt will take place as soon as the one-bit enters the appropriate bit position of the PSWR.

Load PSW. The general form of the *Load PSW* instruction is:

LPSW D1(B1)

The operand, D1(B1), points to a double-word which will be loaded into the PSW register. Bits 40–63 of this double-word should point to the next instruction that will be executed by the CPU.

When an interrupt occurs, the interrupt mechanism (hardware) stores the "old" PSW and "loads" the "new" PSW automatically. The interrupt mechanism, however, cannot restore the "old" PSW. It should, after all, be restored into the PSW register only if the exception which caused the interrupt is "successfully" handled. In that case, control will be transferred back to the program in which the interrupt occurred. Hence the last instruction in the interrupt subroutine should be to load the "old" PSW.

The Address of an I/O Device. We digress for a few paragraphs to show how to find the address of a channel or the address of a device on a particular channel. This discussion is applicable to the last four instructions that we cover in this section.

The general form of the machine language format for the next four instructions—Halt I/O, Test I/O, Start I/O, and Test Channel—is depicted in Figure 17.2. Note that bits 8–15 of the ML instruction are ignored.

FIGURE 17.2 Machine Language Instruction Format

0	7 8	15 16	19 20	31
Opcode		B1	D1	

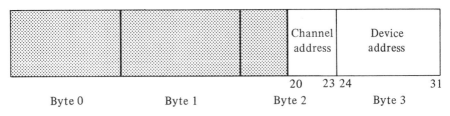

			Channel address	Device address

20   23 24   31

Byte 0   Byte 1   Byte 2   Byte 3

FIGURE 17.3 Addressing a Channel and a Device

The effective address, EF, is determined in the usual way. $EF = C(B1) + D1$. Let us assume, however, in order to simplify our discussion, that EF is 32 bits, or one word in length.

EF is not, of course, an address in MEMORY. It is the address of an I/O device. The low order byte, byte 3, of the effective address (see Figure 17.3) designates the device address. The four bits to the left of byte 3 specify the channel. (Actually only three bits to the left of the device address byte are used.) All other bits in the EF word are ignored.

For instance, the address 00C (in hex) refers to the CARDREADER. The channel is 0; the device address is 0C. The address 191 refers usually to the disk on the selector channel 1.

A programmer generally specifies the effective address of the channel and device in the next four I/O instructions by giving only the displacement in the operand field. Hence $B1 = 0$, which means the value zero will be used instead of the contents of a base register. (Recall that register 0 cannot be used as a base register.)

Test Channel. The general form of the *Test Channel* instruction is:

    TCH D1(B1)

Bit positions 16–23 of the effective address word $(EF = C(B1) + D1)$ specify the channel to test. All other bits of EF are ignored.

The instruction is used to set the condition code. This code is set as follows:

    0 the channel is available
    1 an interrupt is pending in the channel
    2 the channel is operating in the burst mode
    3 the channel is not operational

Test I/O. The general form of the *Test I/O* instruction is:

    TIØ D1(B1)

The Test I/O instruction can be used to clear pending interrupts in a channel which would inhibit the execution of SIO instructions if the interrupts are associated with the addressed device.

The instruction sets the condition code as follows:

0 no interrupt is pending in the channel
1 an interrupt is pending
2 a burst mode operation is in progress
3 the channel is not operational

Bits positions 20–31 of the effective address specify the channel and the device to which the instruction applies.

Start I/O. The general form of the *Start I/O* instruction is:

SIO D1(B1)

An input/output operation is initiated at the device specified by the operand field. The channel and device must, of course, be available.
The condition code is set as follows:

0 I/O operation is initiated
1 some exceptional condition exists in the channel
2 the channel is busy
3 the channel is not operational

If an exceptional condition exists in the channel, the information will be passed to the CPU via the Channel Status Word (see Section 17.4).

Halt I/O. The general form of the *Halt I/O* instruction is:

HIO D1(B1)

The input/output operation going on in the channel and device specified by D1(B1) is stopped.
The condition code is set as follows:

0 an interrupt is pending in the channel; no action is taken
1 some exceptional condition exists in the channel
2 the burst mode operation terminated
3 the channel is not operational

We now turn to a short discussion of channel programming. We note here that execution of a channel program is initiated by the Start I/O instruction. Once initiated, however, the channel program executes independently of the CPU.

17.4 Channel Programming

The great disparity in the speed of input/output devices and the CPU has lead to the development of I/O channels which handle the I/O devices while the CPU executes instructions. (A CPU can execute, for example, up to 50,000 arithmetic instructions in the time it takes to read in a card on the

CARDREADER.) A computer may have several channels attached to it, and each channel may be connected to one or more I/O devices. Hence a good deal of input and output may go on while the CPU is executing its arithmetic or data processing instructions.

The channel, however, executes a program at the behest of the CPU. That is, the CPU initiates the channel program by executing the SIO (Start I/O) command. If the channel is available (free to do the I/O processing), then the channel program will be executed independently of the program being executed by the CPU.

The CPU may still communicate with the channel by HIO (Halt I/O), if it is necessary to stop the channel program. The channel can interrupt the CPU when it completes the I/O program or if some unusual condition occurs during the processing.

The channel may also communicate with the CPU via a double-word location called the Channel Status Word (CSW). The channel may store information (at appropriate times) about the status of the I/O devices and other existing conditions into this double-word, and since this CSW is in MEMORY (location $40_x = 64_{10}$), its contents are accessible to the CPU. Let us now turn to a discussion of how the operations are specified to the channel and how the channel executes its command. This discussion will lead us back to the Channel Status Word. At that time we will give its format and its role in a channel program.

The sequence of commands (instructions are called commands when executed by a channel) is defined by one or more Channel Command Words (CCW). The address of the first CCW in the channel program is given to the channel by the Channel Address Word (CAW). Location $48_x = 72_{10}$ is dedicated by the hardware to this CAW.

When the CPU issues the instruction SIO (Start I/O), the channel fetches the address of the first channel command from location 48_x, or, to say it another way, successful execution of Start I/O causes the channel to fetch the address from the CAW.

The format of the Channel Address Word is given in Figure 17.4. The first nibble is the protection key. If the protection feature is not installed, this field must be set to zero. Otherwise the value in this field is compared to the key in the storage block affected by the channel command. If the keys do not match, the channel program will not be executed.

FIGURE 17.4 Channel Address Word

0 3 4 7 8		31
Protection key	0000	Address of channel command

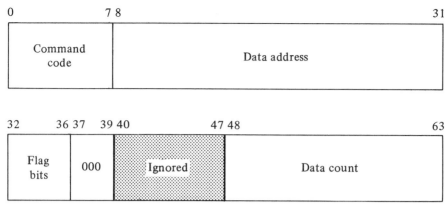

FIGURE 17.5 Channel Command Word

A Channel Command Word is a double-word. It may reside in any appropriate location in MEMORY. It is, of course, the responsibility of the programmer to put the address of the first command of a channel program into the CAW. When the channel completes the execution of a command, it fetches the next command, if necessary, from the double-word location whose address is eight higher than the address of the present command. These addresses need not be contiguous if a Transfer-in-Channel command is used. This command, which is an unconditional branch, makes it possible to form a loop in a channel program.

The general format of a Channel Command Word is given in Figure 17.5.

Command Code. The command code, bits 0–7, specifies one of the six channel commands: READ, WRITE, READ BACKWARD, CONTROL, SENSE, and TRANSFER-IN-CHANNEL. These commands are listed in Table 17.8. (Our discussion will be limited to the READ and WRITE commands.)

Data Address. The data address field specifies the address of the buffer in MEMORY that will be used in the I/O operation.

Data Count. The data count field specifies the number of bytes involved in a READ or WRITE command. As each byte is transmitted, the count is decremented by one and the core address is incremented by one. The transmission of data ceases when the count reaches zero.

Chaining. Two Channel Command Words are said to be *chained* if the channel, after completion of the task specified in the first command, fetches the second. A chain may consist of more than two CCWs. Chaining, however, takes place only between CCWs that occupy successive double-word

TABLE 17.8 Command Codes

Command	Meaning
READ	This command causes data to be read from an I/O device into MEMORY.
WRITE	This command causes data in MEMORY to be written on the selected I/O device.
CONTROL	This type of command is an order to a device and will cause rewinding of a magnetic tape, positioning of read-write heads to a particular cylinder, etc.
SENSE	This command requests the channel to store detailed information about the status of an I/O device.
READ BACKWARD	This command causes the read operation performed by the I/O device to be done in reverse order. Characters, which are read in backwards, will be stored in descending order in MEMORY.
TRANSFER-IN-CHANNEL	This command specifies the address of the next channel command which is to be used by the channel.

locations. All CCWs which are in a single chain are associated with the I/O device that was specified in the SIO (Start I/O) command.

Two types of chaining can occur: the chaining of data and the chaining of commands. *Data-chaining* and *command-chaining* are specified by bits 32 and 33 of the Channel Command Word. If a CCW fails to specify chaining and the CCW is not a transfer-in-channel command, then that CCW is the last one in the channel program.

The Flag Bits. Bit 32 is the *chain-data* flag. If the count of the present CCW reaches zero and the chain-data bit is on, then the next CCW will be fetched. The command code of this new CCW will be ignored. The same operation continues with new flag bits, a new core address, and a new data count.

Bit 33 is the *chain-command* flag. When the chain-command flag is on (equals one) and the chain-data flag is off, the next sequential channel command is fetched. The operation specified by the new command code and the information in the fields of this CCW will be used.

Bit 34 is the *suppress-length-indicator* flag. It will indicate, when on, if the length of the transmitted data is incorrect. If off, no indication will be given. Check the *Principles of Operation* manual for the specifics on this bit since the status of some of the flag bits—the chain-data flag in particular—modify the above statement.

Bit 35 is the *skip* flag. This flag, when on, causes the data field specified in a READ operation to be skipped. The discussion which follows Example 17.2 should clarify the use of this flag bit.

Bit 36 is the *program-controlled-interrupt* flag (PCI). When this flag is on, the channel interrupts the CPU as soon as the CCW has been fetched and the I/O operation has started.

Example 17.2 A Channel Program

	Code	Address	Flag		Count
①	C2	005000	80	00	000A
②	00	000000	90	00	000C
③	00	00500A	00	00	003A

The CCW designated by ① reads the first ten bytes of a card. The data is stored in MEMORY locations 005000–005009. The chain-data flag is on. Therefore, the channel fetches the second command, ②.

We have arbitrarily placed zeros in the command code field of ②, since ① specified data chaining. (Recall that data chaining causes the command code of the next CCW to be ignored. Now ② has the skip flag on, so the next 12 columns of the card will be skipped. The data is "read" but not transmitted into MEMORY.)

The chain-data flag in ② is on. The channel fetches the next CCW, ③. The operation is still READ, even though the command code field is filled with zeros. Why?

Fifty-eight bytes are read and transmitted to 58 consecutive locations starting at 00500A. No data-chaining or command-chaining is specified; therefore, ③ is the last CCW in the channel program.

We note here that bits 40–47 of the channel command word are ignored. Bits 37–39 must be zero for all CCWs except a transfer-in-channel command.

We now return to complete the discussion of the Channel Status Word which we started earlier in this section. We noted then that the channel used this double-word location to store information about the status of I/O devices and other conditions associated with a particular channel program.

The information passed to the CPU by a CSW which is formed by the execution of HIO, TIO, and SIO pertains to the device and the channel addressed by the instruction. The CSW is said to be *stored* when the pertinent information about a channel program is stored into location $40_x = 64_{10}$. This information is available to the CPU at this location until the next interrupt or until another I/O instruction causes the contents of this double-word to be replaced.

The format of the Channel Status Word is given in Figure 17.6. We discuss the meaning of each field immediately following the figure. Space precludes any detailed discussion of the two-byte status field.

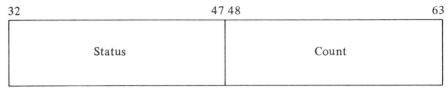

FIGURE 17.6   Channel Status Word

Key Field.   The protection key is copied from the Channel Address Word which is associated with the channel program.

Command Address.   The command address field contains the address of the last Channel Command Word plus eight.

Status.   Each of the 16 bits in this field indicates a condition in the I/O device and the channel that might have caused a storing of the CSW. We omit any discussion of these bits.

Count.   The residual count for the last CCW used before an interrupt occurred is stored in this field.

The following Channel Program Algorithm gives the procedure a system programmer might follow to execute a channel program. The algorithm assumes that the channel is operational.

Channel Program Algorithm

Step 1: Write a set of Channel Command Words to do the desired I/O function.

Step 2: Place the Channel Command Words in consecutive double-word locations.

Step 3: Put the address of the first CCW into the Channel Address Word.

Step 4: Disable the interrupts from all sources associated with the system mask.

Step 5: Put the address of the channel and device into the Start I/O instruction.

Step 6: Issue the Start I/O instruction.

Step 7: If the condition code equals zero, go to step 9.

Step 8: Go to step 6.

Step 9: End.

```
//EXCP    JOB     '3525  26    010    03','  KENNETH W SKEWES      '
          PRINT   NOGEN
          INIT
          OPEN    (CARDIN,,PRINT,OUTPUT)
          EXCP    READ
          WAIT    1,ECB=ECB
          CLI     ECB,X'7F'
          BNE     FAILED
          EXCP    WRITE
          WAIT    1,ECB=ECB
          CLI     ECB,X'7F'
          BE      DONE
FAILED    QDUMP   STORAGE=(IMAGE,IMAGE+80)
DONE      CLOSE   (CARDIN,,PRINT)
          GOBACK
ECB       DS      F
IMAGE     DS      CL80
CCW1      CCW     X'02',IMAGE,X'20',80
CCW2      CCW     X'09',IMAGE,X'20',80
READ      DC      F'0',A(ECB),2F'0',A(CCW1,CARDIN),4F'0'
WRITE     DC      F'0',A(ECB),2F'0',A(CCW2,PRINT),4F'0'
CARDIN    DCB     DSORG=PS,MACRF=E,RECFM=F,IOBAD=READ,DDNAME=SYSIN
PRINT     DCB     DSORG=PS,MACRF=E,RECFM=F,IOBAD=WRITE,DDNAME=SYSPRINT
          END
```

FIGURE 17.7   The EXCP Macro Program

There is a Supervisor macro called Execute Channel Program (EXCP) which enables an application program to execute a channel program. Figure 17.7 has a program which uses EXCP to execute two short channel programs. We suggest the student study this example after reading Topic 1, which is devoted to EXCP.

Computer Notebook

TOPIC 1   The Execute Channel Program Macro

The EXCP (Execute Channel Program) macro is a supervisor macro which can be issued by a user to execute a channel program. The macro instruction will cause a transfer of the CPU to the I/O Supervisor (one of the Operating System routines), which will then see that the specified channel executes the user's channel program.

The user who issues an EXCP must realize, however, that he is bypassing the access method routines. That means the services usually provided by the access method will not be available unless the user provides them himself. QSAM and the other access methods, for instance, check for the "slash-asterisk" card which signifies the end of a data set; the channel does *not*. An EXCP macro user must, therefore, provide his own coding to check for the end of a data set. Failure to do so, when it is necessary, will produce unpredictable results in the user program and in the regular job stream.

Perhaps the easiest way to learn the EXCP macro is to look at a few examples. Therefore, we present two channel programs in our routine. Each of these channel programs is executed by an EXCP macro.

Before we present the examples of EXCP, however, we list and discuss the procedures that a user must perform in his routine before an EXCP macro instruction can be successfully executed. We will refer to these procedures as the *user responsibilities* in the discussion that follows.

1. The user must define a data control block for the data set that is to be retrieved or stored by the channel program. This block must specify the address of an input/output block (see the next item in our list of responsibilities) by using the keyword parameter IOBAD (input/output block address). The MACRF keyword parameter must specify E. The LRECL and BLKSIZE parameters may be omitted since the programmer is bypassing the system access methods.

2. The user must define an input/output block (usually called the IOB). This block (see Figure 17.8) will pass the address of the Event Control Block (usually abbreviated to ECB) to the I/O Supervisor. The IOB also passes the address of the first Channel Command Word and the address of the data control block to the I/O Supervisor.

3. Construct an Event Control Block (ECB) that will be used by the System to return a completion code at the termination of the channel program. The ECB is a full-word. If, after termination of the channel program, the C(ECB) = 7F000000, then the channel program has terminated without an error. If the System returns the completion code 41000000 to the ECB, then the channel program has been terminated because of permanent errors. We suggest that the student consult the *System Programmer's Guide* for the rest of the ECB completion code.

4. The user must issue an OPEN macro instruction so that the data control block defined by the DCB will be initialized.

5. The user must create a channel program. This can be done quite readily by issuing Define Channel Command Word instructions.
   The syntax of *Define Channel Command Word* is:

   name   CCW   OP1,OP2,OP3,OP4

   Note that OP1 is an eight-bit command code. OP2 is the data address field of the CCW (see Figure 17.5). OP3 is bits 32–39 of the CCW. Recall that bits 32–36 are the flag bits and that bits 37–39 must be zero (see Figure 17.5). OP4 is the data count field (see Figure 17.5).
   Bits 40–47 of the CCW that is being constructed are set to zero by the Assembler. Recall that these bits are ignored by the channel.

6. The user must issue an EXCP macro instruction which passes the address of the IOB to the I/O Supervisor.

The programmer should also use the WAIT macro instruction in his routine if his code which follows the EXCP macro depends upon the successful termination of the channel program.

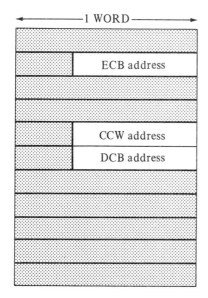

FIGURE 17.8   Input/Output Block Format

The syntax of the WAIT macro instruction used in our examples is:

name   WAIT   ECB = address

The WAIT macro causes the routine to "wait" until the completion of the event specified by the address in the ECB keyword operand has occurred. In other words, the System is told that the program must not continue until the event associated with ECB specified by *address* has been completed.

We suggest that the student "research" the *Data Management and Supervisor Macro Instructions* manual for additional information about the WAIT macro.

Example 17.3

We have repeated for the student's convenience our EXCP Program in Figure 17.9. Recall that this routine executes two channel programs. The first EXCP "reads" in 80 bytes via the CARDREADER. The second prints the card image. The circled numbers are reference numbers for the discussion which follows the figure.

① The OPEN macro initializes the data control blocks which we constructed by the DCB macros in ⑮ and ⑯ .

② The syntax of *Execute Channel Program* is:

   EXCP   IOB

where IOB is the input/output block that contains information about the channel program. The IOB in ② was defined by ⑬

```
          PRINT    NOGEN
          INIT
        ①OPEN     (CARDIN,,PRINT,OUTPUT)
        ②EXCP     READ
        ③WAIT     1,ECB=ECB
        ④CLI      ECB,X'7F'
        ⑤BNE      FAILED
        ⑥EXCP     WRITE
        ⑦WAIT     1,ECB=ECB
        ⑧CLI      ECB,X'7F'
          BE       DONE
FAILED    QDUMP    STORAGE=(IMAGE,IMAGE+80)
DONE      CLOSE    (CARDIN,,PRINT)
          GOBACK
ECB     ⑨DS       F
IMAGE   ⑩DS       CL80
CCW1    ⑪CCW      X'02',IMAGE,X'20',80
CCW2    ⑫CCW      X'09',IMAGE,X'20',80
READ    ⑬DC       F'0',A(ECB),2F'0',A(CCW1,CARDIN),4F'0'
WRITE   ⑭DC       F'0',A(ECB),2F'0',A(CCW2,PRINT),4F'0'
CARDIN  ⑮DCB      DSORG=PS,MACRF=E,RECFM=F,IOBAD=READ,DDNAME=SYSIN
PRINT   ⑯DCB      DSORG=PS,MACRF=E,RECFM=F,IOBAD=WRITE,DDNAME=SYSPRINT
          LTORG
          END
```

FIGURE 17.9 The EXCP Macro Program

③ The WAIT macro instruction informs the System that the program cannot continue until the event specified by the ECB has been completed. The ECB has a "wait" bit. When the wait bit, which is in bit position 0, has been set to zero, then the CPU will be allowed to execute the instructions which follow.

We note that the form of the operand of WAIT is ECB=address. We have chosen ECB as the name of our ECB, hence the second ECB in ECB=ECB is a symbolic address.

④ CLI tests to determine if the channel program has terminated successfully. See the discussion of the ECB in the list of *user responsibilities*.

⑤ BNE causes a branch to a QDUMP routine if the channel program terminated unsuccessfully. Recall that 7F000000 is the completion code for a successful termination of the channel program. We check just the first byte of the ECB.

⑥ EXCP WRITE causes the execution of the second channel program in our routine. See the discussion of ②.

⑦ See the discussion of ③.

⑧ See the discussion of ④.

⑨ We have defined the ECB as one full-word. See item three in the list of user responsibilities.

⑩ The channel will read the data into the 80-byte storage location named IMAGE since that address is specified in the data address field in ⑪.

The channel will print the data from IMAGE since that address is specified in the data address field in ⑫.

⑪ This CCW constructs the first channel command in the channel program specified in ②. We have exactly one Channel Command Word in the channel program. We may have several such commands in a channel program. The subsequent commands must be in consecutive double-word locations. The channel is told to fetch the next channel command by data-chaining or command-chaining.

If a channel program has more than one command, only the address of the first is given in the IOB. See ⑬ .

Compare ⑪ with the syntax of the CCW instruction which was given in item five of the list of user responsibilities.

⑫ See ⑪ .

⑬ The DC labeled READ constructs the IOB for our first channel program. Compare the constants defined in the READ block with the format of the IOB which is given in Figure 17.8.

⑭ The DC labeled WRITE constructs the IOB for our second channel program. See ⑬ .

⑮ The DCB labeled CARDIN constructs the data control block for our first channel program. Notice that MACRF=E and IOBAD=READ have been specified.

⑯ The DCB labeled PRINT constructs the data control block for our second channel program. See ⑮ .

TOPIC 2   A Glimpse at Virtual Memory (I)— Segmentation and Paging

We discuss, in this topic, the concepts of segmentation and paging so that our explanation of *virtual memory* in Topic 3 will have more meaning.

One of the problems that arises in a *multiprogramming environment*[1] is the *fragmentation* of MEMORY. Consider Figure 17.10. The diagram depicts the status of MEMORY after three programs have been introduced into STORAGE. Program X takes up 25,000 bytes of our MEMORY, Program Y and Program Z need 30,000 and 20,000 bytes, respectively.

The nucleus (the Supervisor subroutine) of the Operating System takes up several thousand bytes in the low order address part of MEMORY. There are still 10,000 bytes available, but the two Programs Q and R, which are in a queue waiting for MEMORY space, require 35,000 and 30,000 bytes, respectively. Therefore, 10,000 bytes of MEMORY are being "wasted" at this moment. This phenomenon—the non utilization of MEMORY "space"—is called the fragmentation of MEMORY.

Now suppose Program X completes its processing and is terminated by the Operating System. There are 35,000 bytes available (see Figure 17.11), but these bytes are not contiguous. Therefore, neither Program Q nor Program R can be loaded into MEMORY. Both must wait until the required number of contiguous bytes are available to them. Thus, if no smaller programs have entered the job queue, we have an extreme case of MEMORY fragmentation.

---

[1] The term *multiprogramming* is used when two or more programs are in MEMORY at the same time. The motivation behind the concept of multiprogramming is to maximize the utilization of the computer's resources such as the CPU, the I/O devices, and CORE STORAGE (MEMORY).

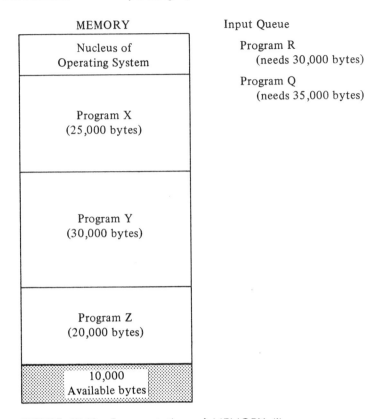

MEMORY

Input Queue

Nucleus of
Operating System

Program X
(25,000 bytes)

Program Y
(30,000 bytes)

Program Z
(20,000 bytes)

10,000
Available bytes

Program R
(needs 30,000 bytes)

Program Q
(needs 35,000 bytes)

FIGURE 17.10 Fragmentation of MEMORY (I)

Segmentation. Is there any way to avoid fragmentation? No. But fragmentation of MEMORY can be reduced by the segmentation of programs. For instance, suppose Program R were divided or segmented into three parts— Segment I, Segment II, and Segment III—so that each part was 10,000 bytes. It is now possible to load our segmented Program R into the available space as shown in Figure 17.12. Notice that some MEMORY is still wasted. That is, we still have fragmentation of MEMORY. (Note that both Program Y and Program Z may be segmented. We have not shown the segments since they are not pertinent to our discussion.)

Does segmentation introduce new problems into our computer system? Yes. The addressing scheme—the method by which CONTROL determines the effective address of an operand—must be modified. We must, in order to explain the method by which the effective address is determined in a segmentation system (and, hence, in a Virtual Memory Operating System), introduce some new concepts.

A program consists of a set of instructions and a set of storage locations into which data is defined or into which data will be stored. The addresses of those instructions and storage locations are said to be in the program's

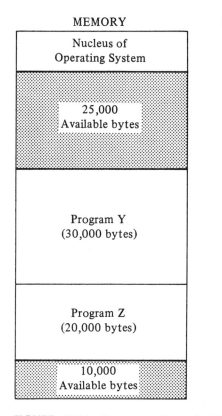

FIGURE 17.11   Fragmentation of MEMORY (II)

address space. In an Assembler Language program, the range between the entry point—STM 14,12,12(13)—and the END statement is that program's address space.

In Topic 1 of the Computer Notebook (Chapter 7) we showed how the relative addresses in a program's address space were *relocated* or *translated* to the absolute addresses at execution time. Recall that this relocation was accomplished by inserting the actual (sometimes called the *relocated* or the *absolute value*) address of the base-location into the implied base register. The act of inserting the absolute address of the base-location into the implied base register relocated all addresses in that program's address space. The program, once the base register points to the actual base-location, is *bound* to the storage locations into which it has been loaded.

This relocation technique, which is used by the System 360/370 Operating Systems, is called *static relocation.* Let us repeat the two most important ideas which define the concept of *static relocation.*

The first important idea to remember with respect to static relocation is that all of the addresses in the program's address space are relocated at load time. (In System 360/370, the relocation is accomplished shortly after the

MEMORY

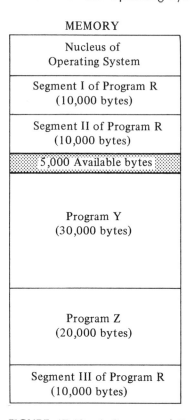

Nucleus of Operating System
Segment I of Program R (10,000 bytes)
Segment II of Program R (10,000 bytes)
5,000 Available bytes
Program Y (30,000 bytes)
Program Z (20,000 bytes)
Segment III of Program R (10,000 bytes)

FIGURE 17.12 A Segmented Program in MEMORY

program gains control of the CPU, that is, during execution.) In a sense, however, we can say that relocation occurs at load time, since no symbolic address, belonging to the program's address space, may be referenced until the relocation has been completed.

The second important fact is that all addresses in the program's address space are relocated exactly once. The program is bound, as stated above, to the storage locations into which it has been loaded.

Another type of relocation, called *dynamic relocation,* is important to our discussion. Under dynamic relocation the effective address of each operand referenced by an instruction is relocated when that instruction is executed. Perhaps the best way to understand this technique of dynamic relocation is to look at an example. Let us consider the addressing structure necessary in each of Program R's source segments. (See Figure 17.12.)

Each segment in Program R has its own address space. The entry point to each segment will be in location 0 of that segment's address space. The address of any other instruction and any data item will be its displacement from the entry point of its segment.

⋮
① A   5,GREEN
② S   5,BLUE
③ M   4,GREEN
⋮

FIGURE 17.13   Some Program R Instructions

①	5 A	5	0	1	03 E 8
②	5 B	5	0	2	03 E 8
③	5 C	4	0	1	03 E 8

Opcode   R1   Index   Segment   Displacement
           field   field   number   in segment

FIGURE 17.14   Segment Field in the ML Instructions

Suppose, for instance, that in Segment I we have a data item named GREEN which has a displacement of 1000_{10} from Segment I's entry point. (In order to simplify our discussion, all addresses in this topic will be given in base 10.) Suppose, further, that the address of BLUE with respect to the address space of Segment II is also 1000_{10}. And suppose that in Segment I we have the instructions listed in Figure 17.13.

It should be obvious that providing CONTROL with the relative address of 1000_{10} for GREEN is insufficient since the relative address of BLUE is also 1000_{10}. What other information must we pass to CONTROL so that the *address translation*[2] of both GREEN and BLUE will result in unambiguous locations?

The Assembler should pass two pieces of information to CONTROL and the Loader subroutine should pass one piece of information. The Assembler should tell CONTROL the segment to which both GREEN and BLUE belong, and, in addition, the Assembler should pass their respective displacements in those segments. The machine language equivalent of the Assembler code of Figure 17.13 might appear as depicted in Figure 17.14.

The Loader, the Operating System subroutine which physically loads the program into MEMORY, must provide CONTROL with pointers to the segment entry points. This might be done in a *segment table*. Figure 17.15 is a diagram of Program R's segment table. The values given in the entry point column are in decimal.

---

[2] The process of determining the effective address of an operand is often called *address translation*.

Segment no.	Entry point
1	8000
2	18000
3	83000

FIGURE 17.15 Program R Segment Table

The effective addresses of the operands can now be found using the formula:

EF = entry point + displacement

The effective addresses for the operands in ①, ②, and ③ of Figure 17.13 are:

GREEN = 8,000 + 1,000 = 9,000
BLUE = 18,000 + 1,000 = 19,000

We note that this address translation occurs only when each instruction is executed. We note further that the segments are not bound to the storage locations into which they have been loaded. If the Operating System deems it worthwhile to move any segment, it may do so. The only updating that is necessary is changing the value in the *Entry Point* column in the Program R Segment Table.

Suppose, for example, that the Operating System finds it necessary to move Segment I to location 40,000. After the move has been completed the Program R Segment Table must be updated. The updated table is depicted in Figure 17.16.

What is the absolute address of GREEN after this relocation has been accomplished?

Paging. Segmentation is not, however, the best solution to the problem of fragmentation. It has been found by empirical methods that division of segments into smaller parts called *pages* reduces still further the amount of fragmentation that will occur in a multiprogramming environment.

A page, unlike a segment, is usually fixed in length. Let us assume, therefore, that the length of a page in the discussion that follows is 2048 bytes.

Figure 17.17 is a diagram of MEMORY. It depicts the status of MEMORY with Program T as a resident. Program T has been divided into two segments of 10,000 and 7,000 byte lengths. The larger segment, Segment I, has been

FIGURE 17.16 Program R Segment Table Updated

Segment no.	Entry point
1	40000
2	18000
3	83000

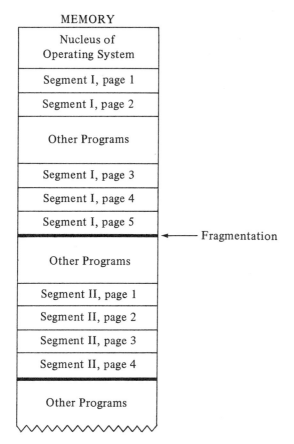

MEMORY

Nucleus of Operating System
Segment I, page 1
Segment I, page 2
Other Programs
Segment I, page 3
Segment I, page 4
Segment I, page 5
Other Programs
Segment II, page 1
Segment II, page 2
Segment II, page 3
Segment II, page 4
Other Programs

◄——— Fragmentation

FIGURE 17.17 The Pages of Program T

subdivided into five pages, while Segment II has been divided into four pages.

Program T does not fill page 5 of Segment I, nor does it fill page 4 of Segment II. The lower portions of these pages are shaded in the diagram. This shaded portion represents unutilized core, or the fragmentation of MEMORY that still exists. (The other programs in MEMORY are not pertinent to our discussion.)

Each page has its own address space. If GREEN has been defined in page 2 of Segment I, then the relative address of GREEN will be the displacement of GREEN from the entry point in page 2. This means that the address translation performed by CONTROL will be slightly more complicated than that performed in our segmentation system.

Since each page has its own address space, the Assembler must encode one additional piece of information into the machine language instruction. The operand's page number must be passed to CONTROL in the instruction. Figure 17.18 illustrates the addressing structure needed in the machine language code in a page-segment system. The machine language code is the answer to the problem posed in Example 17.4.

Example 17.4

We assume that:

1. BROWN has a displacement of 464 in page 1 of Segment II.
2. BLUE has a displacement of 160 in page 3 of Segment I.
3. BLACK has a displacement of 1000 in page 2 of Segment I.
4. Three assembly language instructions in Program T are:

$$\vdots$$

    ① A   5,BROWN
    ② A   5,BLUE
    ③ S   5,BLACK

$$\vdots$$

Give a machine language code for the assembly language instructions in assumption 4. The code should contain an addressing scheme so that the absolute locations referenced by BROWN, BLUE, and BLACK will be unambiguous.

A solution to this problem appears in Figure 17.18.

The Operating System must now provide a pointer in the *Program Segment Table*. It will point to the *Page Entry Point Table* of each segment. The Page Entry Point Table (PEPT) will have a pointer to the entry point of each page. Figure 17.19 is a diagram of the tables required by CONTROL in order to translate the addresses in the machine language code in Figure 17.18.

The Loader will enter the addresses of the Page Entry Point Tables into the page-table address column of the Program Segment Table at load time. The absolute address of each page's entry point will be placed in the appropriate column of the PEPT in the same step. A page is not, however, tied to the locations designated by its entry point in the PEPT. The Operating

FIGURE 17.18 The Page Field in the ML Instructions

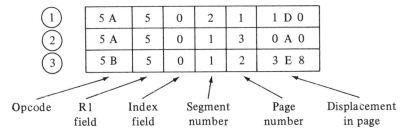

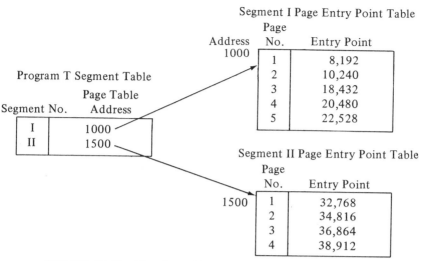

FIGURE 17.19 The Page Entry Point Tables

System may move the page if necessary. The PEPT must be updated to reflect this change. It should be noted that the option to move a page is a consequence of *dynamic relocation*. Recall that under *static relocation* a program is bound to the locations into which it is loaded.

We suggest that the reader find the absolute addresses in MEMORY of BROWN, BLUE, and BLACK of Example 17.4. That is, perform the address translation of the machine language given in Figure 17.18. The correct addresses are given as a footnote at the end of Topic 3.

We note that it is not necessary to have all pages of a program in MEMORY when that program is executing. Only the page which contains the program's entry point need be introduced into MAIN STORAGE to start execution. The other pages can be loaded into MEMORY when they are referenced by the instructions of the page already in MEMORY. A page is loaded into MEMORY only when it is *demanded* by the instruction. This technique is called *demand paging*.

Demand paging is the key to understanding the concept of virtual memory. The first part of the next topic is devoted to an examination of demand paging. In the second half of the topic we look at a Virtual Memory Operating System.

TOPIC 3   A Glimpse at Virtual Memory (II)— Demand Paging and Virtual Storage

A Virtual Memory Operating System gives the user the "feeling" that the computer has available more real MEMORY than actually exists. If the address field used by CONTROL is 24 bits long as in System 360/370, then the Virtual Memory Operating System can simulate a main core size of 16,777,216 bytes.

Since the key to this simulation is *demand paging,* our first subject in this topic will show how the Operating System allocates real MEMORY storage locations under the demand paging technique. (Note: we distinguish between the computer component, MEMORY, and the computer science concept, Virtual Memory, by capitalizing each letter in the component. And, at times, we will preface it by real, as in real MEMORY. We will consider Virtual Memory to be short for Virtual Memory Operating System. Since this is a software item, we capitalize the first letter of each word in its name following the practice adopted in this text. Virtual storage, however, is neither a hardware nor a software item; therefore, none of the letters are capitalized.)

Demand Paging.   We said in Topic 2 that an Operating System which uses a paging technique provides CONTROL with two tables. These tables help CONTROL perform the necessary address translation. Recall that we labeled these tables as the PST (Program Segment Table) and the PEPT (Page Entry Point Table). See Figure 17.19.

The PST pointed to the location of each segment's PEPT. The PEPT had one pointer to the entry point of each page in the segment. The paging technique under discussion at that time had a requirement: all pages which belonged to a program had to be in real MEMORY when the execution of the program began.

Under a demand paging Operating System, however, only the page which contains the entry point to the program needs to be in real MEMORY at execution time. If an operand which belongs to another page is referenced by an executing instruction—we say the page is demanded by the instruction —the Operating System will load (*page-in*) the desired page into MEMORY from auxiliary storage. If the page is already in MEMORY, then, of course, no page-in is necessary. CONTROL will use the two tables—the Program Segment Table and the Page Entry Point Table—to translate the address of the effective operand.

This means that there must be a way to pass information about the status of any page referenced during the execution of a program. CONTROL must be able to determine if any particular page is in CORE. We can pass this information to CONTROL by adding a status bit to the Program Entry Point Table.

Figure 17.20 is a diagram of a modified PEPT used in demand paging. If the bit in the status column is *on* (equals one), then the corresponding page is *not* in MEMORY. If the status bit is *off,* the page is a resident of real MEMORY.

Suppose CONTROL encounters the machine language equivalent of L 5,BLUE in page 1 of Program T. Suppose, further, that the machine language code designates the operand BLUE as defined in the address space of

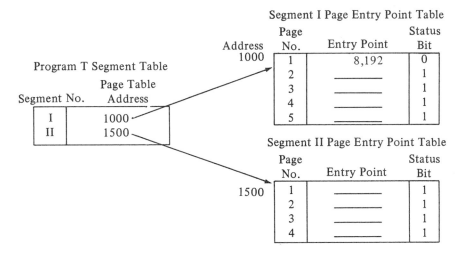

FIGURE 17.20 Status Bit in the Entry Point Tables

Segment I, page 5. Is page 5 in CORE? No. The status bit is on (see Figure 17.20).

CONTROL must *interrupt* Program T. The control of the CPU is transferred to the Operating System which will load (page-in) page 5 from auxiliary storage. Let us now consider how the Operating System does this task.

The Operating System maintains an External Page Table (EXPT) which consists of pointers to the external storage devices (auxiliary storage) where the pages of Program T are stored. The Operating System finds the location of any page that is demanded in MEMORY in the EXPT. Likewise, when a *page-out* (copying a page from MEMORY onto an external device) operation is needed, the EXPT has a pointer to the external storage where the page is stored.

How does the Operating System manage the real MEMORY under demand paging? Or, to be more specific, how does the Operating System provide space for the demanded page, page 5 of Segment I?

Real MEMORY—under a demand paging Operating System—is divided into groups of contiguous bytes called *real-page frames*. These page frames are equal in (byte) length to the pages of the program that will be executed by the CPU. In our example we have divided our programs into pages of 2K bytes in length (K = 1024, 2K = 2048). Hence the real-page frames in our system will be 2K bytes in length also.

The demand paging Operating System maintains a table which we call the *Real-Page Frame Table*. This table contains a good deal of information about the status of the real-page frames and the program pages in those frames. MEMORY and the Real-Page Frame Table are depicted in Figure 17.21.

Real-Page Frame Table

	Frame No.	Program Information	Status Bit	Reference Bit	Page Out Bit
MEMORY					
Frame 1	1	Supervisor 1, 1	1	1	0
Frame 2	2	Supervisor 1, 2	1	1	0
Frame 3	3	Supervisor 1, 3	1	1	0
Frame 4	4	Supervisor 1, 4	1	1	0
Frame 5	5	Program T 1, 1	1	1	1
Frame 6	6	————	1	1	0
Frame 7	7	————	1	0	1
Frame 8	8	————	1	0	0
.	.	————	1	1	0
.	.	————	1	1	0

FIGURE 17.21 The Real-page Frame Table

We now discuss the significance of the *status bit,* the *reference bit,* and the *page-out bit.* Note that the first four frames in MEMORY are occupied by the nucleus (Supervisor) of the Operating System.

The information in row i of the table gives the status of its corresponding real-page frame in MEMORY. The column headed by *Program Information* might list the program name—along with the segment and page numbers— which occupies the corresponding real-page frame in MEMORY.

The status bit, if off, signifies that the real-page frame is available. Whenever a program terminates in MEMORY, the status bit for all real-page frames occupied by that program page are turned off. If the status bit is on, then the corresponding real-page frame contains a page of an "active" program. An active program will have one or more pages in MEMORY at any particular time.

Now suppose that all status bits in the Real-Page Frame Table are *on.* There are no available real-page frames in MEMORY. (Recall that CONTROL encountered the machine language equivalent of L 5,BLUE when Program T was executing. The instruction was on page 1 of Segment I. The operand BLUE was on page 5 of Segment I. The Segment I Page Entry Point Table indicated that page 5 was not in MEMORY. Program T was interrupted. The Operating System has now found that there are no real-page frames available.)

The Operating System must find, however, a real-page frame for any demanded page. Some page, even if the status bit is 1, must be replaced by page 5, the demanded page. The page that is replaced is one whose reference bit is turned off.

The IBM Virtual Memory Operating System turns off the reference bits of those pages which have not been recently referenced. The method is called the "least recently used" rule. Let us repeat the rule. If all status bits in the Real-page Frame Table are on, then the demanded page will replace that page in MEMORY which has been *least recently used*. The reference bits of the least recently used pages will be off.

The Real-page Frame Table of Figure 17.21 indicates that page 5, Segment I of Program T will replace the page in real-page frame 7. Let us now look at the activity that occurs before page 5 is paged in. (Note that Program T's page replaces the page in real-page frame 7 even though that page may be part of an active program.)

Each page in MEMORY is duplicated in an *external-page frame* in auxiliary storage. (Recall that the Operating System maintains an External Page Frame Table for each program which has been introduced into MEMORY. This table has the pointers to each page's external-page frame.)

Since each page is duplicated in its external-page frame, is there any reason to copy the page into the real-page frame before the demanded page is read into its place? No. Not if the page has *not* been changed while it has been a resident of MEMORY.

Suppose, however, that some of the data items in a page which is to be replaced have been modified while that page has been in MEMORY. The back-up (duplicate) page is no longer a true replica. In this case—when a page has been modified while in MEMORY—the Operating System must copy the page from the real-page frame into the external-page frame. But how does the Operating System know that this activity called *page-out,* is necessary?

The *page-out bit* (IBM calls it the *change bit*) indicates the status of the page in MEMORY. If the page-out bit is off, no page out is necessary. The Operating System must, in our example, page-out real-page frame 7. When that is done, page 5 of Segment I will be paged in.

The student will find Example 17.5 informative.

Example 17.5

① M   4,BROWN

We assume that:

1. The status of Program T and MEMORY is as depicted in the Segment I Page Entry Point Table of Figure 17.20 and the Real-Page Frame Table of Figure 17.21.
2. The instruction ① is in Program T, Segment I, page 2.
3. BROWN is a data item on page 4 of the same segment.

The action is:

1. The one in page 4's status bit in the Segment I Page Entry Point Table indicates that a *page-in* is required.

2. The execution of Program T is interrupted.
3. CONTROL requests the Operating System to *page-in* page 4 of Segment I.
4. All status bits in the Real-Page Frame Table are on. No real-page frames are available.
5. The reference bit for real-page frame 8 is off. (Recall that page 5 was read into real-page frame 7. The reference bit of that frame was changed to one.)
6. The page out bit indicates that the present page in frame 8 has not been modified. No page-out is necessary.
7. The External-Page Table is searched for the pointer to the external-page frame in auxiliary storage which contains the demanded page.
8. The demanded page—page 4 of Segment I—is read into real-page frame 8.
9. The Segment I Page Entry Point Table is updated. The page 4 Entry-Point column now contains 14,336.
10. The Program Information Column of the Real-Page Frame Table, row 8, is changed to Program T, Segment I, page 4.
11. The status, reference, and page out bits of frame 8 in the Real-Page Frame Table are set to one, one, and zero, respectively.

The page in and page out activities are I/O operations. Since I/O operations are performed independently of the CPU, other programs will be executing during the paging activity.

The updating of the tables is done with the Operating System in control of the CPU. Therefore, no programs will execute during the updating.

When Program T again regains control of the CPU, the effective address of BROWN will be available for the Multiply instruction.

Virtual Memory. We now discuss the three important elements of a Virtual Memory Operating System: virtual storage, external page storage, and real MEMORY. After this discussion we look at the method used to load a program into virtual storage. Finally, we suggest two areas which the student might research to gain additional insight into the virtual memory concept.

Virtual storage is a concept. It is a simulation of MEMORY. We pointed out earlier in this topic that the Virtual Memory Operating System can simulate a real MEMORY whose size is 16,777,216 bytes (16,384K). Do you recall why? Because the addressing structure in System 360/370 is 24 bits long and, hence, enables CONTROL to reference any address between 0 and 16,277,215 ($2^{24} = 16,277,216$).

These 16,384K (16 megabytes) virtual storage bytes are divided into segments of 64K contiguous bytes (64K = 64 × 1024). Our virtual storage will consist, therefore, of 256 segments. Each segment is divided into sixteen 4K pages.

The Virtual Memory Operating System (VMOS) allocates space in virtual storage by segments, not pages. Fragmentation of virtual storage is very large since the minimum space allocated for any program is 64K.

Real MEMORY is, however, divided into page frames (no segments are involved). Each page frame, we assume, is 4K bytes in length. If we assume we have a real MEMORY of 128K, then we have 32 page frames available. The fragmentation of real MEMORY would occur only when a page frame is not completely "filled" by a program page.

The nucleus of the Operating System, the Supervisor and the Paging Supervisor, would occupy the low order page frames of both virtual storage and real MEMORY. Since the nucleus is a permanent resident of real MEMORY, the nucleus would not participate in the paging activity except as the supervisor of it.

The *external-page storage* contains the actual pages of a program which are assumed to be in virtual storage. The pages of external-page storage must, therefore, be in a one-to-one correspondence with pages of virtual storage. The "locations" in external-page storage which hold the pages for virtual storage are called *slots*.

VMOS (Virtual Memory Operating System) maintains pointers to these slots in the External Page Table. Although the nucleus of the Operating System cannot be paged in or paged out of real MEMORY, back-up copies of these pages may be stored in the slots of external storage.

Figure 17.22 shows the relationship of virtual storage, real MEMORY, and the external page storage. The one-to-one correspondence between virtual storage and external page storage means that they are of the same byte length. Do not, however, form the impression that external page storage is a single auxiliary storage device. The slots may be on one or more auxiliary storage devices.

Although we have chosen to discuss the maximum size of virtual storage allowed by the System 360/370 addressing structure, we might have had our virtual storage only half the size of the one chosen. That is, it is possible to simulate a real MEMORY of 8,192 megabytes. In that case our external page storage requirements would also be reduced by half.

How is a program executed under the Virtual Memory Operating System? First, a program must be loaded into virtual memory storage. Let's see how that is done.

Suppose Program T resides on a job queue waiting for an opportunity to execute. When the computer resources become available, a loader program, a subroutine of VMOS, will physically load Program T into real MEMORY. While in MEMORY, Program T will be formatted into pages. One or more segments in virtual storage will be allocated to these pages.

All of the addresses in the address space of Program T will be *statically relocated* with respect to the address space of the allocated segments in virtual storage. (See Topic 2 of this chapter for the meaning of static relocation.)

Suppose, for instance, that Program T is allocated segment 22 in virtual storage. After the static relocation has been completed, all of the addresses in Program T will be from 0 to 64K with respect to segment 22 in virtual storage.

When these addresses have been relocated, the formatted pages are stored into the external page storage slots which will correspond to segment 22's

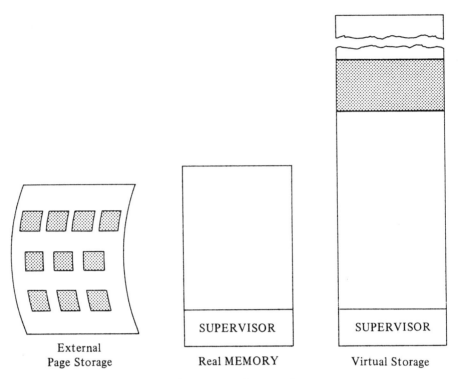

External
Page Storage   Real MEMORY   Virtual Storage

FIGURE 17.22 Virtual Memory Storage System

page frames. The VMOS will update the External-Page Frame Table to reflect the changes that have been made. Program T has now been loaded into virtual storage.

Now that Program T is in virtual storage, its execution will begin when the page which contains its entry point is read into real MEMORY. VMOS, the Virtual Memory Operating System, will update the Real-Page Frame Table to reflect Program T's entry into real MEMORY. Program Q will be given a Segment Table and a Page Entry Point Table so that all addresses can be translated by CONTROL at execution time. (Recall that all addresses in Program T's address space have been relocated with respect to the address space of segment 22 of virtual storage. We also note that the Segment Table and the Page Entry Point Table will be in a Supervisor page in real MEMORY.)

Program T will be executed using the demand paging technique discussed in the early part of this topic. We will not repeat that discussion here.

In our presentation of virtual storage we have developed the concepts without mentioning the problems which arise when the demand paging technique is used. However, in the exercises to this chapter, we do pose two research questions to the student. The first involves the speed of program execution when address translation is done at execution time. The second concerns *thrashing*. Thrashing occurs when the paging activity consumes so much of the computer system's time that little or no useful work is accomplished. We suggest that interested students investigate these two areas to increase their background in the virtual storage concept.

The answer for Example 17.4 is:
  The addresses for BROWN, BLUE, BLACK are 33,232, 18,592, and 11,240, respectively.

EXERCISES

1. Consider the SPIE macro instruction (see Section 17.2). Write a program segment which specifies an interruption exit routine address for an execute, a specification, and a fixed-point divide exception.

2. Find the answers to the following two questions:
   a. What will be the result if a user issues two SPIE macro instructions in the same program?
   b. How does a programmer cancel the effect of a previously issued SPIE macro?
   Use the *Data Management and Supervisor Macros* manual as your reference.

3. What is meant by a *pending* interrupt?

4. What is the difference between the *burst* mode of operation and the *multiplex* mode of operation?

5. What is the difference between the *wait* state and the *stop* state?

6. What program exceptions can the SPM instruction mask?

7. Discuss the "old" and the "new" PSWs.

8. Give all the fields of the program status word that a programmer may modify in the user mode.

9. Assume that bits in the system mask have the following pattern: 11000001.
   a. Can the channel which controls the CARDREADER interrupt the CPU?
   b. Can the computer operator interrupt the CPU?

10. Consider the program interrupts which are listed in the interrupt code table in the *Principles of Operation* manual.
    a. Give the program interrupts in this list that can be masked by SPM.
    b. Give the program interrupts in this list for which the user may specify an interruption exit routine address by the SPIE macro.

11. What action will CONTROL take if a privileged instruction is issued in the user mode?

12. Punch numeric data into a punch card. Create the following mistake in the keypunching: punch the letter O for the number 0 for all occurrences of 0. Now do the following:

    a. Read the card via a channel program (use EXCP).

    b. Correct the card image using the Translate instruction. That is, replace each letter O by a numeric 0.

    c. Punch a new data card using the EXCP macro instruction.

    d. Use EXCP to print the card image of both the old and the new cards.

13. Write a channel program which reads columns 1–15 and 31–45 of a punch card into contiguous bytes in MEMORY. Print the image of the 30 bytes that have been read in. Use the EXCP macro instruction to execute the program.

14. The address translation (dynamic relocation) which goes on in a page-segment system during the entire program execution time will slow the execution of a program. IBM has announced that their virtual memory system has special hardware—the ASSOCIATIVE ARRAY REGISTERS —which is used in the address translation process. These special purpose registers will compensate for the "slow" speed of the dynamic relocation.

    Prepare a paper which discusses the hardware—such as the ASSOCIA-TIVE ARRAY REGISTERS—which is provided by the computer manufacturers to offset the "slow" speed of dynamic translation. (Note: it will be necessary to research in the computer science section of your college library or elsewhere for information about paging systems.)

15. Paging activity—paging in and paging out—may increase to such a level that the computer system performs little, if any, useful work. This situation is known as *thrashing*.

    Prepare a paper (after appropriate research) which discusses the problem of *thrashing* in a Virtual Memory Operating System.

Appendix A

Character	EBCDIC Binary	EBCDIC Hexcode	EBCDIC Cardpunch	BCD Binary Code	BCD Cardpunch
Blank	0100 0000	40	No punch	110 000	No punch
.	0100 1011	4B	12, 8, 3	011 011	12, 8, 3
(	0100 1101	4D	12, 8, 5	111 100	0, 8, 4
+	0100 1110	4E	12, 8, 6	010 000	12
$	0101 1011	5B	11, 8, 3	101 011	11, 8, 3
*	0101 1100	5C	11, 8, 4	101 100	11, 8, 4
)	0101 1101	5D	11, 8, 5	011 100	12, 8, 4
−	0110 0000	60	11	100 000	11
/	0110 0001	61	0, 1	110 001	0, 1
,	0110 1011	6B	0, 8, 3	111 011	0, 8, 3
'	0111 1101	7D	8, 5	001 100	4, 8
=	0111 1110	7E	8, 6	001 011	3, 8
A	1100 0001	C1	12, 1	010 001	12, 1
B	1100 0010	C2	12, 2	010 010	12, 2
C	1100 0011	C3	12, 3	010 011	12, 3
D	1100 0100	C4	12, 4	010 100	12, 4
E	1100 0101	C5	12, 5	010 101	12, 5
F	1100 0110	C6	12, 6	010 110	12, 6
G	1100 0111	C7	12, 7	010 111	12, 7
H	1100 1000	C8	12, 8	011 000	12, 8
I	1100 1001	C9	12, 9	011 001	12, 9
J	1101 0001	D1	11, 1	100 001	11, 1
K	1101 0010	D2	11, 2	100 010	11, 2
L	1101 0011	D3	11, 3	100 011	11, 3
M	1101 0100	D4	11, 4	100 100	11, 4
N	1101 0101	D5	11, 5	100 101	11, 5
O	1101 0110	D6	11, 6	100 110	11, 6
P	1101 0111	D7	11, 7	100 111	11, 7
Q	1101 1000	D8	11, 8	101 000	11, 8
R	1101 1001	D9	11, 9	101 001	11, 9
S	1110 0010	E2	0, 2	110 010	0, 2
T	1110 0011	E3	0, 3	110 011	0, 3
U	1110 0100	E4	0, 4	110 100	0, 4
V	1110 0101	E5	0, 5	110 101	0, 5
W	1110 0110	E6	0, 6	110 110	0, 6
X	1110 0111	E7	0, 7	110 111	0, 7
Y	1110 1000	E8	0, 8	111 000	0, 8
Z	1110 1001	E9	0, 9	111 001	0, 9

Character	EBCDIC Binary	EBCDIC Hexcode	EBCDIC Cardpunch	BCD Binary Code	BCD Cardpunch
0	1111 0000	F0	0	000 000	0
1	1111 0001	F1	1	000 001	1
2	1111 0010	F2	2	000 010	2
3	1111 0011	F3	3	000 011	3
4	1111 0100	F4	4	000 100	4
5	1111 0101	F5	5	000 101	5
6	1111 0110	F6	6	000 110	6
7	1111 0111	F7	7	000 111	7
8	1111 1000	F8	8	001 000	8
9	1111 1001	F9	9	001 001	9

Appendix B

Basic Assembler Language Instruction Set

Mnemonic	Name	Opcode	Type	Form of Operand Implicit	Form of Operand Explicit	Reference
A	Add	5A	RX	R1,S2(X2)	R1,D2(X2,B2)	Section 6.2
AD	Add Double	6A	RX	FLP1,S2(X2)	FLP1,D2(X2,B2)	Section 12.2
ADR	Add Double Register	2A	RR	None	FLP1,FLP2	Section 12.2
AE	Add Single	7A	RX	FLP1,S2(X2)	FLP1,D2(X2,B2)	Section 12.2
AER	Add Single Register	3A	RR	None	FLP1,FLP2	Section 12.2
AH	Add Half-Word	4A	RX	R1,S2(X2)	R1,D2(X2,B2)	Topic 1, Chapter 6
AL	Add Logical	5E	RX	R1,S2(X2)	R1,D2(X2,B2)	See Note 1
ALR	Add Logical Register	1E	RR	None	R1,R2	See Note 1
AP	Add Packed	FA	SS	S1,S2	D1(L1,B1),D2(L2,B2)	Section 13.1
AR	Add Register	1A	RR	None	R1,R2	Section 6.2
AU	Add Unnormalized	7E	RX	FLP1,S2(X2)	FLP1,D2(X2,B2)	Section 12.4
AUR	Add Unnormalized Register	3E	RR	None	FLP1,FLP2	Section 12.4
AW	Add Double Unnormalized	6E	RX	FLP1,S2(X2)	FLP1,D2(X2,B2)	Section 12.4
AWR	Add Double Unnormalized Register	2E	RR	None	FLP1,FLP2	Section 12.4
BAL	Branch and Link	45	RX	R1,S2(X2)	R1,D2(X2,B2)	Section 10.2
BALR	Branch and Link Register	05	RR	None	R1,R2	Section 10.2
BC	Branch on Condition	47	RX	R1,S2(X2)	R1,D2(X2,B2)	Section 10.1

BCR	Branch on Condition Register	07	RR	None	R1,R2	Section 10.1
BCT	Branch on Count	46	RX	R1,S2(X2)	R1,D2(X2,B2)	Section 9.1
BCTR	Branch on Count to Register	06	RR	None	R1,R2	Section 9.3
BXH	Branch on Index High	86	RS	R1,R3,S2	R1,R3,D2(B2)	Section 9.7
BXLE	Branch on Index Less than or Equal to	87	RS	R1,R3,S2	R1,R3,D2(B2)	Section 9.7
C	Compare	59	RX	R1,S2(X2)	R1,D2(X2,B2)	Section 9.5
CD	Compare Double	69	RX	FLP1,S2(X2)	FLP1,D2(X2,B2)	Section 12.4
CDR	Compare Double Register	29	RR	None	FLP1,FLP2	Section 12.4
CE	Compare Single	79	RX	FLP1,S2(X2)	FLP1,D2(X2,B2)	Section 12.4
CER	Compare Single Register	39	RR	None	FLP1,FLP2	Section 12.4
CH	Compare Half-word	49	RX	R1,S2(X2)	R1,D2(X2,B2)	See Note 2
CL	Compare Logical	55	RX	R1,S2(X2)	R1,D2(X2,B2)	Section 9.9
CLC	Compare Logical Character	D5	SS	S1,S2	D1(L,B2),D2(B2)	Section 9.9
CLI	Compare Logical Immediate	95	SI	S1,I2	D1(B1),I2	Section 9.9
CLR	Compare Logical Register	15	RR	None	R1,R2	Section 9.9
CP	Compare Packed	F9	SS	S1,S2	D1(L1,B1),D2(L2,B2)	Section 13.1
CR	Compare Register	19	RR	None	R1,R2	Section 9.5
CVB	Convert to Binary	4F	RX	R1,S2(X2)	R1,D2(X2,B2)	Section 8.1
CVD	Convert to Decimal	4E	RX	R1,S2(X2)	R1,D2(X2,B2)	Section 8.1
D	Divide	5D	RX	R1,S2(X2)	R1,D2(X2,B2)	Section 6.2
DD	Divide Double	6D	RX	FLP1,S2(X2)	FLP1,D2(X2,B2)	Section 12.2
DDR	Divide Double Register	2D	RR	None	FLP1,FLP2	Section 12.2
DE	Divide Single	7D	RX	FLP1,S2(X2)	FLP1,D2(X2,B2)	Section 12.2
DER	Divide Single Register	3D	RR	None	FLP1,FLP2	Section 12.2
DP	Divide Packed	FD	SS	S1,S2	D1(L1,S1),D2(L2,B2)	Section 13.3
DR	Divide Register	1D	RR	None	R1,R2	Section 6.2
ED	Edit	DE	SS	S1,S2	D1(L,S1),D2(B2)	Section 13.4

Appendix B (*continued*)

Mnemonic	Name	Opcode	Type	Form of Operand		Reference
				Implicit	*Explicit*	
EDMK	Edit and Mark	DF	SS	S1,S2	D1(L,B1),D2(B2)	Section 13.4
EX	Execute	44	RX	R1,S2(X2)	R1,D2(X2,B2)	Section 15.2
HER	Halve Single Register	34	RR	None	FLP1,FLP2	Section 12.4
HDR	Halve Double Register	24	RR	None	FLP1,FLP2	Section 12.4
IC	Insert Character	43	RX	R1,S2(X2)	R1,D2(X2,B2)	Section 8.5
L	Load	58	RX	R1,S2(X2)	R1,D2(X2,B2)	Section 6.1
LA	Load Address	41	RX	R1,S2(X2)	R1,D2(X2,B2)	Section 7.5
LCR	Load Complement Register	13	RR	None	R1,R2	Section 6.1
LCDR	Load Complement Double Register	23	RR	None	FLP1,FLP2	Section 12.1
LCER	Load Complement Single Register	33	RR	None	FLP1,FLP2	Section 12.1
LD	Load Double	68	RX	FLP1,S2(X2)	FLP1,D2(X2,B2)	Section 12.1
LDR	Load Double Register	28	RR	None	FLP1,FLP2	Section 12.1
LE	Load Single	78	RX	FLP1,S2(X2)	FLP1,D2(X2,B2)	Section 12.1
LER	Load Single Register	38	RR	None	FLP1,FLP2	Section 12.1
LH	Load Half-word	48	RX	R1,S2(X2)	R1,D2(X2,B2)	Topic 1, Chapter 6
LM	Load Multiple	98	RS	R1,R3,S2	R1,R3,D2(B2)	Section 6.1
LNDR	Load Negative Double Register	21	RR	None	FLP1,FLP2	Section 12.1
LNER	Load Negative Single Register	31	RR	None	FLP1,FLP2	Section 12.1
LNR	Load Negative Register	11	RR	None	R1,R2	Section 6.1
LPDR	Load Positive Double Register	20	RR	None	FLP1,FLP2	Section 12.1
LPER	Load Positive Single Register	30	RR	None	FLP1,FLP2	Section 12.1

LPR	Løad Positive Register	10	RR	Nøne	R1,R2	Section 6.1
LR	Løad Register	18	RR	Nøne	R1,R2	Section 6.1
LTDR	Løad and Test Døuble Register	22	RR	Nøne	FLP1,FLP2	Section 12.1
LTER	Løad and Test Single Register	32	RR	Nøne	FLP1,FLP2	Section 12.1
LTR	Løad and Test Register	12	RR	Nøne	R1,R2	Section 9.4
M	Multiply	5C	RX	R1,S2(X2)	R1,D2(X2,B2)	Section 6.2
MD	Multiply Døuble	6C	RX	FLP1,S2(X2)	FLP1,D2(X2,B2)	Section 12.2
MDR	Multiply Døuble Register	2C	RR	Nøne	FLP1,FLP2	Section 12.2
ME	Multiply Single	7C	RX	FLP1,S2(X2)	FLP1,D2(X2,B2)	Section 12.2
MER	Multiply Single Register	3C	RR	Nøne	FLP1,FLP2	Section 12.2
MH	Multiply Half-wørd	4C	RX	R1,S2(X2)	R1,D2(X2,B2)	Topic 1, Chapter 6
MP	Multiply Packed	FC	SS	S1,S2	D1(L1,B1),D2(L2,B2)	Section 13.3
MR	Multiply Register	1C	RR	Nøne	R1,R2	Section 6.2
MVC	Møve Character	D2	SS	S1,S2	D1(L,B1),D2(B2)	Section 6.3
MVI	Møve Immediate	92	SI	S1,I2	D1(B1),I2	Section 6.3
MVN	Møve Numeric	D1	SS	S1,S2	D1(L,B1),D2(B2)	Section 6.3
MVØ	Møve with Øffset	F1	SS	S1,S2	D1(L1,B1),D2(L2,B2)	Section 13.2
MVZ	Møve Zøne	D3	SS	S1,S2	D1(L,B1),D2(B2)	Section 6.3
N	And	54	RX	R1,S2(X2)	R1,D2(X2,B2)	Section 8.3
NC	And Størage	D4	SS	S1,S2	D1(L,B1),D2(B2)	Section 8.3
NI	And Immediate	94	SI	S1,I2	D1(B1),I2	Section 8.3
NR	And Register	14	RR	Nøne	R1,R2	Section 8.3
Ø	Ør	56	RX	R1,S2(X2)	R1,D2(X2,B2)	Section 8.3
ØC	Ør Størage	D6	SS	S1,S2	D1(L,B1),D2(B2)	Section 8.3
ØI	Ør Immediate	96	SI	S1,I2	D1(B1),I2	Section 7.3

Appendix B (*continued*)

Mnemonic	Name	Opcode	Type	Form of Operand — Implicit	Form of Operand — Explicit	Reference
OR	Or Register	16	RR	None	R1,R2	Section 8.3
PACK	Pack	F2	SS	S1,S2	D1(L1,B1),D2(L2,B2)	Section 8.1
S	Subtract	5B	RX	R1,S2(X2)	R1,D2(X2,B2)	Section 6.2
SD	Subtract Double	6B	RX	FLP1,S2(X2)	FLP1,D2(X2,B2)	Section 12.2
SDR	Subtract Double Register	2B	RR	None	FLP1,FLP2	Section 12.2
SE	Subtract Single	7B	RX	FLP1,S2(X2)	FLP1,D2(X2,B2)	Section 12.2
SER	Subtract Single Register	3B	RR	None	FLP1,FLP2	Section 12.2
SH	Subtract Half-word	4B	RX	R1,S2(X2)	R1,D2(X2,B2)	Topic 1, Chapter 6
SL	Subtract Logical	5F	RX	R1,S2(X2)	R1,D2(X2,B2)	See Note 1
SLA	Shift Left Arithmetic	8B	RS	R1,S2	R1,D2(B2)	Section 8.4
SLDA	Shift Left Double Arithmetic	8F	RS	R1,S2	R1,D2(B2)	Section 8.4
SLDL	Shift Left Double Logical	8D	RS	R1,S2	R1,D2(B2)	Section 8.4
SLL	Shift Left Logical	89	RS	R1,S2	R1,D2(B2)	Section 8.4
SLR	Subtract Logical Register	1F	RR	None	R1,R2	See Note 1
SP	Subtract Packed	FB	SS	S1,S2	D1(L1,B1),D2(L2,B2)	Section 13.1
SPM	Set Program Mask	04	RR	None	R1	Section 17.1
SR	Subtract Register	1B	RR	None	R1,R2	Section 6.2
SRA	Shift Right Arithmetic	8A	RS	R1,S2	R1,D2(B2)	Section 8.4
SRDA	Shift Right Double Arithmetic	8E	RS	R1,S2	R1,D2(B2)	Section 8.4
SRDL	Shift Right Double Logical	8C	RS	R1,S2	R1,D2(B2)	Section 6.2
SRL	Shift Right Logical	88	RS	R1,S2	R1,D2(B2)	Section 8.4
ST	Store	50	RX	R1,S2(X2)	R1,D2(X2,B2)	Section 6.1

STC	Store Character	42	RX	R1,S2(X2)	R1,D2(X2,B2)	Section 8.5
STD	Store Double	60	RX	FLP1,S2(X2)	FLP1,D2(X2,B2)	Section 12.1
STE	Store Single	70	RX	FLP1,S2(X2)	FLP1,D2(X2,B2)	Section 12.1
STH	Store Half-word	40	RX	R1,S2(X2)	R1,D2(X2,B2)	Topic 1, Chapter 6
STM	Store Multiply	90	RS	R1,R3,S2	R1,R3,D2(B2)	Section 6.1
SU	Subtract Unnormalized	6F	RX	FLP1,S2(X2)	FLP1,D2(X2,B2)	Section 12.4
SUR	Subtract Unnormalized Register	2F	RR	None	FLP1,FLP2	Section 12.4
SW	Subtract Double Unnormalized	7F	RX	FLP1,S2(X2)	FLP1,D2(X2,B2)	Section 12.4
SWR	Subtract Double Unnormalized Register	3F	RR	None	FLP1,FLP2	Section 12.4
TM	Test Under Mask	91	SI	S1,I2	D1(B1),I2	Exercise 11, Chapter 15
TR	Translate	DC	SS	S1,S2	D1(L,B1),D2(B2)	Section 15.4
TRT	Translate and Test	DD	SS	S1,S2	D1(L,B1),D2(B2)	Section 15.3
TS	Test and Set	93	SI	S1	D1(B1)	See Note 3
UNPK	Unpack	F3	SS	S1,S2	D1(L1,B1),D2(L2,B2)	Section 8.1
X	Exclusive Or	57	RX	R1,S2(X2)	R1,D2(X2,B2)	Section 8.3
XC	Exclusive Or (Storage)	D7	SS	S1,S2	D1(L,B1),D2(B2)	Section 8.3
XI	Exclusive Or Immediate	97	SI	S1,I2	D1(B1),I2	Section 8.3
XR	Exclusive Or Register	17	RR	None	R1,R2	Section 8.3
ZAP	Zero and Add Packed	F8	SS	S1,S2	D1(L1,B1),D2(L2,B2)	Section 13.2

Note 1

The logical arithmetic instructions—Add Logical, Add Logical Register, Subtract Logical, and Subtract Logical Register—recognize the full-word operands as unsigned binary integers. The logical add instructions put the sum of the first and second operand into the first operand's location. The logical subtract instructions put the *sum* of the first operand and the *2's complement* of the second operand into the first operand's location.

Any carry which results from the addition is lost, but the carry, if any occurred, affects the setting of the code. The condition code schedule follows the logical arithmetic instruction table.

The Logical Arithmetic Instructions

Name	General Form	Action
Add Logical	AL R1,S2	$R1 \leftarrow C(R1)+C(S2)$
Add Logical Register	ALR R1,R2	$R1 \leftarrow C(R1)+C(R2)$
Subtract Logical	SL R1,S2	$R1 \leftarrow C(R1)+C(S2*)$
Subtract Logical Register	SLR R1,R2	$R1 \leftarrow C(R1)+C(R2*)$

$C(S2*)$ is the 2's complement of $C(S2)$.
$C(R2*)$ is the 2's complement of $C(R2)$.

The Condition Code Schedule

$CC \leftarrow 0$ if sum is zero and no carry.
$CC \leftarrow 1$ if sum is not zero and no carry.
$CC \leftarrow 2$ if sum is zero and there was carry.
$CC \leftarrow 3$ if sum is not zero and there was carry.

Note 2

The general form of Compare Half-word is

CH   R1,S2

Compare Half-word compares the contents of S2 with the contents of R1 in the following manner. The contents of the half-word at S2 is fetched, the sign bit of the fetched half-word is propagated to the left for sixteen bits, and then a full-word signed binary integer comparison is made between the two operands.

The condition code is set according to the schedule given below. (Compare Half-word cannot set the code to 3.)

$CC \leftarrow 0$ if $C(R1) = C(S2)$ expanded
$CC \leftarrow 1$ if $C(R1) < C(S2)$ expanded
$CC \leftarrow 2$ if $C(R1) > C(S2)$ expanded

Note 3   Test and Set

The general form of Test and Set is

    TS   S1

    Note that the Test and Set has only one operand.

    The instruction tests the first (leftmost) bit of the byte at S2. The condition code is set to zero if this bit, the leftmost bit, is a 0. If this bit is a 1, then the condition code is set to 1.

    After the test has been made and the condition code has been set, Test and Set stores binary 1's in all bit positions in the byte.

    The instruction is often used to control the sharing of a common memory storage area by two or more programs. Bit position 0 of S2 is the control bit. If this bit position is a 0, then the common storage area is available. A binary 1 in the control bit says that the area is being used by another program.

Note 4

The set of privileged instructions appear in Table 17.7, Section 17.3. These privileged instructions have not been included in the Basic Assembler Language Instruction Set of this Appendix.

Appendix C

This appendix lists several macros which enable a student to get their Assembler Language programs on a System/360 computer with a minimum amount of instruction. Some pertinent information about each macro is given in the notes which follow the code for that particular macro.

The INIT Macro

```
               MACRO
&NAME          INIT
               LCLC    &LABEL
               AIF     ('&NAME' NE '').NAMED
&LABEL         SETC    'SUBPGM'
               AGO     .START
.NAMED         ANOP
&LABEL         SETC    '&NAME'
.START         ANOP
&LABEL         CSECT
               STM     14,12,12(13)
               LR      12,15
               USING   &LABEL,12
               B       A&SYSNDX
S&SYSNDX       DS      18F
A&SYSNDX       LA      11,S&SYSNDX
               ST      11,8(13)
               ST      13,S&SYSNDX+4
               LR      13,11
               MEND
```

INIT Notes

1. The INIT macro establishes a base register, defines an eighteen-word save area, and performs the necessary housekeeping to run a Basic Assembler Language program (see Chapter 10 for a discussion of the above items).

2. The student may give a name to the control section established by the INIT macro. This is done by placing any legitimate symbolic label in the namefield of the INIT macro call statement. Note that if the namefield of the call statement is left blank, INIT pre-empts the label SUBPGM.

3. After execution of INIT, register 13 points to the save area defined by the macro. The student should avoid disturbing this pointer.

The PROLOG Macro

```
              MACRO
&NAME         PROLOG   &END=,&CSIZE=80,&LSIZE=133
              AIF      ('&END' EQ '').NOTE
              CNOP     0,8
&NAME         BAL      1,G&SYSNDX
              DC       A(CARDIN)
              DC       X'8F',AL3(LINEOUT)
CARDIN        DC       5F'0',A(1),AL3(64),XL5'1',A(&END),F'0'
              DC       CL8'SYSIN',X'020050',XL5'1',F'1',A(&CSIZE),F'0'
              DC       3F'1',A(&CSIZE),F'1',XL8'1'
LINEOUT       DC       5F'0',A(1),AL3(64),X'0',2F'1',X'94',3X'0'
              DC       CL8'SYSPRINT',X'2',AL3(80),2F'1',A(&LSIZE),F'0'
              DC       3F'1',A(&LSIZE),F'1',XL8'1'
G&SYSNDX      SVC      19
              MEXIT
.NOTE         MNOTE    '** THE REQUIRED OPERAND "END= " '
              MNOTE    'HAS BEEN OMITTED. **'
              MEND
```

PROLOG Notes

1. PRØLØG defines two data control blocks—CARDIN for the card reader and LINEØUT for the printer.

2. CARDIN—the card reader data control block—has a default logical record length of 80 bytes. Code CSIZE= (when calling PRØLØG) where n is any integer from 1 to 79 if the input records are less than 80 bytes long. Do not code the keyword parameter CSIZE when calling the PRØLØG macro if the default value is acceptable.

3. LINEØUT—the printer data control block—uses the first byte of the print record as a USASI carriage control character. Recall that a blank in the USASI carriage control code specifies a new line.

4. LINEØUT has a default logical record length of 133 bytes (see Note 3). If the output records are less than 132 bytes, specify the number of bytes desired after the equal sign in the keyword parameter LSIZE= when calling the macro. Omit the LSIZE keyword parameter if the logical record length of 133 is acceptable.

5. The keyword parameter END= specifies the address to which control is transferred when the end of cardreader data set is reached. This address must be a symbolic name defined in the problem program. There is no default value. The marco causes an error message to be printed if this end-of-file address is omitted.

6. Both CARDIN and LINEØUT specify the move mode for GET and

PUT, respectively. (See Chapter 14 for a discussion of GET and PUT in the move mode.)

The SETUP Macro

```
                MACRO
&LABEL          SETUP   &END=,&CSIZE=80,&LSIZE=133
                AIF     ('&END' EQ '').NOTE
                AIF     ('&LABEL' EQ '').NONE
&LABEL          CSECT
                AGO     .NEXT
.NONE           ANOP
SUB1            CSECT
.NEXT           STM     14,12,12(13)
                BALR    12,0
                USING   *,12
                LA      11,SAVE&SYSNDX
                ST      11,8(13)
                ST      13,SAVE&SYSNDX+4
                LR      13,11
                BAL     1,ISA&SYSNDX
                DC      A(CARDIN)
                DC      X'8F',AL3(LINEOUT)
SAVE&SYSNDX     DS      18F
CARDIN          DC      5F'0',A(1),AL3(64),XL5'1',A(&END),F'0'
                DC      CL8'SYSIN',X'020050',XL5'1',F'1',A(&CSIZE),F'0'
                DC      3F'1',A(&CSIZE),F'1',XL8'1'
LINEOUT         DC      5F'0',A(1),AL3(64),X'0',2F'1',X'94',3X'0'
                DC      CL8'SYSPRINT',X'2',AL3(80),2F'1',A(&LSIZE),F'0'
                DC      3F'1',A(&LSIZE),F'1',XL8'1'
ISA&SYSNDX      SVC     19
                MEXIT
.NOTE           MNOTE   'THE REQUIRED OPERAND "END= " HAS'
                MNOTE   'BEEN OMITTED'
                MEND
```

SETUP Notes

1. The SETUP macro combines the functions of both INIT and PRØLØG. All the comments given in the notes to INIT and PRØLØG are applicable to SETUP.

The GOBACK Macro

```
                MACRO
&NAME           GOBACK
&NAME           L       13,4(13)
                LM      14,12,12(13)
                BR      14
                MEND
```

The GOBACK NOTES

1. GØBACK "restores" the registers and returns control to the operating system. &NAME may be blank.

The EPILOG Macro

```
          MACRO
&LABEL    EPILOG
          CNOP    0,4
&LABEL    BAL     1,* + 12
          DC      A(CARDIN)
          DC      X'80',AL3(LINEOUT)
          SVC     20
          MEND
```

The EPILOG Notes

1. EPILØG issues a Supervisor call to close the CARDIN and LINEØUT data control blocks created by PRØLØG or SETUP. &LABEL may be blank.

The QDUMP Macro

```
               MACRO
&LABEL         QDUMP &STORAGE=
               PRINT  NOGEN
               OPEN   (USYSNDX,OUTPUT)
               PRINT  GEN
               B      AITI &SYSNDX
USYSNDX        DC     5F'0',A(1),AL3(64),XL5'1',XL5'154',3X'0'
               DC     CL8'SYSPRINT',X'02000020',2F'0',A(882)
               DC     F'0',3F'1',A(125),F'1'
AITI &SYSNDX   BCTR   0,0
               PRINT  NOGEN
          SNAP DCB=USYSNDX,PDATA=(REGS),STORAGE=(&STORAGE(1),&STORAGE(2))
               MEND
```

QDUMP Notes

1. The QDUMP macro creates and opens a data control block for the IBM system macro named SNAP.

2. The QDUMP macro may be used to dump any portion of memory. The user must specify two symbolic addresses in memory following the keyword parameter STORAGE= when calling QDUMP. The two addresses must be enclosed in parentheses, separated by a comma, and the absolute address of the first symbolic name must be less than the absolute address of the second. Consider the examples given below.

Example 1

QDUMP   STORAGE=(BLUE,RED)

will give a dump of memory from the absolute address of BLUE to the absolute address of RED inclusive.

Example 2

QDUMP STORAGE = (BLUE,BLUE+15)

will give a dump of memory from the address BLUE to the address BLUE+15 inclusive.

---

3. The contents of the floating point and the general purpose registers are dumped each time QDUMP is involved.

Index